MOUNTAIN BIKING

UTAH'S

WASATCH FRONT

GREGG BROMKA

Off-Road
PUBLICATIONS
Salt Lake City, Utah

Mountain biking has inherent risks and dangers. Hazards, whether cited in this book or not, can present themselves at any time and under a variety of situations or may occur where they did not exist previously. Every rider must use his/her best judgement to determine where, when, and under what circumstance to ride a particular route to ensure his/her safety, the safety of others, and to minimize environmental impacts.

All routes presented in this book were deemed open to bicycles at the time of publication; *however,* access privileges, management policies, land status, and signage may change without notice. Trails may be rerouted, altered, or closed, thus making the descriptions in this book inaccurate. In the event that a trail crosses private property, the land owner makes no claim that the trail or any portion of his/her property is free of hazards. Trespassing is a serious offense that is punishable by law. Obtain expressed permission from land owners to cross private property. That said, *Ride At Your Own Risk!*

Cover photo: Brad Karren at Sundance Resort

Back cover photos:
Top: Wasatch Crest Trail
Left: Albion Basin
Right: Bonneville Shoreline Trail (Salt Lake)
Bottom: Wasatch Crest Trail

Cover design by Gregg Bromka/Off-Road Publications

First edition, second printing 2005
5 4 3 2
Printed in the United States of America

Comments, corrections, and suggestions are welcome and should be sent to the author c/o Off-Road Publications.

Published by
Off-Road Publications
3009 S 2000 East
Salt Lake City, UT 84109
www.offroadpub.com

ISBN: 0-9624374-4-1
Library of Congress Control Number: 2003093290

Table of Contents

Central Wasatch Rides (Salt Lake)

Southern Wasatch Rides (Orem-Provo-Payson)

West of the Wasatch Rides (Tooele-West Desert)

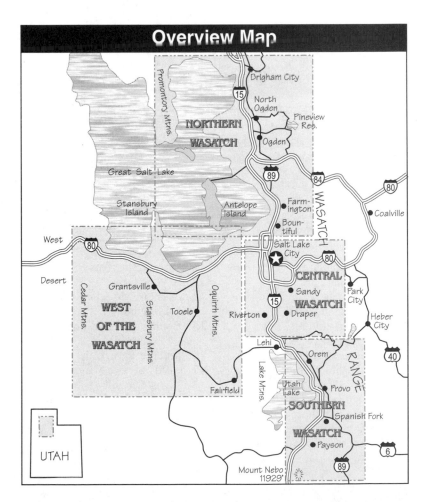

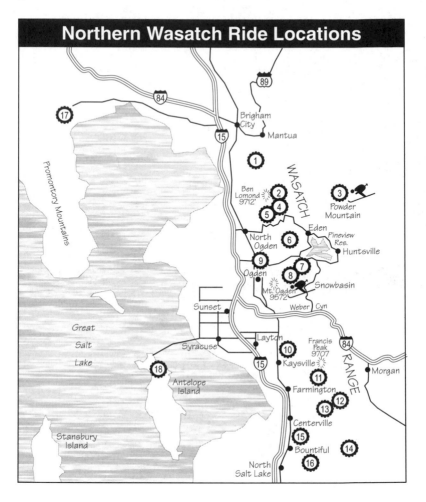

Northern Wasatch Ride Locations

1. Inspiration Point
2. Cutler Flat Park
3. Powder Mountain Resort
4. Ben Lomond Trail
5. Northern Skyline Trail
6. Southern Skyline Trail
7. Wheeler Creek Trail
8. Snowbasin Resort
9. Bonneville Shoreline Trail (Ogden)
10. Bonneville Shoreline Trail (Kaysville-Layton)
11. Farmington Canyon-Francis Peak

12. Farmington Flats
13. Skyline Drive
14. Sessions Mountain-Big Mountain Pass
15. Bonneville Shoreline Trail (Bountiful)
16. Mueller Park Trail
17. Golden Spike National Historic Site
18. Antelope Island State Park

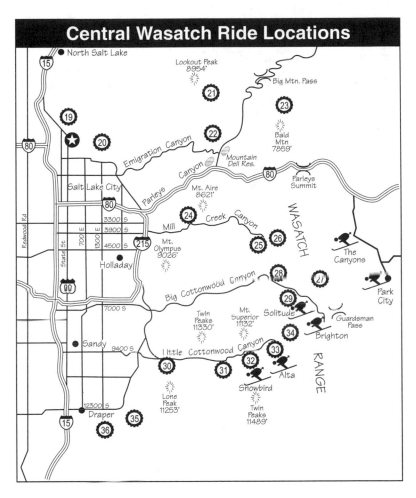

Central Wasatch Ride Locations

19. Bonneville Shoreline Trail (Ensign Peak)
20. Bonneville Shoreline Trail (Salt Lake)
21. Lookout Peak
22. Little Mountain-Mormon Pioneer Trails
23. Mormon Pioneer Trail & Beyond
24. Mill Creek Pipeline Trail
25. Big Water Trail
26. Upper Mill Creek Canyon
27. Wasatch Crest Trail
28. Mill D North Fork-Desolation Trail
29. Solitude Mountain Resort
30. Little Cottonwood Canyon Trail
31. White Pine Trail
32. Snowbird Resort
33. Alta Ski Area
34. Grizzly Gulch to Twin Lakes Pass
35. Upper Corner Canyon Road
36. Bonneville Shoreline Trail (Draper-Sandy)

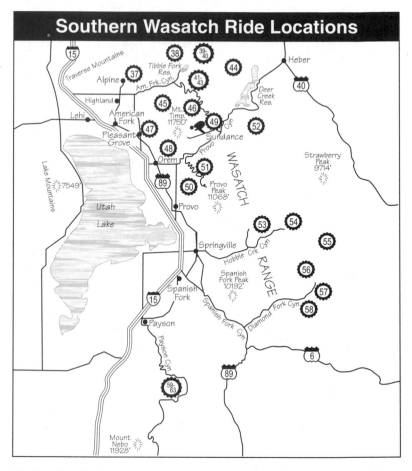

Southern Wasatch Ride Locations

37. Lambert Park
38. Silver Lake Flat Reservoir
39. Ridge Trail 157 North (Ant Knolls-Forest Lake)
40. Ridge Trail 157 (Mill Canyon Peak)
41. Tibble Fork Trail & More
42. Pine Hollow Figure Eight
43. South Fork Deer Creek Trail
44. Upper Provo Deer Creek
45. Timpooneke Road
46. R. A. T. (Ride Around Timpanogos)
47. Grove Creek Trail
48. Bonneville Shoreline Trail (Orem)
49. Sundance
50. Bonneville Shoreline Trail (Provo)
51. Squaw Peak Road
52. Bald Knoll-Windy Pass
53. Hobble Creek Loop
54. Wardsworth Creek
55. Center Trail (Halls Fork-Sixth Water)
56. Sawmill Hollow
57. Diamond Fork Hot Springs Loop
58. Monks Hollow
59. Bennie Creek Cutoff Trail
60. Payson Lakes
61. Jones Ranch-Shram Creek Trails
62. Sheepherder Hill Trail
63. Blackhawk Loop Trail

West of the Wasatch Ride Locations

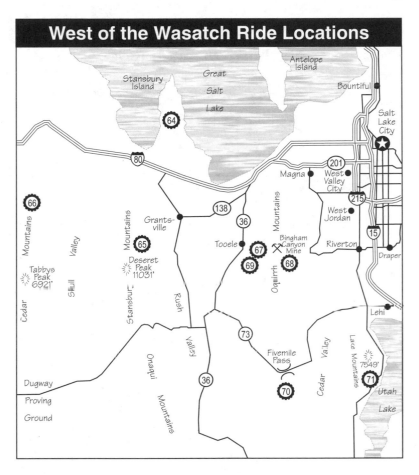

64. Stansbury Island Trail
65. Stansbury Front Trail
66. Cedar Mountains
67. Copper Pit Overlook
68. Butterfield Canyon
69. Settlement Canyon
70. Five Mile Pass
71. Lake Mountains

Ride Guide

Northern Wasatch Rides

Trail Name	Length (miles)	Type	ST	DT	DR	PV	Phys Diff	Tech Diff	Gain (feet)	Dogs	GWT
Farmington Flats	5.5	↻		•	•		E*	1*-3	500	NR	•
BST: Layton-Kaysville	3.6	→	•	•			E*-M	2-3*	500*	L	
Wheeler Creek Trail	10.4	↔	•	•			E*-M*	1*-4*	1500	Y	•
BST: Odgen (Lewis Peak Section)	4.4	→	•	•			M	1*-4*	400*	L	
BST: Bountiful-Centerville	6	→	•	•			M	2-4	600*	L	
Cutler Flat Park	5	↔	•	•			M	2-3+	960	L	
BST: Ogden (Mt. Ogden Section)	6.4	→	•	•			E*-M*	2-4	1200	L	
Mueller Park Trail	13	↔	•				M*	2-3*	1910	Y	
Powder Mountain Ski Resort	5.7	ALL	•	•			M*	2-4	800	L	•
Snowbasin Ski Resort	23*	ALL	•	•			M-S	2-4	2500	L	
Ben Lomond Trail	12	↔	•				S	3-4*	2940	Y	•
Northern Skyline Trail	13	↔	•				S	2-4*	2510	Y	•
Southern Skyline Trail	22.5	↻	•			•	S	2*-4	4200	Y	•
Inspiration Point	27.6	↔			•	•	S	1*-3*	4500	NR	
Skyline Drive	24	→				•	S*	1*-2*	4620	NR	•
Farmington Canyon-Francis Peak	26	↔				•	X	1*-2*	5047	NR	•
Sessions Mountain	14.1	→	•	•			X	3-5	2700	Y	•

Central Wasatch Rides

Trail Name	Length (miles)	Type	ST	DT	DR	PV	Phys Diff	Tech Diff	Gain (feet)	Dogs	GWT
Mill Creek Pipeline Trail	7.2	→	•				E	2-4*	150	Y*	
"Bird" Trail (Snowbird)	2	↔	•	•			E*	2-3	100	N	
BST: Draper	8	→	•	•			E*-M	2-3*	800	L	
Albion Basin Road (Alta)	6.2	↔			•		E*	2	800	N	
Upper Corner Canyon Road	7.6	↔			•		M	1*-2*	1070	L	
Big Water Trail	6.5	↔	•				M	2-3*	1200	Y*	•
Little Cottonwood Canyon Trail	6.5	↔	•	•			M	2-4	1140	N	
Upper Mill Creek/GWT	9.2	↔	•				M	2-3	1340	Y*	•
Solitude X-Country Course	6	↻	•	•			M	2-4	1500	N	
Gad Valley (Snowbird)	2.5	↻	•	•			M*	2-3	700	N	
BST: Salt Lake Section	10	→	•	•			M	1*-3	1300	L	
BST: Ensign Peak Section	5.6	→	•	•			M*	2*-3*	800	L	
Mormon Pioneer Trail	11.2	↔	•				M*	2-3	1600	N	
Mill D North Fork Trail	7.4	↔	•				M*	2-4*	2000	N	
Little Mtn-Mormon Pioneer Trail	14.6	↻	•		•		M*	2-3*	2400	N	
Boulder Basin Trail (Alta)	8.3	↻	•	•			S	2-4*	1800	N	
Germania Pass (Alta)	8.3	↻		•			S	2-4	1900	N	
Grizzly Gulch-Twin Lakes Pass	4.3	→	•	•			S	3-5	1350	N	
Wasatch Crest Trail	15.2	↔	•	•			S	2-4	2600	N	•
White Pine Trail	9.6	↔	•	•			S	2-4	2460	N	
Peruvian Gulch (Snowbird)	8.4	↔	•				S*	3-4	2900	N	
Lookout Mountain	12.4	↻	•	•			S*	2-5	3000	N	•
Mormon Pioneer Trail & Beyond	21.3	↻	•	•		•	X	2-4*	3800	N	•

Type:	Tread:	Physical Difficulty:	Technical Difficulty:
→ One-Way	ST: Singletrack	E: Easy	1: Smooth dirt & gravel roads
↔ Out & Back	DT: Doubletrack	M: Moderate	2: Smooth trails, washboard dirt roads.
↻ Loop	DR: Dirt Road	S: Strenuous	3: Variably choppy trails & dirt roads
	PV: Paved Road	X: Extreme	4: Rough, rutted, rocky trails & dirt roads.
			5: Extremely rough trails & roads--caution!

Rated By Physical Difficulty

Northern Wasatch Rides

Highlights	Tr #	pg
Rolling DT & DR around sunny alpine basin. Steady climb to start, fast descent to end.	12	67
Short but sweet foothills trail. Good spring & fall ride or after work. Views of metro & GSL. Sandy in spots.	10	60
Climb DT in canyon then ST across lush basin. Link to East & Middle Fork or Snowbasin.	7	47
Hand-built STs access aqueduct road north of Ogden Canyon. Goat heads--beware!	9	56
ST & DT along utility corridor on foothills. Good spring & fall ride or when other trails are wet.	15	79
Secret stash of STs in North Ogden Valley. More in the area if you're willing to sniff them out.	2	28
Popular multiuse foothills trail between Ogden-Beus Canyons. Many access points.	9	56
Locals' favorite ST. Ride to Big Rock (easy*) or to Rudys Flat (mod*). Sweet trail! Great for dogs.	16	83
Short, fun race course on hand-built STs. Out of the way--no crowds. Views of Cache Valley.	3	31
Well-crafted, extensive trail system begs to be ridden. Lift service for XC and DH riders.	8	51
Tough, rugged climb to ridge beneath Ben Lomond. Sweet sections too. Views in every direction.	4	35
ST from N. Ogden Divide to Ben Lomond. Steep switchbacking climb then rolling ridgetop trail. Views!	5	39
Climb to Wasatch Crest, descend to N Ogden Divide & link to Pineview Reservoir Trail. Awesome loop!	6	42
Long steady climb to "inspiring" viewpoint of metro, mountains & GSL. Watch for wildlife. Long descent.	1	25
Farmington to Bountiful--the long way! Big views from the top. Utah "Scenic Backway." DH options.	13	70
Biggest continual climb in the Wasatch. Nearly a vertical mile. Spin, spin, spin. How about that descent?	11	63
Remote, rugged, little-used ST. Nasty hike-a-bikes. Why ride it? Because it's there, that's why.	14	75

Central Wasatch Rides

Highlights	Tr #	pg
Old water flume high on side of canyon. Buffed. Final descent is rough & tricky. Scenic, popular.	24	121
Mountain-bike specific trail at Snowbird. Short, fun, scenic. Great summer get away. Ocktoberfest!	32	151
A work in progress & getting longer each year. Hand-built ST to Point of the Mountain.	36	167
Great ride for rookies but high elevation. Picnic at campground or hike to Cecret Lake. Wildflowers galore.	33	155
Good off-season riding or winter riding when frozen. Views of southern Salt Lake valley & Wasatch Front.	35	164
Everyone's favorite, thus popular! Perfect for bikers hitting singletrack for first time. Siesta at Dog Lake.	25	125
Old pipeline route along gushing creek. Easy & tough sections make it a good, quick workout.	30	145
Access route to Wasatch Crest or fun ride by itself. Wooded trail leads to lush basin. Buffed.	26	129
Great XC race course that's fun for mortals. Hill climb options for XC riders or lift service for downhillers.	29	140
Annual Mountain Bout race course. Stunning views. Snowbird is always eventful.	32	151
Popular foothills trail between Emigration-City Creek Canyons. Good climbs. Great views of Wasatch Front.	20	103
Burly climb from City Creek to antennas behind Capitol. Connects to Davis County. Finally complete!	19	99
New & getting popular. Easy at first then tough to Big Mountain Pass. Link to Little Mountain Trail or GWT.	23	116
Tough little climb to secluded alpine lake. Options to Mill Creek & GWT. Popular with hikers.	28	137
Old trail reborn with link to Mormon Pioneer Trail. Seven short, murderous climbs! Good anaerobic training.	22	112
Fun, tough loop on new trail beneath Devils Castle. Scope out Alta's powder shots for next winter.	33	155
Classic climb through classic ski resort on old Rustler Run race course. Those were the days!	33	155
Burly climb from Alta to Brighton via Twin Lakes Pass. Mining relicts. How are you going to get back?	34	160
Classic ridge trail & locals' choice. Stunning views of Big Cottonwood Canyon. Options. Vomit hill awaits!	27	132
Rugged climb to pristine alpine lake. Hiking options to ridge. Backcountry skiers haunt.	31	148
Acid test for hill climbers. Unyielding grind to top of tram. Or take the tram up & freeride down.	32	151
Climb MPT to Big Mountain Pass then west on GWT. Links to seldom-traveled ST w/ wicked descent.	21	108
Climb MPT to Big Mountain Pass then on GWT to Parleys Summit. Sheep Trail descent is sweet. Sick ride!	23	116

Dogs:	Abbreviations:
Y: Dogs allowed	GWT: Great Western Trail
Y*: Dogs allowed with restrictions	BST: Bonneville Shoreline Trail
NR: Route not recommended for dogs	MPT: Mormon Pioneer Trail
N: Dogs not allowed	GSL: Great Salt Lake
L: Dogs must be on leash	

Ride Guide
Southern Wasatch Rides

Trail Name	Length (miles)	Type	Tread ST	DT	DR	PV	Phys Diff	Tech Diff	Gain (feet)	Dogs	GWT
Sundance Ski Resort	20+	ALL	●	●			E-M	2-4	1050	N	
BST: Orem Section	4	→		●	●		E	1*-3	500	Y/L	
Payson Lakes	8.3	Loop	●	●		●	M	2-5	1000	NR	
Silver Lake Flat Reservoir	7.8	↔			●		M	2-3	1200	NR	
South Fork Deer Creek Trail	6.4	Loop	●				M	2-3*	1100	Y	●
Wardsworth Creek Trail	5	↔	●				M	2-3	1080	Y	
Lambert Park	7	Loop	●	●	●		M	2-3	1000	L	
Pine Hollow Figure Eight	8.3	Loop	●			●	M	2-4*	1500	Y	●
Bennie Creek Cutoff Trail	7.9	Loop	●			●	M	3-5	1530	NR	
BST: Provo Canyon Section	4.4	→	●	●			M	2-4	750	L	
BST: Provo-Springville Section	9.8	→	●	●			M	2-4	1250	L	
Jones Ranch-Shram Creek	8.8	Loop	●	●		●	M	2-3	1500	Y	
Monks Hollow	15	↔	●	●			M	2-3	2000	Y	
Sawmill Hollow	11.2	Loop	●	●		●	M	2-4*	1700	NR	
Diamond Fork Hot Springs Loop	15.1	Loop	●	●		●	M*	2-4*	2100	NR	●
Sheepherder Hill Trail	12.7	Loop	●	●	●		M*	2-4*	2000	NR	
Tibble Fork Trail & More	15.2	Loop	●			●	S	1-4*	2800	NR	●
Timpooneke Road	17	↔		●	●		S	1*-3	3000	NR	●
Upper Provo Deer Creek	17.3	Loop	●	●	●		S	2-4*	3000	NR	
Ridge Trail 157 N. (Ant Knolls)	13.7	Loop	●	●	●		S	2-4	2600	NR	●
Center Trail (Halls Fork)	15	Loop	●	●	●		S	2-4*	2300	NR	●
Grove Creek Trail	10.4	↔	●	●			S	3-5	3000	Y	
Blackhawk Loop Trail	17.1	Loop	●		●	●	S	2-3	2400	NR	
Squaw Peak Road	26.8	↔			●		S	1-3	4200	NR	
Ridge Trail 157	14.5	→		●	●		S*	2*-4*	3300	NR	●
Bald Knoll-Windy Pass	22	→	●	●		●	S*	3-5	3500	NR	●
Hobble Creek	42	Loop			●	●	X	2-3*	4500	NR	●
Ride Around Timpanogos (RAT)	33	Loop	●	●	●	●	XX	2-5	6000	NR	●

West of the Wasatch Rides

Trail Name	Length (miles)	Type	Tread ST	DT	DR	PV	Phys Diff	Tech Diff	Gain (feet)	Dogs	GWT
East Grade Tour	3.5	Loop		●	●	●	E	1-2	200	L	
West Grade Tour	14	Loop		●	●	●	E*	1-2	350	L	
Lakeside Trail	5.6	↔	●				E*	2-5	500	L	
Fivemile Pass	11.8	Loop		●			E*	2-4	150	Y	
Elephant Head Trail	2.8	↔	●				M	2-4*	150	L	
White Rock Bay Trail	7.5	Loop		●			M	2-3	650	L	
Mountain View Trail	23	↔	●				M	2	300	L	
Stansbury Island Trail	10.4	Loop	●	●			M	1-4*	1050	L	
Split Rock Bay Trail	11.7	↔	●	●			M*	2-4	1350	L	
Settlement Canyon	8.6	Loop	●	●		●	M*	1-3*	1850	NR	
Copper Pit Overlook	9.8	Loop	●		●		M*	2-4*	2200	NR	
Stansbury Front Trail	10.5	→	●	●			M*	2*-4*	2500	Y	
Lake Mountains	29	Loop		●	●		S	1-3*	3300	NR	
Butterfield Canyon	13.6	↔		●			S	2-3	3000	NR	
Cedar Mountains	55.7	Loop		●	●		X	1-3	4000	NR	

Type:
→ One-Way
↔ Out & Back
Loop

Tread:
ST: Singletrack
DT: Doubletrack
DR: Dirt Road
PV: Paved Road

Physical Difficulty:
E: Easy
M: Moderate
S: Strenuous
X: Extreme

Technical Difficulty:
1: Smooth dirt & gravel roads
2: Smooth trails, washboard dirt roads.
3: Variably choppy trails & dirt roads
4: Rough, rutted, rocky trails & dirt roads.
5: Extremely rough trails & roads--caution!

Rated By Physical Difficulty
Southern Wasatch Rides

Highlights	Tr #	pg
Well-designed STs for XC & downhillers. Lift service. Postcard-perfect scenery. Locals races.	49	226
Hand-built ST links to aqueduct road high above Provo Canyon & beneath Mt. Timpanogos.	48	223
Great intro to Payson Canyon trails w/o committing to longer rides. Passes several lakes.	60	269
Steady DR climb to reservoir backdropped by Alpine Ridge if trails are not your game.	38	184
The hot ride in American Fork Canyon. Short but sweet. Stunning views of Mt. Timpanogos. Take 2 laps.	43	204
Often overlooked ST along babbling brook. Upper stretch is good technical challenge.	54	246
Newly designated open space park & singletrack hotspot. Lots of trails, tricky to follow, excellent riding.	37	181
Variety of trails in American Fork Canyon. Links to Ridge Tr. 157. Challenging descent. Bring a camera.	42	200
Wicked descent off Nebo Loop Rd. Pedal up on pavement--shuttles are for wimps!	59	266
Tricky ST rises above Provo Canyon to old pipeline DT. Views of canyon, mountains & metro.	50	231
Popular foothills trail south of Rock Canyon. Good spring-fall riding. Tricky to follow.	50	231
Blackhawk Trail in reverse; links to trail that sees few bikers. Yet another Payson score.	61	272
ATV trails lead to ridge with views of Southern Wasatch. Smokin' descent. Locals thwarted a dam here.	58	263
Out-of-the-way ride in upper Diamond Fork. ST descent is a fun test of technical skills.	56	253
Classic loop around Diamond Fork with stop at Fifth Water Hot springs. Bathing suit optional.	57	256
New ST on the outskirts of Payson Canyon. Challenging alternative to Blackhawk Loop.	62	275
Links together many STs in American Fork Canyon for bigger tour. Thrilling descent. Fish in lake after.	41	196
Circle around Mt. Timpanogos & sample sections of the GWT. Unparalleled scenery.	45	211
Long climb from Cascade Springs to Wasatch Mountain S.P. Technical ST then speedy DT return.	44	208
No-shuttle version of Ridge Tr. 157. New GWT section, amazing views & wild descent past Forest Lake.	39	187
Seldom-used but bikeable section of GWT. Remote mini adventure. Fun, fast DT descent.	55	249
Painful climb on precarious trail. Big scenic reward of Mt. Timpanogos & Utah Valley from trail end.	47	220
Flagship ST atop Payson Canyon. Insiders' stash now gone mainstream. Always worth the drive.	63	279
Spin, spin, spin. Long climbs = bomber descents. Amazing views of southern Wasatch Front.	51	236
Premier American Fork ST. Buffed & rugged trails. Total backcountry adventure. Huge views. Da 'kine!	40	191
Adventurous backcountry exploit on GWT to remote reaches of Southern Wasatch. Long descent.	52	240
Endurance ride around Hobble Creek basin. Four-wheelers will think you're nuts. Good for training.	53	243
Epic XC-ST tour around icon of Wasatch Range. Beat your chest proudly after this one. Burly!	46	215

West of the Wasatch Rides

Highlights	Tr #	pg
Family fun ride on historic railroad grade. Passes Chinamens natural arch. Views of GSL & Wasatch Front.	17	87
Longer family fun ride on historic railroad grade. Lots of time to ponder life of pioneer days.	17	87
ST on edge of GSL at Antelope Island S.P. Smooth with one rocky section. Very scenic.	18	90
Easier-to-follow version of popular springtime race course. Fast-paced. Good spring fitness ride.	70	308
Spur trail to Split Rock Bay Trail (Antelope Island S.P.). Leads to overlook of bay & lake. Fun trail.	18	90
Loop to Beacon Point (Antelope Island S.P.). Good climb, fast descent. Big view of GSL & Wasatch Front.	18	90
Scenic ST on east side of Antelope Island S.P. to Garr Ranch. Easy but long. Popular with horses.	18	90
ST high on ancient lake shoreline. Tough 1st climb, lively trail, bomber descent. Beautifully desolate.	64	287
Main route at Antelope Island S.P. Two solid climbs & fun descents. Hand-built ST sections. Great sunsets.	18	90
Secret Tooele ST stash. Burly climb yields a rewarding descent. Add-on Dark Trail. Worth the drive.	69	305
DR climb to view of Bingham Canyon Mine. Link to secluded White Pine Trail. Fun w/ gnarly descent.	67	299
ATV trail along Stansbury Mountains foothills. Good workout with many short, tough climbs.	65	291
Burly climb to mountains west of Utah Lake. Smokin' descent. Big views of Southern Wasatch Front.	71	312
Long-winded grind to overlook of Bingham Canyon Mine. Biggest man-made hole on earth. Long descent.	68	302
Near metric century in West Desert. Fast-paced with two solid climbs. Bonk & you're buzzard meat!	66	294

Dogs:
Y: Dogs allowed
Y*: Dogs allowed with restrictions
NR: Route not recommended for dogs
N: Dogs not allowed
L: Dogs must be on leash

Abbreviations:
GWT: Great Western Trail
BST: Bonneville Shoreline Trail
MPT: Mormon Pioneer Trail
GSL: Great Salt Lake

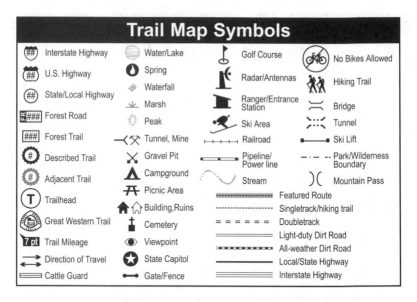

Trail Map Symbols

(##) Interstate Highway	Water/Lake		Golf Course		No Bikes Allowed
(##) U.S. Highway	Spring		Radar/Antennas		Hiking Trail
(##) State/Local Highway	Waterfall		Ranger/Entrance Station		Bridge
### Forest Road	Marsh				
### Forest Trail	Peak		Ski Area		Tunnel
(#) Described Trail	Tunnel, Mine		Railroad		Ski Lift
(#) Adjacent Trail	Gravel Pit		Pipeline/Power line		Park/Wilderness Boundary
(T) Trailhead	Campground		Stream		Mountain Pass
Great Western Trail	Picnic Area		Featured Route		
	Building,Ruins		Singletrack/hiking trail		
7pt Trail Mileage	Cemetery		Doubletrack		
Direction of Travel	Viewpoint		Light-duty Dirt Road		
Cattle Guard	State Capitol		All-weather Dirt Road		
	Gate/Fence		Local/State Highway		
			Interstate Highway		

Acknowledgments

Although publishing this book was a one-man operation, I could not have accomplished it without the assistance of many other persons.

We all must applaud the continual efforts of local, county, state, and federal government agencies who provide us with the trails we ride, including the cities of Ogden, Kaysville, Layton, Farmington, Bountiful, Centerville, Salt Lake, Sandy, Draper, Alpine, Pleasant Grove, Lindon, Orem, Provo, Springville, and Payson; Weber, Davis, Salt Lake, and Utah Counties; Utah State Parks and Recreation; Bureau of Land Management (Salt Lake Field Office); Wasatch-Cache National Forest (Ogden and Salt Lake Ranger Districts); and Uinta National Forest (Pleasant Grove and Spanish Fork Ranger Districts).

High fives go my biker buddies who accompanied me on numerous rides, divulged cherished trail secrets, and patiently stopped for my photographic needs, especially Brad Karren for riding that same stretch of trail two dozen times for the cover photo. Doggie treats to his indefatigable Weimaraners Aspen and Sage.

A technical thanks to Mark Silver and John Zobell for complimentary use of *All Topo Maps: Utah*, which was used to generate the shaded relief profiles of the trail maps.

An overdue thanks goes to Trek Bikes for realizing that the little guys of the mountain biking industry make an impact too. A hard-tail purist is now a full-suspension convert.

Lastly, and always, hugs and kisses to my wife, Tricia, for her unwavering support of my two-wheeled obsession and to my daughter Joanna, who, little does she know it, will be a kick-ass mountain biker some day.

INTRODUCTION

About this Guide

Moab, Crested Butte, Marin County, Durango, Sun Valley, British Columbia—the granddaddies of mountain biking. Fruita, Bend, Flagstaff, Asherville, St. George, and the Black Hills are up-and-coming legends. All of these places are synonymous with mountain biking and are the places that get featured regularly in national mountain biking magazines. In 2001, *Mountain Bike* magazine even named the flat-land towns of Minneapolis, Austin, and Charlottesville as three of the top 10 mountain biking cities in the U.S. Huh? Ever see Salt Lake City, Ogden, or Provo on the covers of national mountain biking mags or touted as "must-go-there" fat-tire destinations? Nope. What gives?

Granted, Salt Lake City gained world-wide recognition for hosting the 2002 Winter Olympic Games, but the Wasatch Front remains the *unsung hero* in the world of mountain biking. We shouldn't complain. While riders (and writers) are making beelines to the hot spots "du jour," we all are quietly relishing our trails in the Wasatch Range, which define the term "mountain" biking. If you're new to the Wasatch Front or if you're a local but first time mountain biker, then all it will take is a few rides to make you raise you brow and exclaim "Whoa! I never knew . . ." Yes, the mountain biking in the Wasatch Range is pretty great and is comparable to all the legendary locales across the country. The icing on the cake is that it's all a stone's throw from a major metropolis. Great trails, easy access, big city life. What more could you want? How about a guidebook that gives you the goods on all these choice trails?

Mountain Biking Utah's Wasatch Front, is more than a revised edition of the previous regional best seller. It's a whole new book with a fresh new look. It's been trimmed down to fit conveniently in a jersey pocket or hydration pack, but it's still comprehensive and utterly detailed. The layout gets a facelift for easier reading. Trail maps sport cutting-edge technology with the addition of shaded relief topography—no more confusing contour lines or blank white backgrounds. Elevation profiles have been included, so you can get a "feel" for the terrain. Every trail has been checked and updated, and most importantly, there are *more trails*—some of which have never been published before. Here's what you'll find.

Northern Wasatch
Skyline Trail continues to serve as the backbone for epic adventures in the mountains above Ogden, and now you can make a neat loop out of the Lewis Peak section by linking to the new Pineview Reservoir Trail. Snowbasin took out all the stops by building over 20 miles of trails on the resort

Part of the ever-expanding Bonneville Shoreline Trail (Bountiful section).

and by offering lift service to cater to downhill riders. But if you like to climb, then you can log 4,000 vertical feet by tying together Wheeler Creek with the newly built East Fork and Middle Fork Wheeler Creek Trails and the trails at Snowbasin—ride from Pineview Reservoir to mountain peaks. Go for it! The Bonneville Shoreline Trail (BST) now stretches three miles north of Ogden Canyon, shows off a tasty little stretch above Kaysville and Layton, and gets new singletrack sections between Bountiful and Centerville.

Central Wasatch
Just when you were getting tired of the same old trails in Salt Lake, several new trails have become all the buzz. The Mormon Pioneer Trail in East Canyon rises from Little Dell Reservoir Recreation Area to Big Mountain Pass, and it serves as the stepping stone for big adventures on the Great Western Trail to Parleys Summit or as a supporting role to the old Little Mountain Trail above Emigration Canyon. The BST received finishing touches above the Avenues and behind Ensign Peak. Now you can ride from Emigration Canyon to Davis County—all on dirt! In Sandy and Draper, the BST is a work in progress. When completed, it will connect Little Cottonwood Canyon to Point of the Mountain with future plans to link to Utah County sections and to the Provo-Jordan River Parkway. Solitude, Alta, and Snowbird Resorts all boast improvements and additions to their trail systems.

Southern Wasatch
The cat's out of the bag in American Fork Canyon now that the Pleasant Grove Ranger District has inventoried all routes in their Mineral Basin Trail System, and you'll get *The Full Monty* on what trails you must ride and what trails you should avoid. The BST expands north and south from Provo Canyon with future extensions proposed from Orem to Pleasant Grove. Sundance continues to expand its well-crafted trail system, which caters to both downhillers and cross-country riders. For lift-served trail riding, it's one of Utah's best kept secrets—until know. And singletrack purists will scotch all their favorite haunts and flock to Payson Lakes to explore the many one-laners harbored in the shadow of Mount Nebo.

West of the Wasatch

Want to ride in early spring or late fall but don't want to drive umpteen hours to southern Utah? Then head West of the Wasatch to find secret singletrack stashes out of Tooele, endless miles of untraveled dirt roads in the Cedar Mountains, and a race course at Five-Mile Pass that is all the rage. Antelope Island State Park continues to offer surprises. The new 11.5-mile Mountain View Trail is geared for novices and is packed with stunning sights of the lake, island, and Wasatch Front.

Fat-Tire Dining Guide

If your philosophy is, "Eat to Ride—Ride to Eat," then you'll appreciate a brand new section: Fat-Tire Dining Guide. Food is an integral part of mountain biking and of the healthy lifestyle it promotes. Food is fuel, food is social, food is good, and you'll find suggestions on where to carbo-load before a ride, to satiate your cravings after a ride, or to enjoy good food and drink on any occasion. These restaurants were selected because they are unique, have an appreciation for mountain biking, and support the Wasatch Front's active outdoor community. Stop in, give them a try, and let them know you saw them in this book. "Bon Appetit!"

Trail Description Format

Trail descriptions have been developed to provide you with all the necessary information to make your bike ride safe and enjoyable. Here's how each trail chapter is laid out:

Just the Facts

These are the bare-bones facts that detective Joe Friday of the television series *Dragnet* would want to know. For some, this is all that is needed.

Location is the proximity of the trail to the nearest town or city.

Length is the total miles to complete the route.

Type is the route's layout. *Out-and-back:* You ride to a distant location and return by retracing your tracks. Mileage is for the entire round trip. *Loop:* You return to the trailhead by continually moving forward and not doubling back on the same trail. *One-way:* You ride to a distant location, where the ride ends. You must arrange a shuttle to return to the trailhead.

Tread is the route's surface, and the miles of each kind of tread for the entire route is given. *Singletrack* is a narrow one lane dirt path—hiking trail or game path. *Doubletrack* is an unimproved dirt road consisting of dual parallel lanes, i.e., a "jeep" road. High clearance or four-wheel-drive may be required. *Light-duty dirt roads* are irregularly maintained native surface roads that are generally suitable for passenger cars when dry but may require four-wheel-drive when wet. *All-weather dirt roads* are improved dirt or gravel roads that are generally suitable for passenger cars when wet. *Paved road* is any secondary, primary, or interstate roadway.

It's a dog's life . . . or is it?

Physically: Physical difficulty is subjective and is relative to other rides in this guidebook only and may differ significantly from that of rides in other locations or other books. *Easy-easy+:* up to 10 miles and/or less than 1,000 feet of elevation gain. Modest fitness and basic handling skills are required. *Moderate-moderate+:* 10-20 miles and/or 1,000-2,000 feet of elevation gain. Are you game for a little adventure? *Strenuous-strenuous+:* 20-30 miles and/or 2,000-3,000 feet of elevation gain. Typically, these rides *go places!* You should be fit and acclimated to high elevations. *Extreme:* over 30 miles and/or more than 3,000 feet of elevation gain. Only elite bikers who have indefatigable fitness and razor sharp skills need apply.

Technically: Technical difficulty is the measure of bike handling skill required, and is based on but not limited to sand, gravel, loose or embedded rocks, ruts, fallen trees or limbs, unusually steep ascents or descents, water bars, water crossings, and cow pies. *Tech 1-1+* is a smooth dirt road. *Tech 2-2+* is a slightly rocky dirt road or mostly smooth singletrack. *Tech 3-3+* is a variably rocky and rutted doubletrack or singletrack that requires you to watch what is beneath your front wheel. *Tech 4-4+* is a very rough doubletrack or singletrack with persistent obstacles that warrant your full attention. Dismounting and walking may be required. *Tech 5-5+* is an extremely rough dirt road or trail that may have severe gradients. Dire consequences can result if you try to ride a section and fail. Hike-a-biking for extended periods is not uncommon.

Gain is the total amount of climbing (in feet) required to complete a ride. On out-and-back rides, you'll have to re-climb every hill you descend, and gain reflects this total elevation.

Dogs: Since many bikers ride with dogs, this is a quick note as to whether a route is "canine compatible." See *Fido Factor* below for more details.

Why Should U Ride This Trail
This sets the tone of a ride and gives you a glimpse into the ride's inner soul. Each ride is unique, and this is where you'll be able to tell if any given ride suits your fancy, your ability, and your desires.

Details

This section presents the turn-by-turn narrative to get you through a ride. Although a painstaking attempt has been made to accurately describe every route, the narratives are not exhaustive. Every biker must assume responsibility for paying attention to his/her surroundings and for having a general sense of direction. Mileages set in bold type (**mX.X**) in "Details" correspond to miles noted on the trail maps. Even if your bike computer differs from the mileages listed, you'll still be able to cross-reference the description to the trail map to determine your whereabouts.

Start young. Ride for life.

Common abbreviations in text:

I-#: Interstate highway
UT #: Utah state highway
GWT: Great Western Trail

US #: Federal highway
FR #: Forest road
BST: Bonneville Shoreline Trail

Know Before You Go

This lists notes, precautions, and hazards that pertain to the trail along with any fees, regulations, and restrictions. *Fido Factor* suggests if a route is appropriate for dogs and includes information on leash regulations, water sources, hazards, and other factors. Know your pet's limit.

Maps & More Information

This section gives the standard USGS (United States Geological Survey) 1:24,000 scale topographic quadrangle(s) for the trail, plus contacts for additional information.

Trailhead Access

This tells you how to drive to the trailhead from the closest town or major roadway.

Trail Maps & Elevation Graphs

Trail maps were computer generated using USGS topographic maps as a base. Mileages inside little black boxes correspond to those set in bold type (**mX.X**) in the "Details" category. The shaded relief aspect of the maps was generated by *All Topo Maps: Utah*, version 7.0 by **iGage**. This software package of digitized topographic maps can be purchased at most major outdoor retailers or by contacting iGage: 1545 S 1100 East, Salt Lake City UT 84105, www.igage.com, (801) 412-0011.

Elevation graphs show the route's change in elevation, distance, and tread surfaces, and note key landmarks or junctions.

STUFF YOU SHOULD KNOW

SHUT UP AND RIDE!

Trail Etiquette

Webster defines *etiquette* as ". . . the forms [and] manners established by convention as acceptable or required for social relations . . ." Etiquette, therefore, applies to both tea parties and mountain biking, and riding responsibly is a subject that cannot be overemphasized. Your every action has an impact on the trail, on the environment, and on how you are perceived by others.

The "Rules of the Trail" by the International Mountain Bike Association (IMBA) provides a simple guideline to riding right. Although it may seem lengthy, it boils down to basic common sense: *Expect and respect* others, and *be kind* to the dirt beneath your tires. Keep trails open by setting a good example of environmentally sound and socially responsible off-road cycling.

Only You Can Prevent
. . . Trail Closures!

1. Ride on Open Trails Only: *Respect* trail and road closures (ask if uncertain); avoid trespassing on private land; obtain permits or other authorization as may be required. Federal and state wilderness areas are closed to cycling. The way you ride will influence trail management decisions and policies.

2. Leave No Trace: Be sensitive to the dirt beneath you. Recognize different types of soils and trail construction; practice low-impact cycling. Wet and muddy trails are more vulnerable to damage. When the trailbed is soft, consider other riding options. This also means staying on existing trails and not creating new ones. Don't cut switchbacks. Be sure to pack out at least as much as you pack in.

3. Control Your Bicycle: Inattention for even a second can cause problems. Obey all bicycle speed regulations and recommendations.

4. Always Yield the Trail: Let your fellow trail users know you're coming. A friendly greeting or bell is considerate and works well; don't startle others. Show your respect when passing by slowing to a walking pace or even stopping. Anticipate trail users around corners or in blind spots. Yielding means slow down, establish communication, be prepared to stop if necessary, and pass safely.

《   Enough said!

Give horses lots of room by stepping off the trail and waiting for them to pass.

5. Never scare animals: All animals are startled by an unannounced approach, a sudden movement, or a loud noise. This can be dangerous for you, others, and the animals. Give animals extra room and time to adjust to you. When passing horses, use special care and follow directions from the horseback riders (ask if uncertain). Running cattle and disturbing wildlife is a serious offense. Leave gates as you found them or as marked.

6. Plan ahead: Know your equipment, your ability, and the area in which you are riding—and prepare accordingly. Be self-sufficient at all times, keep your equipment in good repair, and carry necessary supplies for changes in weather or other conditions. A well-executed trip is a satisfaction to you and not a burden to others. Always wear a helmet and appropriate safety gear.

Granted, this may seem like a lot to remember when your sole objective is to pedal through the woods for a while. If anything, remember this one point every time you ride: Just because you *can* doesn't mean you *should!*

Policies, Rules, & Regulations

Trail Access Policies
United States Forest Service and Bureau of Land Management: The Wasatch-Cache and Uinta National Forests and the Salt Lake Field Office of the Bureau of Land Management maintain an open policy toward mountain bike use. Bicycles are allowed on all roads and on trails that are posted open to bicycles. Be aware that trails and roads may not be constructed or maintained specifically for bicycles and that you may encounter motor vehicles on some routes.

Riding skillfully is *cool*. Riding recklessly is *lame*.

Wilderness Areas: Mountain bikes are *not* allowed in state and federal wilderness areas. Pertaining to the area of coverage in this guidebook, these include the Mount Olympus, Twin Peaks, Lone Peak, Mount Timpanogos, Mount Nebo, and Deseret Peak Wildernesses.

Mill Creek Canyon: *Recreational Use Fee:* A fee is charged per vehicle upon exiting Mill Creek Canyon ($2.25 per vehicle). Bicyclists and pedestrians who do not drive up Mill Creek Canyon are not charged the fee, currently. Contact the Public Lands Information Center at REI for additional information: (801) 466-6411.

Odd-Even Day Trail Access Policy: Mountain bikes are allowed on upper Mill Creek Canyon trails on *even-numbered* calender days. Mountain bikes are not allowed on upper Mill Creek Canyon trails on *odd-numbered* calender days. Upper Mill Creek Canyon trails are defined as Big Water, Little Water, and Upper Mill Creek/Great Western Trail. This regulation does not apply currently to Mill Creek Pipeline, Wasatch Crest, Mill D North, or Desolation Trails.

City Creek Canyon: Policies are strict and violators can be cited.
During summer months (Memorial Day through the end of September)
- Foot traffic is allowed on the canyon's paved road and dirt trails every day.
- Motor vehicles are allowed on the canyon's paved road by permit only on odd-numbered calender days.
- Bicycles are allowed on the canyon's paved road on odd-numbered calender days and are prohibited on holidays regardless of the odd-even status. Bicycles are not allowed off the paved road, except on the Bonneville Shoreline Trail (BST). Bicycles are allowed on the BST every day.
- Pets must be leashed at all times. Pets are not allowed past the water treatment plant about 2.5 miles up the canyon road.

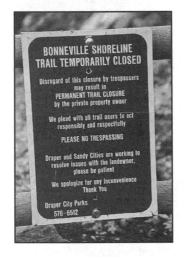

Top: Upper Mill Creek Canyon. Middle: Bonneville Shoreline Trail (Sandy Section). Bottom: Bonneville Shoreline Trail (Salt Lake Section--Sunnyside to Pipeline).

During winter months (end of September to Memorial Day):

- Vehicles are prohibited.
- Ski and bicycle travel is not encouraged on the paved road because of heavy machinery and snow removal equipment used to access the water treatment plant.

Corner Canyon Preservation District, Draper: Vehicle, bicycle, and horse use within the Corner Canyon Preservation District is limited to Lower Corner Canyon Road, Upper Corner Canyon Road, Mt. Baldy Trail, Jacob's Ladder Trail, and Cherry Canyon/Bear Canyon Loop Trail. Foot travel within the Limited Use area is restricted to designated trails. Public use of private lands within the Preservation District is prohibited, except by consent of the owner.

American Fork Canyon/Alpine Scenic Highway: The Uinta National Forest has implemented a recreational use fee for UT 92/Alpine Scenic Highway between American Fork Canyon and Provo Canyon and for the Cascade Springs area. Vehicles must pay a fee when entering the area: $3 per vehicle for a three-day pass.

Ski Areas: Mountain bike use within ski areas that operate under permit by the Wasatch-Cache National Forest is restricted to established roads and to trails designated open to mountain bikes. Obey all signs restricting travel. All lifts, structures, buildings, and summer homes are private property. Be watchful of activity on slopes above you. Maintenance operations and heavy machinery may be present at any time. Powder Mountain and Sundance are privately owned ski resorts and have additional and specific policies. Portions of Snowbasin exists on privately owned land.

Dogs and Mountain Biking in the Wasatch Front
It's safe to say that dogs and mountain biking go hand in hand, but just because you are on a dirt road or trail does not mean your pet can run free.

Wasatch-Cache and Uinta National Forests: Pets must be leashed at all times at campgrounds, trailheads, parking areas, picnic grounds, and all developed areas within the national forest. On trails, it is required that dogs be under control at all times, and it is recommended that your pet be leashed. You are required to clean up after your pet. Pick it up and dispose of it properly, or at least kick it off the trail.

Weber, Davis, Salt Lake, and Utah Counties: County ordinances state that pets must be leashed and under the owners' control at *all* times within county limits. The exceptions are designated off-leash areas and parks. For example, off-leash areas in Salt Lake County are Memory Grove, Herman Frank's Park, Lindsey Gardens, Jordan Park, and Atherton Park. At the time of publication, Tanner Park and Parley's Nature Park were *not* designated off-leash county areas.

Mill Creek Canyon (Salt Lake County): In addition to national forest and Salt Lake County regulations, the following rules apply. Dogs must be leashed on all trails in Mill Creek Canyon on even-numbered calender days. Dogs may be off leash on all trails on odd-numbered calender days.

Your pet must be under control at all times. Remember, bikes are allowed on upper Mill Creek Canyon Trails (Big Water, Little Water, and Upper Mill Creek/Great Western Trail) on even-numbered calender days. If your dog accompanies you when you bike these trails, your dog must be leashed! Contact the Public Lands Information Center at REI for updates: (801) 466-6411.

Watershed Areas: Bicycles are not restricted from any canyons that provide culinary water to the Wasatch Front; however, domestic animals (pets, horses, and grazing animals) are not allowed in Big Cottonwood and Little Cottonwood Canyons, Mountain Dell Canyon, and portions of City Creek Canyon, except by special permit. Domestic animals are currently allowed in Mill Creek Canyon.

Planning Your Ride

The trails in the Wasatch Range vary from short jaunts just out of town to remote backcountry treks. While it is reasonable to adjust your preparedness for each ride, never underestimate your need for water and food, the prospect of rapidly changing weather, and the possibility of having to address a mechanical or health-related emergency.

Water and Food
Water and food are essential to life, and the lack of either one can turn the most blissful ride into an agonizing nightmare. Play it safe and overestimate your consumption of both; the added weight is trivial. Remember the cyclists' axiom: Eat before you feel hungry, drink before you feel thirsty. Consume food and water at regular intervals, rather than one large binge midway through the ride.

Tools and Repair Equipment
Some people ride with just the shirt on their back, others seem to pack a complete hardware store. Learn the basic on-trail repair techniques, or ride with someone who has. Don't wait for a mishap on the trail to realize how little you know about your bike. Carry the "basic tool kit" at least, which can be stuffed easily into a small under-the-saddle pack:
- Tire levers
- Patch kit
- Spare tube
- Frame-mount pump or compressed air cartridge

Now consider these extras:
- Multi-purpose tool
- Chain tool
- Crescent wrench, pliers, or vise grips
- Flat head and/or Phillips screwdrivers
- Hex and socket wrenches

- Spoke wrench
- Duct tape
- Pocket knife

Still more stuff:

Spare brake and derailleur cables, chain lube, sunscreen, lip balm, water purification tablets, toilet paper, and zipper-top bags for left over snacks. And don't forget money, in case you need a bribe for a lift.

A word of advice: It's reasonable to share the load if you ride with a group, but stay close together or regroup often. It does little good for the lead rider to be carrying the pump and patch kit if another rider is a mile behind with a flat. If you ride solo, you may have to carry the whole works.

Accessories & Emergency Gear:
- Lock
- Cyclometer
- Camera
- Waterproof jacket
- Waterproof matches or lighter
- Compass and map
- Flashlight or headlamp
- Plastic whistle
- Emergency blanket
- First aid kit
- Cell phone

Clothing

Clothing is a personal matter and varies from no fashion to high zoot. Regardless, consider function as well as style.

- Helmet: Today's helmets are incredibly lightweight, well ventilated, and utterly vogue. Like the American Express Card, "don't leave home without it."
- Padded bicycling shorts and gloves: Whether skin-tight lycra or cargo style, padded bike shorts cushion the bumps and prevent chaffing and blistering where you need it most.
- Shirt: Synthetic materials are preferred over cotton because they wick moisture away from your skin and dry quickly.
- Shoes: Lightweight hiking boots or mountain biking shoes provide support both in the pedals and on the trail.
- Extra layers: Layering is the key to maintaining a comfortable body temperature and preventing excessive perspiration while exercising, especially in cool or damp weather. Wear layers of synthetic materials next to the skin and a nylon or breathable-weatherproof shell on the outside. Cotton sweat pants and sweaters are poor choices, especially for rainy weather.

- Rainwear: Afternoon thunderstorms during the summer are common in the Wasatch Range, even if the morning sky is cloud free. Pack along lightweight rainwear or at least a garbage bag—just cut three holes for your head and arms.
- Eye wear: Sunglasses and sport shields are highly fashionable and protect your sensitive eyes from the sun's harmful rays, passing branches, and flying debris. Make sure glasses are fastened securely with a retention strap.
- Sunscreen: Sunscreen is a must because the Wasatch Range is considered high elevation. Exposed skin can burn in less than one hour. Use a sunscreen with a minimum SPF (sun protection factor) of 15.

Potential Hazards

Health-related problems can result from lack of preparedness, inadequate physical conditioning, and plain misfortune. Weather conditions in the Wasatch Range can vary between the extremes depending on the season: sweltering valley heat to cool moist forests to frigid wind-swept ridges and peaks. Plan for current and forecasted weather conditions.

Lightning: During the summer, afternoon thunderstorms are common and they can be violent. Don't be fooled by the morning's cerulean sky. If lightning is proximal and strikes are frequent, get off ridges quickly. Seek shelter at lower elevations in valleys, between boulders in rocky slopes, or in heavily forested areas. Avoid shallow caves, open meadows, lone trees, or isolated tree clusters. Separate yourself from your bike. Then get low: sit or lie down.

The best protection against being caught in a thunderstorm is to start your ride early and complete it by midafternoon. Always carry some form of rainwear.

Hypothermia: The lowering of the body's core temperature is not just a winter-related health. Frigid mountain rains, wind blowing across exposed or wet skin, and lack of food and water can attenuate the onset of hypothermia. Symptoms include feeling deep cold, numbness, shivering, poor coordination, slowing of pace, and slurred speech. Advanced symptoms include blueness in the skin, fingers, or lips; severe fatigue; irrationality and disorientation; and decreased shivering followed by stiffening of muscles.

Treat a hypothermic victim by seeking shelter and warmth. Replace wet clothes with dry clothing, or cover the victim with wind-proof materials. Encourage the victim to ingest food and warm fluids or to move at a slow and steady pace to raise body temperature.

Heat exhaustion: *Hyper*thermia (raised body temperature) is caused by exposure to hot environments and overexertion. Blood vessels in the skin become so dilated to promote internal cooling that blood to the brain and

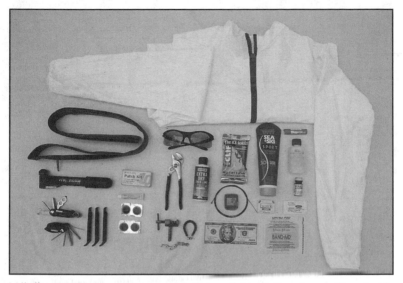

Left: the essentials; middle: more stuff; top: lightweight waterproof/breathable jacket--O2 Rainwear.

other vital organs is reduced to inadequate levels. Symptoms include nausea, dizziness, mild confusion, headache, slight temperature elevation, and dehydration. Cool the victim by seeking shade or by wetting the victim and fanning vigorously, and encourage drinking cool fluids.

Altitude sickness: Ascending to high elevations (nearly all of the Wasatch Range) without acclimating may produce headaches, fatigue, loss of appetite, drowsiness, and apathy. (It's about the same feeling as a hangover.) Treatment includes rest, adequate consumption of fluids and food, and pain relievers. If you're visiting from low elevations, proceed slowly at first or allow an extra day to adjust to the new environment.

Bad Water: Water does not have to be visually polluted to be bad. Mine wastes, bacteria and viruses, or *Giardia lamblia* can pollute water. Giardia, which is introduced to surface waters from animal and human waste, causes intestinal distress, cramps, and loss of appetite. Symptoms can last for weeks if not treated medically. Avoid all surface waters and carry plenty of water with you; otherwise, treat the water by boiling it for 10-15 minutes, purifing it through a filtration device, or disinfecting it with chemicals (Potable Aqua, Globaline, or iodine).

Hunting Season: Big-game hunting season in Utah runs from early September through the end of October, and much of the Wasatch Range is prime deer and elk habitat. Avoid the opening and closing days of hunting season, stay on main dirt roads, forfeit remote singletracks, and wear brightly colored clothing. Contact the Utah Division of Wildlife Resources for more information: (801) 538-4700, www.wildlife.utah.gov.

REGIONAL SETTING

Shape of the Land

To the eye of the casual tourist or the discerning geologist, Utah's diverse and stunning scenery is largely the product of grand scale accumulations of layered rocks: from the burnt umber sandstones of southern Utah's canyon country to the glaciated peaks of northern Utah's mountainlands. Lehi F. Hintze, in *Geologic History of Utah,* effectively summarizes Utah's physiographic evolution into six broad phases.

The oldest period, **Phase I**, occurred one billion to 350 million years ago (Late Precambrian to Devonian Periods). A pervasive western sea invaded Nevada and Utah and laid a thick wedge of shoreline sands, offshore muds, and deep-water limestones over the crystalline rocks of North America's Precambrian Shield, or craton. These sedimentary rocks are seen in the ridge-forming Big Cottonwood Formation; the bold face of Mount Olympus; and the conspicuous tan quartzite escarpments bolstering Ben Lomond, Wil-lard Peak, and Lewis Peak near Ogden.

A wedge of Cambrian quartzite underlies Willard Peak.

The craton's Precambrian rocks are well hidden in Utah, but you'll see outcrops if you pedal up Farmington Canyon or onto Antelope Island. These 1.6-billion-year-old metamorphic rocks, called the Farmington Complex, are characterized by crinkled bands of light and dark minerals cut by pink granitic rocks, which attest to the intense heat and pressure found deep within the earth.

Deposition was still the theme of **Phase II**, 350 million-200 million years ago (Mississippian to Early Triassic Periods). During this time, a sequence of mountain-building events gave rise to the Ancestral Rocky Mountains. As these highlands were uplifted, they were viciously attacked by erosion, and large quantities of sediment filled nearby depositional basins. The Oquirrh Basin in northwestern Utah received over 25,000 feet of limy sediments. Deposits were thinner in the Wasatch. Most notable are the white and gray Mississippian marbles in Big and Little Cottonwood Canyon, including the Hellgate Cliffs across from Snowbird.

The Wasatch Range creates a formidable backdrop to the cities of northern Utah.

In **Phase III**, 200 million to 80 million years ago (Late Triassic to Early Cenozoic Periods), the 3000-mile-long Sevier Orogenic Belt uplifted western Utah and eastern Nevada. Compressional forces in the earth's crust thrust massive sheets of rocks along near horizontal fault planes for great distances, resulting in older rocks lying on top of younger rocks. The rocks comprising Mount Timpanogos, for example, were shoved nearly 30 miles eastward from the Oquirrh Basin along the Charleston-Nebo Thrust Fault.

The deep ocean that once inundated western Utah would never return, and eastern Utah became a low, oscillating shoreline flushed periodically by shallow seas. Much sediment was deposited in southeastern Utah, including what geologist William L. Stokes refers to in *Geology of Utah* as the Great Sand Pile. These cliff-forming sandstones are showcased in many of southern Utah's national parks and make up the frictional rolling surface of Moab's famed Slickrock Bike Trail. The Nugget Sandstone (a co-relative of the renowned Navajo Sandstone) fingered into the Wasatch and was quarried from Salt Lake's Red Butte Canyon. This flesh-tone stone was used in many historic buildings, including Fort Douglas, which served as the athletes' village for the 2002 Winter Olympics.

Phase IV, 80 million to 40 million years ago (Late Cretaceous to Early Tertiary Periods), was a period of renewed tectonic activity as the North American continental plate pulled farther away from the African continental plate and the Atlantic Ocean widened. The Rocky Mountains and parts of southern Utah were uplifted during the Laramide Orogeny, but the Wasatch Range remained topographically low and received only stream deposits from nearby highlands. During this time, the Weber, Provo, and Spanish Fork Rivers may have established their seemingly impossible courses across the now formidable Wasatch Range.

Phase V, 40 million to 25 million years ago (Oligocene Period), was the age of fire, and Utah was invaded by igneous intrusions and volcanic eruptions. The Little Cottonwood Stock, which forms the gray cliffs at the mouth of Little Cottonwood Canyon, was the material of choice for construction of the L. D. S. Salt Lake Temple in the late 1800s. Today, its steadfast handholds lure technical rock climbers. Miners flocked to upper Big and Little Cottonwood Canyons to reap the semi-precious metals that mineralized from the Alta and Clayton Stocks. Over the Wasatch, Park City sounded a silver siren as well. Despite the prosperity found in the Wasatch, the Oquirrh Mountains were the richest on earth with the excavation of Kennecott's Bingham Canyon Copper Mine.

The ancient shoreline of Lake Bonneville forms a noticeable bench on the Brigham City foothills.

It wasn't until **Phase VI**, 25 million years ago (Late Tertiary), that Utah's mountains received their current topographic expressions. Regional uplift hoisted Utah and the Intermountain West over a mile upward, and the rivers of southeastern Utah—Green, Colorado, and San Juan—dug deep convoluted courses into the Colorado Plateau.

The Wasatch Range marks the dividing line between the Rocky Mountains to the east and the Basin and Range to the west. Geologists have estimated the maximum displacement along the Wasatch Fault to be about 15,000 vertical feet, and recent earthquake data suggest that the Wasatch Range may still be on the move.

The Quaternary Period of Phase VI (the last 1.6 million years) is the latest chapter in geologic history and is marked by two significant events: the proliferation of mammals, including the emergence of modern man, and the Great Ice Age.

As the earth's climate cooled, continental glaciers crept southward from the Arctic into the northern United States. Melt water from the expanding and thawing ice sheets coupled with copious precipitation inundated western Utah's low valleys and coalesced into an enormous freshwater body known as Lake Bonneville. At its maximum size, Lake Bonneville was 145 miles wide, 346 miles long, and 1,050 feet deep. By contrast, the Great Salt Lake, the evaporative offspring of Lake Bonneville, averages about 15 feet deep. The Bonneville Shoreline Trail, along with trails on Antelope Island and Stansbury Island, take advantage of nature's craftsmanship by following the wave-cut shoreline of Lake Bonneville.

Although Utah escaped the southernmost advance of continental glaciers, its mountains were the sites of smaller alpine glaciers. Rivers and bowls of ice gouged the high peaks of the Wasatch Range into biscuitboard topography. The Wasatch's longest glacier, Little Cottonwood Canyon, flowed nearly 12 miles from Albion Basin to the shore of Lake Bonneville.

When you're out on your mountain bike, keep in mind that although the foundation of Utah's diverse scenery extends back to the opening sentence in the encyclopedia of geologic time, when the earth itself began to form, the topography you see today took shape during the last page of the last chapter. Modern man's existence in Utah is but the last syllable of the last word in this geologic treatise. Perhaps it is this incomprehensible span of time that fosters our deep reverence for Utah's stately mountains, vast deserts, and mighty rivers.

Crossroads of the West

While pedaling your alloy-spoked two-wheeled steed through the Wasatch Range, it's easy to think of yourself as a time traveler, for many of Utah's trails and roads are the historic paths crossed centuries ago by Native Americans, Spanish friars, frontiersmen, and westward-bound emigrants. Whether spurred by the quest for freedom, intrigued by promises of fortune, or compelled by discovery, early travelers converged upon northern Utah, which became the "Crossroads of the West."

Utah's First Inhabitants
Utah's first trail blazers were the Desert Archaic tribes, who lived in Utah about 9,600 B.C. to 400 A.D. They were replaced by the Fremont and Anasazi Indians, who prospered until the thirteen century. The Anasazi settled in grand cliff dwellings in the Four Corners area, whereas the Fremont roamed east-central Utah and ventured as far west as the Wasatch Range.

For uncertain reasons, the Fremont people disappeared from Utah and were replaced later by Shoshoni-speaking Indians: The Goshutes, an isolated western band, lived in the barren Great Basin, hunting small game and gathering native plants and insects. The Ute Indians occupied a large portion of north-central Utah and parts of Colorado. The Timpanoguts tribe settled in Utah Valley, and they would be the first Indians encountered by white men who wandered to the Wasatch Front.

European Arrival
The first account of Europeans in Utah was the 1776 trek of Spanish friars Dominguez and Escalante, who were appointed with establishing a route between missions in New Mexico and California. Their route of choice led them into western Colorado and then across Utah's vast Uinta Basin. In Utah, they wrote of pleasant valleys, good pastures, and all the conveniences for a settlement, recounts William B. Smart in *Utah Trails*.

Establishing a settlement was not the friars' immediate goal, however, so they forged west across the southern Wasatch Range and emerged from Spanish Fork Canyon to present-day Utah Valley. Here, they caught first sight of Utah Lake, which they called "Nuestra Señora de la Merced of the Timpanogotzis," or Lake of Our Lady of Mercy of the Timpanogotzis. Unable to establish a promising route westward from central Utah, the padres were compelled to abandon their expedition and return to New

Artist's depiction of a trappers' rendezvous. (Photo: Utah State Historical Society)

Mexico. Their retreat stands today as one of history's great treks, for the party faced innumerable hardships while crossing the badlands along the Arizona-Utah border and the Colorado River where Lake Powell now resides.

The New Frontier

Many years would pass before Native Americans in Utah would encounter European descendants, when Anglo-American trappers scurried through northern Utah in search of beaver pelts during the early 1820s. While exploring the Bear River, trapper Jim Bridger was credited with the honor of laying first eyes upon the Great Salt Lake, although Peter Skene Ogden, Jedediah Smith, and Etienne Provost were close on his heels.

Smith, in particular, was bent on exploring, and his aim was to trap the length of the elusive Buenaventura River, which he believed flowed from the Great Salt Lake to the Pacific Ocean. He never found the Buenaventura; instead, he wrote of a barren and destitute country without grass or water. He was describing Utah's west desert.

Westward Ho

Others would follow and expand upon the trappers' western routes, including government survey parties lead by Captain John C. Fremont, who mapped tracts of Utah's heartland and first explored Antelope Island.

By 1840, the business of trapping fur dwindled, so some trappers focused on establishing trading posts along the dusty Oregon Trail. The Oregon Trail stayed north of Utah, thus pioneer emigrants paid little interest to the Utah territory. In 1846, Lansford W. Hastings, who was eager to capitalize on a more direct wagon route to California, convinced a caravan lead by George and Jacob Donner to travel his "cutoff" trail around the southern shore of the Great Salt Lake.

The Donner party pressed through Echo Canyon to present-day Henefer in good time, but then it took the group 16 exasperating days to hack their way 36 miles up East Canyon, over Big Mountain Pass, and down Emigration Canyon to the Salt Lake Valley. This exhausting task coupled with the agony of crossing the Salt Desert's crusted mud flats precluded later disaster, for an early autumn blizzard caught the caravan in the Sierra Nevada Range. Only half of the 87-member party survived. Those who did ate their boots, harnesses, and the flesh of those who had perished, recounts Ward J. Roylance in *Utah: A Guide to the State.*

In Search of Zion
The impetus for the Mormon movement differed from that of other west-bound emigrants, for theirs was a flight from religious persecution, rather than the pursuit of fur, gold, or fertile farmlands promised in Oregon and California. Mormon beginnings took place about 1820 in a small upstate New York town, where young Joseph Smith received a series of divine revelations and professed that his was the only true Church of Christ.

Smith's preachings garnered skepticism, opposition, and fear from neighbors who soon learned Smith endorsed polygamy, or plural marriage. Smith's church was forced to move numerous times throughout the Midwest. Smith realized that he and his thousands of followers had to seek peaceful isolation in a region ". . . where the Devil cannot dig us out," quotes Don and Betty Martin in *Utah Discovery Guide.*

Smith drew up plans for an exodus to the Rocky Mountains. He never led his congregation westward, however, because he was arrested and was later murdered by an angry Illinois crowd. Senior apostle Brigham Young succeeded Smith and assumed leadership of the journey.

In April 1947, Young lead his Pioneer Company of 144 men, three women, and two young boys out of the Midwest. He saw no seclusion in the golden state of California. Instead, he had a vision of an isolated valley ringed by mountains on the edge of the Great Basin.

The Mormons veered south from the well-traveled Oregon Trail along the faint trail pursued by the Donner party the previous year. Where it took the exhausted and embittered Donner party 16 days to travel 36 miles to the Salt Lake Valley, Brigham Young's group took only four. On July 24, 1847, Brigham Young proclaimed they had reached the "right place" and would build their temple to God. Ironically, the Mormon Trail also put Young's refuge on a main thoroughfare for California-bound gentiles.

Crossroads of the West
During the 1850s, stage coaches drawn by six fast horses provided regular service for passengers and freight between east and west, but they proved to be an inefficient means of communication. "Young wiry orphans" rode like the wind for the Pony Express in 1860 and used portions of the estab-lished Mormon Trail between Missouri and California.

The overland mail route was doomed from the start because the of high costs to run it, winter's blizzards, and hostile Indians. Despite its speed and reliability, the Pony Express lasted only 18 months and was replaced by the Overland Telegraph of 1861.

Left: Statue at Main Street and North Temple, dedicated to Brigham Young and the Mormon Pioneers. Church of Jesus Christ of Latter Day Saints Salt Lake Temple in background. Right: East meets west with the transcontinental railroad on May 10, 1869. (Photo: Utah State Historical Society.)

A year later, the Central Pacific and Union Pacific Railroads expand ed their tracks east and west, respectively, with the mission of completing a single rail line across the country. Again, following the routes pioneered by natives, trappers, and emigrants, the railroads crossed northern Utah and met head to head west of Ogden. On May 10, 1869, the Golden Spike at Promontory Summit completed 1776 miles of desert, rivers, and mountains as the Atlantic and Pacific Oceans were linked by rail.

The completion of the transcontinental railroad coincided nicely with the Wasatch's blossoming mining era, which began with a silver strike near present-day Alta (Little Cottonwood Canyon) in 1864 by Colonel Patrick E. Connor. A few years later, his soldiers unearthed a vein of silver-, lead-, and gold-laden quartz in the hills surrounding Parleys Park—renamed Park City in 1872. Instantly, Park City was placed on the map. Over the next two decades, Park City became one of the wealthiest mining districts in the Rocky Mountains. The bonanza brought an ethnically diverse influx of miners, and the Mormons would see their land of Zion infringed upon once again.

By the late 1800s—with mining towns booming, the steam engine chugging from coast to coast, and both Mormons and gentiles inhabiting the Salt Lake Valley—northern Utah was propelled from an age of discovery into an era of expansion. In the years to come, many pioneer trails would become asphalt corridors for commerce and tourism, and where Brigham Young envisioned physical, religious, and economic isolation for his Mormon congregation, a major metropolitan center would sprout.

Although our daily lives today may seem overwrought with technology and modernism, we can still hop on our mountain bikes and celebrate those romantic days when pioneer travelers blazed the original trails through Utah.

NORTHERN WASATCH

NORTHERN WASATCH

1
Inspiration Point

JUST THE FACTS

Location:	Mantua, 5 miles east of Brigham City
Length:	27.6 miles
Type:	Out-and-back
Tread:	22.6 miles doubletrack, 5 miles dirt road
Physically:	Strenuous (long, sustained climb; big elevation gain)
Technically:	2-3⁺ (variable gravel, washboards, and rocks)
Gain:	4,500 feet
Dogs:	Not recommended: possible traffic, too long

GO □
NO ■ | JAN | FEB | MAR | APR | MAY | JUN | JUL | AUG | SEP | OCT | NOV | DEC |

WHY SHOULD U RIDE THIS TRAIL *As its name suggests,* Inspiration Point will leave you awestruck by the dynamic and diverse terrain that defines northern Utah. Below your feet, the Wasatch Front is one big chunk of fractured rock that has been uplifted dramatically above the far-reaching levelness of the Great Salt Lake valley, and more than 100 miles of the range can be seen stretching from the Idaho border to Salt Lake. Wildlife, including moose, are drawn to the fertile, flower-dotted slopes of Willard Canyon. Got bike lights? They'll come in handy if you hang out until sunset when Inspiration Point lives up to its name. Since this long-winded ride is wholly on dirt roads, it's more a test of endurance than technical prowess.

Details

From Mantua's Wyatt Park, head south on the paved road, following the sign for Willard Basin/Inspiration Point. In a half mile, the road turns to light-duty dirt with variable gravel and washboards (tech 2). A left turn across Box Elder Creek (**m2.5**) begins the steep switchbacking climb up the mountain's side to Willard Basin (tech 2-3⁺). As elevation increases, oak mixes with aspen and pine then with fir, through which cooler breezes filter. Stay left at the junction for Perry Reservoir (**m7.7**), and angle up several ascending traverses to a road junction on the edge of Willard Basin (**m10.0**). Here, you can view fertile Cache Valley far to the north.

Fork left and descend gradually into the basin (right heads to Grizzly Peak—an easy, scenic diversion). Pass a primitive Forest Service campground; then circle north around the basin's edge. A small glacier once rested in this cirque, but it didn't flow far. The lower canyon's conspicuous V-shape is an indication of erosion by stream flow rather than glacial scouring. As you cross over the lip of the basin, you'll be shocked by your first view of the Wasatch Front. Chug up to Inspiration Point for more jaw-dropping sights.

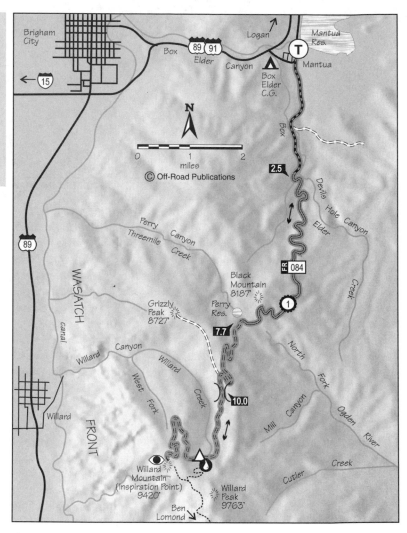

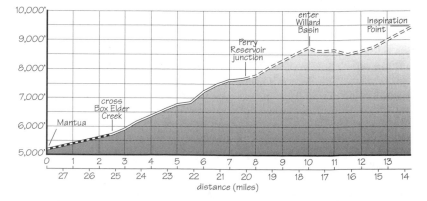

Option: (Inspiration Point-Ben Lomond)

There are 2.5 miles of ridge-top singletrack (one-way) between Inspiration Point and Ben Lomond. The trail is moderately difficult but rates tech 3⁺-5 since it receives little regular maintenance. Along the way, you'll cross above ragged, ex-humed terrain and shadow-filled crevasses.

Moose are known to inhabit Willard Basin.

From Inspiration Point, head southward on the old jeep road; then branch right to stay just below the ridge. In the small saddle ahead, take the uppermost trail along the ridge. Connect with another trail that contours across the western face of Willard Peak. The trail crosses a small point then follows the ridge south through a meadow to Ben Lomond.

Naturally, you can keep heading south from Ben Lomond on Northern Skyline Trail and descend to North Ogden Divide for a total ride distance of 26 miles, but you'll need a vehicle shuttle to return to Mantua.

Know Before You Go

- To knock off a few miles of mundane dirt road, drive about 3 miles south of Mantua and park alongside the road. Perry Reservoir is a good trailhead for a moderate-rated ride to Willard Basin, but high clearance is recommended for the dirt road approach.
- The potability of spring water at the primitive campground in Willard Basin is uncertain.
- *Fido Factor:* Dogs are not recommended because of the long distance, lack of water, and possible vehicle traffic.

Maps & More Information

- USGS 1:24,000: Mantua, Utah
- Public Lands Information Center (at REI): (801) 466-6411
- Wasatch-Cache National Forest (Ogden Ranger District): (801) 625-5112, www.fs.fed.us/r4/wcnf/unit/ogden/index.shtml

Trailhead Access

From I-15, take Exit 364 (Brigham City, Logan). Travel east on UT 89/91 and up Box Elder Canyon. Just past the Box Elder Campground, turn right for Mantua, and park at Wyatt Park in .5 mile.

NORTHERN WASATCH

JUST THE FACTS

2
Cutler Flat Park

Location:	Ogden Valley, 12 miles north of Pineview Reservoir
Length:	5.0 miles
Type:	Out-and-back w/ loop
Tread:	3.8 miles singletrack, 1.2 mile doubletrack
Physically:	Moderate (short in miles but a few good climbs)
Technically:	2-4 (smooth doubletracks, undermaintained & semi-primitive singletracks)
Gain:	960 feet
Dogs:	On leash

	JAN	FEB	MAR	APR	MAY	JUN	JUL	AUG	SEP	OCT	NOV	DEC
GO □ NO ■												

How far would you go for a choice one-lane trail? If you're a singletrack purist, you would likely go to the ends of the earth, but you need only go as far as Ogden Valley to ride the secluded trails at Weber County's Cutler Flat Park. This little circuit follows unnamed trails on the eastern foothills of Willard Peak. Small meadows explode with wildflowers in the summer, and thickets of oak and maple become a fire storm of color in the autumn. Although the trails are undermaintained, they have a surprisingly smooth flow. If you like this little loop and want to log more miles, simply take another lap or ride back in reverse.

Details

On the north side of the Bowery Picnic Area (big sloping meadow), pick up a dirt road that descends to Cutler Creek and goes around a gate. The road crosses over the creek, follows alongside it, and then bends north up North Fork Ogden River. In .2 mile, fork left on an unsigned singletrack that rises moderately up a small cool hollow. The trail steepens to a solid low-gear pump as it switchbacks twice and follows up a subtle ridge overlooking Bowery Flat. The mostly hard-packed dirt tread provides adequate grip for your rear tire (tech 2-3). Fork right on a singletrack .7 mile up from the road to loosely contour the hillsides through dense groves of oak and maple and to cross small meadows; you'll return by descending the trail that forks left and stays along the ridge overlooking Bowery Flat and Cutler Creek. Gradually, the tight track bends right and descends to the North Fork doubletrack (**m1.9**). If this ride is not your cup of tea, then coast down the road back to Bowery Flat. To continue, go left and climb the doubletrack for .1 mile; then fork left on a dirt lane that provides access to Arc Smith Ranch. (The North Fork road ends at a gate in .4 mile.)

Next you tackle the route's toughest climb—a moderate[+] grind that gains 250 feet in .4 mile. A few hundred yards past Arc Smith Ranch, fork left on a well-worn singletrack that contours above a hollow. Some choppy tread and exposed roots will keep your riding style honest (tech 3-4).

Angle into the hollow, and rise up to a junction at a small divide overlooking Cutler Creek (**m3.0**). To close this loop, fork left, climb over a low timbered knoll, and descend on lively but choppy tread to a previous junction where you then retrace your tracks to Bowery Flat.

For an alternate route back to the picnic area, descend from the small divide (**m3.0**) to Cutler Creek. You'll have to ford the creek, which can be deep and swift in spring; by autumn you can hop across on rocks. Go left to descend alongside the creek and past vent covers for a buried water line. Angle uphill to the right, and exit through a gate to a dirt road that serves as access to a buried water tank. On your left is a secret singletrack that drops back to the picnic area through dark dank timber flanking Cutler Creek. Hold on tight; it's a wild little ride (tech 4⁺).

! Know Before You Go

- Cutler Flat Park is primarily a group picnic and camping area (fee area) with water taps and outhouses. Individual sites are limited. There is

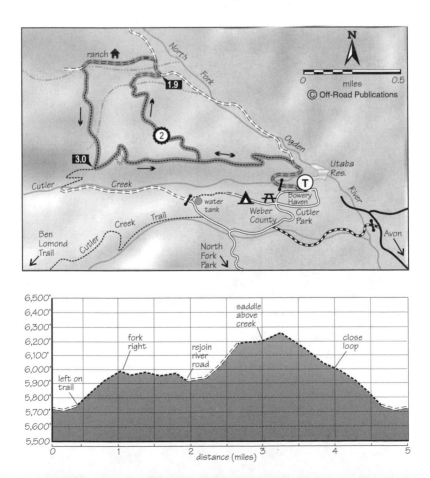

NORTHERN WASATCH

no fee for day use, provided you do not occupy a campsite and park on the north side of the Bowery Flat away from the picnic area.

• *Fido Factor:* Trails are dog friendly, but you should leash your pet in the picnic/camping area.

? Maps & More Information

• USGS 1:24,000: Mantua, Utah
• Weber County Parks and Recreation: (801) 399-8491

Trailhead Access

From I-15, take Exit 347 (12th South Street, Ogden Canyon, Recreation Areas), and travel east on UT 39. At the top of Ogden Canyon, cross the Pineview Reservoir dam on UT 158 for Eden, Liberty, and Powder Mountain. (Alternatively from Salt Lake City, take Exit 324 off I-15 for South Ogden. Travel north on US 89 to South Ogden, and then go east on I-84 to

Score some sweet singletrack in North Ogden Valley.

Exit 92 for Mountain Green. Take Trappers Loop Road/UT 167 to UT 39 at Pineview Reservoir. Go left on UT 39 to the dam and then cross it onto UT 158.) Turn left at the junction for Powder Mountain Ski Area (signed "Old Highway 162"), travel 3 miles, and turn left on 4100 North at a T-junction in Liberty. Go right/north on 3300 East at the four-way stop toward North Fork and Avon. In 1.5 miles, fork left for Weber County North Fork Park. Take North Fork Road 2 miles, and turn left for Cutler Flats. Go right at a T-junction then left to reach the big meadow of Bowery Flats. Park across the field alongside the road that descends to the river.

3
Powder Mountain Resort

JUST THE FACTS

Location:	17 miles northeast of Ogden
Length:	5.7-mile loop
Type:	3.1 miles singletrack, 2.6 miles doubletrack
Tread:	Loop
Physically:	Moderate (short rocky climb on dirt road, aggressive climb up Mushroom Trail)
Technically:	2-4 (pebbly dirt roads; smooth & rocky singletracks)
Gain:	800 feet
Dogs:	On leash

GO ☐
NO ■ | JAN | FEB | MAR | APR | MAY | JUN | JUL | AUG | SEP | OCT | NOV | DEC |

WHY SHOULD U RIDE THIS TRAIL

If you're feeling singed during the dog days of summer, then head to Powder Mountain to cool your head and revitalize your soul on fast-paced doubletracks and fun-filled singletracks. This route follows the 2002 Pedal Powder mountain bike race course on a double loop around the resort's summit. Mountain goat genes are not required because Powder Mountain's "summit" at Hidden Lake Lodge is a broad rolling highland not a chise̶̶̶̶̶̶̶̶̶̶ ̶̶̶̶̶̶̶̶̶̶re are no long-winded climbs on this route, but there̶̶̶̶̶̶̶̶̶̶̶̶̶̶̶̶̶̶̶̶̶̶̶̶s that will pump up your heart and inflate yo̶̶̶̶̶̶̶̶̶̶̶̶̶̶̶̶̶̶̶̶̶̶̶ntain delivers big time with sights of Og̶̶̶̶̶̶̶̶̶̶̶̶̶̶̶̶̶̶ Range, and Cache Valley. Wildflowe̶̶̶

TRAILS CLOSED

Navigation̶̶̶̶̶̶̶̶̶̶̶̶̶̶̶̶̶̶̶̶̶̶̶̶s are rarely signed, but since̶̶̶̶̶̶̶̶̶̶̶̶̶̶̶̶̶̶̶̶̶̶e is little risk of getting lost. N̶̶̶̶̶̶̶̶̶̶̶̶̶̶̶̶̶̶̶̶̶e and learn about the trails the "easy" way.̶̶̶̶̶̶̶

From the double wh̶̶̶̶̶̶̶̶̶̶̶̶̶̶̶̶̶̶̶̶̶ right fork and climb gradually on a pebbly doubletrack. A̶̶̶̶̶̶espite precedes a more lengthy but modest climb up to the relay towers. Freewheel briefly, and climb once again to a low rounded knoll where you should look for Ed's Singletrack forking right (may be unsigned, **m1.1**). If you reach a fork in the road, you went .2 mile too far.

Ed's meanders gradually off the treeless summit through a blanket of mountain sage and wildflowers; then it angles downhill more steeply (tech 3-4). Some turns are sharp, rough, and unannounced, so don't daydream. Intersect a doubletrack, and take the road to the right across a broad bench pocketed with aspens. Fork left at a Y-junction, now on a southeast bearing. In .2 mile, fork left from the road on Meadow Singletrack (may be unsigned). If you miss the turn, you'll head southeast to White Rock Basin, so named for the conspicuous bleach-white quartzite knolls in the distant. (In fact, that's a good destination if you want to add on a few miles. You'll find gaping views of Ogden Valley from the road's end.)

Appropriately named, Meadow Trail crosses a sloping field of grass on a near level keel before _____ intersection of doubletracks that is very near to Ed's Si_____ ___rk, and climb gradually on the doubletrack. J_____ ___d gets despairingly rutted, fork right or _____ ____nsigned). Pump hard briefly then con_____ ___ a deep timbered canyon. The potpou_____ ___edging the path give the trail its nam_____ ___es you to an intersection with the do_____ __. Go left and climb a sharp, rough hill. _____ __r Shortcut Singletrack forking right (may_____ ___ch a T-junction with a doubletrack, you miss_____ ___enough, then go to the T-junction, fork right, and retra____ y___cks past the relay towers and back to the trailhead.) Shortcut Singletrack contours around the knoll and inter-

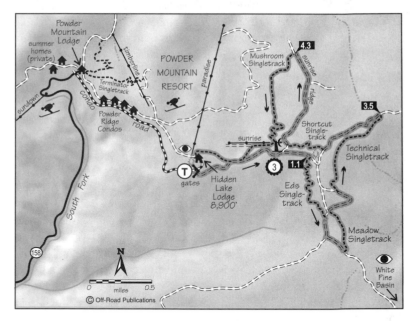

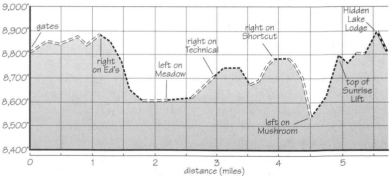

sects a double-track coming off the north side of the relay towers. Go right and descend at highway speeds out Sunrise Ridge. Stay left/straight at a Y-junction, drop more steeply on rugged tread, and watch closely for Mushroom Singletrack forking left (may be

Heading down Ed's Singletrack . . . in haste.

unsigned, naturally, **m4.3**) ding toward a sign for the ski run Picnic after tur

Mushroom Sing ss Mushroom Valley (tech 2⁺-4) and up Valley fills a huge agrarian void north ins and Bear River Range. Descend a v) for a half dozen lift towers, and fo at pops up a small steep embankment ain ridge road, and retrace your outgoing n one last trail, pump hard up to Hidden La e dirt road back to the gates and trailhead to wrap ther lap? How about four? That's how many pro racers have to ride, and they do it in about one hour forty minutes. Ouch!

TRAILS CLOSED

Option: Terminator Singletrack

Racers who competed here in years past are quick to strike a chord about the legendary Terminator Singletrack and of the toll its steep radical switchbacks took on "over-zealous" bikers. Unfortunately, Terminator has fallen to disrepair. You can still ride it, and it's still as wild as a desert stallion, but the tread is overgrown and eroded in spots. And keep in mind that if you make the descent, you'll have to chug up the gravelly Condo road to return to the Hidden Lakes Lodge trailhead.

Meadow Trail.

NORTHERN WASATCH

To find it, start at Hidden Lakes Lodge and descend westward on the steep gravelly doubletrack t̶o̶ ̶[̶ ̶]̶ ̶4̶)̶. Go counterclockwise around the summit of Timberli̶[̶ ̶]̶ ̶[̶ ̶]̶der the lift. The road banks right at a sign for R̶u̶[̶ ̶]̶ ̶[̶ ̶]̶a̶ left turn. (You can see the trail right bel̶[̶ ̶]̶ you'll have to snoop around to find th̶[̶ ̶]̶'s embankment. The path rounds a lo̶[̶ ̶]̶ Lift, and then drops you down four n̶[̶ ̶]̶s̶ gone "tilt" (tech 5). Cross Extermin̶t̶o̶[̶ ̶]̶xit to Powder Mountain Lodge.

But wait, there̶[̶ ̶]̶wder Mountain Lodge, angle right, cross Drif̶[̶ ̶]̶the woods again. Another set of remarkable turns (tec̶[̶ ̶]̶across lower Drifter and to the base of Timberline Lift. Pump up the service road to Powder Mountain Lodge then up the Condo road to return to the Hidden Lakes Lodge trailhead.

! Know Before You Go

- Powder Mountain is private property. Public recreational use is allowed from June 1-August 15. The trails are closed at other times. Stay on designated trails and roads to avoid trespassing.
- Obey all signs restricting parking.
- Camping (undeveloped) is allowed by permit only and requires a fee.
- There is no lift service during the summer.
- Helmets must be worn at all times.
- *Fido Factor:* Pets must be leashed at all times.

? Maps & More Information

- USGS 1:24,000: Browns Hole, Hunstville, James Peak, and Sharp Mountain, Utah.
- Powder Mountain Resort: (801) 745-3772, www.powdermountain.com
- Intermountain Cup Mountain Bike Race Series: www.intermountaincup.com

Trailhead Access

From Ogden, take UT 39 up Ogden Canyon, cross the Pineview Reservoir dam, and travel on UT 158 to Eden. Continue on UT 158 for 7.3 miles up South Fork Canyon (steep). Go right on a dirt road for Powder Ridge and the condos (Powder Mountain Lodge is straight ahead) for 1.3 miles to a Y-junction and two white steel gates. Park alongside the road, but do not block the gates. Hidden Lakes Lodge is up the left fork; the ride begins on the right fork.

4
Ben Lomond Trail

JUST THE FACTS

Location:	25 miles northeast of Ogden at Weber County North Fork Park
Length:	12 miles
Type:	Out-and-back
Tread:	All singletrack
Physically:	Strenuous (one big, tough climb)
Technically:	3-4⁺ (rough, rocky, rutted switchbacking trail w/ enticing amounts of smooth running tread)
Gain:	2,940 feet
Dogs:	Yes

GO □
NO ■ | JAN | FEB | MAR | APR | MAY | JUN | JUL | AUG | SEP | OCT | NOV | DEC |

WHY SHOULD U RIDE THIS TRAIL?

Ben Lomond Trail is the main route to the namesake mountain icon of the northern Wasatch Range. Steep grades and often-rugged tread will test your brute strength, stamina, and tenacity. The optional ascent to the summit of Ben Lomond itself is arguably the toughest mile of singletrack in the Wasatch. Rewards? Making it to the top is reward enough, but the views of Ogden Valley to the east, Great Salt Lake to the west, Ogden metro below, and 100 miles worth of the Wasatch Range will steal your breath away—what little you have left that is.

Details

Pick up the Ben Lomond Trail (BLT) at the stone monument, and cross a footbridge just past the "Mixed Shrub Community" interpretive sign. This lower section is downright nasty with rock rubble littering the entrenched tread (tech 4-5), and the stout oak brush adds insult to injury by scraping your exposed skin and offering little shade from the beating sun. Persevere. Periodically, the trail smooths and passes through shade-giving aspens. As you round turn number four, your withered tongue will stretch out to the ribbons of water cascading down the mountain's bare rock slopes from Cold Spring, but the cool drips are too distant to provide refreshment. Keep chugging up eight more turns; then take a well-deserved break by enjoying the sights of Ogden Valley from the "Overlook" trail that spurs right from a saddle. Pass the Cutler Spring Trail forking right (**m5.0**, see Option), and pump hard up a quick succession of turns. Pass Bailey Cabin Spring, and rejoice when you reach the old wooden trail sign on the ridge (**m6.0**).

Rejoice nothing. Your trip is not "officially" complete until you bag the summit of Ben Lomond. Other than to boast that you "rode" to the top, there's little reason to endure the agony of pedaling your bike up. You're better off stashing your rig and taking to foot. You may end up walking more than riding anyway. Midway, you'll face "Satan's Serpent" (author's name)—seven improbable turns. Make the effort because the view from the top is the finest in northern Utah, and it's all downhill.

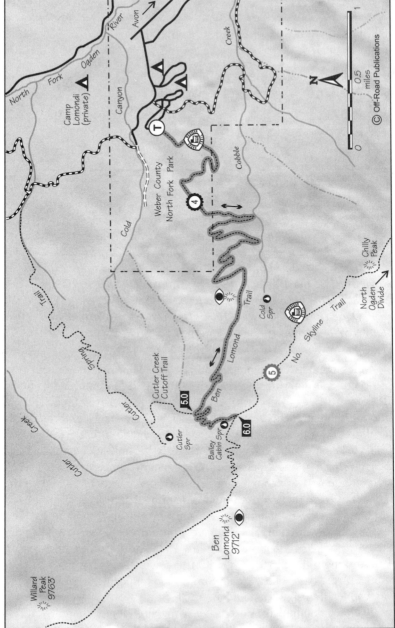

Option: Cutler Spring Trail

The mostly flat, 1.2-mile (out-and-back) Cutler Spring Trail leads to a natural seep cupped within a pristine bowl beneath Ben Lomond. One-half mile out, fork left at a junction signed "Wasatch Crest Trail 1.5, North Fork Park 6.5," and descend gently to the spring. Return the opposite way and descend BLT. You can descend Cutler Spring Trail, but be forewarned, it's one wicked drop loaded with rocks (tech 4-5). You'll take a beating if your bike is not of the "freeride" variety. Go right on dirt roads at the bottom to return to the BLT trailhead. Don't even think about riding up!

! Know Before You Go

- Ben Lomond Trail is also popular with hikers and equestrians, especially on weekends and holidays. Expect and respect other users.
- North Fork Park has a developed campground (fee area) with water taps and outhouses. There is no fee for day use, provided you do not occupy a campsite.
- *Fido Factor:* Trail is dog friendly, but there are no water sources along the route, and Bailey Cabin Spring is unreliable. Remember, your dog can't coast on the downhill, so don't over work it on the uphill.

? Maps & More Information

- USGS 1:24,000: North Ogden, Utah
- Public Lands Information Center (at REI): (801) 466-6411
- Wasatch-Cache National Forest (Ogden Ranger District): (801) 625-5112, www.fs.fed.us/r4/wcnf/unit/ogden/index.shtml
- Weber County Parks and Recreation: (801) 399-8491

Trailhead Access

Via North Ogden Divide: From I-15, take Exit 352 (North Ogden), and travel east on UT 134. Turn right on US 89 for North Ogden/Ogden then immediately left on UT 235 for North Ogden. Turn left/north on 400 East (Washington Boulevard), travel uphill to 3100 North, and turn right/east for North Ogden Canyon. Cross North Ogden Divide, descend to the junction of 4100 North and 3300 East (stop sign), and go left/north on 3300 East. Travel 1.5 miles and fork left for North Fork Park. Follow more signs for Camping Area-Horse Stalls, and park near the stone monument.

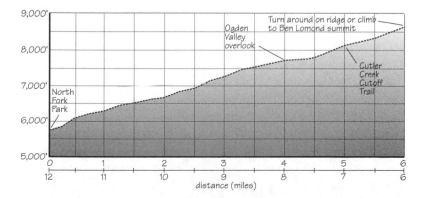

Chief and Joe descend Ben Lomond Trail

Via Ogden Canyon/Pineview Reservoir: From I-15, take Exit 347 (12th South Street, Ogden Canyon, Recreation Areas), and travel east on UT 39. At the top of Ogden Canyon, cross the Pineview Reservoir dam on UT 158 for Eden, Liberty, and Powder Mountain. (Alternatively from Salt Lake City, take Exit 324 off I-15 and travel north on US 89 toward South Ogden for about 10.5 miles. Go east on I-84 to Exit 92 for Mountain Green. Take Trappers Loop Road/UT 167 to UT 39 at Pineview Reservoir. Go left onto UT 39 to the dam and then cross it onto UT 158.) At the junction for Powder Mountain Ski Area, turn left (signed "Old Highway 162"), and travel 3 miles to a T-junction with 4100 North in Liberty. Go left/west then right/north on 3300 East at the four-way stop toward North Fork and Avon. Proceed as described above.

5
Northern Skyline Trail

JUST THE FACTS

Location:	North Ogden Divide, 3.5 miles east of North Ogden
Length:	13 miles
Type:	Out-and-back
Tread:	All singletrack
Physically:	Strenuous (steep, rough climb with rolling ridge-top singletrack)
Technically:	2-4⁺ (choppy, narrow trail w/ steep exposures; smoother tread on ridge)
Gain:	2,516 feet
Dogs:	Yes

GO ☐
NO ■ | JAN | FEB | MAR | APR | MAY | JUN | JUL | AUG | SEP | OCT | NOV | DEC |

WHY SHOULD I RIDE THIS TRAIL?

Kindred to Ben Lomond Trail from North Fork Park, Northern Skyline Trail, too, provides access to Ben Lomond but from North Ogden Divide. Like Ben Lomond Trail, Northern Skyline rises quickly through a multitude of angular switchbacks where brute strength and finesse are prerequisites; however, Northern Skyline then serves up smooth-rolling ridge-top singletrack. It's no easier overall, just a different twist on a similar theme. The optional ascent to Ben Lomond's summit rewards you with a stunning view of the Ogden metro and of the thousands of feet of rock the Wasatch Fault has uplifted above the Great Salt Lake valley.

Details

The trail is remarkably smooth at first as it weaves through stands of oak, maple, and pine. After a short distance, though, the turns become more angular, the tread gets choppy, and the trail crosses steep, sunny slopes (tech 3-4⁺). Elevation is gained quickly, and you'll need good balance coupled with raw power to conquer the initial 10 switchbacks without faltering. Southern Skyline Trail, alter ego to Northern Skyline Trail, can be seen across North Ogden Divide dropping dramatically from Lewis Peak.

Leaving North Ogden Divide far below, the narrow trail makes a long ascending traverse up the east side of the ridge. The path is less rugged, but you'll still need to keep your eye on your front wheel. That's tough to do with such a big view of Ogden Valley tugging for your attention.

After crossing over to the ridge's west side (**m4.2**), you'll revel in smoother tread and easier pedaling as the trail rounds Chilly Peak (tech 2). Again, there's no time for day dreaming because the path crosses steep slopes that bolster Ben Lomond. Notice how uplift and faulting have tilted and juxtaposed these once flat laying rocks: "tectonics," as geologists call it.

A short, rugged section on the north side of Chilly Peak may force you to hoof it briefly (tech 4⁺-5) and then you encounter what locals call "The Wall." More ridge-top rolling takes you to the old wooden trail sign and the route's turnaround point at the base of Ben Lomond (**m6.5**). Head southeast and up to the small knoll to enjoy endless views in nearly every direction—or, legs and psyche willing, tackle the ascent to Ben Lomond's summit.

Option: Ben Lomond Summit

Wolf down an energy bar, and glug a bottle of water, for this "side trip" demands every ounce of energy. It's 1,000 vertical feet and 1.2 miles

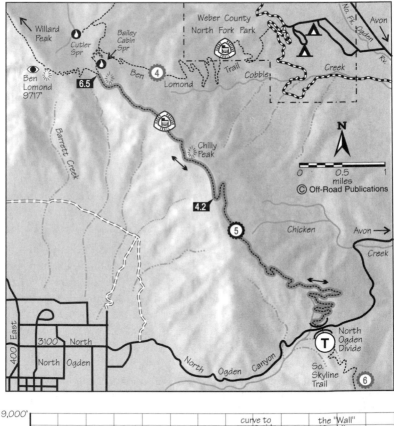

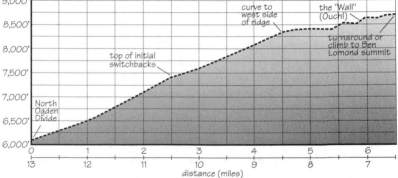

NORTHERN WASATCH

Left: It's a long way down to North Ogden. Right: Returning from Ben Lomond.

from the old trail sign to the summit (2.5 miles round trip). The trail's steep grade, loose rocks, and two dozen switchbacks are hell on wheels. Midway to the top, the trail snakes through "Satan's Serpent" (author's name), a series of seven devilish switchbacks. Even the most gifted biker will find *riding* the entire way extremely challenging. Stashing your bike and hiking to the top is the best choice for most mortals. But, make the effort; the views are worth every drop of sweat, and then it's all downhill.

! Know Before You Go

- Northern Skyline Trail is open to foot, bike, horse, and motorcycle travel, and use can be heavy on weekends. Expect and respect others.
- North Ogden Divide Trailhead has an outhouse but no water taps.
- *Fido Factor:* Trail is dog friendly, but there are no water sources along the route, and Bailey Cabin Spring is unreliable. Remember, your dog can't coast on the downhill, so don't over work it on the uphill.

? Maps & More Information

- USGS 1:24,000: North Ogden, Utah
- Public Lands Information Center (at REI): (801) 466-6411
- Wasatch-Cache National Forest (Ogden Ranger District): (801) 625-5112; www.fs.fed.us/r4/wcnf/unit/ogden/index.shtml

Trailhead Access

From I-15, take Exit 352 (North Ogden), and travel east on UT 134. After one mile, turn right on US 89 for North Ogden and Ogden; then turn left immediately on UT 235 for North Ogden. Turn left/north on 400 East (Washington Boulevard); travel through the stop light then uphill to 3100 North, and turn right/east (signed "North Ogden Canyon"). Travel through residential areas then up North Ogden Canyon to North Ogden Divide.

NORTHERN WASATCH

JUST THE FACTS

6
Southern Skyline Trail

Location:	5 miles east of Ogden; 1.4 miles north of Pineview Res. dam
Length:	22.5 miles
Type:	Loop (clockwise)
Tread:	19.3 miles singletrack, 3.2 miles paved road
Physically:	Strenuous (long taxing climb, sharp descent, large elevation gain)
Technically:	2⁺-4⁺ (climb is packed dirt, gravel, and rocks w/ a few sharp turns; descent to N. Ogden Divide is steep w/ eroded tread; Pineview Trail is smooth
Gain:	4,200 feet
Dogs:	No for loop, yes for out-and-back

GO □
NO ■ | JAN | FEB | MAR | APR | MAY | JUN | JUL | AUG | SEP | OCT | NOV | DEC |

WHY RIDE THIS TRAIL / SHOULD U

Southern Skyline Trail is the alter ego to Northern Skyline Trail. You'll climb for many miles up a sunny mountainside and then out along a breezy ridge. But, rather than retrace your tracks to the trailhead, you can now loop back on almost all singletrack by first descending to North Ogden Divide and then linking with Indian and Pineview Trails. This makes for what is arguably the best loop ride in the northern Wasatch and one that truly defines the term "mountain biking." If you take the spur to Lewis Peak, you'll see vistas of the Great Salt Lake, Ogden metropolis, and block-faulted Wasatch Range that will make you shudder with awe.

Details

From the parking area, cross the highway and pedal southward about 100 yards to a dirt road. The trail is marked by a carsonite post with a Great Western Trail (GWT) decal. Start out in a good climbing gear because the trail begins with a deceptively steep ramp. Then it rises moderately above rough-cut limestone cliffs that encase Ogden Canyon (tech 2⁺-3⁺). Take the short spur to Lookout Point for a refreshing view of Pineview Reservoir (**m2.0**).

A mile farther, the trail levels briefly but becomes very choppy (tech 4). Ogden Valley spreads out below you like an agrarian quilt. The path then curves onto northeastern slopes and passes through a canopy of shade-giving foliage; there's even a bit of downhill to offset the steady climbing thus far. However, it's short lived; so don't get used to it. You'll resume climbing strenuously in short order (tech 3⁺).

As the trail wraps around the head of Goodall Canyon, Mount Ogden rears its stony crown above lesser peaks and deep bowls of Snow Basin Ski Area. Ignore a right fork tagged for the GWT, unless you want to make a shortcut to the North Ogden Divide descent. Keep chugging uphill until you reach the main ridge (**m7.0**). Glorious views of North Ogden, Ben Lomond, and the Great Salt Lake are your just rewards.

To reach Lewis Peak, head left/south along the ridge, and fork right where a left choice is signed "Dead End." Descend on choppy tread, climb through a small aspen grove, and pump up to the humble summit of Lewis Peak (**m9.3**). Arguably, the vista from Lewis Peak outshines that from Ben Lomond because you are looking *at* Ben Lomond and the ragged cliffs that support it.

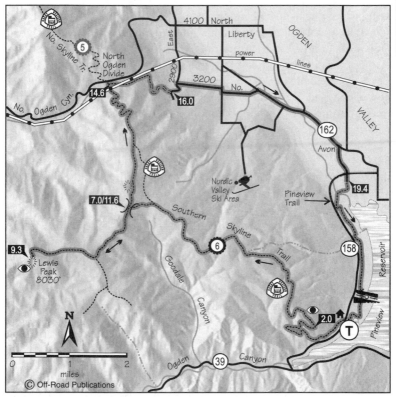

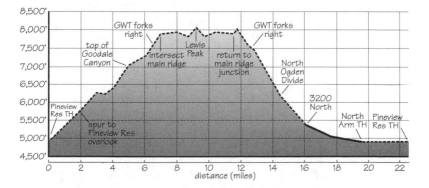

Return from Lewis Peak to the ridge junction (**m11.6**), and take the trail north, or if you're pooped, just coast back home. Take the right fork around the small peak (cheater route), and descend straightaway to the junction with the GWT forking right. This is your last chance to return to Pineview via Southern Skyline.

Going on? Stay straight through this junction and square up for the steep, rugged drop to North Ogden Divide (tech 3⁺-4⁺). Be friendly to the trail by keeping your wheels rolling, and be friendly to other trail users by keeping your head up and yielding.

Take a moment to read the interpretive monument at North Ogden Divide about how Native Americans, trappers, and pioneer settlers traveled historical trails through this area (**m14.6**); then pick up the Indian Trail at a carsonite post to the left of the stone sign. The route is an old power line road, but it rides like singletrack (tech 3⁺). Bend right into the trees at a viewing bench, and continue on doubletrack. Without much warning, the track exits to a paved road (**m16.0**).

Take the road down to a T-junction, and go right on what becomes 3200 North. Go straight at the four-way junction with 3500 East, and glide into Ogden Valley. Take Highway 162 right to Eden, and fork right on UT 158. Duck into the North Arm Trailhead just around the bend to pick up the Pineview Trail (**m19.4**).

Built in 2001, the Pineview Trail slips between the reservoir's shore and the highway for a mellow little cool down to the day's adventure. There's one small climb, a few quick turns, and lots of smooth tread (tech 2). However, the trail-side weeds can grow tall and whack at your sides if they haven't been cut back recently.

Exit to a dirt parking area, and pick up the trail just before the highway junction. Ride behind a mobile home park, cut through the Ogden Pineview Yacht Club, and cross the Port Ramp boat launch. Wind around a field of tall grasses, and return to Pineview Trailhead.

Option: The Skyline Olympiad
Tie together Southern and Northern Skyline Trails with Ben Lomond Trail for a 29-mile, Olympic-caliber, trans-Wasatch trek. (See respective chapters.) This fat-tire marathon is reserved for off-road experts, endurance junkies, and "mountain-bike-or-die" hammerheads whose penchant is *big* elevation gain—nearly 7,000 feet (including the 1,000-foot gruntwork to the summit of Ben Lomond). Subtract about 4 miles if you don't bag Lewis Peak and 2 miles if you skip Ben Lomond, but that's cheating. Add on about 10.3 miles if you ride from North Fork Park back to Pineview. Consider caching food and water midroute at North Ogden Divide. Masseuse, please!

Option: Pineview Trail
You don't have to scale an entire mountain to score the sweet little ride along the shore of Pineview Reservoir. Built in 2001 by the Ogden

Top: Chugging up from Pineview Reservoir.
Middle: Joe and Jared take five at Lewis Peak.
Bottom: Pineview Reservoir Trail.

Ranger District, the Pineview Trail is well-suited for families or anyone looking for an easy time on true singletrack. There are some gravelly sections, one tiny but sharp hill, a few tight turns to test your balance, and lots of smooth-running tread (tech 2). Best of all, it's nearly flat, dog friendly (be cautious when riding through the boat dock and yacht club), and a stone's throw from the reservoir. Distance between North Arm and Pineview Trailheads is 3.4 miles. Easy.

! Know Before You Go

- Southern Skyline Trail is popular with hikers, mountain bikers, equestrians, and motorcyclists, especially on weekends and holidays. Be especially cautious of trail users when descending to North Ogden Divide.
- Get an *early* start during midsummer because the incessant sun makes the climb a blast furnace by midmorning.
- A water tap and outhouse are at the Pineview Trailhead. North Ogden Divide has an outhouse but no water tap.
- *Fido Factor:* The loop version is not dog friendly because of the long distance, lack of water, and paved roads. Out-and-back to Lewis Peak is dog friendly, but there are no reliable water sources, and the climb can be taxing. Remember, man's best friend can't coast downhill.

? Maps & More Information

- USGS 1:24,000: Huntsville and North Ogden, Utah
- Public Lands Information Center (at REI): (801) 466-6411
- Wasatch-Cache National Forest (Ogden Ranger District): (801) 625-5112; www.fs.fed.us/r4/wcnf/unit/ogden/index.shtml

Trailhead Access

From I-15, take Exit 347 (12th South Street, Ogden Canyon, Recreation Areas). Travel east on UT 39 then up Ogden Canyon. At the canyon's top, turn left on UT 158 for Eden, Liberty, and Powder Mountain, and cross Pineview Reservoir's dam. Pineview Trailhead is 1.4 miles farther.

Alternatively from Salt Lake City, take Exit 324 off I-15 and travel north on US 89 toward South Ogden for about 10.5 miles. Go east on I-84 to Exit 92 for Mountain Green. Take Trappers Loop Road/UT 167 to UT 39 at Pineview Reservoir. Go left onto UT 39 to the dam and then cross it onto UT 158. The trailhead is 1.4 miles farther.

7
Wheeler Creek Trail

JUST THE FACTS

Location:	5 miles east of Ogden; top of Ogden Canyon
Length:	10.4 miles
Type:	Out-and-back
Tread:	6.6 miles singletrack, 3.8 miles doubletrack
Physically:	Moderate (E⁺ to Art Nord TH; M-M⁺ to Maples CG)
Technically:	2-4⁺ (some gravel & rock to Art Nord TH; packed dirt, loose tread, rocks, on tight singletrack to Maples CG)
Gain:	1,500 feet (to Maples CG)
Dogs:	Yes

GO ☐
NO ■ | JAN | FEB | MAR | APR | MAY | JUN | JUL | AUG | SEP | OCT | NOV | DEC |

WHY SHOULD U RIDE THIS TRAIL

With its proximity to Ogden, relatively low elevation, and biker-friendly tread, Wheeler Creek Trail is one of Ogden's most popular multiuse trails. It's a great ride to start or end your bike season or to sneak out on whenever time is short. The steady climb up the canyon will challenge novice riders but won't break them. The upper singletrack to Maples Campground will test all riders with a variety of conditions. The entire ride is especially scenic because the trail is locked tightly within the canyon early on and later opens to broad views of Mount Ogden and attendant peaks. New in 2002 were the East and Middle Fork Trails. Combined, they offer a 4.1-mile side loop from the Art Nord trailhead.

Details

From the gated trailhead, the route begins up Wheeler Canyon on an old one-lane dirt road, also known as Art Nord Drive. Smooth, packed dirt is the norm, but there are patches of gravel and chipped bedrock as well (tech 2⁺). No bother. The narrow gorge is tightly embraced by terraced limestone cliffs on the east slope and dense fir on the west. Its tumbling creek nourishes stream-side shrubs, wildflowers, and other riparian hideaways from which the refrains of song birds drift. One mile up, the main fork of Wheeler Creek disappears up Ice Box Canyon to the right, and Art Nord Drive follows the (usually) dry East Fork. At **mile 1.7**, you pass the stone memorial to Art Nord and come to the gate at the upper trailhead. Novice riders can turn around here and freewheel back down the canyon. Those continuing to the Maples trailhead should dive off the embankment on the signed trail and cross the creek, which may dry up by midsummer.

The path splits immediately (steep left, contour right), rejoins in 200 feet, and curves through a small hollow. Struggle around a remarkably tight left turn, and climb moderately to a small divide (tech 2) that serves up a magnificent view of Mount Ogden and of Snowbasin's ski runs that hosted the 2002 Winter Olympics downhill course. Coast freely down a hummocky meadow, but get ready to dismount where the trail drops into a

NORTHERN WASATCH

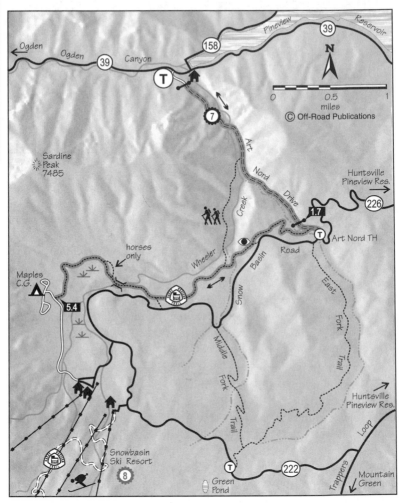

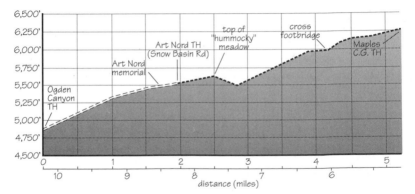

rocky gulch. Ahead, you'll climb on intermittently choppy tread (tech 3-4$^+$) for over a half mile before crossing a footbridge and then continuing up through patterned maple and aspens. Stay left at a junction where horses are directed to the right, and walk your bike across a well-crafted footbridge over upper Wheeler Creek. The horse trail rejoins and the combined path, now deeply entrenched, passes a small pond and rounds a wetlands area. A stealth rider may spy moose and other wildlife lurking here. A gradual but sustained climb through mixed timber takes you to the Maples trailhead (**m5.4**). Except for the climb back up the hummocky meadow to that small divide, the return is all downhill.

Option: East Fork and Middle Fork Wheeler Creek Trails

In the fall of 2001, the Ogden Ranger District began construction of these trails, These two trails, built in 2001, make for a fine loop, but individually, both serve as connectors to Snowbasin's trail network. At 3.0 miles (gain 900 feet) and 1.3 miles (gain 450 feet), respectively, both trails showcase wide treads, sustainable grades, and biker-friendly turns.

For a moderate loop ride, start at the Art Nord trailhead, and pick up East Fork Wheeler Creek Trail about 200 feet west of the parking area. The path rises moderately while passing through a mix of oak, maple, and aspen (tech 2$^+$). In 1.5 miles, it enters a broad meadow where several small drainages converge. Boardwalks and footbridges keep the trail high and dry. Two pairs of well-crafted switchbacks take the path up through a grove of aspens before intersecting Middle Fork Trail. If you continue .1 mile more, you exit to the Green Pond trailhead. Otherwise, take the spirited Middle Fork Trail (tech 2$^+$) down the small tight canyon for 1.3 miles to Snowbasin Road (no developed trailhead). Nicely done Ogden Ranger District. To close the loop, you must pedal the road 1.4 miles to the Art Nord trailhead.

! Know Before You Go

* Wheeler Creek Trail can be very warm at midday during midsummer.
* Because of the main trail's popularity, please descend at prudent speeds, and respect other trail users.
* All trailheads have outhouses but no water taps.
* *Fido Factor:* The entire route is dog friendly and has good water sources, but getting to or exiting from Middle Fork Trail requires over a mile of paved road.

? Maps & More Information

* USGS 1:24,000: Huntsville and Snow Basin, Utah. East Fork and Middle Fork Trails are not shown.
* Public Lands Information Center (at REI): (801) 466-6411
* Wasatch-Cache National Forest (Ogden Ranger District): (801) 625-5112; www.fs.fed.us/r4/wcnf/unit/ogden/index.shtml

Left: Wheeler Canyon. Right: Wheeler Creek Trail, backdropped by Mount Ogden and Snowbasin.

Trailhead Access

From I-15, take Exit 347 (12th South Street, Ogden Canyon, Recreation Areas). Travel east on UT 39 then 5 miles up Ogden Canyon. Park alongside the highway on the right immediately before the Pineview Reservoir dam or at the bottom of the short dirt road (parking is limited).

To reach the Art Nord trailhead, continue past the Pineview Reservoir dam on UT 39 for 2.8 miles, and turn right on UT 226 for Snowbasin Ski Area. Take Snowbasin Road 3.8 miles to the trailhead parking area.

Alternatively from Salt Lake City, take Exit 324 off I-15 and travel north on US 89 toward South Ogden. After about 10.5 miles, go east on I-84 to Exit 92 for Mountain Green. Take Trappers Loop Road/UT 167 north, and fork left at the divide on UT 222 for Snowbasin and National Forest Access. The Green Pond trailhead is 1.2 miles, Snowbasin's main entrance is 2.4 miles, Snowbasin's lower entrance is 3.1 miles (access to the Maples trailhead), and the Art Nord trailhead is 6.3 miles. To reach the lower Wheeler Canyon trailhead, continue on Trappers Loop Road over the summit to Pineview Reservoir. Turn left onto UT 39 and drive 3.9 miles to the trailhead, which is on the left and immediately past the dam. (The lower turnoff for Snowbasin Road is .9 mile from Trappers Loop.)

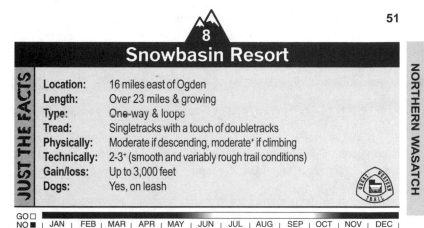

8
Snowbasin Resort

JUST THE FACTS

Location:	16 miles east of Ogden
Length:	Over 23 miles & growing
Type:	One-way & loops
Tread:	Singletracks with a touch of doubletracks
Physically:	Moderate if descending, moderate+ if climbing
Technically:	2-3+ (smooth and variably rough trail conditions)
Gain/loss:	Up to 3,000 feet
Dogs:	Yes, on leash

GO □
NO ■ | JAN | FEB | MAR | APR | MAY | JUN | JUL | AUG | SEP | OCT | NOV | DEC |

WHY SHOULD U RIDE THIS TRAIL

After hosting the downhill and alpine combined events of the 2002 Winter Olympic Games, Snowbasin has made its mark as a world-class ski resort. Now, the "Basin" is striving to become a year-round recreational destination by building an extensive trail system for hikers and mountain bikers. More than a dozen trails totaling 26 miles have been constructed with more on the drawing board. Cut by machine and then polished by hand, these well-crafted singletracks take you on fun, fast-paced downhill runs—not radical, white-knuckle drops—from treeless alpine bowls through timbered slopes to sunny, scenic meadows. If you like to climb, then you'll enjoy many of the resort's trails because they were built to biker friendly specifications, but most will want to "get a lift" on the Needles Express Gondola and cruise down to the base.

Details

With over a dozen trails to choose from at Snowbasin, you can spend days exploring all the possibilities. Here's a breakdown of what you'll find.

Trail No. 1 (Needles): 7 miles, moderate, tech 2+

Needles Trail is the heart of Snowbasin's trail system. It's a fast, mostly smooth "descending traverse" that starts at Needles Lodge at the gondola summit and zigzags under Strawberry Express Lift. After a brief stretch on a service road, it resumes on singletrack across the lower mountain to Grizzly Center. Up high, you'll get a close-up view of the Sisters formation; midway down, you'll gaze across the fertile Morgan Valley, and near the bottom, you'll cross lush meadows and penetrate stands of stately aspens. Add on No. 10 (Last Chance Trail) near the top of Becker Lift for more cross-country-style singletrack, passing or adding on Green Pond Loop before returning to lower Needles Trail. Combine all three and you'll rack up nearly 11 miles.

Trail No. 2 (Moonshine Trees): .3 mile, moderate, tech 3

This little side loop to Needles Trail is tucked away in an aspen-clad hollow—the kind of secret-stash singletrack where bootleggers would want to hide *their* secret stash.

Trail No. 3 (Porcupine Trail): 6 miles, moderate⁺, tech 3-4

If you mastered Needles Trail, then head out Porcupine Trail next. Like Needles Trail, Porcupine is a never-ending descent from the gondola summit to Grizzly Center. But Porcupine Trail harbors more challenging

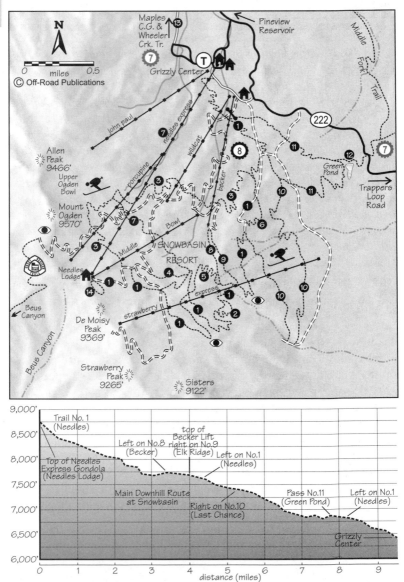

Bill leads the gang to the top of Snowbasin on "Needles Trail."

conditions with rougher tread and innumerable switchbacks. While it's nothing daunting, good handling skill are recommended. The route takes off from Needles Trail just down from Needles Lodge and cuts under the famed Needles Formation. Mount Ogden looms overhead as the trail traverses Mount Ogden Bowl and then descends under Porcupine and Needles Lifts. A winding traverse takes you across the ski runs and mid-mountain elevations; then, a sudden twisting drop connects with lower Needles Trail, which you take to Grizzly Center.

Trail No. 4 (Philpot Ridge): .6 mile, moderate, tech 4

This quick, wild drop connects with Diamond (No. 5). Freeriders and expert cross-country types will get a kick out of it.

Trail No. 5 (Diamond): .9 mile, moderate, tech 4

Nine rocky switchbacks drop off a ridge and connect to Becker Trail (No. 8). Take Becker Trail down to lower Porcupine (No. 3) and to lower Needles Trail (No. 1) for a fast thrilling descent. But don't pass up the great overlooks of the lower resort and of the distant Pineview Reservoir/ Huntsville area.

Trail No. 6 (Sunshine): .5 mile, strenuous, tech 3+

This trail offers an adventurous side track to the otherwise tame Needles Trail. Sunshine Trail serves up rough tread and tight turns through thick brush. Rejoin with Needles (No. 1) and take it to the base.

NORTHERN WASATCH

Ron heads down Last Chance Trail.

Trail No. 7 (Middle Bowl): 1 mile, moderate, tech 3

Middle Bowl Trail connects Needles Trail (No. 1) with Porcupine Trail (No. 3) and crosses the middle of Mount Ogden Bowl along the way. The trail traverses through timber and across ski runs where views are spectacular.

Trail No. 8 (Becker): .5 mile, easy, tech 2+

Becker Trail offers a mid-route traverse from Needles (No. 1) to Porcupine (No. 3) on a mellow single-track and a choppy dirt road. Take Becker downhill from Needles to get quickly to the base, or take Becker uphill from Porcupine to make an extended cross-country ride to the base via Last Chance (No. 10).

Trail No. 9 (Elk Ridge): .2 mile, moderate, tech 3

Like Becker, Elk Ridge is a mid-route traverse between Needles and Porcupine Trails. Combine Becker and Elk Ridge for a long, smooth, traversing side loop to Needles (No. 1).

Trail No. 10 (Last Chance): 2.2 miles, moderate, tech 2-3

Instead of making a beeline to the resort base on Needles, veer off onto Last Chance for more than 2 miles of cross-country-style singletrack. After traversing ski runs under Strawberry Lift, Last Chance rolls through thickets where moose are known to hide. Rejoin with Needles to descend to the base or veer off onto Green Pond Trail for still more cross-country singletrack. Needles-Last Chance-Green Pond Trails make up the longest ride at Snowbasin with over 10 miles of excellent singletrack.

Trail No. 11 (Green Pond): 4 miles, moderately easy, tech 2+

Green Pond Loop stays on the resort's lowest slopes and winds through thick timber and passes a placid pond that lures wildlife. Easy grades and smooth trail make this a good choice for strong novice riders looking for a cross-country-style ride. Ride it by itself or add it on to Needles and Last Chance Trails.

Trail No. 12 (Snowbasin): .5 mile, moderate, tech 3

This trail links Snowbasin's trail system at Green Pond with East Fork and Middle Fork Wheeler Creek Trails on the national forest, which in turn link to Wheeler Creek Trail at the Art Nord trailhead on Snowbasin Road. Whether you're a cross-country purist or a rabid downhiller, Snowbasin Trail is the crucial link to a 3,700-foot masochistic hill climb or epic descent between the Basin's Needles Lodge at the gondola summit and Pineview Reservoir. (See the chapter "Wheeler Creek Trail.")

Trail No. 13 (Maples): .5 mile, moderate, tech 3
Like Snowbasin Trail, Maples connects the trails at Snowbasin Resort with those on the surrounding national forest. This trail leads from Grizzly Center to Maples Campground where the Maples Trail rolls to Wheeler Creek Trail at the Art Nord trailhead off Snowbasin Road.

Trail No. 14 (Cirque Practice Loop): .3 mile, moderately easy, tech 2+
Take a lap around the Cirque Practice Loop to check out your bike before taking flight down the resort's many trails.

! Know Before You Go

- Needles Express Gondola operates 9 A.M.-6 P.M. Friday through Sunday from the end of May through September, weather permitting. Call for lift ticket prices. Grizzly Center at the base has bike rentals, sports retail shop, day-use services, and a cafe. The Needles Lodge atop Needles Express Gondola serves casual lunch and full-service dinner Friday-Sunday.
- Helmets must be worn at all times when biking at Snowbasin.
- Be alert to traffic on dirt roads and to maintenance operations at any place and any time, especially on the slopes above you.
- *Fido Factor:* Dogs must be leashed at all times. (Horses are allowed on dirt roads only.)

? Maps & More Information

- USGS 1:24,000: Ogden and Snowbasin, Utah
- Snowbasin Resort: (801) 620-1000, www.snowbasin.com
- Wasatch-Cache National Forest (Ogden Ranger District): (801) 625-5112; www.fs.fed.us/r4/wcnf/unit/ogden/index.shtml

Trailhead Access

From Ogden, drive 7.8 miles on UT 39 up Ogden Canyon, and turn right on UT 226/Snowbasin Road. Continue another 7 miles to the lower parking at Grizzly Center.

From Salt Lake City, take Exit 324 (South Ogden) from I-15, and drive about 11 miles on US 89 to I-84. Travel east on I-84 for 4.6 miles, and take Exit 92 for Huntsville and Ski Areas. Travel 7.1 miles on UT 167 (Trappers Loop Road) to the summit, fork left on UT 222, and drive 3.1 miles to the lower parking area at Grizzly Center.

9

Bonneville Shoreline Trail (Ogden)

Location:	Ogden foothills
Length:	6.4 miles (Mount Ogden section); 4.4 miles (Lewis Peak section)
Type:	One-way or out-and-back
Tread:	Singletracks & doubletracks
Physically:	Moderate (short, steep hills to reach "shoreline;" murderous climb between Strongs & Beus Canyons)
Technically:	2-4⁺ (sandy & rocky singletracks & doubletracks)
Gain:	1,600 feet (Mount Ogden), 1,400 feet (Lewis Peak): out-and-back
Dogs:	Yes, on leash

GO ☐
NO ■ | JAN | FEB | MAR | APR | MAY | JUN | JUL | AUG | SEP | OCT | NOV | DEC |

WHY SHOULD I RIDE THIS TRAIL *If the thought of riding along the edge of a lake seems too leisurely, then Ogden's Bonneville Shoreline Trail (BST) will surprise you. Granted, you can center the bubble of a carpenter's level on the shore of the ice age lake, but its elevated terrace is several hundred feet above its successor, the Great Salt Lake, and the bench has since been broken by mountain-front canyons. Consequently, there are plenty of ups and downs in between the flats. Throughout the ride, you'll find staggering views of the Ogden metropolis below and of the Wasatch Range overhead.*

Details

For the sake of simplicity, the BST is described from Ogden Canyon, although there are many trailheads. The Mount Ogden section heads south for 6.4 miles to Beus Canyon; the Lewis Peak section heads north for 4.4 miles to the Ogden Nature Center-North.

Mount Ogden Section

From Rainbow Gardens, hop on the Rainbow Trail, and climb the twisting path (tech 2-3) across grassy meadows and through oak and maple, passing the peculiar Corkscrew Trail along the way. At the signed junction under the power lines, the trail heads east toward the mountains and up a sandy stretch. Before you continue, however, take the gravel road north for a .8-mile, out-and-back trip to the overlook of Ogden Canyon. It's easy. When you return, struggle up the sandy trail, and go through a four-way junction of trails. (The Indian Trail forks left, but bicycle travel is not recommended; the right fork follows a side route of the BST.)

Contour along the base of the ledgy foothills (tech 2-3), and wind through Taylor Canyon, passing junctions for 22ⁿᵈ Street and 27ᵗʰ Street trailheads. About .5 mile farther, you come to the signed junction for the 29ᵗʰ Street trailhead. Descend to 29ᵗʰ Street if you want to take a lap around Mount Ogden Park; otherwise, continue straight on the wide, sandy path, and climb steeply into Waterfall Canyon. Tip-toe across the creek, and

NORTHERN WASATCH

continue south on a contour to Strongs Canyon. Upon exiting Strongs Canyon, the BST joins with a doubletrack for a few hundred feet then forks left on a gently rising singletrack—initially.

Round two switchbacks, and begin the steep, punishing climb over to Beus Canyon (tech 4⁺). The reward for your effort is a bird's eye view of the Ogden metropolis, the Great Salt Lake, and the Wasatch Front. Strongs

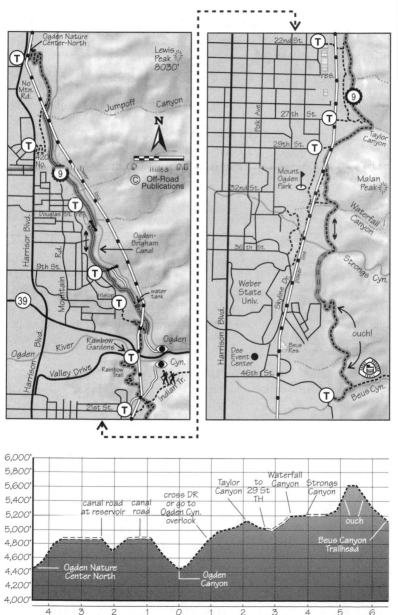

NORTHERN WASATCH

Ben Lomond backdrops a section of Ogden's Bonneville Shoreline Trail.

Peak and Mount Ogden bear down with a weighty presence; Ben Lomond is the mammoth chunk of rock to the north. If you descend to Beus Canyon Trail, you'll have to make the nasty climb back over the top again. Try this variation when returning to Rainbow Gardens. On the north side of Strongs Canyon, fork left on a singletrack that descends along the creek for .5 mile. Fork right on the Mount Ogden Bike Trail, and roll through a canopy of oak and maple to the 29th Street trailhead. Climb the short path up to the BST, and resume your ride northward.

Lewis Peak Section
The trail begins at the mouth of Ogden Canyon near a brick maintenance building. Tight singletrack finds a creative way across the steeply faced foothills (tech 2+-3+), forks right at a junction for the Hislop Drive trailhead, and rises up to the Ogden-Brigham Canal service road. Go right to a scenic overlook of Ogden Canyon, return, and then head north on the road (tech 1+) to a fenced-in water tank. Fork left about .7 mile past the tank to descend a rutted and rough doubletrack (tech 3) because the canal road ends ahead at a rocky bluff.

Climb quickly to regain the canal road on the east side of a fenced-in reservoir, and ride northward on the smooth, wide dirt lane. On the north side of the reservoir, you pass a path forking left that drops to the Douglas Street trailhead. Stay on the canal road for 1.2 miles to its end at another rocky bluff. Retrace your tracks, or test your handling skill by descending the hand-cut trail to the Ogden Nature Center-North. The return climb is strenuous and tech 3-4+, but you must applaud the efforts of those who built this section through the bouldery terrain. Another option is to descend to the 420 Harrison Boulevard trailhead. You'll find this trail about 200 feet south of where the canal road ends. Descend southward on a fun, fast singletrack (tech 2+), and exit to Harrison Boulevard across from the St. James Catholic Church. The return climb is moderate.

❗ Know Before You Go

• The BST is immensely popular, so expect and respect other trail users.
• Wading or swimming in the canal is dangerous and prohibited.

- Rattlesnakes are known to inhabit these warm foothill areas.
- Goatheads grow among these foothills and on some trails. If your tires pick up one of these multiple-spiked seeds, then they will have invariably picked up several. Don't pull them out. Often times they yield a slow leak, and you might be able to limp home or to the trailhead on a soft tire. Patching a tube is problematic because small holes can go unseen. The solution is to use tire liners, tube sealant, or "self-healing" tubes.
- *Fido Factor.* Dogs must be leashed, and you are required to clean up after your pet.

A choice section of hand-built singletrack on the Ogden BST.

? Maps & More Information

- USGS 1:24,000: Ogden, Utah
- Public Lands Information Center (at REI): (801) 466-6411
- Wasatch-Cache National Forest (Ogden Ranger District): (801) 625-5112, www.fs.fed.us/r4/wcnf/unit/ogden/index.shtml
- Weber Pathways: (801) 393-2304, http://www.weberpathways.org/
- Bonneville Shoreline Trail Committee: www.bonneville-trail.org; (801) 816-0876

Trailhead Access

Ogden Canyon trailhead: From I-15, take Exit 347 for 12th South Street, and travel to the mouth of Ogden Canyon. There are several places to park: off Valley Drive for the Ogden River Parkway, behind Rainbow Gardens at the Rainbow Trail, or on the north side of the highway.

Other Mount Ogden section trailheads: Beus Canyon: A paved parking area is 1 mile east of Harrison Boulevard on 46th South Street. Other trailheads/access points are at the ends of 22nd South, 27th South, and 29th South Streets and where 36th South Street bends and becomes Skyline Drive. All are accessed from Harrison Boulevard/UT 203.

Other Lewis Peak section trailheads: Parking areas are at the end of Douglas Street (350 South), at 420 North Harrison Boulevard, and at Ogden Nature Center-North (1175 North Mountain Road, an extension of Harrison Boulevard). Other trailheads/access points are at the east end of 9th Street and at Hislop Drive, two blocks south of 9th Street.

Bonneville Shoreline Tr. (Kaysville-Layton)

NORTHERN WASATCH

JUST THE FACTS

Location:	Kaysville foothills
Length:	3.6 miles one-way; 7.2 miles out-and-back
Type:	One-way or out-and-back
Tread:	3.1 miles singletrack, .5 mile dirt road
Physically:	Moderate (steep, sandy climb from East Mountain Wilderness Park, rolling trail on "shoreline," quick climbs through gulches)
Technically:	2-3⁺ (soft sand trails w/ rocky patches)
Gain:	500 feet (Kaysville trailhead to Fernwood trailhead)
Dogs:	Yes, on leash

GO☐
NO■ | JAN | FEB | MAR | APR | MAY | JUN | JUL | AUG | SEP | OCT | NOV | DEC |

Why Should U Ride This Trail? *Kaysville and Layton* have hopped aboard the Bonneville Shoreline Trail (BST) band wagon and have done commendable jobs of building several miles of quality singletrack along the ancient lake's wave-cut terrace. This stand-alone section runs just over 3.5 miles from East Mountain Wilderness Park to Fernwood Picnic Grounds. Along the way, the route takes you high on the brushy foothills of the Wasatch Range and through thickly forested, creek-fed canyons. Views of the metropolitan valley below, the Great Salt Lake afar, and the mountains overhead will provide ample "eye candy" for sightseers while the diversity of sandy and buffed tread, smooth glides, and hardy climbs will appeal to all pedal pushers.

Details

Squeeze through the boulders at the entrance to East Mountain Wilderness Park, and follow the sandy one-lane road along the Vita-Course (tech 2). Bust out some push-ups and chin-ups while you're at it! In .5 mile (next to the incline leg lift station), fork right on the signed BST, and climb steeply on sandy, rocky tread (tech 3⁺). Cross Holmes Creek in Webb Canyon on a sturdy footbridge, and keep your momentum going for the quick climb that follows. In short order, you'll reach the shoreline bench and roll smoothly across brushy slopes that provide sweeping views of the Wasatch Front and of the Great Salt Lake (tech 2).

The trail passes above private homes on Twin Peaks Circle (no public access) and comes to a Y-junction. Left is a nasty little drop over bedrock steps (tech 5); right is a less-threatening descent over eroded log bars (tech 4). Go right! A sweet section of trail leads to a footbridge over North Fork Holmes Creek in Adams Canyon and penetrates a patch of conifers that is as dark and dank as the Pacific Northwest. Come to a junction upon exiting the gulch. Right continues on the BST (**m2.0**); left descends the steep, sandy switchbacks to the East Side Drive trailhead.

An immaculate, smooth-rolling section passes above a gravel pit; then the trail dips sharply and is followed by a steep, sandy, rough descent. You'll curse this climb on the return. Descend to Snow Creek (no

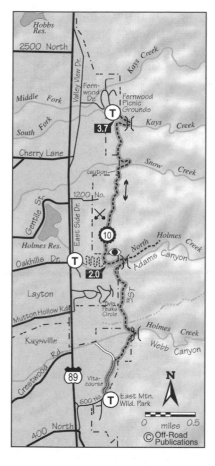

footbridge), and dismount for the quick portage up the steep opposing embankment. Cross the footbridge over South Fork Kays Creek, and roll into Fernwood Picnic Grounds (**m3.7**). About-face, and retrace your tracks. Use caution on the final descent from Webb Canyon to East Mountain Wilderness Park because of the sandy, rocky conditions (tech 3⁺).

Naturally, you can start from Fernwood Picnic Grounds just as easily. In fact, it's much easier. If your goal is to ride the whole trail out-and-back, however, then start from East Mountain Wilderness Park. You'll begin with the toughest climb, but end with a big descent.

Options: Baer Creek and Farmington Creek Sections

There are more miles to log from the Baer Creek and Farmington Creek trailheads. Go check them out, and see what you think. These sections are discontinuous because of private property developments in Fruit Heights and Kaysville. To reach the Baer Creek trailhead, take Nichols Road off US 89, go left on Mountain Road, turn right on East Oaks Drive, and fork left at 1800 East. At the road's end, take the one-lane drive uphill to the parking area. The BST actually starts back downhill in the brush at the end of 1800 East. To reach the Farmington

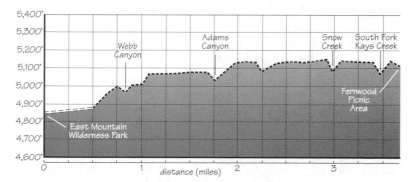

Creek trailhead, take Exit 327 (southbound) or Exit 326 (northbound) from I-15. Go right on Main Street/UT 106 then left on 600 North. Turn left on 100 East, and enter Farmington Pond Park at the mouth of Farmington Canyon. The trailhead is at the horse trailer parking area on the right.

! Know Before You Go

- Expect and respect other trail users.
- Midday temperatures during midsummer can reach 100 degrees Fahrenheit, so carry ample water.
- Rattlesnakes might inhabit these warm foothill areas.
- *Fido Factor:* Dogs must be leashed within city limits.

? Maps & More Information

- USGS 1:24,000: Kaysville, Utah
- Public Lands Information Center (at REI): (801) 466-6411
- Wasatch-Cache National Forest (Salt Lake Ranger District): (801) 943-1794, www.fs.fed.us/r4/wcnf/unit/ogden/index.shtml
- Davis County Department of Community and Economic Development: (801) 451-3278, www.co.davis.ut.us
- Bonneville Shoreline Trail Committee: www.bonneville-trail.org; (801) 816-0876

) Trailhead Access

East Mountain Wilderness Park: From US 89 in Kaysville, turn east on 400 North. Go north on 1300 East, bend right on 600 North, and go to its end. The park is just past the animal shelter and before the gun club.

Fernwood Picnic Grounds: Take Valley View Drive from US 89 (at

either Cherry Lane or about 2800 North), turn east on Fernwood Drive, and go to its end. The BST heads south from a row of boulders at the upper parking area. This is also the trailhead for the GWT.

East Side Drive trailhead: Take 1200 North off US 89, and turn right/south on East Side Drive. The trailhead is in .5 mile. This access trail is one long hike-a-bike because it rises very steeply around a dozen tight, sandy switchbacks.

BST: Kaysville-Layton section.

11
Farmington Canyon to Francis Peak

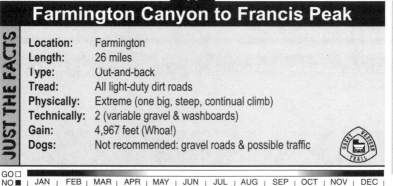

JUST THE FACTS

Location:	Farmington
Length:	26 miles
Type:	Out-and-back
Tread:	All light-duty dirt roads
Physically:	Extreme (one big, steep, continual climb)
Technically:	2 (variable gravel & washboards)
Gain:	4,967 feet (Whoa!)
Dogs:	Not recommended: gravel roads & possible traffic

GO □												
NO ■	JAN	FEB	MAR	APR	MAY	JUN	JUL	AUG	SEP	OCT	NOV	DEC

WHY SHOULD U RIDE THIS TRAIL?

If you've ever traveled I-15 between Salt Lake City and Ogden, no doubt you've seen the two big white FAA radar spheres atop Francis Peak above Farmington. If you've ever wondered how to get up there, here's the way. The ride up Farmington Canyon to Francis Peak is the longest continual hill climb in the Wasatch Front, netting just 53 feet short of a vertical mile. There are tougher, steeper climbs around, like Snowbird's Hidden Peak, but none can dethrone Francis Peak as the kingpin of climbs. As you can imagine, the views from the top are circumambient, with sights north and south along the Wasatch Crest, east of Morgan Valley and the Uinta Mountains beyond, and west of the Great Salt Lake. So, if you feel the urge to climb, then go big and climb up to Francis Peak.

Details

From Farmington Pond Park, find 100 East and take it north into Farmington Canyon. Pass the Bonneville Shoreline Trail forking right on the aqueduct service road. Pavement turns to dirt after the road crosses over the creek to officially begin your off-road climb, and the initially steep grades will call upon your lowest gears.

Directions for the next 7 miles are pretty simple—up! The grade averages about six percent, so it's a perfect off-road spin. The road is packed dirt with light gravel or rock chips (tech 2), and the switchbacks can get fairly choppy and washboarded, especially during prolonged dry spells (tech 3+).

If you're training for the races, then put your nose to the handlebar and grind away. But if you lift your eyes from the front wheel, they'll fall upon long views of the Great Salt Lake and upon road-side rock cuts striped with white, gray, black, and pink metamorphic rocks. Part of the Farmington Complex, this gneiss (pronounced "nice") dates back over 1.5 billion years and represents the continent's oldest rocks—what geologist's call the continental core or "basement."

The grade slackens a bit past Sunset Campground, and you'll scamper easily to the gated junction where Skyline Drive heads right to Bountiful Peak (**m8.0**). Fork left, bend across Left Fork Creek, and stay straight at the maintenance building. Up ahead and on the edge of Whipple Creek, the road's 13-percent grade will put the hurt on both your stamina and psyche. Stay left at a junction, and curve over to the ridge's west side. Stay left again at a second junction (right heads to Smith Creek Lakes, see

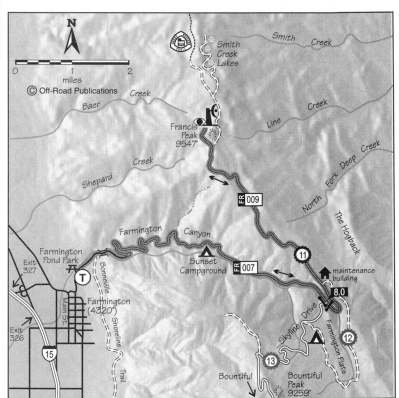

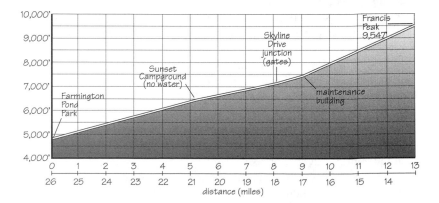

Option), and pump hard up the ride's last and steepest pitch to the radar spheres. Well done! Soak up the view, take a nap, and then let gravity do its thing.

Naturally, you don't *have* to start in Farmington. You can knock off the first 8 miles by driving up Farmington Canyon and parking at the junction where Skyline Drive forks right for Bountiful Peak (steel gates). The remaining miles to the peak are still tough.

Option: Smith Creek Lakes

While you're up here, add on about 7 miles (out-and-back) to Smith Creek Lakes. This trio of tarns (cirque lakes) hides just below the ridge north of Francis Peak. From Francis Peak, backtrack about .5 mile to a junction. Turn sharp left, follow the jeep road north along the ridge, and fork right to descend to Smith Creek Lakes (tech 3-4). (Ignore the next right-hand fork; it drops steeply and ends at some sort of experimental station.) The doubletrack rounds the first lake and rolls over to the second and third lakes before it descends eastward to destinations unexplored.

For a bird's eye view of the lakes, return to the ridge road and pedal north. Where the road ends, hike out the Great Western Trail then up to the crest. The Great Western Trail continues out the ridge and descends Kays Creek, but be forewarned; it's remarkably steep and insanely rough. Rumor has it that the "gravity crowd" uses Baer Creek Trail for downhill training runs. Look before you leap!

❗ Know Before You Go

- Be alert to motorists, and stay to the far right side of the road, especially when rounding blind curves.
- Farmington Canyon is blazing hot at midday during midsummer. Start very early, or skip the canyon climb and drive up 8 miles to the junction where Skyline Drive forks right. Similarly, Farmington Canyon is a great early season ride because it receives copious sun and melts out early.
- Weather will be cool and breezy atop Francis Peak, and thunderstorms can roll in at a moment's notice. Be prepared. The lightning rods at the peak suggest this is no place to be during an electrical storm.
- Don't go snooping around the radar facility. A posted sign reads, "Warning . . . loss of human life may result from service interruption. Facility is protected by an intrusion detection alarm system. WARNING!!!" (Note the three exclamation marks.)
- *Fido Factor:* Dogs are not recommended because of long miles, vehicle traffic, hard dirt and rock road surfaces, and lack of water.

❓ Maps & More Information

- USGS 1:24,000: Bountiful Peak, Farmington, Kaysville, Peterson, UT
- Public Lands Information Center (at REI): (801) 466-6411

Smith Creek Lakes.

- Wasatch-Cache National Forest (Salt Lake Ranger District); (801) 733-2660; www.fs.fed.us/r4/wcnf/unit/slrd/index.shtml

🏃 Trailhead Access

Northbound on I-15, take Exit 322 for Farmington, Lagoon Drive. Drive north into Farmington on 2nd West and turn right on State Street. Turn left/north on 100 East, which leads into Farmington Canyon. Park at Farmington Pond Park at the mouth of Farmington Canyon (open daylight hours); otherwise, start from town for the full vertical effect. (Alternatively, take Exit 324 off I-15 for US 89 and South Ogden. Shortly after the off ramp, turn right/east onto Park Lane [formerly Burke Lane]. Turn right at the intersection with UT 106, which becomes Main Street in Farmington. Turn left on 600 North then left again on 100 East, which leads into Farmington Canyon.

12

Farmington Flats

Location:	8 miles east of Farmington (top of Farmington Canyon)	
Length:	5.5 miles	
Type:	Loop (clockwise)	
Tread:	1.7 miles of dirt road, 3.8 miles of doubletrack	
Physically:	Easy (gentle to moderate hills)	
Technically:	2-3 (variable gravel, washboards, and rocks; fast, gravelly descent)	
Gain:	500 feet	
Dogs:	No for loop; yes for out-and-back	

JUST THE FACTS

GO □
NO ■ | JAN | FEB | MAR | APR | MAY | JUN | JUL | AUG | SEP | OCT | NOV | DEC |

The Farmington Flats loop is a great little introduction to mountain biking and is perfect for the fat-tire neophyte or a family outing. A spirited jeep road carries you around a shallow basin tucked beneath the subtle landform of Bountiful Peak. A quiet, meandering creek impeded by beaver ponds cuts across the basin's luxuriant, grass-filled meadows, and a midroute campground is ideal for a picnic. Keep in mind that the route is at moderately high elevation, so first-time riders or flatlanders may find the ride a tad more difficult. Go slow; stop and rest; and enjoy this easily accessed wedge of the Wasatch high country.

Details

From the junction where Skyline Drive forks right to Bountiful Peak at the top of Farmington Canyon (steel gates), take the left fork up toward Francis Peak. You'll return on Skyline Drive. The smooth climb is easy at first and then becomes moderate for about .5 mile (tech 1+). The Great Salt Lake can be seen in the distance through the deep gap of Farmington Canyon. At the white maintenance building (**m0.9**), turn sharply right on a doubletrack. (The Francis Peak road continues straight/north.)

After a bit more climbing, the road levels and follows around Farmington Flat's eastern perimeter through stands of aspens and across sunny slopes (tech 2+). A few potholes, ruts, and rocks in the road are of little consequence but may rudely awaken a daydreaming biker. A number of jeep roads branch to the left on the loop's southern end. Each ends after a mile or so but is worth pursuing if you want to tack on a few extra miles or test your handling skills. (Obey all signs restricting travel, as some roads are closed to restore vegetation.)

Wrap around the basin, and pedal up a short rocky hill (tech 3+). Pass Bountiful Peak Campground and come to the junction with Skyline Drive (**m4.7**).To complete the loop, stay straight/right for a fast gravelly descent back to the trailhead. Don't let gravity get away from you.

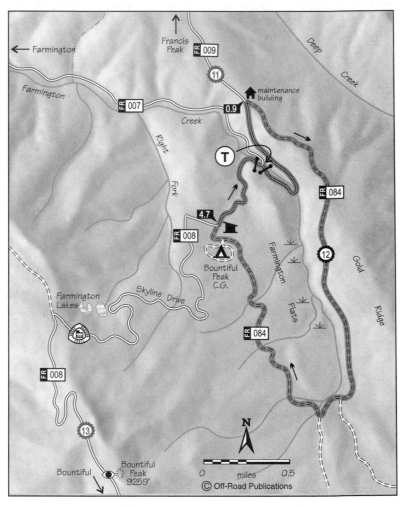

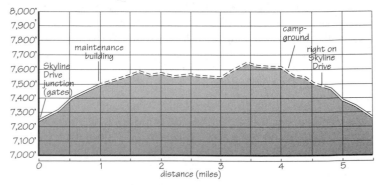

To add on more miles, take Skyline Drive 1.5 miles to the tranquil and secluded Farmington Lakes, or 3.8 miles up to Bountiful Peak for a gigantic view of northern Utah. The former is easy⁺ and gains 400 feet; the latter is moderate⁺ and gains almost 1,700 feet.

❗ Know Before You Go

- Be alert to vehicular traffic on all roads, especially on Francis Peak Road and Skyline Drive.
- Bountiful Peak Campground has water taps, picnic tables, and outhouses.
- Be prepared for cool or rapidly changing alpine weather.
- *Fido Factor:* Dogs are not recommended on the loop because of possible vehicle traffic on Francis Peak Road and Skyline Drive. The Farmington Flats jeep road is dog friendly. Just ride out-and-back from its junction with either Francis Peak Road or Skyline Drive.

❓ Maps & More Information

- USGS 1:24,000: Bountiful Peak, Utah
- Public Lands Information Center (at REI): (801) 466-6411
- Wasatch-Cache National Forest (Salt Lake Ranger District); (801) 733-2660; www.fs.fed.us/r4/wcnf/unit/slrd/index.shtml

Trailhead Access

Northbound on I-15, take Exit 322 for Farmington, Lagoon Drive. Drive north into Farmington and turn right on State Street. Turn left/north on 100 East, which leads into Farmington Canyon. (Alternatively, take Exit 324 off I-15 for US 89 and South Ogden. Take Park Lane [formerly Burke Lane] to UT 106 and turn right (becomes Main Street). Turn left on 600 North then left again on 100 East, which leads into Farmington Canyon.

Park 8 miles up the canyon at a small pullout where Skyline Drive forks right to Bountiful (steel gates). Farmington Canyon road is light-duty dirt with variable gravel, rock, and washboards and is generally suitable for passenger cars.

The Great Salt Lake recedes from view as you pedal up Farmington Canyon.

13
Skyline Drive

Location:	Farmington to Bountiful, the long way
Length:	24 miles
Type:	One-way
Tread:	All-weather dirt roads throughout
Physically:	Strenuous (never-ending climb; never-ending descent)
Technically:	2-3 (variable gravel, rock chips, and washboards)
Gain:	4,620 feet
Dogs:	Not recommended

GO ☐
NO ■ | JAN | FEB | MAR | APR | MAY | JUN | JUL | AUG | SEP | OCT | NOV | DEC |

WHY SHOULD YOU RIDE THIS TRAIL? *Skyline Drive takes you from the warm metropolitan valley up to a cool alpine ridge and then back down again. Along this designated Scenic Backway, you'll find outstanding views of the Great Salt Lake, its shoreline wetlands, and the Bountiful metro. Rough-cut Wasatch peaks,* which tower over Salt Lake City miles away, crack the southern horizon while more modest summits define the northern sky. You'll climb for what seems an eternity to reach Bountiful Peak, but as we all learned in Introductory Physics "what goes up must come down," and the tour concludes with an interminable, blazing-fast descent.

Details

This route can be ridden in either direction with little change in difficulty, but Farmington to Bountiful has its perks. Although the entire road is dirt, Farmington Canyon seems to have a bit less gravel and washboards, making it better for climbing. The Bountiful side is more open and thus more scenic, so your eyes are kept plenty busy while descending. The mileage from Farmington is listed first followed by the mileage from Bountiful.

It's all uphill from the mouth of Farmington Canyon. As you cross over the creek, check out the banded rocks lining the road. This is gneiss (pronounced "nice"), and it's a *nice* example of the metamorphosed Farmington Complex. These rocks are among the continent's oldest, dating back 1.5 billion years, and were formed by intense heat and pressure deep within the earth long before they were uplifted to the surface for you to view.

You'll settle into a low gear right from the start because the grade at the bottom is among the steepest, and the road can be rough with gravel and washboards (tech 3). The grade lessens and the surface smooths a bit after a couple of switchbacks (tech 2). Past Sunset Campground, the road levels still more for an easy spin to the junction where Francis Peak Road forks left at the steel gates (**m7.8/16.2**).

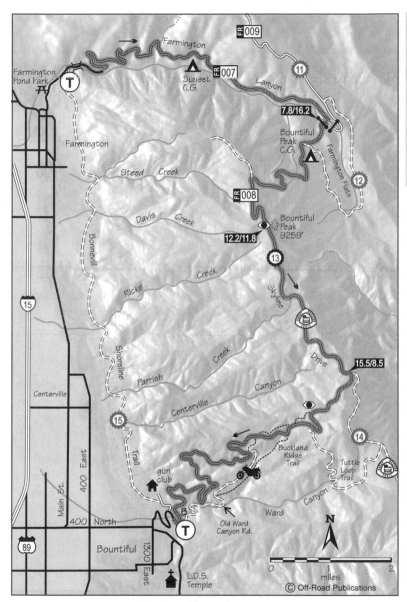

Fork right on Skyline Drive for Bountiful, and continue climbing past Bountiful Peak Campground (water taps). Pass the trail to Farmington Lakes, and pump harder up the ridge to Bountiful Peak for a bird's eye view of northern Utah (**m12.2/11.8**).

It's all downhill from Bountiful Peak (tech 2-3)! Pass two dirt roads branching to the right (they lead to the old Parrish Creek research area), and stay right at the unsigned Sessions Mountain Road (**m15.5/8.5**).

Take a quick stop at a small pullout a mile farther to view forested Centerville Canyon below, and then let gravity continue to pull you down to the valley. Pass Tuttle Loop Trail (**16.2/7.8**), Buckland Ridge Trail (**17.6/6.4**), and Old Ward Canyon Road (**m19.1/4.9**), and end the tour beneath the whitewashed Bountiful "B" (**m24.0/0.0**).

Option: Farmington Canyon

Not only is Skyline Drive a big ride, but it requires a vehicle shuttle also. If neither suits your fancy, then try a shortened 15.6-mile, out-and-back ride in Farmington Canyon to where the road splits (see **m7.8**). Although the elevation gain is a hefty 2,630 feet, the climb is moderate⁺ because technical difficulty is low. Just use your granny gear. This is a good early season ride because Farmington Canyon catches lots of sun and melts out early.

Option: Bountiful "B"

Similarly, you can pedal up Skyline Drive from Bountiful just as easily. Try going 7.5 miles to the Centerville Canyon Overlook or 8.5 miles to the Sessions Mountain Road turnoff (3,000-foot gain). If you go for the gusto and set your sights on Bountiful Peak, you'll log 12 miles and gain nearly 4,000 feet. Regardless, the climb is long and steady, and the gravelly washboards can get tedious.

Option: Skyline-Bonneville Shoreline Trail Loop

Of course, if a vehicle shuttle is not available and/or you have *plenty* of energy to burn, Skyline Drive can be ridden as a 32-mile loop by adding in the Bonneville Shoreline Trail between Bountiful and Farmington. (See "Bonneville Shoreline Trail: Bountiful.") The loop is rated extreme.

Option: Skyline Drive Downhill Course (Buckland Ridge Trail-Old Ward Canyon Road)

Gravity thrill seekers and downhillers in training can test their "moxie" and the durability of their long-travel dualies on a variety of rough—really rough—ATV trails just off Skyline Drive. Those on light-weight cross-country rigs will get thrashed around pretty good.

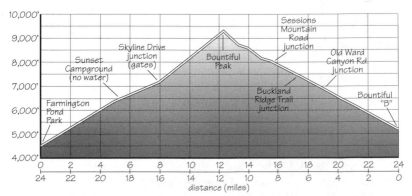

Drive 7.5 miles up Skyline Drive from the Bountiful "B" to a pullout on the left overlooking Centerville Canyon (.5 mile past the Tuttle Loop Trail). You'll find an ATV path dropping off the steep embankment at the end of the guardrail. This fast, smooth-running section (tech 3) spits you out on the road in .5 mile. Coast down Skyline Drive about .5 mile, drop into the Buckland Ridge Trail, and hold on tight. The "trail" is one big high-banked rut filled in with rock rubble (tech 4+) and has two vicious bedrock drops (tech 5+). You'll intersect Old Ward Canyon Road in 1.7 miles (doubletrack, tech 3+); take it left and down to a grassy bench. Go left, drop to another

Letting it all hang out on Buckland Ridge Trail.

bench, and go left again for the final drop to the parking area below the Bountiful "B." Another run, anyone? For a shorter shuttle, just jump on at the Old Ward Canyon Road trailhead.

If you chum around in the right circles, or just hang out at the Bountiful "B" on any Sunday, the DHers will clue you into other nearby free-ride routes, like the "V" Trail, Parrish Creek Trail, and a secret singletrack descent coming off of Old Ward Canyon Road. The latter was used in the 2002 Bountiful Bomber Downhill Race, which is part of the Go-Ride Utah Downhill Race Series. Contact Team Go-Ride, a new downhill specific bike shop in Salt Lake City, for more information.

! Know Before You Go

- Be alert to motorists and OHVs at all times, and stay to the far right.
- Be prepared for cooler temperatures at the top and for quickly changing alpine weather. Snow drifts typically block the road above Farmington Lakes well into June.
- *Fido Factor:* Dogs are not recommended because of long distance, hard graveled roads, and possible vehicle traffic.

? Maps & More Information

- USGS 1:24,000: Bountiful Peak, Farmington, and Peterson, Utah
- Public Lands Information Center (at REI): (801) 466-6411
- Wasatch-Cache National Forest (Salt Lake Ranger District); (801) 733-2660; www.fs.fed.us/r4/wcnf/unit/slrd/index.shtml
- Team Go-Ride: 801-474-0081; www.go-ride.com

NORTHERN WASATCH

On any Sunday . . .

Trailhead Access

Farmington Canyon: Northbound on I-15, take Exit 322 for Farmington, Lagoon Drive. Drive north into Farmington and turn right on State Street. Turn left/north on 100 East, which leads into Farmington Canyon. (Alternatively, take Exit 324 off I-15 for US 89 and South Ogden. Take Park Lane [formerly Burke Lane] to UT 106 and turn right (becomes Main Street). Turn left on 600 North then left again on 100 East, which leads into Farmington Canyon. Park at Farmington Pond Park or just up the canyon where the Bonneville Shoreline Trail forks right on the aqueduct service road (**m0.0/24.0**).

Bountiful: From I-15, take Exit 321 (Bountiful, 400 North), and travel east on 400 North/UT 131. Turn left/north on 1300 East, and wind through a residential area. Stay right at the junction of Eagle Ridge Drive and 1500 East, and park in the big dirt lot just after the pavement turns to dirt beneath the Bountiful "B" (**m24.0/0.00**).

14
Sessions Mountains

JUST THE FACTS

Location:	12 miles east of Bountiful and 14 miles northeast of Salt Lake City
Length:	14.1 miles
Type:	One-way
Tread:	8.6 miles singletrack, 5.5 miles doubletrack
Physically:	Strenuous⁺ (rough trails, steep climbs w/ portaging)
Technically:	3-5 (good doubletracks; rough, seldom-used singletracks)
Gain:	2,700 feet
Dogs:	No, watershed

GO □
NO ■ | JAN | FEB | MAR | APR | MAY | JUN | JUL | AUG | SEP | OCT | NOV | DEC |

WHY SHOULD U RIDE THIS TRAIL?

If you would walk barefoot over burning coals willingly or step into the ring with the heavyweight champ, then you would know what this trail is all about—pain and suffering. The Great Western Trail takes a logical course between Bountiful's Skyline Drive and East Canyon's Big Mountain Pass, but the many insanely steep and rugged segments will leave you dazed and confused. So why ride this trail? If you're looking for an adventure, have a tolerance for hike-a-biking, and have become bored with other Wasatch offerings, then you just might love this trail. You'll venture to remote areas of the Wasatch Range and see angles of these mountains that few bikers can claim to have experienced. If you add on other trails and paved roads, then can ride right into Salt Lake City on the same route that the Mormon Pioneers did over 150 years ago.

Details

This ride starts out friendly enough with many miles of relatively tame doubletrack on the Sessions Mountain road (tech 2-3), except for one small hill of chunky rocks shortly past the Tuttle Loop Trail junction (tech 4). Descend into a small elevated valley, and come to a turnaround where the road appears to end (**m4.3**).

Drop down the torn-up doubletrack (tech 4⁺) to a small pass in the timber. Do not descend the ATV path down the canyon to the left/east from the saddle. Who knows where it goes? Instead, go right a few feet then left to continue on the signed GWT. A short murderous climb greets you and forces you to hoof it. You'll pedal and push along the GWT for a mile on choppy, eroded tread (tech 3-5) to a high point overlooking the head of Bountiful's Mill Creek Canyon with Grandview Peak in the distance (**m5.4**). This is a crucial deciding point, one where you might consider the lyrics of a song by the rock band, The Clash: *"Should I stay or should I go?"*

Let's go! A wickedly steep descent on loose, rubbly, entrenched tread (tech 5) takes you to a saddle at the top of Mill Creek Canyon. Yes, it's the same canyon that eventually comes out at Mueller Park in Bountiful, but *do not* be tempted by the inviting track heading down the canyon. Who knows what perils it holds? Instead, put your bike on your shoulder and portage up the 25-percent-plus grade out of the saddle on the GWT. Once up on the ridge, the pedaling is easier, but it's by no means easy. The undulating trail crosses the headwater basin of Mill Creek Canyon and is littered with baby-head rocks that have eroded from the substrate. Sheep are ranged throughout this area, so beware of false trails branching from the main route.

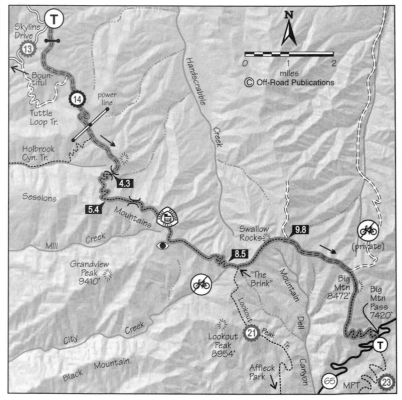

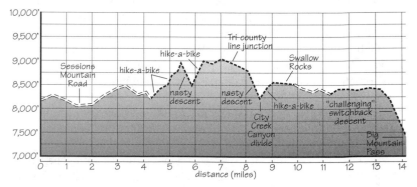

After bending east around a knoll where Morgan, Salt Lake, and Davis Counties converge, the GWT crosses the head of City Creek Canyon and serves up impressive views of Grandview Peak in the foreground and of Salt Lake's Mill Creek ridge in the distance. An eastward bearing along the ridge takes you to another precipitous descent (tech 5) down five treacherous switchbacks to a peaceful meadow at the top of City Creek Canyon (**m8.5**). Now you must undo the elevation loss with another painful portage up to an unsigned junction know as "The Brink." Here, the overgrown Lookout Peak Trail takes off to the right. The "well worn" GWT, on the other hand, is

It's just another "day at the office" for the author. Ho-hum.

quite obvious, and you'll hike-a-bike up remarkably steep grades for another quarter mile. Alas, the trail levels, contours high above the top of Mountain Dell Canyon, but stays just below small caves called Swallow Rocks.

Intersect a doubletrack (**m9.8**), and take it right/east along the ridge for 1.6 miles; then fork right on singletrack tagged for the GWT, and hoof it one last time. Consolation for your effort is the wide-spread view across the Mountain Dell Watershed. Climb one more hill, and then square up for the pin-ball drop through a dozen steep, tight turns to Big Mountain Pass. If you placed your shuttle vehicle here, then you're done; otherwise, follow one of the options listed below.

Option: Mormon Pioneer Trail (MPT)

Tack on an extra 6 miles of sweet downhill singletrack by taking the MPT off Big Mountain Pass through Affleck Park and down to Little Dell Reservoir Recreation Area (tech 2-3$^+$). (Do not take the "Original Trail" on the north side of the pass, or you'll end up on the dirt East Canyon Road.) From Little Dell, you can continue freewheeling another 2.5 miles down UT 65/East Canyon Road to I-80 and another 6 miles down I-80 to Salt Lake City at Foothill Drive.

Option: Affleck Park to Emigration Canyon

If you still have some life left in your legs and haven't bonked upon reaching Big Mountain Pass, then your ride is only half over, or half begun. You can ride all the way to Salt Lake City along the path the

Mormon Pioneers blazed over 150 years ago. Whereas it took Brigham Young and his followers a couple of days to travel these 12 miles, you can knock them off in a couple of hours.

First, descend the MPT 2.6 miles to Affleck Park. Cross the vehicle bridge over the creek, go right toward Area 3, and pick up the Birch Springs Trail at a brown steel gate. The grooved path (tech 3$^+$) rises steeply for .5 mile to a four-way junction of unsigned trails in a small saddle. Little Mountain Trail goes left and Lookout Peak Trail goes right—both uphill. Go straight to descend the forever-neglected Killyon Canyon. Both rough and smooth tread (more of the former and less of the latter) take you to the paved Pinecrest Road and then to Emigration Canyon Road. Pedal and coast 6 miles down Emigration Canyon to Salt Lake City. Note: You can park a vehicle at the Sunnyside Avenue trailhead for the Bonneville Shoreline Trail (see "Bonneville Shoreline Trail: Salt Lake"). Lower Killyon Canyon is private property, so obey any signs restricting public use.

! Know Before You Go

- Portions of this route are remote, confusing, and exceptionally difficult. Plan accordingly and travel well equipped.
- Be prepared for rapidly changing alpine weather.
- Cell phone reception is good throughout this ride.
- *Fido Factor:* Trail is not dog friendly. Dogs are not allowed between "The Brink" and Big Mountain because the trail enters the Mountain Dell Watershed.

? Maps & More Information

- USGS 1:24,000: Bountiful Peak, Fort Douglas, and Mountain Dell, Utah
- Public Lands Information Center (at REI): (801) 466-6411
- Wasatch-Cache National Forest (Salt Lake Ranger District); (801) 733-2660; www.fs.fed.us/r4/wcnf/unit/slrd/index.shtml

Trailhead Access

To the Skyline Drive trailhead: From I-15, take Exit 321 in Bountiful, and travel east on 400 North/UT 131. Turn left on 1300 East, and wind through a residential area to Skyline Drive. The light-duty dirt road has variable amounts of rocks, gravel, and washboards. It's suitable for passenger cars but rough locally. Travel 8.5 miles up Skyline Drive to the Sessions Mountain road forking right (might not be signed), and park at the turnaround near the Forest Service information board. (The left fork is the continuation of Skyline Drive to Bountiful Peak and Farmington Canyon.)

To the Big Mountain Pass trailhead: From Salt Lake City, take I-80 up Parleys Canyon for 6 miles to Exit 134 (Mountain Dell, East Canyon). Drive 8.2 miles up UT 65 to Big Mountain Pass.

Bonneville Shoreline Trail (Bountiful)

JUST THE FACTS

Location:	Bountiful-Centerville foothills
Length:	6 miles; 12 miles-out-and-back
Type:	One-way or out-and-back
Tread:	2.7 miles singletrack, 3.3 miles doubletrack
Physically:	Moderate (short, steep climbs & persistent sand)
Technically:	2-4 (sand, gravel, & rocks)
Gain:	1,200 feet (out-and-back)
Dogs:	Yes, on leash

GO ☐
NO ■ | JAN | FEB | MAR | APR | MAY | JUN | JUL | AUG | SEP | OCT | NOV | DEC |

WHY SHOULD U RIDE THIS TRAIL

Bountiful and Centerville have joined other Wasatch Front communities by adding several miles of hand-built singletrack to the ever-growing Bonneville Shoreline Trail (BST). Three miles of nonmotorized trails supplemented by several miles of fast-paced doubletracks take you along the Wasatch foothills, where you'll find wide-sweeping vistas of the Great Salt Lake, the valley's metropolis, and the nearby mountains. Because the old shoreline is quite sandy and the area receives copious sunshine, it dries rapidly after it rains. It's also an excellent choice during the fall and the spring, too, when snow has closed trails at higher elevations. You can even sneak out during the winter.

Details

To tap into the new singletrack section, start out from the dirt staging area under the Bountiful "B," and return north through the neighborhood to the intersection of Skyline Drive and Eagle Ridge Drive. Go right and take the dirt road that accesses the gun club. The trail starts about 200 feet before the gun club gate near a cement structure.

The trail splits immediately. Although the left fork is signed for the BST, take the right fork tagged for hikers, horses, and bikers. This hand-cut singletrack slips across the brushy foothills and descends gradually for .8 mile before intersecting a dirt road on a switchback. (From here, the BST roughly follows the pipeline service road.) Go left/south from the road's curve on a narrow doubletrack signed for the BST (that's the route you skipped previously); then fork right in 50 feet to catch more singletrack heading northward. Squeeze between pegmatite boulders, flow through hip-tall wheat grass, and cross the dirt road, which is now angling downhill into a gulch. The singletrack bends around a fenced-in underground tank and crosses Centerville Canyon on a new wooden footbridge. Pop up to the dirt road next to a fenced-in reservoir (**m1.9**).

Head north for .2 mile to where the road veers left and descends into another gulch. Stay straight at the bend, go through a row of boulders, and hop onto more singletrack. Now, the trail winds through Parrish Creek and crosses another footbridge. Pop out to the dirt road again, and head

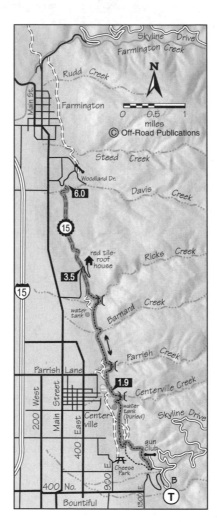

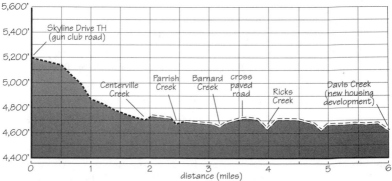

Left: In the weeds. Right: A new singletrack section high above the city.

north past a Forest Service sign stating that motorized uses are restricted in the area. This is the end of the singletrack and the signed BST, currently. To continue, take the dirt road downhill into Barnard Creek; then pedal and push up a long, steep, sandy hill to regain the shoreline bench. Stay straight at a Y-junction (the main road dips through a gulch again) to catch a crude trail that crosses a tall cement retaining wall over Ricks Creek. Once on the other side, stay right/straight at a Y-junction, and intersect a paved drive (private) that leads up to a seclusive home with a red tile roof. If you take the left fork on the dirt road by mistake, you'll simply intersect the paved drive down lower. Go to the road's right-hand bend, and resume northbound on the dirt pipeline road (**m3.5**).

You can ride for 2.5 miles more on the pipeline road, dipping through gulches and climbing back up to the shoreline, until the road ends at a new housing development called Hughes Estates (**m6.0**). Turn around and retrace your tracks back to Bountiful.

At the time of publication, the BST was blocked off by private property in the vicinity of Davis Creek Canyon at the end of Woodland Drive. Davis County is working with land owners to allow public access to the continued pipeline utility road so the BST can connect to Farmington Canyon 2 miles away. Until then, obey all signs restricting travel.

❗ Know Before You Go

- Private property borders much of the BST. Stay on the trail to avoid trespassing, and obey all signs restricting travel.
- Rattlesnakes are known to inhabit these warm foothills.
- *Fido Factor:* Dogs must be leashed within Davis County; otherwise, the route is canine compatible.

NORTHERN WASATCH

Impressive bridge work on the Bountiful-Centerville BST.

? Maps & More Information

- USGS 1:24,000: Bountiful Peak and Farmington, Utah
- Public Lands Information Center (at REI): (801) 466-6411
- Wasatch-Cache National Forest (Salt Lake Ranger District): (801) 733-2660; www.fs.fed.us/r4/wcnf/unit/slrd/index.shtml
- Davis County Department of Community and Economic Development: (801) 451-3278, www.co.davis.ut.us
- Bonneville Shoreline Trail Committee: www.bonneville-trail.org; (801) 816-0876

Trailhead Access

From I-15, take Exit 321 (Bountiful, 400 North), and travel east on 400 North/UT 131. Turn left/north on 1300 East, and wind through a residential area. Stay right at the junction of Eagle Ridge Drive and Skyline Drive, and park where pavement turns to dirt beneath the Bountiful "B". You can access the BST from Bountiful City's Cheese Park at 900 East and 1300 North and from Parrish Lane in Centerville.

▲▲ 16
Mueller Park Trail

JUST THE FACTS

Location:	2 miles east of Bountiful
Length:	13 miles
Type:	Out-and-back
Tread:	All singletrack
Physically:	Moderate (steady climb w/ a few rough sections)
Technically:	2-3$^+$ (some rocky sections & tight turns, but lots of buffed tread)
Gain:	1,910 feet
Dogs:	Yes

GO ☐
NO ■ | JAN | FEB | MAR | APR | MAY | JUN | JUL | AUG | SEP | OCT | NOV | DEC |

WHY SHOULD U RIDE THIS TRAIL?

The Mueller Park Trail epitomizes the metro-to-mountains transition for which the Wasatch Front is famed. Instantly, you'll turn your back on the suburban jungle and become immersed in the tranquil backcountry. You won't find staggering views of mountain peaks along this route because, for the most part, the trail is embraced by serene woods. Spirited sounds of nature drift from the timber, and a rich, earthy bouquet envelops your senses. There are, however, good views of the Great Salt Lake and the metropolitan valley from selected locations. And to top it off, the constantly turning singletrack is one of the finest in the Wasatch and is reason enough why you should ride this trail.

Details

Pick a low gear because the trail rises quickly up a series of stretched-out switchbacks right after crossing the footbridge. Thereafter, the trail heads generally eastward into the mountains, rising steadily and weaving through several wooded hollows (tech 2-3). Between these hollows, the path curves out across sunny hills where you can look down into Mill Creek Canyon. About 2.0 miles up, you cross the treeless swath of the Kearns pipeline. After crossing a couple of footbridges over lightly flowing creeks, you come to a right-hand switchback that marks the overlook at Big Rock (**m3.5**). This is a good turnaround for those not wishing to go the distance. (Go straight a few feet for the view; make the right turn to continue up.)

Now, the path steepens a bit and is noticeably more choppy in places (tech 2$^+$-3$^+$), or maybe it's just that the choppy spots make the trail seem steeper. Oak gives way to aspen and fir as elevation increases and temperatures cool. Cross a footbridge over a creek, and keep chugging up the trail. A nice little downhill stretch that gives your legs a respite and a trio of tight turns signify the top is just over a mile away. You can start your final sprint to Rudys Flat after crossing a mucky spring area covered by boardwalks (**m6.5**). Take a break before coasting back down, or cuddle against a shady pine and doze away the afternoon.

NORTHERN WASATCH

Option: Mueller Park Loop

Instead of riding back down on Mueller Park Trail, try descending North Canyon and then looping back to Mueller Park on paved roads. Total distance is about 13.5 miles. North Canyon Trail is a bit steeper and more technical than Mueller Park Trail, and the rutted doubletrack down in the canyon bottom can swallow you whole if you're not careful.

From Rudys Flat, follow the singletrack west, and curve left through a small saddle. Nice view of the Great Salt Lake, huh? The trail is pretty rough along this section (tech 3-4) and stays choppy until it drops into the conifers where it smooths considerably. About 2.5 miles down, the trail joins the North Canyon jeep road. The rough and deeply rutted doubletrack (tech 3-4) parallels the creek for about a mile then reaches paved Canyon

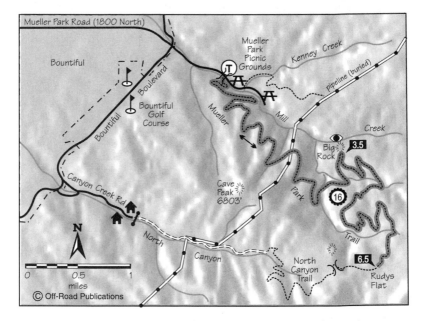

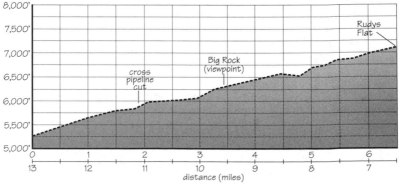

Mueller Park Trail takes you from metro to mountains and back again.

Creek Road. Glide downhill, turn right on Bountiful Boulevard, pedal past the golf course (is your helmet still on?), and then turn right on Mueller Park Road. The parking area is about one-half mile uphill.

Option: North Canyon Loop

The climb from Mueller Park to Rudys Flat is perfect for intermediate-level bikers. Stronger riders wanting to build powerful legs should try climbing to Rudys Flat via North Canyon, hence riding the North Canyon Loop in reverse (see above). The jeep road is a handful with its steep grade, rough tread (tech 2⁺-4) and periodic deep ruts. Reward for your effort is the sweet descent on Mueller Park Trail. Which is the best direction for the loop? Ride both ways and decide for yourself.

❗ Know Before You Go

- Mueller Park Trail is *very* popular with mountain bikers, hikers, and equestrians and is open to motorcycles.
- Control your speed, and remain attentive to other trail users. You *will* meet others at some point, and *you* are required to yield. It's good form! Be able to stop *safely* within the distance you can see down the trail and around a curve.

NORTHERN WASATCH

Buffed!

- Mueller Park Picnic Ground (fee area) has water taps, outhouses, and picnic tables; overnight camping is prohibited.
- *Fido Factor:* The trail is dog friendly and has reliable water sources. Leash and control your pet in the parking area.

? Maps & More Information

- USGS 1:24,000: North Salt Lake, Utah
- Public Lands Information Center (at REI): (801) 466-6411
- Wasatch-Cache National Forest (Salt Lake Ranger District); (801) 733-2660; www.fs.fed.us/r4/wcnf/unit/slrd/index.shtml

Trailhead Access

From I-15, take Exit 318 (2600 South, Bountiful), and travel east on 2600 South. After crossing 200 West, 2600 South bends north and becomes Orchard Drive. Turn right on 1800 South (becomes Mueller Park Road), and travel 2.3 miles to Mueller Park Picnic Ground. The trail begins at the wooden bridge over Mill Creek.

17
Golden Spike National Historic Site

JUST THE FACTS

Location:	30 miles west of Brigham City
Length:	East Grade Tour: 3.5 miles; West Grade Tour: 14 miles
Type:	Loops
Tread:	Pavement & dirt roads
Physically:	Easy+ (gentle hills, smooth dirt & gravel roads)
Technically:	1-2 (gravel on dirt roads)
Gain:	East Grade Tour: 200 feet; West Grade Tour: 350 feet
Dogs:	On leash

GO ☐
NO ■ | JAN | FEB | MAR | APR | MAY | JUN | JUL | AUG | SEP | OCT | NOV | DEC

Although the great pioneering, steam-driven days of the first Transcontinental Railroad are gone, the legacy of that time lives on at Golden Spike National Historic Site. The site houses exact replicas of the Jupiter and 119 locomotives that met on May 10, 1869, linking the east and west coasts by continuous rail service. A small museum recaptures the excitement of this pivotal event in the West's romantic history, and annually, on May 10, the Golden Spike Ceremony is reenacted. Both the East and West Grade Tours follow portions of the original rail beds that have been converted to smooth-riding, one-lane dirt roads. Since the tracks' grades never exceeded an average two-percent, these routes are perfect for novice bikers and families.

Details

As you pedal these routes, let your imagination wander back to the late 1860s when smoke-belching locomotives chugged across Utah to the first head-to-head meeting of railroads from the East and West. Across 1,776 miles of mountains, prairies, deserts, and rivers, the railroads' workers placed 2,000 wooden cross ties per mile. Upon the ties, iron men laid 200 pairs of iron rails, each weighing 560 pounds. Spikers fastened the rails into place: three blows to each spike, 10 spikes to the rail, 400 rails, 4,000 spikes, 12,000 blows to the mile. Such was the rhythm of the Grand Anvil Chorus.

East Grade Tour
This loop begins 3.2 miles east of the Visitor Center. (Add on 6.4 miles, out-and-back, by riding to the trailhead.) Turn off the paved road at the East Grade Tour sign, and park near the Last Cut. As you pedal along the railroad bed, you'll find the combined beauty of the Great Salt Lake and the grandeur of the northern Wasatch Front especially stunning. It's easy to trace the terraced shorelines that ancient Lake Bonneville etched into the nearby hills. A mile from the trailhead, you pass the 30-foot-high Chinaman's Arch—a natural memorial to the thousands of Chinese who worked for the Central Pacific Railroad. Shortly thereafter, turn left on the paved highway, and return to the trailhead.

NORTHERN WASATCH

Left: Echoes of the Great Anvil Chorus. Right: Chinaman's Arch.

Big Fill Walk

You can log about 8 more miles (out-and-back) by veering from the East Grade Tour and seeking out the Big Fill Walk. This section of railroad bed is closed to vehicles, so you will find plenty of solitude. Along the way, you'll pass the Big Fill and Big Trestle sites—two laborious methods of spanning a deep ravine—and caves that were used to house railroad workers and their families.

West Grade Tour

From the Visitor Center, pedal west on the paved road, which turns to dirt. As you approach the North Promontory Mountains, the Central Pacific's remnant railroad grade parallels the roadway. The road forks twice; stay right following signs for West Grade Tour. The Great Salt Lake's cerulean water appears in the distance like an oasis, but to pioneer travelers, its high salinity and salt-encrusted shoreline were wretched blights. Two miles from the road's second fork, turn right on the signed West Grade Tour, and double back along the rail bed (**m7.2**). Wooden ties still scatter the hillsides, and you'll pass through cut and fill excavations. A sign boasts a record track-laying pace of "Ten Miles in One Day." Follow the main road back to the Visitor Center after the West Grade Tour ends.

! Know Before You Go

- Vehicles are allowed on both the East Grade and West Grade Tours.
- Temperatures can be very warm, and insects can be bothersome from midspring through early fall.
- The Visitor Center is open daily (9:00 A.M.-5:30 P.M) The Visitor Center is closed Mondays and Tuesdays from October 21-April 30 and on New Year's Day, Thanksgiving, Christmas.
- Entrance fee is $4 for bicycles, $5 per vehicle (May 1-mid September), and $7 per vehicle (mid September-April 30).
- Other than vending machines, restrooms, and picnic areas, there are no visitor services at the National Historic Site.
- A re-enactment of the "Driving of the Golden Spike Ceremony" is held

annually on May 10. A Railroaders Festival is held annually on the second Saturday of August.

- *Fido Factor:* Pets must be on a leash at all times.

? Maps & More Information

- USGS 1:24,000: Golden Spike Monument, Lampo Junction, Sunset Pass, and Thatcher Mountain, SW, Utah
- National Park Service (Golden Spike National Historic Site): (435) 471-2209; www.nps.gov/gosp/index.htm

Trailhead Access

From I-15, take Exit 368 (Golden Spike NHS, Corrine), and travel west on UT 13. After 2.5 miles, fork left on UT 83 following signs for Golden Spike NHS and Thiokol. Travel 17.5 miles, and then turn left toward Promontory and Golden Spike NHS. Fork right a few miles ahead, and continue 3 miles to Golden Spike NHS. (The road forking left leads to Promontory Point.)

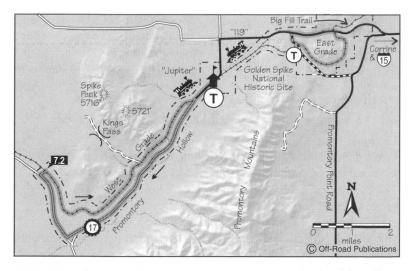

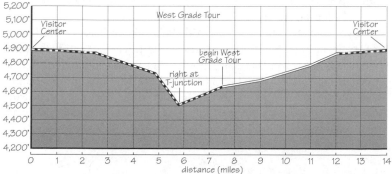

18
Antelope Island State Park

NORTHERN WASATCH

JUST THE FACTS

Location:	25 miles northwest of Bountiful
Length:	Up to 28 miles
Type:	Loops & out-and-backs
Tread:	19.5 miles singletrack, 8.5 miles doubletrack
Physically:	Easy$^+$-moderate$^+$ (see below)
Technically:	1$^+$-5 (sandy doubletracks, smooth & rocky singletracks)
Gain:	(see below)
Dogs:	On leash

GO □
NO ■ | JAN | FEB | MAR | APR | MAY | JUN | JUL | AUG | SEP | OCT | NOV | DEC |

Utah is not a place where you would expect to mountain bike around an island. But you can, and Antelope Island State Park is the place. The island floats amidst the Great Salt Lake's ever-blue water, and from the saddle of your bike you'll hear waves lap against the shore, smell the salty air, see flocks of waterfowl gather on mud flats then take to synchronous flight, and, perhaps, spy antelope and bison roaming distant pastures. From the island's bony crest, you'll marvel at the circumambient view of the lake, island, sky, distant mountains, and metropolitan valley. Although the island seems secluded, it has a rich human history. Trails on Antelope Island range from leisurely jaunts to heart-pounding, backcountry escapes, so there is something for everyone.

Details

Lakeside Trail

Lakeside Trail is the perfect introduction to the varied trails and terrain hosted by Antelope Island State Park. The easiest approach is to start at the White Rock Bay group camping area and ride to Bridger Bay Campground then back for a 5.6-mile out-and-back trip. The

> **Lakeside Trail:**
> 5.6 miles, out-and-back, easy$^+$, tech 1$^+$-5, 100-foot gain

lake-edge path starts out as smooth, packed sand (tech 2), but then it threads through a boulder field about 2 miles out (tech 4-5). You'll have to dismount and portage a bit. It's a small price to pay for the ever-changing views and for the dreamy glide on the return.

If you loath backtracking, then ride Lakeside Trail as a 5.5-mile loop by first heading up the dirt road from White Rock Bay and then riding paved roads to Bridger Bay Campground. Pick your way through the rock garden on the trail, and then feel the salty breeze flow through your helmet as you coast back to the trailhead. To take in the best panorama from Antelope Island, tack on the heart-pumping climb to Buffalo Point. There, you can enjoy a char-broiled bison burger at the snack stand.

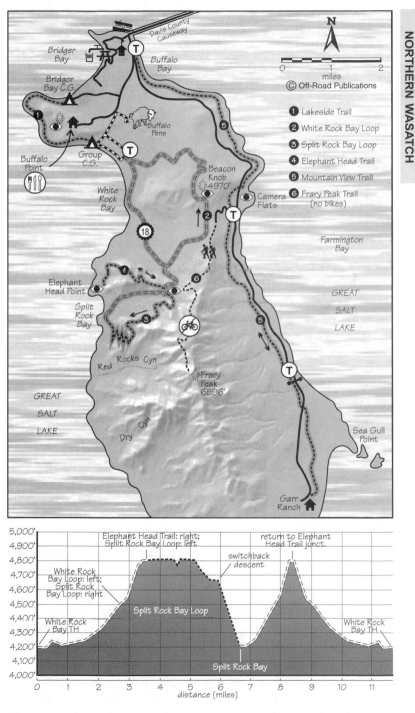

Key

1 Lakeside Trail
2 White Rock Bay Loop
3 Split Rock Bay Loop
4 Elephant Head Trail
5 Mountain View Trail
6 Frary Peak Trail (no bikes)

© Off-Road Publications

Map labels: Davis County Causeway, Bridger Bay, Buffalo Bay, Bridger Bay C.G., Buffalo Pens, Buffalo Point, Group C.G., White Rock Bay, Beacon Knob 4970', Camera Flats, Farmington Bay, GREAT SALT LAKE, Elephant Head Point, Split Rock Bay, Red Rocks Cyn, Frary Peak 6596', Dry Cyn, GREAT SALT LAKE, Sea Gull Point, Garr Ranch

Elevation profile labels: Elephant Head Trail: right; Split Rock Bay Loop: left; return to Elephant Head Trail junct.; switchback descent; White Rock Bay Loop: left; Split Rock Bay Loop: right; Split Rock Bay Loop; White Rock Bay TH; Split Rock Bay; White Rock Bay TH; distance (miles)

NORTHERN WASATCH

The aptly named Mountain View Trail.

White Rock Bay Loop

Head south from the backcountry trailhead on doubletrack, and cross White Rock Bay (tech 2-3). As the road curves up the sloping plain, it rises deceptively and summons your lowest gears. Go left at the junction, slog through patches of drift

> **White Rock Bay Loop:**
> 7.5 miles, loop, moderate, tech 2-3⁺, 650-foot gain

sand, and power up to the low treeless ridge for a sweeping view across Farmington Bay to the Wasatch Front. Pedal and push up one more short but rugged hill to reach Beacon Knob.

The descent begins on a curving course that turns southward with segments of pedaling and freewheeling; then it dives quickly down an incline (tech 3⁺) alongside a fence before making a beeline back to the trailhead. You can reach high speeds along the descent, and you never know what booby traps might await in the sandy tracks, so ride cautiously. Also, be ready to yield to other trail users, especially equestrians. They have the right of way.

Split Rock Bay Loop

This is Antelope Island's premier trail, which boasts several miles of hand-built singletrack. Two hardy climbs are countered by two thrilling descents on both smooth and rugged tread. Don't let speed blur your vision, for there is much to see. The loop

> **Split Rock Bay Loop:**
> 11.7 mile loop with out-and-back, moderate⁺, tech 2-4, 1350-foot gain

is an outdoor geologic classroom. You'll brush by metamorphic Precambrian rocks that are over 1.5 billion years old, ride along the wave-cut shoreline of the ice age Lake Bonneville, and view distant block-faulted mountains that define the Basin and Range Province. A variety of plants, birds, and animals complete your natural interlude.

Head south from the backcountry trailhead across White Rock Bay, and pump steadily up to the main junction (tech 2-3). Stay right

Hand-built singletrack highlights the Split Rock Bay Loop.

and keep chugging up to the Split Rock Bay overlook. If you ride the loop clockwise, you'll embark on singletrack that contours along the Lake Bonneville shoreline (tech 2⁺) and descend multiple switchbacks to Split Rock Bay (tech 2⁺-4). The climb out is direct and strenuous on a rutted, sandy doubletrack (tech 3⁺). Counterclockwise, you first make a beeline descent on the sandy doubletrack to Split Rock Bay and then climb continually up rocky and tempered singletrack to the shoreline bench for an easy contour. Which direction is best? You'll have to ride both ways and judge for yourself.

Elephant Head Trail

To ride the Elephant Head Trail, you must first climb 3.2 miles and gain 610 feet to the Split Rock Bay overlook. There, the Elephant Head Trail follows a small ridge to a rocky point overlooking arcuate

Elephant Head Trail:
2.8 miles, out-and-back, moderate, tech 2-4⁺, 150-foot gain

white-sand beaches. There are some tricky sections along the way (tech 4⁺) and one short sharp climb, but the rest is pretty tame (tech 2⁺). All said, the entire round trip from the backcountry trailhead is 9.2 miles. The trail's namesake formation, which resembles a pachyderm drinking from the Great Salt Lake, is best seen from Split Rock Bay, so you'll have to add on that loop as well for the full effect (14.5 miles).

Mountain View Trail

This is the park's newest addition to its trail system, and it is just right for aspiring mountain bikers who shy away from tire-bashing trails. The 11.5-mile-long Mountain View Trail is a wide biker-friendly singletrack that follows the island's east

Mountain View Trail:
23 miles, out-and-back, moderate, tech 2, 300-foot gain

shoreline and leads to the historic Garr Ranch. The Wasatch Front is your constant companion, and over 60 miles of peaks can be seen running from North Ogden's Ben Lomond to Draper's Lone Peak. The tread is usually smooth, packed dirt and sand, but if horses have been on the trail when it

NORTHERN WASATCH

was wet, their hooves often leave teeth-chattering pock marks.

Since the trail crosses the paved ranch road three times, you can always seek soothing blacktop if the going gets rough. Note: Mountain View Trail and the paved ranch road are closed at 6 P.M. from trail mile 9.0 (road mile post 8) to the ranch. Mountain View Trail is closed to use from May 15-June 1 for pronghorn fawning in the area.

! Know Before You Go

- The park is open every day at 7 A.M. and closes about an hour after sunset: 10 P.M. May-Labor Day; 9 P.M. September and April; 7 P.M. in October; and 6 P.M. November-March. The Visitor Center is open 10 A.M. to 5 P.M. daily, year-round.
- Day-use fees are $8 for motorists; $4 for bicyclists, in-line skaters, and others who do not drive across the Davis County Causeway (2003). Camping fees are extra.
- You must fill out and carry a permit to use the backcountry trails from the White Rock Bay trailhead (permit is free and self-service).
- All users must stay on designated trails. Off-trail use is prohibited.
- Open fires and overnight camping are not allowed in the backcountry.
- It is unlawful to harass wildlife and to remove, alter, or destroy plants, minerals, cultural and natural features.
- Mountain bikers must yield to hikers and equestrians.
- Trail users must be off the trails by park closing times.
- Backcountry trails are closed the last week of October for the annual bison roundup.
- There are hot showers (free) and water taps at the day-use area north of Bridger Bay Campground.
- Insects can be intolerable from mid-May through September. Use repellant liberally. Midday temperatures during summer can exceed 100 degrees Fahrenheit.
- *Fido Factor:* Pets must be leashed and under physical control always.

? Maps & More Information

- USGS 1:24,000: Antelope Island North, Antelope Island South, and Buffalo Point, Utah
- Antelope Island State Park: (801) 773-2941, www.stateparks.utah.gov/

♪ Trailhead Access

From I-15, take Exit 335 (Syracuse, Freeport Center). Travel 7 miles west on UT 108 to the park's toll booth/entrance, and cross the Davis County Causeway. Fork left/south on the park's loop road. The Mountain View Trail is immediately on the left; otherwise, turn left at the Buffalo Point junction, and then fork right on a dirt road that goes downhill to the backcountry trailhead at White Rock Bay.

Fat-Tire Dining Guide (Northern Wasatch)

c (less than $5)	2-Go Take Out
$ ($5-$10)	Delivery
$$ ($10-$15)	Serves Beer
$$$ (over $15)	Serves Wine
B: Open for Breakfast	Serves Liquor
L: Open for Lunch	Patio Dining
D: Open for Dinner	

American & Grilles

Dylans
981 E 12th Street
Ogden, UT 84404
(801) 393-4545
200 N Main Street
Kaysville, UT 84037
(801) 496-7777
c-$, B L D (M-Su), 2-Go

The best quick-serve restaurant in Ogden. This popular, locally owned restaurant serves hearty and "heart-healthy" food mountain bikers crave, featuring made-to-order sandwiches prepared with grilled halibut and chicken breast, fresh sliced turkey, and roast beef. We have a great salad bar, our smoothies are blended with fresh fruits, and breakfast is fast but still made from scratch. Located near the mouth of Ogden Canyon and on route to and from your favorite Ogden trails.

Union Grill
2501 Wall Ave at Historic Union Station
Ogden UT 84401
(801) 621-2830
$-$$, L D (M-Sa)

The Union Grill adds just the right touch of chic to the historical setting of Ogden's famous railroad station. A successful blend of vibrant colors, art deco inspired stained glass, and a tantalizing menu, makes this eating establishment a must in Ogden. Its the perfect place for a special night out or to kick back and relax after mountain biking.

Bakeries & Delis

Great Harvest Bread Co.
43 E 500 South
Bountiful, UT 84010
(801) 296-2524
272 25th St
Ogden UT 84401
(801) 394-6800
4848 S Harrison Blvd
Ogden UT 84405
(801) 476-4605
www.greatharvest.com
c-$, B L D (M-Sa), 2-Go

Whether you are gearing up for a morning singletrack or cooling down after a wicked ride, Great Harvest Bread Co. has you covered. We're up early grinding our fresh whole wheat flour to bake the finest breads, cinnamon rolls, muffins, cookies, granola and a variety of other healthy snacks for better nutrition and energy. Stop in for a huge free slice of bread with real butter and honey. With many stores along the Wasatch Front, you are sure to find a Great Harvest bakery near your favorite trail.

Brewpubs & Taverns

Roosters 25th St. Brewing Company
253 Historic 25th St.
Ogden UT 84403
(801) 627-6171
www.roostersbrewingco.com
$-$$, L D (M-Su), 2-Go

Upscale, Upbeat, and Eclectic. After kayaking in Weber Canyon, biking in the foothills and mountains of Ogden, or skiing the Olympic downhill at Snowbasin, Roosters is *your* destination for exceptional brews, excellent food, patio seating, and a great time. Proud recipient of the *Salt Lake Magazine* 2002 Utah Dining Award "Best Restaurant in Northern Utah."

Cafes

Eats of Eden
2595 N Hwy 162
Eden UT 84310
(801) 745-8618
www.ovba.org/eats.html
$, L D (T-Sa), 2-Go 🏠 ☂

Located just north of Pineview Reservoir and near the many bike trails of Upper Ogden Valley is Eats of Eden. It's a great casual restaurant to get something tasty to eat, from burgers to pasta and salads. They make pizza from scratch and homemade bread for sandwiches and to accompany pasta and soup. Relax in the dining room or enjoy the view from the patio. This popular little bistro is perfect for a relaxing lunch or a fun night out.

Greek

The Athenian
252 25ᵗʰ Street
Ogden UT 84401
(801) 621-4911
$-$$, L D (M-Sa), 2-Go 🚗 🏠 ☕ ☂ ☂

Good times and superb Greek and American cuisine can be found at The Athenian. The wide array of menu selections, from appetizers to combo plates to specialties, are authentic and made from the finest ingredients. Try traditional dolmathes, souvlaki, and gyros, or let your taste buds explore Greek spaghetti, beeftekia, Greek stew, or moussaka. The atmosphere is casual, so come as you are, but it's also quaint and romantic for a special occasion. Featuring belly dancers every Thursday night!

University Broiler & Grill
4342 S Harrison Blvd.
Ogden UT 84403
(801) 392-2525
$, L D (M-Sa), 2-Go 🏠

Serving Greek food the way the Gods like it, including souvlaki, gyros, lamb kabobs, spiced lemon chicken, and pastas, plus American favorites like burgers, steak sandwich, and BBQ chicken and ribs. Seafood lovers will enjoy halibut, trout, and shrimp; or go meatless with vegetarian gyro, hummus, and dolmathes. All grilled for good health and served fast. Located just downhill from WSU and Ogden's Bonneville Shoreline Trail. Go Wildcats!

International & Eclectric

Nico's Restaurant and Lounge
2401 Washington Blvd.
Ogden UT 84401
(866) 394-9400, (801) 395-8424
www.ogdenplazahotel.com
$-$$, B L D (M-Su), 2-Go 🏠 ☕ ☂

Located downhill from the 22nd Street Bonneville Shoreline Trailhead and in the Ogden Plaza Hotel, Nico's Restaurant and Lounge offers a full variety of classic American dishes and internationally influenced specialties. So if you want to refuel after a ride or build up those carbos the night before—in culinary style—come in and enjoy everything from our classic Philly Sandwich to Herbed Cream-Three Cheese Penne or a selection of grilled fresh fish.

Italian

Boccia's D'Italia
5647 S Harrison Blvd.
S Ogden UT 84403
(801) 452-0193; www.boccias.com
$, L D (M-Sa), 2-Go 🏠 ☕ ☂ ☂

Nothing satisfies the hunger of a mountain biker like Italian food. Boccia's serves old-world fare that is straight from Sicily via New York's Little Italy, including spaghetti marinara, chicken or eggplant parmigiana, raviolis, garlic shrimp linguine, and the ever popular "Italian Trio." New York style pizzas, calzones, subs, and wraps. A sweet ride deserves just rewards, and all of our desserts are homemade. On a group ride? Order our "family style" dinner and feed the whole team. Abbondanza!

Juice Bars

Jamba Juice
1944 N Woodland Park Dr.
Layton, UT 84040
(801) 779-1200; www.jambajuice.com
c-$, B L D (M-Su), 2-Go

Jamba creates delicious, nutritious, all-natural, energizing fruit smoothies and juices. Each refreshing drink provides 3-6 servings of fruit to get you on your way to Five-A-Day! Also boosted with vitamins, minerals, anti-oxidants, phytonutrients, and optional protein powder. Have a Jamba Bread or Jamba Pretzel for whole-grain nutrition. Together, Jamba offers a perfect light meal before or after a ride and to promote a healthy, happy life. "Your body is a temple, littering is strictly prohibited!"

Mexican & Southwestern

Burrito Grande Mexican Food
3836 Washington Blvd.
South Ogden UT 84403
(801) 334-0122
c-$, L D (M-Su), 2-Go

Hungry? Waste no time. Get the best tasting Mexican food in Ogden from Carlos. We serve made-from-scratch tacos, chimichangas, and burritos, plus combination plates and vegetarian selections—all prepared from traditional recipes. We cook with pure vegetable oil for better health. Dine in, take-out, or drive through. If you like to ride hard and "go big," then go to Burrito Grande!

New York Burrito Gourmet Wraps
755 W Antelope Drive
Layton UT 84041
(801) 774-8687
www.newyorkburrito.com
c-$, L D (M-Sa), 2-Go

Eat like a king for the about the price of a burger and fries. Our huge warm tortilla wraps are stuffed full of wholesome ingredients for your healthy lifestyle: cajun shrimp, marinated steak, mango chicken, or savory vegetables; even pastrami for those who are home-sick for the east coast. Custom designed with your choice of beans, lettuce, tomatoes, sour cream, and cheeses. Located just east of I-15 from Exit 335 (Antelope Island).

Pizza

The Pie
1225 Country Hills Rd.
Ogden, UT 84403
(801) 627-1920
www.thepie.com
c-$$, L D (M-Su), 2-Go 🍴

Voted "Best Pizza in Utah" 12 years straight. Our dough is hand rolled and hand tossed in Pie standard, New York (thin) or Chicago (thick) styles. We use the highest quality meats, vegetables, gourmet toppings, and a blend of 100% whole milk Mozzarella, Parmesan, and Romano cheeses. Salads, "zappis," baked subs, and a large beer selection, too. We offer live music, and kids are always welcome!

Vegetarian

Sage's Cafe
473 East 300 South
SLC UT 84111
(801) 322-3790
www.sagescafe.com
$-$$, L D (W-Su), 2-Go 🍴 🍷

Sage's provides an eclectic, cross-cultural menu featuring organic foods and a fresh selection of worldly flavors—all created in house. We offer an impressive selection of beer and wine, triple certified coffees, a great tea menu, fresh pastries, raw foods, and a unique atmosphere. Nightly Chef's Specials feature the freshest seasonal produce. Voted "Best Vegetarian" by *City Weekly*, 2002.

CENTRAL WASATCH

Bonneville Shoreline Trail (Ensign Peak)

19

JUST THE FACTS

Location:	2 miles north of Salt Lake City: City Creek Cyn. to N. Salt Lake
Length:	5.6 miles one-way (11.2 miles out-and-back)
Type:	One-way, or out-and-back
Tread:	3.2 miles singletrack, 2.4 miles doubletrack
Physically:	Moderate⁺ (steep climb from City Creek Cyn. to Ensign Peak & from Jones Hollow to the radio towers)
Technically:	2⁺-3⁺ (good tread but switchbacks are notoriously tight and steep)
Gain:	1,000 feet (City Creek to NSL); 500 feet (NSL to City Creek)
Dogs:	Yes, on leash

GO ☐
NO ■ | JAN | FEB | MAR | APR | MAY | JUN | JUL | AUG | SEP | OCT | NOV | DEC |

CENTRAL WASATCH

"Trail closed. No Trespassing. Violators will be prosecuted." This is what recreationists faced over the years when biking, running, or walking the foothills above the State Capitol and behind Ensign Peak. Finally, after years of legal battles over a dead-end trail, the Bonneville Shoreline Trail is now a through-trail between City Creek Canyon and North Salt Lake. Public access has been secured and recreationists can once again wander the foothills to take in some of the best views of the Wasatch Front. This is no "easy" through-trail because only a small amount actually follows the flat ancient shoreline. You really have to want those views because you must tackle steep hills and tricky switchbacks to get them. Your efforts will not be in vain.

Details

Pick up the Bonneville Shoreline Trail (BST) on the west side of City Creek Canyon Road at its junction with Bonneville Boulevard. The BST follows the old cross-country ski trail just above the paved canyon road, rising moderately (tech 2-3) through a corridor of brushy oak and maple. After 1 mile, the BST forks left. Do not continue on the ski trail because bikes are prohibited past the BST junction. You know you are on route when you start climbing steeply through dense oak and maple and have to creep (or walk) around a half-dozen remarkably sharp turns (tech 4-5). The trail cuts under cliffs of reddened sandstone conglomerate and overlooks the private Eagle Gate community, which had contested the trail's alignment in court. City, state, and federal agencies prevailed, and the trail was completed up to the ridge behind Ensign Peak. It's steep, though, and the switchbacks near the top ease the grade only a bit (tech 3⁺). Go left on the ridge to reach Ensign Peak and a panoramic view of Salt Lake Valley; go right then veer left to continue on the BST on a rolling contour over to the radio towers' access road. Go right on the dirt road, and climb to the divide at the towers (**m3.4/7.8**).

CENTRAL WASATCH

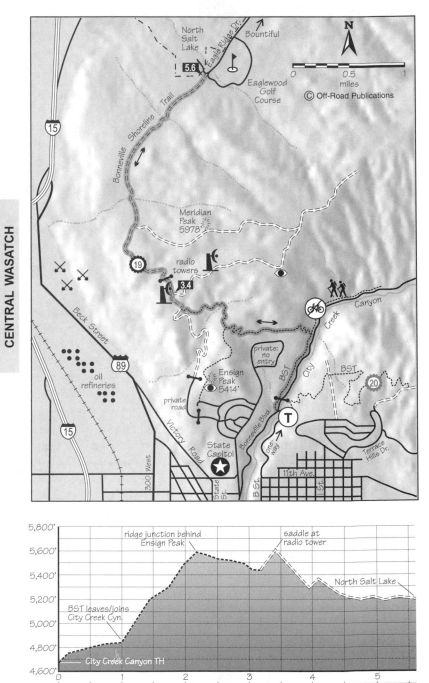

Descend the choppy doubletrack (tech 3⁺) around a gate and into Jones Canyon, keeping in mind that you'll have to climb back up on the return trip. Climb out of the hollow on a rutted doubletrack (tech 2⁺) and freewheel swiftly to a broad grassy plain that is the ancient lake's wave-cut shoreline. The trail ends at Eagle Ridge Drive in North Salt Lake. (Trail-head access is subject to change or may be closed because of residential developments.) Turn around and retrace your tracks.

Option: City Creek Canyon Overlook

When you reach the divide at the radio towers, you can climb the dirt road to the right past more towers and to the ridge overlooking City Creek Canyon. The hills are steep and gravelly, which makes them excellent training climbs for racers. Remember, bikes are not allowed off road in City Creek Canyon, so do not descend any trails or roads into the canyon or you risk being arrested.

Top: Amy and Tricia roll past a showcase of flowers on the BST. Bottom: The BST offers superlative views and sweet singletrack.

Option: City Creek Canyon Road

City Creek Canyon Road is one of Salt Lake City's classic road rides, but fat tire cyclists, runners, and pedestrians enjoy the curving lane, too. The first 3.2 miles to the water treatment plant are easy⁺ and gains 700 feet for a rolling 4-percent grade. Beyond, the road narrows to one lane and rises more steeply for 2.6 miles more to its end at Rotary Park. Total round-trip distance is just over 11.5 miles with a total gain of 1,350 feet.

CENTRAL WASATCH

Option: Mueller Park Marathon

Anyone looking for a day-long ride at relatively low elevations can link the BST with Bountiful's Mueller Park-North Canyon Trails for a 29-mile cross-country circuit. When you reach Eagle Ridge Drive in North Salt Lake, go right past Eaglewood Golf Course and onto Bountiful Boulevard. To climb North Canyon Trail, go right on Canyon Creek Road; to climb Mueller Park Trail, continue past Bountiful City Golf Course and go right on Mueller Park Road. Then, return the way you came on the BST to City Creek Canyon. Total gain is around 3,500 feet. So good!

Know Before You Go

- Rattlesnakes are know to inhabit these warm foothills.
- *Fido Factor:* Dogs are required to be leashed on the BST.

City Creek Canyon Use Policies (Memorial Day-September 31):
- Bicycles are allowed on the paved City Creek Canyon Road on odd-numbered calender days but are prohibited on holidays regardless of odd-even status.
- Motor vehicles (reservations only) are allowed on even-numbered calender days.
- Foot traffic is allowed all the time.
- Bicycling off the paved road is prohibited, except on the BST.
- Bicycles must stay to the right side of the road and obey the posted speed limit.
- Dogs must be leashed and cannot go beyond the water treatment plant.

Maps & More Information

- USGS 1:24,000: Fort Douglas and Salt Lake City North, Utah
- Public Lands Information Center (at REI): (801) 466-6411
- Wasatch-Cache National Forest (Salt Lake Ranger District): (801) 733-2660; www.fs.fed.us/r4/wcnf/unit/slrd/index.shtml
- Bonneville Shoreline Trail Committee: www.bonneville-trail.org, (801) 816-0876
- Salt Lake City Mayor's Office Administrative Affairs: (801) 535-7704

Trailhead Access

First, make your way through Salt Lake City to the Avenues (north of North Temple), and travel to the intersection of B Street and 11th Avenue. Drive north on Bonneville Boulevard Loop (one-way, east to west) to where it intersects City Creek Canyon Road. Parking is limited. Additional parking, but still limited, is up City Creek Canyon Road at the gate.

20

Bonneville ShorelineTrail (Salt Lake)

JUST THE FACTS

Location:	Salt Lake foothills: Emigration Canyon to City Creek Canyon
Length:	10 miles one-way; 20 miles out-and-back
Type:	One-way or out-and-back
Tread:	6.6 miles singletrack, 3.4 miles doubletrack
Physically:	Moderate (steep climbs required to get to the "shoreline")
Technically:	1$^+$-3$^+$ (Smooth-running tread w/ choppy sections; dips & tight curves in gulches)
Gain:	1,600 feet (Sunnyside-City Crk); 1,300 feet (City Crk-Sunnyside)
Dogs:	Yes, on leash

GO ☐
NO ■ | JAN | FEB | MAR | APR | MAY | JUN | JUL | AUG | SEP | OCT | NOV | DEC |

CENTRAL WASATCH

This section of the Bonneville Shoreline Trail between Emigration and City Creek Canyons is the cornerstone of the entire 95-mile-long trail. It's more than a simple recreational corridor for pedestrians, joggers, and bicyclists; it serves as a buffer between the ever-rising tide of urbanism and the invaluable open spaces bordering Salt Lake City. Come March and the first warm weekend of spring it brings, the Bonneville Shoreline Trail is a veritable magnet for mountain bikers who long to shake off the winter blues and move their legs in circles once again. The unobstructed views of city and mountains are unparalleled. And best yet, the trail itself is a sweet blend of smooth-running tread, short but challenging climbs, and rewarding descents.

Details

With a dozen access points and a myriad of off-shoot trails, this section of the Bonneville Shoreline Trail (BST) can be confusing to navigate, but half the fun is exploring and creating your own favorite circuit, (see "Add-Ons").

Gear down and rev up the rpms because the first hill from the Sunnyside Avenue Trailhead is a little bruiser. Follow alongside the log fence, passing a singletrack forking right, and merge with a dirt road coming up from This is the Place State Park. Come to a T-junction and go left on another dirt road. (*Add On* by taking that bypassed singletrack to the right. It contours above the mouth of Emigration Canyon and widens to doubletrack in Rattlesnake Gulch. Turn left on a dirt road and you'll rejoin the main route at the T-junction.) Pass a doubletrack forking right, descend a couple hundred feet, and *then* fork right on singletrack. Roll uphill gradually, passing still more trails forking right, and squeeze through the gap in the wire fence on the pipeline corridor (**m1.0/9.0**). (*Add On* by taking that previous doubletrack. It rises moderately at first then ends with a painfully steep but ridable pitch to the top of the "four-rollers" [tech 4$^+$] on the gas pipeline corridor. They take you to the gap in the fence.)

Take the left most of two doubletracks and make a beeline past the entrance to Red Butte Garden and Arboretum and to paved Red Butte

Canyon Road (**m2.0/8.0**). Are you with me? (*Add On* by taking the right doubletrack from the fence gap. It bends through Georges Hollow and runs parallel to and above the main route. At the junction with Skyline Trail, go left and descend to the Arboretum's entrance. Skyline Trail is another *Add On,* but it's steep, eroded, and nasty [tech 4-5].)

Go up the paved road for a few hundred feet, fork left on a paved drive signed "Dead End," and then go right immediately on a doubletrack that rises sharply to the power lines and onto the ancient shoreline. (*Add On* by heading up Red Butte Canyon Road and taking one of several connector trails to the left/north. They eventually take you up to the power lines, if you know the right combination. Go play and see.) Dip through a gulch; then take either the contour trail (tech 3) or the free-fall plunge (tech 5) through Battle Gulch. Finally, descend a switchbacking singletrack and go right on a wide dirt road to the mouth of Dry Gulch (**m3.5/6.5**). (Access to Popperton Park and 11th Avenue is via the paved path heading west from Dry Gulch.)

Onward to City Creek Canyon. This section is also called the Steiner Centennial Trail for the generous grants made by the Steiner Foundation in 1996, Utah's statehood centennial. Dry Gulch is one of two significant climbs on the BST. (The other is the climb out of City Creek Canyon when going west to east.) Head straight up the gulch for 1 mile then bank left and chug up to a scenic saddle and overlook of Limekiln Gulch (**m4.7/5.3**). Wind through several gulches, go right at a T-junction, and climb sharply beneath Twin Peaks where the 2002 Winter Olympic rings shined brightly. Here, the true nature of the shoreline is revealed with a long mile of near level trail, although technically the trail was built above the actual lake level. You get the idea, though.

Come to a saddle (**m7.0/3.0**) where the gas pipeline crosses and people tend to congregate, and take the main doubletrack downhill. (*Add On* by descending the infamous Bobsled Trail [tech 4]. Dive down the pipeline, turn right, and swoop down high-banked curves in a narrow gulch. Upon intersecting a doubletrack, take it right, exit to a paved road in a residential area, and go right again to reach Terrace Hills Drive. Or, cross the doubletrack to continue on lower Bobsled.) In a half mile and under the power lines, watch for the BST forking right into the oak brush. (Continuing down the doubletrack leads to the Terrace Hills Drive trailhead.) Wind through more gulches on buffed singletrack and veer left on a doubletrack to descend sharply to the edge of a fenced-in water tank. Go right on an entrenched doubletrack with Salt Lake's central business district at your

CENTRAL WASATCH

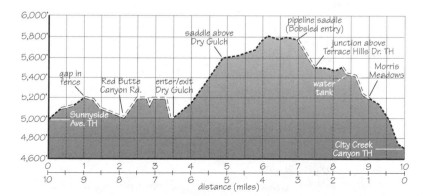

CENTRAL WASATCH

feet and descend to a four-way junction of tracks in Morris Meadows. Go straight through for the final drop to the City Creek Canyon trailhead (**m10.0/ 0.0**). Trim your speed and ride courteously because the corners are blind and the last pitch is steep.

If you didn't set up a shuttle, you'll have to get back to the Sunnyside Avenue trailhead by either retracing your tracks (no easy task) or by taking paved roads (an easier task).

Here's tips for the road route with the least amount of traffic. Take Bonneville Boulevard southeast, and turn left on 11th Avenue. A designated bike lane edging the road takes you 1.6 miles to Virginia Street (1345 East) and Popperton Park. Go downhill one-half block, and turn left on Fairfax Road at Primary Children's Hospital. Bend right (downhill), and go left on Federal Heights Drive. Pedal uphill to North Campus Drive, and turn right

Top: Plump wildflowers adorn the foothills during spring. Bottom: Want views? You'll find them on Salt Lake's BST.

then left immediately on Wasatch Drive. At the four-way stop light with Hempstead, go left and ride through Fort Douglas, continuing on Stover to the BST at Red Butte Canyon (**m2.0** above). Retrace your tracks to the Sunnyside trailhead.

! Know Before You Go

- Because the BST is so popular, it's imperative that mountain bikers adhere to trail etiquette.
- Yield to foot traffic. Slow to a walking pace or stop alongside the trail to

allow pedestrians to pass; make your presence known with a friendly greeting.

- Obey travel restrictions and trail closures; respect private property.
- Avoid riding during wet conditions to prevent trail damage.
- Control your bike. Excessive speed poses a threat to fellow trail users and skidding is "bad form."
- Rattlesnakes are know to inhabit these warm foothills, so stay alert.
- *Fido Factor:* Trail is dog friendly but water sources are lacking. Salt Lake County Ordinance requires dogs to be leashed on the BST.

? Maps & More Information

- USGS 1:24,000: Fort Douglas and Salt Lake City North, Utah
- Public Lands Information Center (at REI): (801) 466-6411
- Wasatch-Cache National Forest (Salt Lake Ranger District): (801) 733-2660; www.fs.fed.us/r4/wcnf/unit/slrd/index.shtml
- Bonneville Shoreline Trail Committee: www.bonneville-trail.org, (801) 816-0876
- Salt Lake City Mayor's Office Administrative Affairs: (801) 535-7704

Trailhead Access

Sunnyside Avenue: From the intersection of Foothill Drive (1950 East) and Sunnyside Avenue (850 South) take Sunnyside 1 mile east and park at the east gate to This is the Place State Park, opposite Crestview Drive and Hogle Zoo.

City Creek Canyon trailhead (and other access points): From the Sunnyside Avenue trailhead, return to Foothill Drive and take it right/north then west (becomes 500 South) to 1300 East. (Red Butte Canyon access: From Foothill Drive, turn right on Wasatch Drive, right on Hempstead, travel through Fort Douglas on Stover, and park at the lot for Red Butte Gardens and Arboretum.)

Turn right/north on 1300 East, go right on South Temple, and turn left on Virginia Street (1345 East). Turn left/west on 11th Avenue opposite Popperton Park (trail access to Dry Gulch). Take 11th Avenue to the intersection with B Street, and go right on Bonneville Boulevard (one-way) to the City Creek Canyon trailhead. Additional parking is up City Creek Canyon Road. (Terrace Hills Drive access: Turn right from 11th Avenue opposite the fire station at about 1000 East, drive up Terrace Hills Drive [steep!] to its end, and park roadside. Morris Reservoir access: From 11th Avenue, go up I Street, fork left on Northhills Drive, and curve right on 18th Avenue. The small parking area is just east of the L. D. S. church.)

21
Lookout Peak

JUST THE FACTS

Location:	11 miles northeast of Salt Lake City
Length:	12.4 miles
Type:	Loop (counterclockwise)
Tread:	Singletrack w/ a touch of doubletrack
Physically:	Strenuous (steep climb on MPT, hike-a-biking on GWT, semi-primitive trails w/ bushwhacking & route finding thereafter)
Technically:	2-5 (gravelly tread on MPT; eroded, rocky tread on GWT; narrow, overgrown singletrack w/ a rocky & rutted descent)
Gain:	3,000 feet
Dogs:	No, watershed

GO ☐
NO ■ | JAN | FEB | MAR | APR | MAY | JUN | JUL | AUG | SEP | OCT | NOV | DEC |

WHY RIDE THIS TRAIL   *Completed in 2001, the Mormon Pioneer Trail (MPT) serves as the backbone for several rides around the Mountain Dell basin. The Lookout Peak loop circles the canyon's western slope on mostly rugged singletracks. You'll climb steadily on the MPT to Big Mountain Pass* then hike-a-bike up the Great Western Trail before encountering a variety of conditions. The Lookout Peak section follows a seldom traveled path that can be a thrilling technical challenge or a bike-on-shoulders portage depending on your ability and trail's seasonal conditions. You'll need route-finding skills, tolerance and stamina for harsh terrain, and a solid sense of adventure, or this could be a mountain bike nightmare come true. Of course, the spectacular views might ease any hardships endured.

Details

From the interpretive plaques at Affleck Park, take the dirt road north (don't cross the bridge over the creek). It ends shortly and the Mormon Pioneer Trail takes over. Initially, the climb is moderate, and the path cuts across small fields separated by thick stands of hardwoods. After crossing the highway, the path angles upward more steeply and gets pebbly (tech 3+) until the switchbacks ease the grade. Read the plaque on the stone monument at Big Mountain Pass (**m2.6**), and imagine the exaltation of weary Mormon Pioneers when they gained similar views of the Salt Lake Valley during their 1847 trek.

Cross the highway, and start hoofing up the Great Western Trail (GWT). The grade is severe, the tread can be hammered, and the dozen turns are humorously tight. Don't blow up here trying to ride it all because there's lots of tough trail ahead. The GWT bends north, skirts Big Mountain, and descends to join a doubletrack that you take along the ridge for nearly 2 miles. At Swallow Rocks (shallow caves eroded from outcrops of nodular rocks), fork left from the doubletrack onto the GWT, which becomes brushy singletrack contouring high above the canyon (**m6.8**). (The

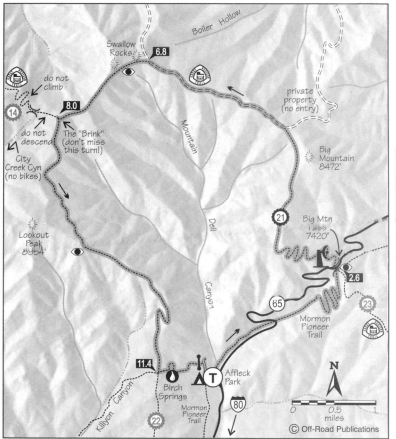

Boiler Hollow

Swallow
Rocks   **6.8**

do not
climb

8.0
The "Brink"
(don't miss
this turn!)

(14)

do not
descend

City
Creek Cyn
(no bikes)

Lookout
Peak
8954'

Mountain

Dell

Canyon

private
property
(no entry)

Big
Mountain
8472'

21   Big Mtn
Pass
7420'

2.6

(23)

(65)   Mormon
Pioneer
Trail

11.4

Birch
Springs

T   Affleck
Park

(22)   Mormon
Pioneer
Trail

(80)

N

0   0.5   1
miles

© Off-Road Publications

CENTRAL WASATCH

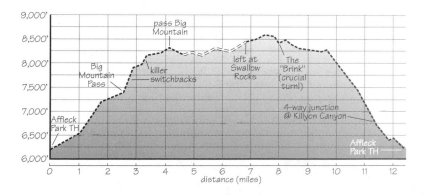

CENTRAL WASATCH

The smooth-rolling Mormon Pioneer Trail precedes a "variety" of trail conditions on the rest of the Lookout Peak loop.

doubletrack turns northward to destinations unknown.) Beyond, the trail plunges radically down a slope of loose, chunky rock (tech 5), and then drops severely again (**m8.0**). Stop!

This is a crucial junction called "the Brink." The old trail sign no longer exists, so you must watch for the following indicators: pink squares painted on aspens, a yellow "no trespassing" sign, and a tree on the right etched "Ono Salazar," really! Now, fork left/south on a faint, overgrown trail that crosses a low, rounded hill; you may have to bushwhack. (If you miss this turn, you'll drop dismally to the very head of City Creek Canyon then face a near vertical and exceptionally painful hike-a-bike section. Eventually, the GWT crosses the Sessions Mountains to Skyline Drive near Bountiful Peak—no man's land.) Head southward across a second treeless hill, angling above two small depressions of red soil, and descend to a saddle. Here, the more-evident Lookout Peak trail heads south into the aspens.

The Lookout Peak trail is not regularly maintained and is kept evident only by occasional equestrians, roaming deer, and fool-hearted adventurists like yourself. Expect overgrown brush, deadfall, and lots of roots (tech 3$^+$-5). Fortunately, the trail is nearly level. Cross a subtle, open ridge where you can look back at Swallow Rocks and Big Mountain, duck into the aspens, and come to a second ridge that extends from Lookout Peak.

Head southeast down the ridge. Steep grades and scores of loose rocks can make the descent pretty nasty (tech 3^+-5). After a mile, the trail becomes a deep rut as it dives down a pair of switchbacks and cuts through the haunting char-blackened trees remnant of the 1988 Emigration Canyon wildfire. Come to a four-way junction of trails in a small clearing at the head of Killyon Canyon (**m11.4**), and fork left to descend a rutted doubletrack-turned-singletrack past Birch Springs to Affleck Park.

! Know Before You Go

- Mormon Pioneer Trail is a popular nonmotorized trail, so expect and respect other trail users.
- Affleck Park is a fee-use area: $5 for day-use or overnight camping. There are outhouses but no water taps.
- Sheep ranching is common around Big Mountain.
- *Fido Factor:* Dogs are not allowed on this route because it is within the Mountain Dell Watershed.

? Maps & More Information

- USGS 1:24,000: Mountain Dell, Utah
- Public Lands Information Center (at REI): (801) 466-6411
- Wasatch-Cache National Forest (Salt Lake Ranger District): (801) 733-2660; www.fs.fed.us/r4/wcnf/unit/slrd/index.shtml
- Salt Lake City Watershed Management: (801) 483-6705, www.slcgov.com

♪ Trailhead Access

From I-80, take Exit 134 for Emigration and East Canyons and Mountain Dell (located 6 miles east of Salt Lake City and 11 miles west of Park City from Kimball Junction/Exit 145). Drive 4.6 miles on UT 65 to Affleck Park. Pay the park fee or park along the highway at your discretion.

CENTRAL WASATCH

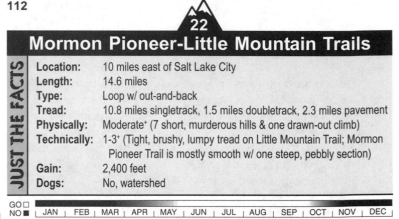

22
Mormon Pioneer-Little Mountain Trails

Location:	10 miles east of Salt Lake City
Length:	14.6 miles
Type:	Loop w/ out-and-back
Tread:	10.8 miles singletrack, 1.5 miles doubletrack, 2.3 miles pavement
Physically:	Moderate+ (7 short, murderous hills & one drawn-out climb)
Technically:	1-3+ (Tight, brushy, lumpy tread on Little Mountain Trail; Mormon Pioneer Trail is mostly smooth w/ one steep, pebbly section)
Gain:	2,400 feet
Dogs:	No, watershed

GO ☐
NO ■ | JAN | FEB | MAR | APR | MAY | JUN | JUL | AUG | SEP | OCT | NOV | DEC |

WHY SHOULD U RIDE THIS TRAIL

Old trail teams up with new trail on what will likely become one of Salt Lake's most popular rides. The long-forgotten Little Mountain Trail at the top of Emigration Canyon gets a lease on life by linking up with the new Mormon Pioneer Trail, debuted by the Salt Lake Ranger District in 2001. Little Mountain Trail remains one of the hardest short courses around with its seven short but murderous climbs. Mormon Pioneer Trail is a hand-crafted, government issue trail that rises steadily from Little Dell Reservoir Recreation Area to Big Mountain Pass. The whole ride is one tough cookie, but it's easy to custom fit the trail to your ability by breaking it down into components of varying difficulty.

Details

Pick up the trail behind the outhouses at the UT 65 trailhead, and coast 0.2 mile to a plank footbridge. Here, the route becomes doubletrack, which flows as freely as the creek at your side. The parallel lanes are entrenched at times and can clip your pedals on the down stroke (tech 2+). Also, you'll have to dodge overhanging branches like a knight in a jousting match. Stay straight on a grassy, overgrown track where the main route veers left across a meadow. Exit to a green gate and connect with a gravel path. Turn sharp right past the boat ramp to take the paved access road to the entrance of Little Dell Reservoir Recreation Area. Go left on the highway; then fork right for Emigration Canyon, and climb moderately to Little Mountain Summit (**m4.3**).

The low-gear climb (No. 1) on the old fire-break road past the red gate is just a teaser of what lies ahead. The dual track narrows to singletrack along the rolling scenic ridge then rises up a half dozen biker friendly switchbacks (No. 2). Catch your breath before entering the oak brush because you'll have to pump hard on pebbly tread up climb No. 3 (tech 3+). Get the feel of it?

A quick descent on grooved, eroded tread (tech 3+) through the prickly oak brush is barely long enough for you to catch your breath before you are power-stroking again up the fourth interval. Climb number five is steeper yet, six is a breeze, but the clayey tread can be powdery, slimy, or choppy depending on conditions. Cross the meadow under the power lines and gear down for the seventh hill, which comes in three ever-steepening stages. Ugh! A free-fall drop takes you to a four-way junction of trails (**m7.6**). Go right to descend on variably rutted singletrack (tech 3⁺) past Birch Springs and to Affleck Park. (Left descends Killyon Canyon and crosses private property on the way.) Go right on the dirt road to the bridge over the creek (**m8.6**). If you've had enough, then simply hop on

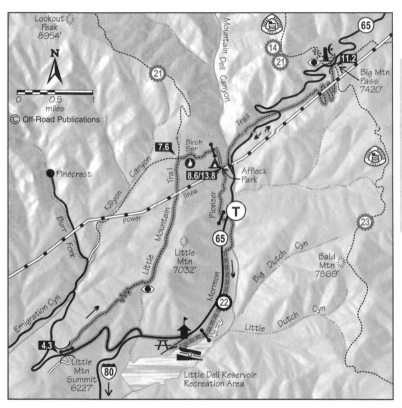

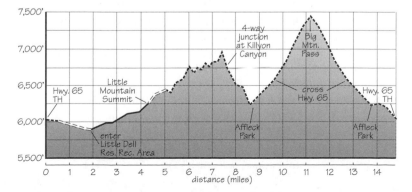

the MPT and take it back to the highway trailhead; otherwise, cross the bridge and take the dirt lane left at the interperative signs describing the Mormon Pioneers' Road to Zion. The trail resumes at the road's end. The well-groomed path rises moderately (tech 2$^+$) through groves of oak and maple and crosses small meadows. Cross the highway (look both ways, naturally), climb more aggressively through the oak, and then pump harder yet up pebbly tread (tech 3-4). The grade eases when the switchbacks begin, but the half-dozen turns themselves are tight and difficult to negotiate. At Big Mountain Pass (**m11.2**), you can read another plaque describing the Mormon's trek and gaze down to the valley that Brigham Young declared to be "the right place."

Freewheel back to Affleck Park (be cautious of and courteous to uphill travelers, naturally), cross the bridge, and connect with the lower MPT (**m13.8**). You'll climb a touch then descend gradually on lumpy tread (tech 2$^+$) and across open slopes back to the highway trailhead.

Option: Little Mountain Trail Loop

If you skip the long climb up to Big Mountain Pass, you can make a moderate 9.4-mile loop on Little Mountain and the lower section of the MPT. Keep in mind that you still must tackle the seven murderous climbs on Little Mountain Trail.

Option: Mormon Pioneer Trail, proper

If you skip Little Mountain Trail you can ride up-and-back on the MPT. Here's the breakdown. Little Dell Reservoir to the UT 65 trailhead is rated easy at 2.2 miles. The UT 65 trailhead to Affleck Park is moderate at 1.1 miles. Affleck Park to Big Mountain Pass is 2.6 miles and is rated moderate$^+$ because of the steep climb from the highway crossing to the summit. Do the math, guage your ability, and go ride.

! Know Before You Go

- Mormon Pioneer Trail is a very popular trail for hikers and bikers. Control your speed, tread lightly, and yield to other users, especially when descending. MPT is not a downhiller's test track!
- If you park at Little Dell Reservoir Recreation Area, you must pay the entrance fee. Bicyclists who ride into or out of the park do not have to pay the fee. Additional rules and regulations apply.
- Affleck Park offers day use and overnight camping for $5.00 for individual sites. Fees for the group areas are higher. There are outhouses but no water taps.
- *Fido Factor:* Dogs are not allowed in the Mountain Dell Watershed.

? Maps & More Information

- USGS 1:24,000: Mountain Dell, Utah
- Public Lands Information Center (at REI): (801) 466-6411

John, Brad, and James head up the second of seven murderous climbs on Little Mountain Trail.

CENTRAL WASATCH

- Wasatch-Cache National Forest (Salt Lake Ranger District): (801) 733-2660; www.fs.fed.us/r4/wcnf/unit/slrd/index.shtml
- Salt Lake City Watershed Management: (801) 483-6705, www.slcgov.com
- City Creek and Affleck Park Reservations: (801) 483-6797

Trailhead Access

From Salt Lake City, take I-80 about 6 miles up Parleys Canyon to Exit 134 (Mountain Dell, East Canyon). Go left/north on UT 65 for 2.9 miles to Little Dell Reservoir Recreation Area then 1.7 miles farther to the highway trailhead and parking area for the Mormon Pioneer Trail (outhouses on right). You can park and embark from several other locations.

23

Mormon Pioneer Trail & Beyond

JUST THE FACTS

Location:	6 miles east of Salt Lake City
Length:	21.3 miles
Type:	Loop (clockwise)
Tread:	17.1 miles singletrack, 1.7 miles doubletrack, 2.5 miles paved road
Physically:	Extreme (steady climb to Big Mtn. Pass, sharp climbs on ridge)
Technically:	2-4+ (smooth & choppy tread to Big Mtn. Pass; rugged tread on ridge; overgrown but smooth grassy descent)
Gain:	3,800 feet
Dogs:	No, watershed

GO □
NO ■ | JAN | FEB | MAR | APR | MAY | JUN | JUL | AUG | SEP | OCT | NOV | DEC |

WHY SHOULD I RIDE THIS TRAIL?

Three trails, *each with a distinct personality, are tied to-gether for this 21.3-mile loop around the Mountain Dell watershed, located only a few miles east of Salt Lake and up Parley's Canyon. After a few warmup miles on pavement, you'll embark on the Mormon Pioneer Trail, and climb on singletrack to Big Mountain Pass. There, the Great Western Trail traces the county line along the Wasatch Crest to Parley's Summit. Although the ridge seems subdued from afar, it packs a punch with a multitude of long-winded and short stinging climbs on both rough and smooth trail. Your legs might scream "uncle" when you reach Parley's Summit, and the prospect of coasting down Interstate 80 may look all-too inviting. But don't succomb to pavement because you can sneak back into the wilds and rip down one of the Wasatch's secret singletrack stashes.*

Details

Start out easy because there are lots of miles ahead of you, and it's far too early to redline your heart rate while climbing the mile-long straightaway up UT 65. Pass the turnoff for Emigration Canyon, and duck into the Little Dell Reservoir Recreation Area (**m2.5**; no fee for bicycles). To access the Mormon Pioneer Trail (MPT), go down the paved access road, turn sharply left to go past the boat ramp, and then take the pebbly trail to some picnic tables. Go left at a green steel gate and onto a grassy doubletrack. (You can go straight on the more obvious doubletrack into the big meadow, but it requires several confusing turns to get back on route.) In 0.2 mile, you join with and continue on a well-worn doubletrack just below the highway. The grooved track rises gently through a corridor of cottonwoods (tech 2+) to a footbridge, where the route turns to singletrack and exits to the highway trailhead. Cross the road, and pick up the MPT near a gate.

Climb moderately on lumpy tread (tech 2+) to Affleck Park. Go right, cross the bridge, and follow the dirt road left past the interpretive plaques describing the Mormon Pioneers' Road to Zion (**m5.5**). The trail resumes at the road's end.

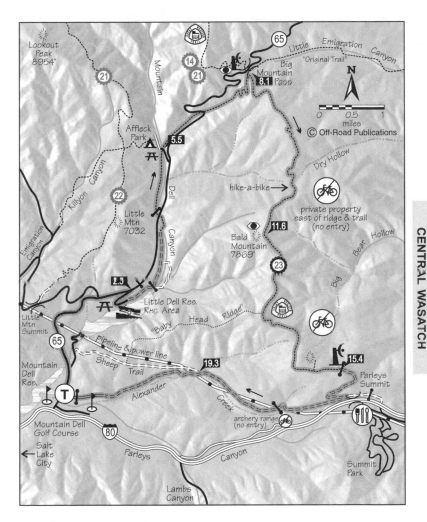

CENTRAL WASATCH

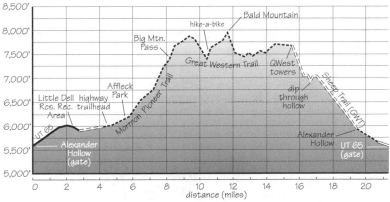

CENTRAL WASATCH

Your destination is still a long way off when you reach the top of Bald Mountain.

The well-groomed path rises moderately (tech 2⁺) through thick oak and across small meadows. Cross the highway and climb more aggressively on pebbly tread (tech 3-4), knowing that the trail eases when it starts to switchback under the power lines. Reach Big Mountain Pass (**m8.1**), and read the interpretive plaque on the monument. Can you imagine the hardships endured by Brigham Young and his Mormon Pioneers on their transcontinental trek in 1847?

Feeling fresh? If not, then make an about face, coast back to your car, and resolve to conquer this route another time. Legs willing, take the GWT up a pair of grueling climbs that are barely ridable. A rolling section offers distant views of the Mill Creek ridge and of the valley that Brigham Young declared to be the right place; then it dives down a pair of rough hills (tech 4) and crosses a sloping meadow at the top of Dry Hollow. Don't bother trying to ride the upcoming hill; it's so steep and so hammered that it's wise to save your energy (tech 5⁺). Grind up several short intense hills through dense deciduous and coniferous growth, taking comfort in the smooth respites in between (tech 2⁺-4). A nasty climb on small loose rocks brings you to the loop's high point atop a treeless summit aptly named Bald Mountain (**m11.6**). Spend some time here to admire the sights of the Mill Creek ridge, distant Salt Lake Valley, and shimmering reservoir far below.

Still feeling fresh? If not, you might be in trouble because the GWT takes a less than direct course to Parley's Summit. There is still lots of elevation to gain and some sections are extremely rugged, like the drop off of Bald Mountain (tech 4⁺); however, there are segments of singletrack that will replace any grimace with a mile-wide grin. The GWT is not marked, but it's quite evident. Still, watch for a junction about 1.6 miles south of Bald Mountain and atop a short painful climb. Don't get duped into taking a faint trail forking right. It leads to "Baby Head Ridge" and drops steeply over loose rocks the size of a newborn's noggin toward Mountain Dell. It's nasty (tech 5⁺). Enough said! So, stay straight/left and descend an eroded stretch (tech 4⁺) to stay along the main ridge (tech 3-4). You can breathe easy when the whole route swings eastward, levels, and smooths to a mile-long thread of silk that ends at the Qwest relay towers (**m15.4**).

Take the rutted double-track downhill (tech 3). Where it bends left and you can see the Brake Test Area sign on Interstate 80 below, fork right on a grassy lane for the Sheep Trail. "This is no trail," you'll likely bark, as did I on my recon. Many of life's finest pleasures come in disguised packages, right? Descend abruptly to where a pipeline is exposed, go around the gate, and

Joe drops off Bald Mountain; Mill Creek ridge in the background.

CENTRAL WASATCH

struggle up one last hill. There's no shame in walking at this point. Level out for a bit; then freewheel in wild abandon down Alexander Hollow. You can't get lost because the route is tagged with pipeline markers every couple hundred feet, and the only enticing turnoff is signed "danger keep out, archery range." The overgrown track is surprisingly smooth (tech 3), but be leery of unseen dips covered by the grass and sharp water bars. A bit over 2 miles down and in a flat grassy clearing (**m19.3**), fork left down the hollow on an initially faint singletrack that becomes as smooth as "budda." (If you start climbing under the power lines you missed the turn.) Singletrack widens to pebbly doubletrack, and the nearby golf course signals the ride's end.

Option: Mormon Pioneer Trail or Sheep Trail only

If this loop sounds a bit daunting, then no problem. Skip the GWT and target either the front or back ends of this loop, both of which are rated moderate. MPT is a fine 11.2-mile out-an-back ride in itself. The descent from Big Mountain Pass is worth every drop of sweat to reach it. Alternatively, spin up I-80 to Parley's Summit and descend the Sheep Trail back to Mountain Dell for a 12-mile loop. Hesitancy while descending the grassy track on your first go will turn to fevered freewheeling on returns flights.

CENTRAL WASATCH

Are we having fun yet? Stacy and Inge glide down Alexander Hollow.

Know Before You Go

• This is a long, grueling ride with no water sources or easy bailouts once you're committed to the GWT.
• Be prepared for rapidly changing alpine weather.
• Mormon Pioneer Trail is quickly becoming one of the most popular trails in the Central Wasatch, so ride courteously and tread lightly.
• *Fido Factor:* Dogs are not allowed in the Mountain Dell Watershed, which includes the GWT.

? Maps & More Information

• USGS 1:24,000: Mountain Dell and Big Dutch Hollow, Utah
• Public Lands Information Center (at REI): (801) 466-6411
• Wasatch-Cache National Forest (Salt Lake Ranger District): (801) 733-2660; www.fs.fed.us/r4/wcnf/unit/slrd/index.shtml
• Salt Lake City Watershed Management: (801) 483-6705, www.slcgov.com

Trailhead Access

From Salt Lake City, take I-80 about 6 miles up Parley's Canyon to Exit 134 (Mountain Dell, East Canyon) and go left/north on UT 65. Park alongside the road near the steel gate posted "Salt Lake City Watershed" just past the entrance to Mountain Dell Golf Course. Do not block the gate.

24
Mill Creek Pipeline Trail

Location:	Lower Mill Creek Canyon
Length:	7.2 miles
Type:	One-way
Tread:	All singletrack
Physically:	Easy (mostly flat, w/ one steep, rough descent)
Technically:	2-4$^+$ (mostly smooth tread w/ some rocks; steep, exposed slopes edge the trail; descent in Rattlesnake Gulch is tricky)
Gain:	150 feet; Loss: 1,460 feet
Dogs:	Yes, restrictions

GO ☐
NO ■ | JAN | FEB | MAR | APR | MAY | JUN | JUL | AUG | SEP | OCT | NOV | DEC |

Mill Creek Pipeline Trail is the perfect ride for those wanting to experience the joy of singletrack but without having to scale entire mountains. The path follows an old water flume line high on the side of Mill Creek Canyon, curving into forested hollows and out across sunny slopes. Views of Mill Creek Canyon and the distant Salt Lake Valley are plentiful. Water flows downhill and so does the Pipeline Trail with the lion's share no more turbulent than a trickling brook, but the descents down Burch Hollow and Rattlesnake Gulch are more like tumbling rapids and a gushing waterfall, respectively. Neither should dissuade a prudent novice biker. No shuttle? No problem. With four trailheads on Mill Creek Canyon Road, Pipeline Trail can be ridden as loops of varying difficulty.

Details

Don't get duped into taking Lambs Canyon or Mount Aire Trails from the Elbow Fork trailhead. The signed but inconspicuous Pipeline Trail ducks into the trees about 100 feet down from the parking area. After an initially rough section of small angular rocks (tech 3), the trail smooths to hard-packed dirt (tech 2). Still, you must concentrate on your front wheel because the trail is narrow, and the canyon's slopes brush by your right shoulder and drop sharply beneath your left pedal. Eyes forward; don't look down! The pedaling is more comforting farther on as the path runs through a tunnel of oak, maple, and knee-high grasses. A pronounced right bend that affords good views of Porter Fork, Mount Raymond, and Gobblers Knob across the canyon announces the initial descent into Burch Hollow. Roll through an archway of timber and descend gingerly through six sharp switchbacks (tech 3$^+$) to the Burch Hollow junction (**m2.9**). Be cool, not lame—Ride it, don't slide it!

The Burch Hollow trailhead is a couple hundred feet to the left; the Pipeline Trail continues right/west, contouring the canyon's steep slopes once more (tech 2$^+$). Portions are sunny and treeless; others are enveloped by a wooded canopy. After a mile the trail splits without warning;

CENTRAL WASATCH

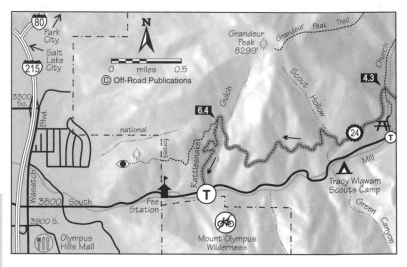

stay right and power up a steep slope. (Straight is a dead end.) Catch your breath and plunge down a sharp shot edged by wooden planks, which keep the trail from being undercut by the steep-walled canyon below. One-half mile farther, you reach a footbridge over Church Fork (**m4.3**). To bailout, turn left to descend steeply on dirt then on a paved drive to Mill Creek Canyon Road; otherwise, continue straight on Pipeline Trail.

Over the next 2 miles, the trail continues weaving into forested hollows and out across treeless slopes where views are incredible. Come to the junction in Rattlesnake Gulch (**m6.4**), and square up for the sharp drop to the trailhead. Do your best to not skid when dropping over the rocks, skittering over the gravel, and rounding the angular turns (tech 4).

The trail continues past Rattlesnake Gulch for another mile to a viewpoint of the entire Salt Lake Valley that is truly inspirational, but getting there means exiting the national forest and crossing private property. Obey any signs restricting travel.

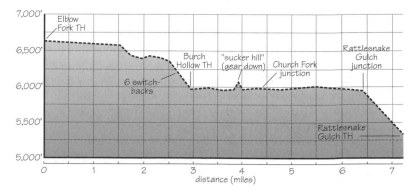

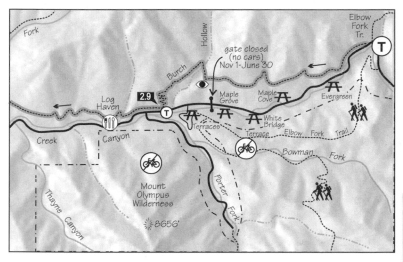

Option: Pipeline Trail Loops

When riding Pipeline Trail as a loop, keep in mind that Mill Creek Canyon Road is steepest between Burch Hollow and Elbow Fork with a near 10-percent grade at the very end.

- Rattlesnake Gulch-Elbow Fork Loop: 11.9 miles, 1,460-foot gain, moderate
- Rattlesnake Gulch-Burch Hollow Loop: 7.2 miles, 830-foot gain, easy[+]
- Church Fork-Elbow Fork Loop: 7.9 miles, 950-foot gain, moderate
- Church Fork-Burch Hollow Loop: 3.2 miles, 300-foot gain, easy
- Burch Hollow-Elbow Fork Loop: 4.8 miles, 650-foot gain, moderate

! Know Before You Go

- Ride cautiously, courteously, and at prudent speeds because the trail is very popular and sight lines are limited.
- This trail is a scorcher at midday during midsummer.
- Mill Creek Canyon is a fee-use area. Each vehicle must pay the fee upon exiting the canyon ($2.25). Bicyclists and pedestrians are not charged a fee, currently.
- Mill Creek Canyon Road is closed to vehicles above Maple Grove Picnic Area (4 miles from the fee station) from November 1-June 30.
- The canyon's odd-even day access policy does not apply to this trail.
- *Fido Factor:* The trail is dog friendly, but dogs must be leashed on this trail on even-numbered calender days.

CENTRAL WASATCH

Three riders appear destined for doom and be swallowed up by the shadowy depths of Mill Creek Canyon . . . Not!

❓ Maps & More Information

* USGS 1:24,000: Mount Aire and Sugarhouse, Utah
* Public Lands Information Center (at REI): (801) 466-6411
* Wasatch-Cache National Forest (Salt Lake Ranger District): (801) 733-2660; www.fs.fed.us/r4/wcnf/unit/slrd/index.shtml

🚶 Trailhead Access

If traveling south on I-215, take Exit 4 (3900 South), turn left on 3900 South and go to the intersection with Wasatch Boulevard; if traveling north on I-215, take Exit 4 (3900 South, 3300 South) and go to the intersection of 3900 South and Wasatch Boulevard. For both ways, drive one block north to 3800 South, and turn right/east on Mill Creek Canyon Road. The fee station is in .7 mile. Rattlesnake Gulch is .7 mile past the fee station. Leave one vehicle here and shuttle 4.7 miles up Mill Creek Canyon Road to the Elbow Fork trailhead.

25

Big Water Trail

JUST THE FACTS

Location:	9.5 miles up Mill Creek Canyon
Length:	6.5 miles
Type:	Out-and-back
Tread:	All singletrack
Physically:	Moderate (steady climb w/ a few choppy spots & roots)
Technically:	2-3⁺ (Lots of buffed tread; some tight turns, rocks, & roots)
Gain:	1,200 feet
Dogs:	Yes, leash restrictions

GO □
NO ■ | JAN | FEB | MAR | APR | MAY | JUN | JUL | AUG | SEP | OCT | NOV | DEC |

CENTRAL WASATCH

WHY SHOULD U RIDE THIS TRAIL?

*Since the beginning of time (in mountain bike years), the Big Water Trail to Dog Lake has been **the** ride for bikers who were ready to dabble in the blissful realm of singletrack. Two decades later, Big Water is still a lo-cals' favorite. Why? It's not because of jaw-dropping moun-tain vistas or long miles across hill and dale; rather, Big Water Trail is a moderately mellow climb through fragrant timber dashed with summer-time wildflowers that ends at a secluded pond canines call their own. Except for a few tricky bits, the bulk of the trail is like "budda." Although it's often busy, you'll be compelled to ride Big Water time and again.*

Details

Catch Big Water Trail from the lower of the two parking lots and pick a low gear because the first climb is the trail's toughest. In .5 mile, the GWT enters from the left, and the two trails become one. Cross the footbridge over Big Water Gulch .5 mile farther, and wiggle up a series of switchbacks through opaque conifers. On the return, you'll feel like Luke Skywalker riding his space scooter through the Forests of Endor in *Return of the Jedi*. After banking hard right at a small knoll, the GWT forks left for upper Mill Creek Canyon and the Wasatch Crest (**m1.5**); Big Water Trail continues straight.

About a mile farther, Big Water Trail crosses Little Water Trail at a four-way junction. Stay straight and then round a right-hand switchback. Keep chugging, you're almost there. Pass Little Water Trail, which merges from the right, and come to the junction with the Desolation Trail in a small clearing (**m3.1**). This is the "top" of the trail, but to reach Dog Lake you must descend the gravelly path left about 100 yards. (You can ride the Desolation Trail about .5 mile to the Mount Olympus Wilderness. It's a fun little trail, but remember bicycles are not permitted in the wilderness.)

Take a break at the lake while man's best friend dives in on a mission to round up all those logs floating about. Although the return descent may invite unbridled speed, pull back on the reigns and resist the urge. Don't jeopardize everyone's access privileges for 15 minutes of selfish bliss.

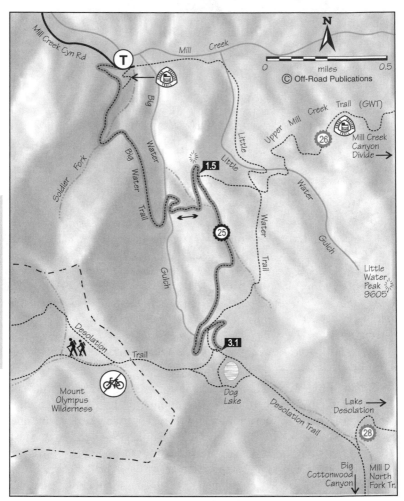

CENTRAL WASATCH

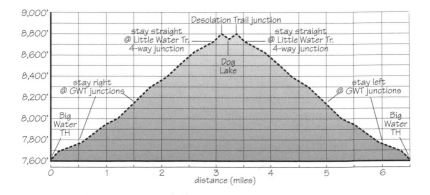

Is it real or is it . . .
Monet?

Option: Desolation Trail to Lake Desolation

Desolation Trail runs 2.3 miles from Dog Lake to Lake Desolation. This option is strenuous because of the steep, rough hill down to and then up from Mill D North Trail plus the steady climb to Lake Desolation. (See "Mill D North Fork Trail.") To tally additional miles, climb from Lake Deso to Wasatch Crest Trail/GWT. There you can head out-and-back along the ridge to the south or loop back to the Big Water trailhead by heading north and descending through upper Mill Creek Canyon. This loop is 13 miles and gains about 2,600 feet. (See "Wasatch Crest Trail" and "Upper Mill Creek Canyon.") Dogs are not allowed on this loop because it enters the Big Cottonwood Canyon Watershed.

Option: Little Water Trail

Little Water Trail takes off from the upper parking lot and intersects Big Water Trail near its top. Little Water Trail is steep, rough, and strenuous and is not recommended for mountain bikes. To lessen the billowing dissension between competing user groups, stay to the Big Water Trail, and let hikers and equestrians enjoy Little Water Trail.

! Know Before You Go

- The Big Water Trail is one of the most popular and thus crowded trails in the Wasatch Range, and so it's imperative that mountain bikers yield to hikers and equestrians. Make your presence known with a friendly greeting.
- Avoid riding during wet conditions to minimize trail damage.
- Control your bike. Excessive speed poses a threat to fellow trail users, and skidding is "bad form."
- Mountain bikes are allowed on Big Water Trail, Little Water Trail, and Upper Mill Creek/GWT on even-numbered calender days from July 1 to October 31. Mountain bikes are not allowed on odd-numbered calenders days. Between November 1-June 30, bikes are allowed every day, (trail conditions permitting), but you must ride up from where Mill Creek Canyon Road is closed at Maple Grove Picnic Area.
- Mill Creek Canyon Road is closed to vehicles above Maple Grove Picnic Area from November 1-June 30 (4 miles from the fee station).
- Mill Creek Canyon is a fee-use area. Vehicles pay the fee upon exiting the canyon ($2.25). Bicyclists are not charged a fee, currently.
- *Fido Factor:* Trail is dog friendly but not if you are riding your bike because dogs must be leashed on even-numbered calender days (bike days). Dogs can be off leash on odd-numbered calenders days. Contact the Public Lands Information Center at REI, or visit www.millcreekfidos.org for updates.

? Maps & More Information

- USGS 1:24,000: Mount Aire, Utah
- Public Lands Information Center (at REI): (801) 466-6411
- Wasatch-Cache National Forest (Salt Lake Ranger District): (801) 733-2660; www.fs.fed.us/r4/wcnf/unit/slrd/index.shtml
- Mill Creek F.I.D.O.S. (Friends Interested in Dogs in Open Spaces): www.millcreekfidos.org

) Trailhead Access

If traveling south on I-215, take Exit 4 (3900 South), turn left on 3900 South, and go to the intersection with Wasatch Boulevard; if traveling north on I-215, take Exit 4 (3900 South, 3300 South) and go to the intersection of 3900 South and Wasatch Boulevard. For both ways, drive one block north to 3800 South, and turn right/east on Mill Creek Canyon Road. The fee station is in .7 mile. Drive 9 miles past the fee station to where the road ends at the double parking lots.

Upper Mill Creek Canyon

JUST THE FACTS

Location:	Top of Mill Creek Canyon
Length:	9.2 miles
Type:	Out-and-back
Tread:	Singletrack & doubletrack-that-rides-like-singletrack
Physically:	Moderate (steady climb w/ a few short, steep hills)
Technically:	2-3⁺ (lots of buffed tread w/ a few rocky, rutted zones)
Gain:	1,340 feet
Dogs:	Yes, restricted

| GO ☐ | | | | | | | | | | | | |
| NO ■ | JAN | FEB | MAR | APR | MAY | JUN | JUL | AUG | SEP | OCT | NOV | DEC |

WHY SHOULD U RIDE THIS TRAIL? *The Great Western Trail is your link to the Wasatch Crest Trail if you choose to start from Mill Creek Canyon instead of Big Cottonwood Canyon. The Crest Trail aside, upper Mill Creek is a fine ride by itself. It begins on the mellow Big Water Trail then veers up the canyon's headwaters on slightly more-demanding singletrack. The climb is steady with a couple of short, steeper ramps thrown in for good measure. Dense timber shields the bulk of the trail from the brightness of day, but wildflowers bob their petaled heads in the upper canyon's sun-kissed meadows. If you make easy work of Big Water Trail, then, as Chef Emeril Lagasse would say, "kick it up a notch" on the Great Western Trail in upper Mill Creek Canyon.*

Details

There are three routes that provide access to the Great Western Trail (GWT) into upper Mill Creek Canyon: Little Water Trail (steep, eroded, and nasty), GWT itself (short, steep, but ridable), and Big Water Trail (most biker friendly of the bunch). Let's take Big Water; you can try the other two later.

Catch the Big Water Trail from the lower parking lot, and gear down for its smooth but moderately steep introductory climb (tech 2). Thereafter, you'll welcome easier grades. In .5 mile, the GWT enters from the left, and the two trails become one. Cross the footbridge over Big Water Gulch, scamper up a series of switchbacks, and fork left on the GWT just after making a hard right turn near a low knoll **(m1.5/7.7)**. The GWT is smooth (tech 2⁺) but rises steeply to where it crosses Little Water Trail; then it mellows as it flows through shadow-filled timber. Singletrack widens to an old doubletrack shortly after you pass a sign stating that Lake Desolation is 3.8 miles farther. Cross the lightly flowing creek a couple of times, and pump hard up a set of quick, sharp climbs that take you to the Mill Creek Canyon divide and to the north end of the Wasatch Crest Trail **(m4.6)**. The Canyons Resort is just over the edge. Turn around and freewheel back to the trailhead, or pursue the options below.

Option: Upper Mill Creek-Desolation Trail Loop (13 miles, strenuous, tech 2-4⁺, 2,600-foot gain)

This is a Wasatch mini-classic, linking together upper Mill Creek/ GWT, Wasatch Crest, Desolation, and Big Water Trails.

From the Mill Creek Canyon divide (**m4.6** above), head right/south on the Wasatch Crest Trail for a steady, strenuous climb on rutted doubletrack (tech 3⁺). Pass two overlooks of The Canyons Resort, and then face a nasty hill that has become nastier over time (tech 5). Hoof it. There are a few tricky rock hops atop the climb before you reach the Big Cottonwood Canyon Watershed boundary (no dogs past this point).

Ready for more? Glide down to the Desolation Trail junction, fork right (Wasatch Crest/GWT goes left to Guardsman Road in Big Cotton- wood Canyon), and drop down choppy, eroded tread to Lake Desolation (tech 3-4⁺). A bouldery drop in the timber (tech 4⁺) is followed by smoother tread that slips through magnificent aspens and skirts delicate meadows. Another wickedly rugged drop (tech 4⁺) takes you to the Mill D North

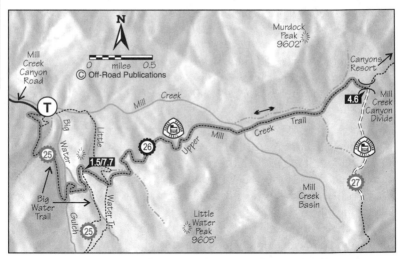

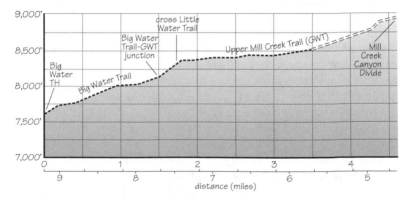

Trail junction. Now you've done it. There's no turning back, so pedal and push up the rutted, gravelly path to Dog Lake (tech 4⁺). Go up the small hill on the right side of the lake to the junction, and freewheel 3.2 miles down Big Water Trail to wrap it up. (See "Wasatch Crest Trail.")

Option: Wasatch Crest Trail

To sample the Wasatch Crest Trail's sweet singletrack, you must first hoof it up the "spine" from the Desolation Trail junction. Thereafter, you'll drool over the 2.8 miles of ridge-top singletrack and the colossal views of the central Wasatch Range. A good turnaround is where the singletrack ends at the national forest boundary. (See "Wasatch Crest Trail.")

Know Before You Go

- Mountain bikes are allowed on this trail on *even-numbered* calender days from July 1 to November 1. Mountain bikes are not allowed on *odd-numbered* calenders days. Other times of the year, you can ride every day (trail conditions permitting) but you must pedal up the paved road from the gate closure at Maple Grove Picnic Area.
- GWT is very popular; yield to others and ride at prudent speeds.
- Mill Creek Canyon is a fee-use area. Vehicles pay the fee upon exiting the canyon ($2.25). Bicyclists are not charged a fee, currently.
- Mill Creek Canyon Road is closed to vehicles above Maple Grove Picnic Area from November 1-June 30 (4 miles from the fee station).
- *Fido Factor:* Trail is dog friendly but not if you are riding your bike because dogs must be leashed on even-numbered calender days (bike days). Dogs can be off leash on odd-numbered calenders days. Contact the Public Lands Information Center at REI, or visit www.millcreekfidos.org for updates.

Maps & More Information

- USGS 1:24,000: Mount Aire and Park City West, Utah
- Public Lands Information Center (at REI): (801) 466-6411
- Wasatch-Cache National Forest (Salt Lake Ranger District): (801) 733-2660; www.fs.fed.us/r4/wcnf/unit/slrd/index.shtml
- Mill Creek F.I.D.O.S. (Friends of Dogs in Open Spaces): www.millcreekfidos.org

Trailhead Access

If traveling south on I-215, take Exit 4 (3900 South), turn left on 3900 South, and go to the intersection with Wasatch Boulevard; if traveling north on I-215, take Exit 4 (3900 South, 3300 South), and go to the intersection of 3900 South and Wasatch Boulevard. For both ways, drive one block north to 3800 South, and turn right/east on Mill Creek Canyon Road. The fee station is in .7 mile. Drive 9 miles past the fee station to where the road ends at the double parking lots.

27
Wasatch Crest Trail

JUST THE FACTS

Location:	16 miles up Big Cottonwood Canyon
Length:	15.2 miles
Type:	Out-and-back
Tread:	9.2 miles singletrack, 6 miles doubletrack
Physically:	Strenuous (short climbs, long climbs, easy climbs, tough climbs; two short portages)
Technically:	2-4 (smooth-running tread w/ some chop; two portages are tech 5)
Gain:	2,600 feet
Dogs:	No, watershed

GO □
NO ■
| JAN | FEB | MAR | APR | MAY | JUN | JUL | AUG | SEP | OCT | NOV | DEC |

WHY SHOULD U RIDE THIS TRAIL

The Wasatch Crest Trail between Big Cottonwood and Mill Creek Canyons is the premier mountain bike ride in the central Wasatch Range. You'll climb through sun-dappled woods, cross the tops of luxuriant basins, and trace the open crest of "the Backbone of Utah." There are steep hills to conquer, many miles to log, and tricky sections that require a full repertoire of bike-handling skills. And there's a boatload of sweet singletrack. When your attention isn't glued to the trail, it's drawn to long views of the magnificent alpine architecture that define these mountains. It's a must-do ride for locals, newcomers, and visitors alike who are acclimated, have good strength and endurance, and have mastered basic skills.

Details

There are two entry points to the Wasatch Crest, Guardsman Road at the top of Big Cottonwood Canyon and upper Mill Creek Canyon. The former is described here (see "Upper Mill Creek Canyon" for the latter).

From Guardsman Road, the task at hand is to conquer the long-winded doubletrack climb to the Crest Trail, proper. This is a two-step process. First is the steady .8-mile "wake-up" grind to Scotts Pass (tech 2⁺), which will jump start your heart better than a double shot of espresso. Second is the grueling, low-gear pump up what locals affectionately call "Vomit Hill" (**m1.2**). You might feel like you'll blow up (or blow chunks) by the time you reach the top (tech 3⁺).

Head west on the stony doubletrack, while admiring the glacially cut granite peaks and deep bowls of Brighton and Solitude Ski Areas in upper Big Cottonwood Canyon. Take the low road past the transmission antenna shack to cross the top of USA Bowl—a popular backcountry ski destination—and stay left when you approach another antenna on Scott Hill. Zoom across a ridge-top meadow to the national forest boundary and to where singletrack begins (**m2.5/12.7**).

The tight track (tech 2-3) rolls just below the ridge through pockets of fir and crook-neck aspens then out across meadows that afford tremen-

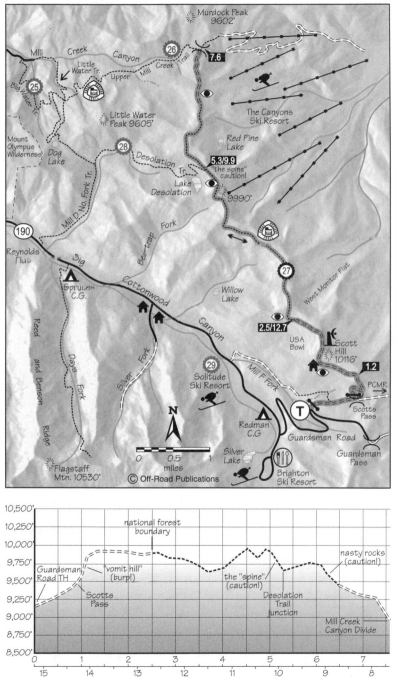

CENTRAL WASATCH

Murdock Peak
9602'

Mill   Creek   Canyon

Little
Water Tr.

Upper   Mill   Creek   Trail

26

7.6

25

Big Water Tr.

The Canyons
Ski Resort

Little Water
Peak 9605'

Red Pine
Lake

Mount
Olympus
Wilderness

Dog
Lake

28

Desolation   Tr.

5.3/9.9
"the spine"
caution!

Lake
Desolation

9990'

Mill D. No. Fork Tr.

Bee-trap   Fork

190

Reynolds
Flat

Dig

Spruces
C.G.

Cottonwood

Willow
Lake

West Monitor Flat

27

2.5/12.7

USA
Bowl

Scott
Hill
10116'

1.2

PCMR

Scotts
Pass

Reed   and   Benson   Ridge

Days   Fork

Silver   Fork

29

Solitude
Ski Resort

Mill F Fork

T

N

Redman
C.G

Guardsman   Road

Guardsman
Pass

Flagstaff
Mtn. 10530'

0   0.5   1
miles

© Off-Road Publications

Silver
Lake

Brighton
Ski Resort

10,500'
10,250'
10,000'
9,750'
9,500'
9,250'
9,000'
8,750'
8,500'

national forest
boundary

"vomit hill"
(burp!)

Guardsman
Road TH

Scotts
Pass

the "spine"
(caution!)

Desolation
Trail
Junction

nasty rocks
(caution!)

Mill Creek
Canyon Divide

15   14   13   12   11   10   9   8
0   1   2   3   4   5   6   7

distance (miles)

Left: Solitude's Honeycomb Cliffs backdrop the Wasatch Crest.
Right: Bob slips through a grove of crook-neck aspens.

dous views of Big Cottonwood Canyon. Mount Raymond and Gobblers Knob separate Big Cottonwood Canyon from Mill Creek Canyon. The riding is fast and smooth, except for some choppy stutter bumps. You'll encounter one drawn out .4-mile climb that will make you work hard in low gear; it's a raging descent on the return leg.

High above Lake Desolation, you'll come to the "spine" where competing glaciers gnawed the divide's red Paleozoic substrate to a narrow rib. Unless you're an expert trials rider, you're best off dismounting and walking (tech 5). This is a popular turnaround because if you're riding out-and-back, you'll just have to hoof up these jags later on.

Stay right on the GWT at the junction with Desolation Trail (**m5.3/ 9.9**), and rise up to the Big Cottonwood Canyon Watershed boundary. Singletrack reverts to doubletrack after a short nasty descent (tech 4+), which will require portaging on the return. Pass two viewpoints overlooking The Canyons Resort and freewheel speedily to a small meadow at the Mill Creek Canyon divide and turnaround point (**m7.6**). Revenge is bittersweet. All those hills that made you sweat on the way in are tantalizing descents on the way out, and vice versa.

Option: Lake Desolation Loop (16-mile loop, moderate+, tech 2-4+, 3,600-foot gain)

Make a loop ride out of the Crest Trail by linking together Mill F, Desolation, and Mill D North Trails for what is arguably the *fourth* best ride in the central Wasatch.

Start at Reynolds Flat/Mill D North Trail (9 miles up Big Cottonwood Canyon), and pedal up the highway 6.8 miles to the Guardsman Road

Joe finds a line down
the "spine" high above
Lake Desolation.

trailhead. (If you're an off-road purist, head up Mill F instead. Take the paved drive opposite Solitude Resort's main entrance, and veer right on doubletrack after passing by summer homes. Stay straight/left at the double steel gates, and continue climbing steadily on singletrack. You'll intersect the doubletrack that connects Guardsman Road and Scotts Pass. Warning, heed any and all "no trespassing" signs.)

Follow the main description to the Desolation Trail junction (**m5.3**). Descend eroded trail (tech 4) to Lake Deso, head due west into the conifers, and square up for a quick nasty drop over boulders and roots (tech 4⁺). Better trail (tech 2⁺) weaves through glorious aspens that edge moist meadows before dropping viciously on severely eroded tread (tech 4⁺) to the Mill D North Trail junction. Take Mill D North Trail (tech 3) down to Reynolds Flat. Be alert to hikers and yield the trail, please.

Option: Canyon to Canyon (12 to 24 miles, one-way, moderate⁺, tech 2-4, 2,000-foot gain)

If you have a shuttle and if it's an *even-numbered* calender day (no bikes on upper Mill Creek Canyon Trails on odd-numbered days), then you can ride from Big Cottonwood Canyon to Mill Creek Canyon for what is arguably the *third* best ride in the Central Wasatch.

Start at Guardsman Road, and head out the Crest Trail. When you reach the Mill Creek Canyon divide (**m7.6** above), descend the GWT (tech 2-3) to the Big Water trailhead for a 12-mile ride. Then, either tuck-n-glide down Mill Creek Canyon Road (21-mile ride), or tack on the Mill Creek Pipeline Trail (24-mile ride). Avoid paying the canyon's fee by parking your shuttle at the park-and-ride lot at 3900 South and Wasatch Boulevard.

Option: Big Cottonwood-Mill Creek Loop (21-mile loop, extreme, tech 2-4⁺, 4,200-foot gain)

Hate riding out-and-back or loath setting up shuttles? Then tackle a 21-mile loop by starting at Reynolds Flat, riding up to the Wasatch Crest and over to Mill Creek Canyon, as described previously, and riding back to Big Cottonwood via Big Water and Mill D North Trails. This is arguably the *second* best ride in the Central Wasatch. Remember, upper Mill Creek Canyon trails are open to bikes on *even-numbered* calender days.

From Reynolds Flat/Mill D North Fork Trail, pedal up to Guardsman Road via either the highway or Mill F (see Option: Lake Desolation Loop, previously), and head out the Crest Trail. When you reach the Mill Creek Canyon divide (**m7.6** above), descend the GWT (tech 2-3) through the four-way junction with Little Water Trail and to the T-junction with Big Water Trail. Chug up to Dog Lake (tech 2$^+$), and descend the steep, gravelly Desolation Trail (tech 4$^+$) to the junction with Mill D North Trail. Take Mill D North (tech 3) down to Big Cottonwood Canyon at Reynolds Flat. Awesome!

Option: City to City (30 miles, one-way, extreme, tech 2-4, 3,500-foot gain)

"What's the *best* ride in the central Wasatch," you say? Park City to Salt Lake City! Start at Park City Mountain Resort, and climb Spiro, Powerline, and Shadow Lake Trails up to Scotts Pass; then take the Crest Trail over to Mill Creek Canyon (bikes allowed on *even-numbered* calender days only). Descend to Salt Lake City via the GWT and Mill Creek Pipeline Trail. Epic!

! Know Before You Go

- Be prepared for rapidly changing alpine weather.
- The Wasatch Crest is very popular; expect and respect other users.
- Bikes are allowed on Big Water Trail, Little Water Trail, and Upper Mill Creek/GWT on *even-numbered* calender days from July 1 to November 1. Bikes are not allowed on *odd-numbered* calenders days.
- *Fido Factor:* Dogs (and horses) are not allowed in the Big Cottonwood Canyon Watershed.

? Maps & More Information

- USGS 1:24,000: Brighton, Mount Aire, and Park City West, Utah
- Public Lands Information Center (at REI):(801) 466-6411
- Wasatch-Cache National Forest (Salt Lake Ranger District): (801) 733-2660; www.fs.fed.us/r4/wcnf/unit/slrd/index.shtml

Trailhead Access

From I-215, take Exit 6 (6200 South, Ski Areas), and travel east on 6200 South then south on Wasatch Boulevard to 7200 South/Fort Union Boulevard. Take Big Cottonwood Canyon Road/UT 190 14 miles, and fork left on Guardsman Road (1.3 miles past Solitude and .5 miles before Brighton). Park along the road's edge 2 miles up Guardsman Road on the second right-hand switchback. Take the dirt road down to the red gate, lift your bike over, and you're off. Do not block the dirt road or gate.

28
Mill D North Fork-Desolation Trail

JUST THE FACTS

Location:	9 miles up Big Cottonwood Canyon
Length:	7.4 miles
Type:	Out-and-back
Tread:	All singletrack
Physically:	Moderate+ (steady, steep climb w/ several short hike-a-bikes)
Technically:	2+-5 (good tread but steep, rugged sections require hike-a-biking)
Gain:	1,980 feet
Dogs:	No, watershed

GO □
NO ■ | JAN | FEB | MAR | APR | MAY | JUN | JUL | AUG | SEP | OCT | NOV | DEC |

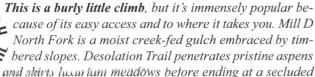

This is a burly little climb, but it's immensely popular because of its easy access and to where it takes you. Mill D North Fork is a moist creek-fed gulch embraced by timbered slopes. Desolation Trail penetrates pristine aspens and skirts luxuriant meadows before ending at a secluded alpine pond cupped beneath the Wasatch Crest. There are a handful of rugged sections that will make you hoof it on the way up and clench your handlebars with white knuckles on the way down. But it's worth it because there is plenty of smooth-flowing trail, too. If you ski the backcountry, then you'll know this route well and the classic powder shots it harbors.

CENTRAL WASATCH

Details

Get into a granny gear and rev up the rpms because the hill at the trailhead can be a real bravado buster. Beyond, the trail rises quickly above Big Cottonwood Canyon and affords sporadic but impressive views of Mill D South Fork, Kesler Peak, and Reed and Benson Ridge across the canyon. There are several problematic spots where roots and rock can toss you around (tech 4); then the path mellows to a steady pump after it enters the gulch, proper (tech 3). The slopes enclosing the gulch are classic powder runs.

Fork right at the Desolation Trail junction (Dog Lake is uphill to the left), and hoof it up the steep, gravelly, eroded trail **(m1.8/5.6)**. Before you have time to mutter unspeakables, you're back in the saddle spinning through fluttering aspens that edge a broad meadow. Climb steadily for about a mile on good tread (tech 2+); then push up another bouldery slope in a stand of conifers (tech 5). Lake Desolation is over the hill **(m3.7)**.

Like nearby Dog Lake, Lake Desolation has no surface outlet. It simply drains through the loose glacial deposits that underlay it.

Option: Wasatch Crest Trail

You can tack on several miles of prime singletrack up on the Wasatch Crest Trail, but first you have to conquer a half-mile-long, rugged climb up several switchbacks. Once on the ridge, ride south to Scott Hill or north to

CENTRAL WASATCH

Aspen leaves sprinkle the Desolation Trail like gold doubloons.

Mill Creek Canyon. Remember, bikes are allowed on upper Mill Creek Canyon trails on *even-numbered* calender days only. (See "Wasatch Crest Trail" and "Upper Mill Creek Canyon.")

Option: Mill D North-Mill Creek Loop

If you pooh-pooh yet another out-and-back ride, try this strenuous 13-mile loop (3,500-foot gain). Along the way you'll experience some of the best singletracks the central Wasatch has to offer.

From Lake Desolation, pedal and push .5 mile up to the Wasatch Crest Trail/GWT (tech 3⁺-4⁺). Follow the GWT 2.3 miles north to the Mill Creek Canyon divide, and descend the GWT 3.1 miles through upper Mill Creek Canyon to the Big Water Trail. (Remember, bikes are allowed on upper Mill Creek Canyon trails on *even-numbered* calender days only.) Climb the moderately mellow Big Water Trail 1.6 miles to Dog Lake (tech 2⁺), descend .5 mile to the Mill D North Fork-Desolation Trail junction (tech 4⁺), and retrace your tracks back down to the Mill D North Fork trailhead. What a ride!

! Know Before You Go

- These trails are extremely popular with hikers and sight lines are limited, so *please* descend cautiously and courteously.
- Swimming is not allowed in Lake Desolation because this area is a watershed.
- Bikes are allowed on upper Mill Creek Canyon trails on *even-numbered* calender days only.
- *Fido Factor:* Dogs are not allowed in the Big Cottonwood Canyon Watershed.

❓ Maps & More Information

- USGS 1:24,000: Mount Aire and Park City West, Utah
- Public Lands Information Center (at REI): (801) 466-6411
- Wasatch-Cache National Forest (Salt Lake Ranger District): (801) 733-2660; www.fs.fed.us/r4/wcnf/unit/slrd/index.shtml

🥾 Trailhead Access

From I-215, take Exit 6 (6200 South, Ski Areas). Go east on 6200 South then south on Wasatch Boulevard to 7200 South/Fort Union Boulevard. Drive 9 miles up Big Cottonwood Canyon/UT 190 to Reynolds Flat. Mill D North Fork Trail is at the "Meeting of the Glaciers" sign.

CENTRAL WASATCH

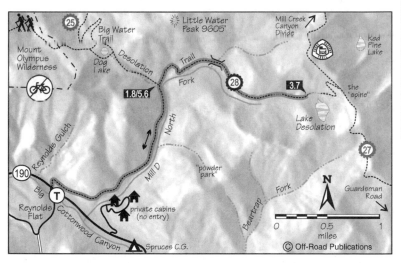

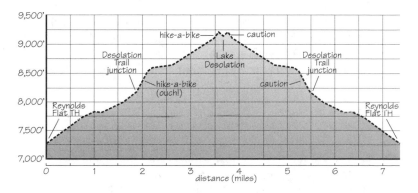

29
Solitude Mountain Resort

JUST THE FACTS

Location:	13 miles up Big Cottonwood Canyon
Length:	Up to 14 miles
Type:	Cross-country and lift-served trails and dirt roads
Tread:	5.9 miles singletrack, 8.1 miles dirt roads & doubletracks
Physically:	Easy+ w/ lift service, moderate+ w/o lift service.
Technically:	2-4 (smooth & rough trails; gravelly, rocky, & steep dirt roads)
Gain:	Varies with route
Dogs:	No, watershed

GO ☐
NO ■ | JAN | FEB | MAR | APR | MAY | JUN | JUL | AUG | SEP | OCT | NOV | DEC |

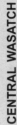

WHY RIDE THIS TRAIL / SHOULD ?

Nestled beneath the formidable Honeycomb Cliffs in up-per Big Cottonwood Canyon, Solitude Mountain Resort offers a quality, compact trail system flaring out from its modest but refined Tyrolean-style village. Sunrise Lift provides up-service to a number of rolling downhill runs that cater to first-time bikers and seasoned veterans alike. If you snub the lift, you'll quickly discover that Solitude's smooth-flowing and lightly aggressive singletracks are laid out with the cross-country rider in mind. Weekends bring live music, a tasty barbeque, and festive socializing to a canopied venue at the resort's base. So, come up to Solitude and let your spirit soar like the resort's mascot eagle.

Details

Easy Trails

#1 Roundhouse Road (2.9 miles, one-way): First-time bikers will find a mellow introduction to Solitude's trails by coasting from the top of Sunrise Lift down to the resort base on the wide dirt Roundhouse Road (#1).

Go right upon exiting Sunrise Lift, fork left on singletrack (#1) at the junction with Kruz'r Trail (#5), and cut across a small meadow below Lake Solitude. There's a small rocky drop preceding the meadow, so use caution. The doubletrack descends steeply past the base of Summit Lift (tech 3) then mellows for a smooth traverse through mixed timber (tech 1+). Enter a broad meadow (Main Street ski run), and pass the Roundhouse Restaurant. From there the road is paved periodically but descends rather steeply to the base.

Moderate Trails

#2 Serenity Trail (3.7 miles, one-way): If you have a solid grasp of basic singletrack riding, then veer off Roundhouse Road onto Serenity Trail (#2), descend 1.6 miles to near the Moonbeam Center, and then climb gradually for .3 mile up to the Village, all on singletrack.

Exit Sunrise Lift, and veer left at the junction with Kruz'r Trail; then cut across the meadow below Lake Solitude, and take Roundhouse Road

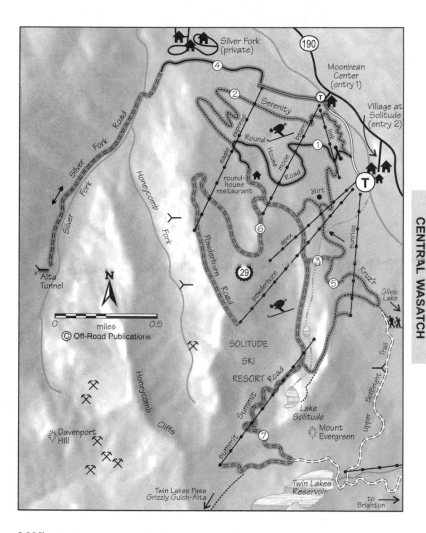

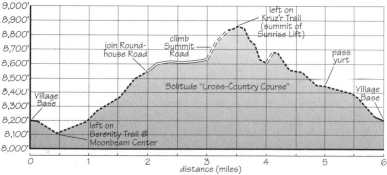

Cruising down Kruz'r Trail.

down past the base of Summit Lift (tech 3). Just past Roundhouse Restaurant, fork left on Serenity (#2). Serenity is a tight one-lane path that meanders across ski runs and through pockets of timber that separate them. A trio of sharp, rough turns drops steeply under Eagle Express Lift and is followed by an "active traverse" that will test your skills (tech 3-4). Just uphill from Moonbeam Center, fork right on singletrack, and zig-zag up a gentle ski run to the Village base.

#3 Apex Trail (1.8 miles, one-way): Apex Trail makes getting back to the base a bit easier by shortcutting the more rugged sections of Kruz'r Trail. You'll encounter some tricky switchbacks near the bottom, so you should have a good grasp of bike skills.

Exit Sunrise Lift, and veer left at the junction with Kruz'r Trail; then cut across the meadow beneath Lake Solitude, and take the Roundhouse Road down past the base of Summit Lift (tech 3). Just around the bend, fork right on Apex Trail (#3), and wind down through thick aspen groves. Go left on Kruz'r to descend almost a mile across ski runs and through patches of trees. Watch out for the tight switchbacks near the bottom; they can be rough and can surprise an unsuspecting biker (tech 4).

#4 Silver Fork Road (5 miles, out-and-back): Silver Fork Road offers strong novice riders a chance to venture away from the lifts and wander up a quiet canyon on a tame doubletrack.

If you start at the Village, ride past the base of Sunrise and Apex Lifts, and intersect the paved Roundhouse Road. Fork right at the steel gate, and descend the singletrack (tech 2) down a mellow ski run next to Link Lift to Moonbeam Center. Cut across the parking area, and continue on a road past the base of Eagle Express Lift. After passing through the Silver Fork summer homes area, the road bends up Silver Fork Canyon and turns to pebbly dirt (tech 2⁺). Stay right at the first junction past the creek crossing, but fork left at the second junction. Climb steadily for about .5 mile to the old Alta Tunnel; return on the same route.

Advanced Trails:

#5 Kruz'r Trail (2.9 miles, one-way): Kruz'r Trail is no laid-back "cruiser"; rather, it's a fast-moving singletrack from the summit of Sunrise Lift to the Village that requires good skills. It has been the cornerstone of the annual Chris Allaire Memorial Mountain Bike Race hosted by Solitude, and racers love the action it delivers.

Exit Sunrise Lift, and fork right on Kruz'r Trail (#5). You'll cross under the lift on smooth trail then fork sharply left for a fast, descending traverse (tech 3-4). There's a short climb on doubletrack to the junction with Apex Trail (#3) followed by more exciting singletrack that is complicated with sweeping turns, creek crossings, and exposed roots. A set of sharp switchbacks drops you to the paved Roundhouse Road, which you take to the base.

#6 Powderhorn Road (8 miles, out-and-back): Think you're hardcore? The 1,500-foot climb to the top of Powderhorn Lift is a raw test of your power and mental fortitude.

Start at the Village base and climb the steeply rising Roundhouse Road to the junction under Moonbeam Lift. Fork right on doubletrack (tech 3), grind up under Eagle Express Lift, and then pump hard to the lift's summit. Don't quit there. Claw your way up the rest of the rough gravelly road to the summit of Powderhorn Lift (tech 4). Nicely done; you've earned your bragging rights.

#7 Summit Road (8.3 miles, out-and-back): Think you're *really* hardcore? The Summit Lift Road is about as tough as hill climbs come with a 2,000-foot gain in just over 4 miles from the resort's base. You can embark from the top of Sunrise Lift, but that's cheating.

Start from the Village base for the full effect by heading up Round-house Road first. From the base of Summit Lift, the going gets tough and doesn't let up until you reach the top (tech 3-4). Extend your climb by taking the trail up to Twin Lakes Pass to gaze into the tops of Big and Little Cottonwood Canyons. Upon descending, link up with the SolBright Trail for a rock n' roll descent past old mines high above Brighton's Silver Lake. Return to the Village on Kruz'r Trail.

Solitude Cross-country Course (6.0-mile loop, 1,500-foot gain): Lifts are for wimps. Link together Solitude's best trails for this sweet cross-country loop on mostly singletrack.

Start at the Village and ride past the bases of Sunrise and Apex Lifts to Roundhouse Road. At the gate, fork right on singletrack (tech 2), and wind down close to Moonbeam Center. Climb Serenity Trail (tech 3-4) up to Roundhouse Road (tech 1⁺), and take it over to the base of Summit Lift.

CENTRAL WASATCH

Climb briefly but steeply on Summit Road (tech 3), and catch the singletrack across the meadow below Lake Solitude. Kruz'r Trail is your way back to the base. There's never a dull moment because the trail packs together tight tread, dips and roots, fast straightaways, and snap-judgement turns. It's everything a race course should be.

! Know Before You Go

- Trails are open every day for biking and hiking. There is no trail-use fee if you do not ride the chairlift.
- Sunrise Lift operates Thursday-Friday 1 P.M.-6 P.M. and Saturday-Sunday 10 A.M.-6 P.M., weather permitting. Lift prices are single ride: $6; all day or 5-ride pass: $24; children 6 and under are free with a paying adult. Hours and prices are subject to change.
- Children under 12 must be accompanied by a parent or legal guardian.
- Bike rentals are available at the Village base.
- Helmets must be worn at all times when biking.
- Stay on designated roads and trails, obey travel restrictions, and be aware of heavy machinery and summer maintenance operations.
- Mountain bikers must yield to hikers. Excessive speed is not allowed.
- Be prepared for quickly changing alpine weather.
- Do not approach or harass wildlife; animals can be unpredictable and dangerous.
- Solitude operates a full-service restaurant, bar/cafe, small general store, and outdoor barbeque (weather permitting) Wednesday-Sunday. Disk golf is available also.
- *Fido Factor:* Dogs are not allowed in the Big Cottonwood Canyon Watershed.

? Maps & More Information

- USGS 1:24,000: Dromedary Peak and Brighton, Utah
- Public Lands Information Center (at REI): (801) 466-6411
- Wasatch-Cache National Forest (Salt Lake Ranger District): (801) 733-2660; www.fs.fed.us/r4/wcnf/unit/slrd/index.shtml
- Solitude Mountain Resort, 12000 Big Cottonwood Canyon, Solitude UT 84121; (801) 534-1400; www.skisolitude.com

Trailhead Access

From I-215, take Exit 6 (6200 South, Ski Areas). Travel east on 6200 South then south on Wasatch Boulevard to 7200 South/Fort Union Boulevard. Travel 12.8 miles up Big Cottonwood Canyon on UT 190 to entry #2 for Solitude Mountain Resort (Village at Solitude).

30

Little Cottonwood Canyon Trail

JUST THE FACTS		
	Location:	Mouth of Little Cottonwood Canyon
	Length:	6.5 miles
	Type:	Out-and-back
	Tread:	Doubletrack & a touch of singletrack
	Physically:	Moderate (short, steep, rough climbs interrupt the overall moderate grade)
	Technically:	2-4 (packed dirt & loose sand w/ some rocky sections)
	Gain:	1,140 feet
	Dogs:	No, watershed

GO □
NO ■ | JAN | FEB | MAR | APR | MAY | JUN | JUL | AUG | SEP | OCT | NOV | DEC |

WHY SHOULD U RIDE THIS TRAIL?

Little Cottonwood Canyon Trail is a fun, quick, hardy ride that is both scenic and historic. Although you're just a stone's throw from the canyon's highway, the forest's earthy bouquet, the air's stillness, and the creek's mono- tonic churning provide a riparian buffer between you and the intrusions of urbanism. During the pioneer era, Little Cottonwood Canyon offered its natural riches to hard rock miners, stone cutters, timber mills, and settlers. Many of their diggings and doings can still be seen along the trail today.

Details

Before you head out, take a stroll along the Temple Quarry Nature Trail (bikes are not allowed on the paved path), and read the plaques describing the local history. During the mid-1800s, Mormon pio- neers quarried the Little Cottonwood Stock (quartz monzanite) to build the Salt Lake Temple. Look for chisel marks on the huge boulders. If you scan the canyon's craggy slopes with binoculars, you might spot mountain goats scurrying about. Also, the rock's frictional surfaces and steadfast cracks are a rock climber's delight. There's good bouldering along the trail, so pack your climbing shoes. The trail follows both the flume of the Murray Hydroelectric Power System, built in the 1920s, and the old railroad that serviced Alta during its mining boom days in the late 1800s.

Now, hop on your bike, and pedal east on the gravel path alongside the paved walkway. Go around a steel gate, cross the paved access road for Wasatch Resorts (private property, stay on route), and continue on a wide gravel road. Go around another gate on the left/north side of the hydroelectric plant. Pass through a third gate, and then cross a small bridge to Little Cottonwood Creek's south bank. The trail is now doubletrack. Pass an old pavilion that has fallen prey to vandals; struggle up a steep, bouldery section (tech 3⁺), and stay right at a junction. The left fork crosses a footbridge over the creek and exits to the highway at the power station. The trail smooths briefly, varies between singletrack and doubletrack, and passes many stream-side picnic spots.

Cross a hefty footbridge over the creek, swing around a steel gate, and come to a junction (**m2.8**). Left leads up to the highway at a road-side turnout signed "Little Cottonwood Trail." If you stay straight, you can continue climbing for another half-mile (tech 4) until the trail peters out near a pair of stone ruins across the creek. Return the way you came, or duck out to the highway for a speedy glide to the trailhead. (The Salt Lake Ranger District is analyzing the possibility of extending the trail to connect with existing trails at Snowbird and Alta.)

! Know Before You Go

- This route crosses parcels of private property. Stay on the main trail, and obey all signs restricting travel.
- Do not wade or swim in Little Cottonwood Creek. The current can be dangerously swift.
- This route can be very hot at midday during midsummer.
- *Fido Factor:* Dogs are not allowed in the Little Cottonwood Canyon Watershed.

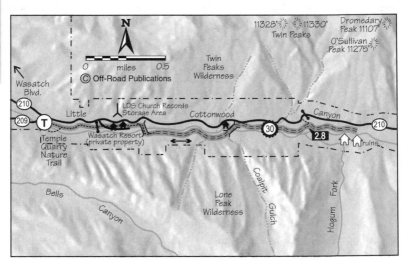

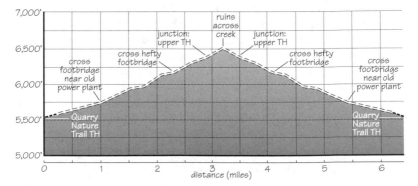

CENTRAL WASATCH

Tricia crosses a bridge over Little Cottonwood Creek.

❓ Maps & More Information

- USGS 1:24,000: Draper and Dromedary Peak, Utah
- Public Lands Information Center (at REI): (801) 466-6411
- Wasatch-Cache National Forest (Salt Lake Ranger District): (801) 733-2660; www.fs.fed.us/r4/wcnf/unit/slrd/index.shtml

🚶 Trailhead Access

From I-215, take Exit 6 (6200 South, Ski Areas.) Travel east on 6200 South then south on Wasatch Boulevard and UT 210. Follow signs for Alta and Snowbird to Little Cottonwood Canyon. Turn right at the canyon's flashing billboard, and park at the Temple Quarry Nature Trail.

▲▲ 31
White Pine Trail

JUST THE FACTS

Location:	5.5 miles up Little Cottonwood Canyon
Length:	9.6 miles
Type:	Out-and-back
Tread:	Doubletrack
Physically:	Strenuous (steep, steady climb w/ hike-a-bike sections)
Technically:	3-5 (rugged doubletrack, talus sections, deadfall)
Gain:	2,460 feet
Dogs:	No, watershed

GO☐
NO■ | JAN | FEB | MAR | APR | MAY | JUN | JUL | AUG | SEP | OCT | NOV | DEC |

WHY SHOULD U RIDE THIS TRAIL?

White Pine Trail captures the rugged beauty of the central Wasatch Range. Rugged is the climb up this glacial tributary to Little Cottonwood Canyon. Beautiful is shimmering White Pine Lake and the steep-walled cirque in which it rests. Since this route is adjacent to the Lone Peak Wilderness, you can be assured it excels in alpine scenery. Wear shoes that are comfortable out of the pedals, for there are many rough sections that require hike-a-biking. Also, there are opportunities to hike above the lake to the surrounding ridges.

Details

Catch the paved path next to the outhouses, and drop down to the footbridge over Little Cottonwood Creek. The route heads up a steep gravel-and-rock doubletrack for a mile to the White Pine-Red Pine trail junction. Some sections rate tech 4 and are a good sampling what lies ahead. Turn left for White Pine and climb in earnest.

Take a break at the first switchback to absorb the grandeur of these mountains. Across the canyon, Twin Peaks, Dromedary Peak, and Mount Superior give a rough-cut profile to the Big Cottonwood Ridge. Even a geologic layman can easily trace the unconformity between the older maroon-brown rocks capping the ridge (Precambrian-age Big Cottonwood

White Pine Lake.

Formation) and the younger gray igneous rocks that intruded them (Tertiary-age Little Cottonwood Stock). White Pine Canyon is a "hanging valley," which was carved by a glacial tributary to the main Little Cottonwood ice sheet.

The road flattens and even descends a bit be-

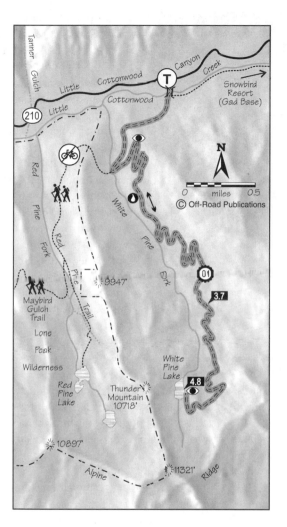

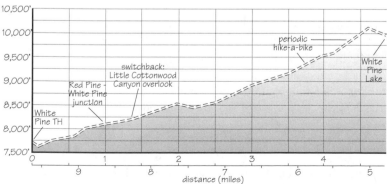

Returning from White Pine Lake.

yond a pair of upcoming turns, and you'll splash through springs that flow across the road and coalesce into small ponds in the meadows below. During winter, backcountry skiers cherish the slopes above you for being prime powder stashes, but they must respect them for being active avalanche zones as well, as can be attested by trees that have been snapped at half mast.

More climbing brings you to a broad wildflower-decked meadow then to a nasty hill clogged with boulders (tech 5, **m3.7**). Now the going gets tough. Near timberline, the doubletrack bends through several switchbacks and crosses talus slopes. If you portage your bike and persevere, you can ride the rest of the way to White Pine Lake (**m4.8**).

Know Before You Go

- The first mile to the White Pine-Red Pine trail junction is heavily traveled by hikers accessing the Lone Peak Wilderness, so share the trail and ride courteously. The parking lot can fill up on weekends.
- Mountain bikes are prohibited in wilderness areas, so don't even think about heading up Red Pine Trail.
- Be prepared for rapidly changing alpine weather.
- Snowbird Resort offers overnight accommodations, dining, and bike rentals and has emergency medical facilities.
- *Fido Factor:* Dogs are not allowed in the Little Cottonwood Canyon Watershed.

Maps & More Information

- USGS 1:24,000: Dromedary Peak, Utah
- Public Lands Information Center (at REI): (801) 466-6411
- Wasatch-Cache National Forest (Salt Lake Ranger District): (801) 733-2660; www.fs.fed.us/r4/wcnf/unit/slrd/index.shtml

Trailhead Access

From I-215, take Exit 6 (6200 South, Ski Areas). Travel east on 6200 South then south on Wasatch Boulevard and UT 210. Follow signs for Snowbird and Alta. The White Pine trailhead is 5.5 miles up Little Cottonwood Canyon from the flashing billboard.

32
Snowbird Resort

JUST THE FACTS		
Location:	6.6 miles up Little Cottonwood Canyon	
Length:	Up to 11 miles (see below)	
Type:	Out-and-back & loops (see below)	
Tread:	10 miles of doubletracks, 1 mile of singletrack	
Physically:	Gad Valley Loop: moderate$^+$; Bird Trail (singletrack): moderate; Peruvian Gulch: strenuous$^+$	
Technically:	3-4$^+$ (packed dirt with gravel, rocks, & roots on roads & trails)	
Gain:	Depends on route chosen (see below)	
Dogs:	No, watershed	

GO ☐
NO ■ | JAN | FEB | MAR | APR | MAY | JUN | JUL | AUG | SEP | OCT | NOV | DEC |

WHY SHOULD U RIDE THIS TRAIL *Renown for its legendary ski terrain, Snowbird Resort offers a wide variety of fat-tire opportunities as well. Novice riders can explore Snowbird's "lowlands" on its mountain bike-specific singletrack, the Bird Trail. Stronger riders will be challenged by the Gad Valley Loop or by venturing up to midmountain levels. Then there is the legendary King/Queen of the Mountain Hill Climb up Peruvian Gulch to Hidden Peak. Lastly, freewheelers can catch a lift on the tram and coast down to the resort base. Mountain biking or not, the "Bird's" perpetually festive beat, award-winning restaurants, and refined accommodations make it a world-class summer destination.*

Details

The "Bird" Trail

The Bird Trail takes you from the Plaza to Gad Valley on a singletrack built with mountain bikes in mind. You'll slip through stands of fir and cross Big Emma ski run on a nearly level keel, but you'll have to negotiate a pair of challenging switchbacks. Chances are good that you'll spy deer and smaller animals peering at you from their wooded hideouts.

> **The "Bird" Trail:**
> 2 miles, out-and-back, moderate, tech 2-3$^+$, 100-foot gain

Saddle up at the Plaza, cross the skier bridge over Little Cottonwood Creek, and take the service road downhill to the right. Fork left immediately on a doubletrack signed for Gad Chairs, and climb a couple hundred feet to the Bird Trail, which forks right. You're off. A potpourri of rocks, roots, and dips will test your balance, and the switchbacks can be a handful for first timers. When you reach the Gad Valley road, you can turn around or continue for a short distance more. Note: The White Pine Connector Trail, which continues west, is steep and very rough (tech 4$^+$).

Gad Valley Loop

This is the core of the annual Snowbird Mountain Bout mountain bike race, and it takes you to the resort's mid-elevations on singletrack and doubletrack.

> **Gad Vallley Loop:**
> 2.5-mile loop, moderate$^+$, tech 3$^+$, 700-foot gain

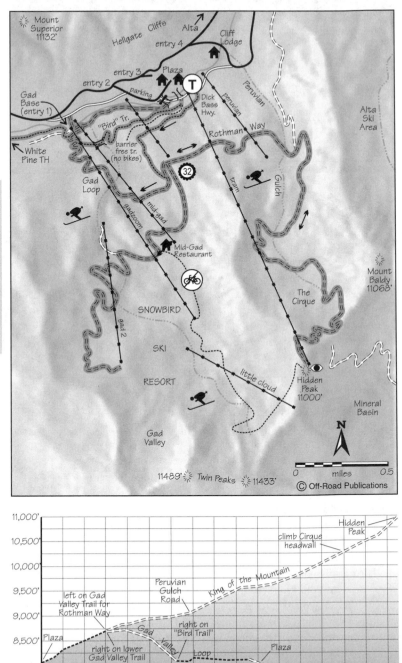

A pack of racers goes full throttle up the Bird Trail.

From the Plaza, cross the skier bridge, and attack the Dick Bass Highway Trail. It's roughest and toughest at the bottom (tech 4) but smooths and moderates farther on (tech 2⁺). Quickly, you rise high above the resort base and come eye-to-eye with the gray-and-white-banded Hellgate Cliffs across the canyon. Mount Superior is the cockscomb roost towering above all. Intersect Gad Valley Trail (doubletrack), and take it right across Big Emma ski run, where you'll descend rapidly around rocky turns (tech 3⁺). Fork right on the Bird Trail before you reach the lift's base. Climb a pair of rugged turns, and return to the Plaza on friendly tread.

Tack on 5 miles, out-and-back, by climbing into upper Gad Valley. Instead of crossing Big Emma, fork left, and climb gradually to the top of Wilbere Lift; then fork right to climb Gad Valley Trail to Mid Gad Restaurant. Descend toward Gad II Lift, fork left on doubletrack, and climb steeply to the lift's summit for up-close views of Twin Peaks.

Peruvian Gulch

The climb from the Plaza to Hidden Peak is one of the toughest in the Wasatch, gaining over 3,000 feet in a bit more than 4 miles. That's an average 13-percent grade. Whoa!

Peruvian Gulch:
8.4 miles, out-and-back, strenuous⁺, 3,000-foot gain

Start by climbing Dick Bass Highway Trail. Fork left on Gad Valley Trail, pass the summit of Wilbere Lift, and follow Rothman Way ski run over to the Peruvian Gulch Road to resume climbing in earnest. Catch a short respite across Chips and Primrose Path ski runs, and then inch your way up the Cirque around steep, rough switchbacks. Don't falter because there's a tram-full of gawkers overhead. Be sure to hang out at the summit to absorb both the top-of-the-world views and the congratulations from dumb-struck tourists.

❗ Know Before You Go

Steve climbs the Dick Bass Highway during the annual Snowbird Mountain Bout Race. Hellgate Cliffs in background.

• The tram runs daily from 11 A.M. to 8 P.M., July to October, weather permitting. The last tram (up) for mountain bikes is at 5 P.M. A single ride tram pass is $10/person; an all-day, unlimited-use tram pass is $14/person.

• Helmets must be worn at all times when biking.

• Bike rentals are available at Snowbird Ultimate Mountain Outfitters (on the Plaza).

• Be prepared for rapidly changing weather, including extreme temperature variations and afternoon rain storms with possible lightning.

• Be alert to traffic on the dirt roads and to maintenance operations at any place and any time, especially on the slopes above you.

• *Fido Factor:* Dogs are not allowed in the Little Cottonwood Canyon Watershed.

❓ Maps & More Information

• USGS 1:24,000: Dromedary Peak, Utah
• Snowbird Ski and Summer Resort: (801) 933-2222, www.snowbird.com
• Snowbird Activity Center: (801) 933-2147
• Public Lands Information Center (at REI): (801) 466-6411

Trailhead Access

From I-215, take Exit 6 (6200 South, Ski Areas). Travel east on 6200 South then south on Wasatch Boulevard and UT 210. Follow signs for Alta and Snowbird. Snowbird Ski and Summer Resort is 6.6 miles up Little Cottonwood Canyon from the flashing billboard. Take Entry Level 2 for the Plaza and tram.

CENTRAL WASATCH

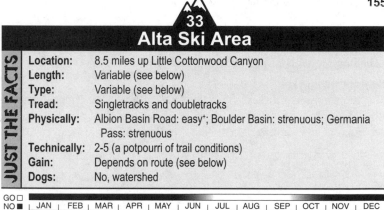

33
Alta Ski Area

JUST THE FACTS		
	Location:	8.5 miles up Little Cottonwood Canyon
	Length:	Variable (see below)
	Type:	Variable (see below)
	Tread:	Singletracks and doubletracks
	Physically:	Albion Basin Road: easy⁺; Boulder Basin: strenuous; Germania Pass: strenuous
	Technically:	2-5 (a potpourri of trail conditions)
	Gain:	Depends on route (see below)
	Dogs:	No, watershed

GO ☐
NO ■ | JAN | FEB | MAR | APR | MAY | JUN | JUL | AUG | SEP | OCT | NOV | DEC

WHY SHOULD YOU RIDE THIS TRAIL? *Don't turn your back on Alta Ski Area after the "Greatest Snow on Earth" has melted because the ski mountain is a locals' favorite summertime destination, too. Located at the top of Little Cottonwood Canyon and in the heart of the central Wasatch, Alta is an alpine showcase of formidable peaks, naked rock, and flower-fed meadows that lure hikers, campers, car tourists, and mountain bikers alike. Novice bikers will likely feel the lung-constraining effects that come with high elevation, so the Albion Basin Road is well suited. The new Boulder Basin singletrack takes advanced bikers past Catherines Pass and into the clutch of the famed Devils Castle area before descending the length of Albion Basin. Riders with strong lungs and big guns can test their resolve against the Germania Pass loop—a classic climb through a classic resort.*

▌Details

Albion Basin Road

If not for the near 9,000-foot trailhead elevation, Albion Basin Road would be one of the easiest rides in the Wasatch Range. Thus, first time riders and visitors will want to ride slowly not only to allow their bodies to acclimate but also to fully appreciate the basin's geologic complexity and natural beauty.

> **Albion Basin Road:**
> (6.2 miles, out-and-back, easy⁺, tech 2, dirt road, 800-foot gain)

The road is all-weather dirt and gravel with variable washboards, and the elevation gain is straightforward. You'll share the route with vehicles, but the speed limit is low and drivers are generally courteous. Your destination is Albion Basin Campground with an optional hike to a secluded glacial tarn called Cecret Lake. During midsummer, blooming wildflowers make a rainbow look pale.

Start from where the paved road ends (Albion Day Lodge), and simply follow the all-weather Albion Basin Road. Two looping switchbacks and a moderately easy grade take you along the base of Mount Wolverine and high above Albion Basin to the parking area for Catherines Pass Trail. Take a look at the plaque that points out Alta's prominent features. The

road then levels and enters the campground. Take a lap on the campground road, or park (and lock) your bike and hike the .75-mile-long Cecret
Lake Interpretive Trail (no bikes allowed). Return the opposite way.

Boulder Basin Trail

This loop combines three trails—Albion Meadows, Catherines Pass, and
Boulder Basin—and takes you on an up-close tour of Alta's classic powder runs. If you've never skied Alta, you'll gain instant respect for the

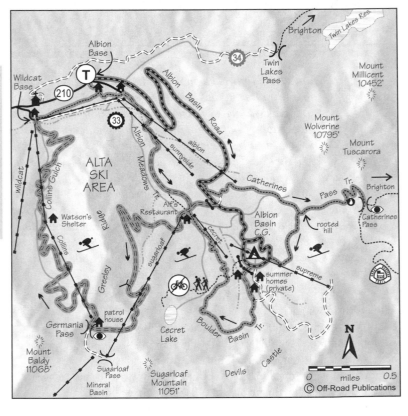

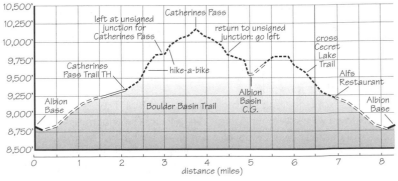

Left: Catherines Pass Trail. Right: Boulder Basin Trail.

slogan "Alta is for Skiers." Parts of the loop may be unsigned, so you might have to snoop around a bit to find your way.

Boulder Basin Trail
(8.3-mile loop; 4 miles singletrack, 4.3 miles doubletrack; strenuous; tech 2⁺-5; 1,800-foot gain.)

Starting from where the paved road ends (Albion Day Lodge), descend the paved drive, and pick up the old doubletrack next to the maintenance building. You'll climb steadily on soft gravel (tech 2⁺-3⁺) for over a mile to a T-junction near Alf's Restaurant. Go left, intersect the Albion Basin Road, and take it left to the Catherines Pass parking area. Be sure to view the plaque that silhouettes the basin's features. Now take Catherines Pass Trail past the top of Sunnyside and Albion Lifts. Although the trail has been rerouted out of the main gulch, it's still rugged (tech 3⁺-5) and will require periodic hike-a-biking. Watch for an unsigned path forking right where the main trail moderates (you'll take it after returning from the pass); stay left and hoof up a steep rooted slope in the conifers. More wickedly steep climbing up a gulch is followed by a friendly climb around a moist basin and up to Catherines Pass.

Return to that unsigned junction after you descend that rooted hill and go left. It widens to doubletrack and drops quickly under Supreme Lift to the campground road at site No.16. (Please respect campers.) Take the road left, cross a bridge, and fork left on a gated doubletrack posted open to hikers but closed to vehicles. Stay left through the summer homes; then fork right on a faded doubletrack that rises sharply to the run-out of the famed Devils Castle. Look up and you'll see that there is no lift access to the bowl; skiers have to hike and traverse diligently to "get the goods."

Julie and Bart cross Albion Basin.

Boulder Basin Trail lives up to its name with choppy tech 4 conditions; then it smooths as it bends west and descends into the trees. Lively freewheeling takes you through the heart of the lush basin, across the Cecret Lake Trail (closed to bikes), and past garage-size limestone boulders near the base of Supreme Lift. A few sharp turns, one long boardwalk, and a smooth trail take you to Alf's Restaurant where you retrace your tracks to the base.

Germania Pass

If you reminisce about the days when bikes were rigid, day-glow was the rage, and lycra helmet covers were vogue, then you need to ride the Rustler Run race course up Albion Basin and down Collins Gulch for old time's sake. If you're not an old-school hold out, then the scenery alone is worth your effort.

Germania Pass:
(8.3-mile loop, doubletrack, strenuous, tech 2⁺-4, 1,900-foot gain)

Start from the Wildcat base, and ride either the Alta Trail or the service road along the rope tow to the Albion Base. Climb the Albion Meadows Trail (gravelly doubletrack, tech 3) for just over a mile to Alf's Restaurant, and go right to the base of Sugarloaf Lift. Now you climb!

The old miners' road rises steeply beneath Greeley Ridge, crosses Backside bowl, and curves around Glory Hole basin. You can practically count the hundreds of turns skiers make coming off the ridge above. You'll power stroke in your lowest gear under Sugarloaf Lift and up to a T-junction with the Germania Pass cutoff road. Evidence of glaciation is startling, from the deep bowls rimmed by craggy mounts to the long claw marks left on smooth naked rock. Go left to Sugarloaf Pass to peer into

Snowbird's Mineral Basin bowl and catch an eye-popping view of Mount Timpanogos; then head to Germania Pass, and hunker down for a wild descent.

The rubbly service road (tech 3-4) curves down through Ballroom bowl to the mid station of Collins Lift at Watson's Lodge. More brake-smoking descending takes you down beneath the legendary Alf's High Rustler run and back to the Wildcat base. All the while, Superior Peak with its ragged cockscomb crown towers over the canyon. Pop into Goldminers Daughter for a frosty beverage (open Thursday-Sunday), and give cheers to this classic tour and to bemoan the thought that expert racers used to have to ride two laps!

! Know Before You Go

- Be aware of work crews and heavy machinery at all times, especially on the slopes above you.
- Summer cabin areas are private property.
- Ride only designated trails, do not ride through meadows, and do not shortcut trails.
- *Fido Factor:* Dogs are not allowed in the Little Cottonwood Canyon Watershed.

? Maps & More Information

- USGS 1:24,000: Dromedary Peak and Brighton, Utah
- Public Lands Information Center (at REI): (801) 466-6411
- Wasatch-Cache National Forest (Salt Lake Ranger District): (801) 733-2660; www.fs.fed.us/r4/wcnf/unit/slrd/index.shtml
- Town of Alta: (801) 363-5105, www.townofalta.com
- Alta Ski Area: (801) 359-1078, www.alta.com

Trailhead Access

From I-215, take Exit 6 (6200 South, Ski Areas). Travel east on 6200 South then south on Wasatch Boulevard and UT 210. Follow signs for Alta and Snowbird. Drive 8.5 miles up Little Cottonwood Canyon Road from the flashing billboard to the end of the pavement at Alta's Albion Day Lodge.

CENTRAL WASATCH

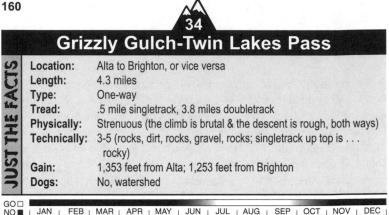

34
Grizzly Gulch-Twin Lakes Pass

Location:	Alta to Brighton, or vice versa
Length:	4.3 miles
Type:	One-way
Tread:	.5 mile singletrack, 3.8 miles doubletrack
Physically:	Strenuous (the climb is brutal & the descent is rough, both ways)
Technically:	3-5 (rocks, dirt, rocks, gravel, rocks; singletrack up top is . . . rocky)
Gain:	1,353 feet from Alta; 1,253 feet from Brighton
Dogs:	No, watershed

GO □
NO ■ | JAN | FEB | MAR | APR | MAY | JUN | JUL | AUG | SEP | OCT | NOV | DEC |

If you have to "canyon hop" between Big Cottonwood *and Little Cottonwood Canyons, whether by necessity or desire, then this is the way. Don't think you can actually pedal the whole way because there are seriously steep, rugged sections that will force even elite riders to hoof it at least briefly. As burly as this ride is, you'll gain immense satisfaction and reap tremendous visual rewards when you crest Twin Lakes Pass and peer into the tops of the competing canyons. How do you get back to where you started? Hitch a ride down one canyon and up the other, or chew a stick of Wrigley's gum and "double your pleasure."*

Details

Alta to Brighton

Head up the steep dirt road between the Shallow Shaft restaurant and Our Lady of the Snows Center; then fork right on a doubletrack signed "Alta-Brighton Trail" (tech 3). Glance over your shoulder for a fine view of Alta's Collins Gulch area, faced by the infamous Alf's High Rustler ski run. The route splits shortly ahead; stay straight and along a nearly level stretch of road. "Piece of cake," you say?

Stay straight at the next junction, ignoring the roads forking right and left. Attack a gravelly hill, pass between a pair of mine tailings, and then fork right on a doubletrack. This area was the once-prosperous mining camp of Michigan City, where precious metals were mined over a century ago. Cross under the power lines and face the route's most dreadful section—a protracted hill of barren, ledgy bedrock that is dashed liberally with loose dirt and rock (tech 4-5). Push, drag, and carry your bike. No whining! Remember, miners traveled this route diligently with mules and wagons while carrying a ton of tools and ore—they were a resilient bunch. Fork right on a faded doubletrack after passing under the power lines again. It rises steeply to the twin power line towers atop Twin Lakes Pass, elevation 9,993 feet (**m2.1**). If former Utah Jazz center, Mark Eaton, was to stand at the pass, the top of his head would break the ten-grand mark by four inches.

Press on or retreat? If the former, then descend the narrow, rough singletrack northeastward (tech 4). After .5 mile, you reach Solitude's Summit Lift Road. Turn right and descend to the junction with the upper SolBright Trail. To reach Brighton, veer right/east on upper SolBright, and descend a short rocky pitch (tech 4[+]) to the Twin Lakes Reservoir dam near the summit of Evergreen Lift. Follow the jeep road below the dam down to the base of Majestic Lift and to Brighton.

Brighton to Alta

From the base of Millicent Lift, go around a steel gate and head up the steep, gravelly doubletrack (tech 4). In just under a mile, the road splits; take the right fork to the summit of Evergreen Lift on the north side of the Twin Lakes Reservoir dam.

Push up a rock-studded path, and connect with the upper SolBright Trail. Follow it uphill .5 mile to Solitude's Summit Lift Road then .2 mile more to where the road turns sharply right at resort signs for Dynamite,

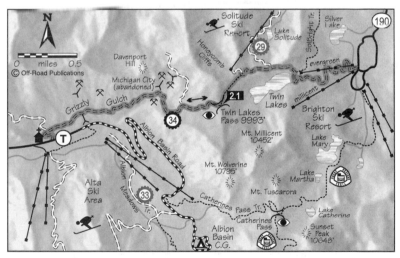

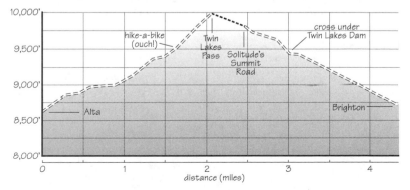

Hoofing it up Grizzly Gulch to Twin Lakes Pass.

SolBright, and Brighton. Hike up a faint path rising up the road's steep embankment. The .5-mile-long bouldery singletrack (tech 4⁺) takes you to Twin Lakes Pass (**m2.1**). When walking seems more sensible than pedaling, take the opportunity for sightseeing; there's plenty.

From the pass, head down the gravelly, rutted trail, which widens to a weathered doubletrack. When you intersect a better doubletrack, fork left and pass under the power lines. You know you're on the correct track if you soon face a menacing descent chock-full of boulders, bedrock, and boulders on bedrock (tech 5). Thereafter, the road passes through mine sites and goes between a pair of mine tailings; stay straight on the near-level road. Fork left at the sign for "Alta-Brighton Trail," and exit to the Town of Alta between the Shallow Shaft restaurant and Our Lady of the Snows Center.

Option: Catherines Pass (6.3 miles, one-way, strenuous, tech 3-5, 1,500-foot gain)

If you're the type who loaths riding out-and-back, then circle back to your starting point via Catherines Pass, keeping in mind that the Alta side is "less unridable" than the Brighton side. From Alta, climb the Albion Meadows Trail to the Catherines Pass trailhead on the Albion Basin Road. Catherines Pass Trail has several short portages; otherwise, it's quite ridable, albeit strenuous. The pass is reached in 4.1 miles. The descent to Brighton is another story. It's half as long and twice as rugged. Entire families of granite boulders will gang up on you and force you to hoof it, voluntarily or not. There are some sweet sections in between the dismounts, though.

From Brighton, start out on the Lake Mary Trail between the lodges at the main base area. You'll get a "feel" for the trail in short order as you pick your way up a steep rock garden. Then you'll savor every inch of smooth tread because there isn't much of it. Take the left fork at the Lake Mary junction to continue pedaling and pushing up past Lake Catherine. The final ascent to Catherines Pass is a mandatory bike-on-shoulders portage. Ouch! Rejoice; the descent to Alta is all ridable (tech 3-4⁺).

Collins Gulch of Alta Ski Area. Alf's High Rustler run is to the left.

CENTRAL WASATCH

❗ Know Before You Go

- Be prepared for rapidly changing alpine weather and the possibility of afternoon thunderstorms. There is little shelter on this route.
- *Fido Factor:* Dogs are not allowed in the Little Cottonwood Canyon and Big Cottonwood Canyon Watersheds.

❓ Maps & More Information

- USGS 1:24,000: Dromedary Peak and Brighton, Utah
- Public Lands Information Center (at REI): (801) 466-6411
- Wasatch-Cache National Forest (Salt Lake Ranger District): (801) 733-2660; www.fs.fed.us/r4/wcnf/unit/slrd/index.shtml

Trailhead Access

To Alta: From I-215, take Exit 6 (6200 South, Ski Areas). Travel east on 6200 South then south on Wasatch Boulevard to 7200 South/Fort Union Boulevard and Big Cottonwood Canyon Road/UT 190. Continue south on Wasatch Boulevard and UT 210, following signs for Alta and Snowbird. Drive 8.5 miles up Little Cottonwood Canyon Road from the flashing billboard to the end of pavement at the Albion base.

To Brighton: Same as above, but travel 16 miles up Big Cottonwood Canyon Road/UT 190 to Brighton Ski Resort. Park and embark from the base of Evergreen Lift.

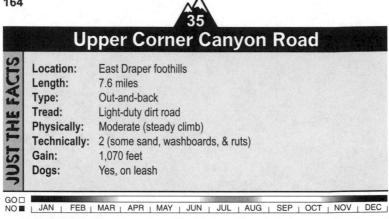

35
Upper Corner Canyon Road

JUST THE FACTS

CENTRAL WASATCH

Location:	East Draper foothills
Length:	7.6 miles
Type:	Out-and-back
Tread:	Light-duty dirt road
Physically:	Moderate (steady climb)
Technically:	2 (some sand, washboards, & ruts)
Gain:	1,070 feet
Dogs:	Yes, on leash

GO □
NO ■ | JAN | FEB | MAR | APR | MAY | JUN | JUL | AUG | SEP | OCT | NOV | DEC |

Despite travel restrictions and trail closures in the Corner Canyon Preservation District in the 1990s, Upper Corner Canyon Road remains open to public use. It's a great ride to loosen up the legs in the early season or to squeeze in a few last-minute miles in the late season. The dirt road angles gradually up the east Draper foothills beneath the broad shoulders of Lone Peak and offers a sweeping panorama of the southern Salt Lake Valley. The road serves as an anchor for the Bonneville Shoreline Trail where additional miles can be logged north to Sandy, west to Point of the Mountain, and south to Alpine. Just choose a direction and ride.

Details

The route is straight forward—ride until you reach the top. You won't be tempted to do otherwise because all the old trails that once branched from the road are posted closed. The only exception is the Bonneville Shoreline Trail (BST), which is open to nonmotorized use. By and large, the road rises at a steady, moderate grade on packed dirt with periodic sand and washboards (tech 2-3) that become more pronounced during dry spells. Novice riders will find the climb to be a pleasant low-gear spin; stronger riders can easily peg their anaerobic threshold by pushing a harder gear. About 3 miles from the trailhead, the road curves through Corner Canyon, where the creek flows lightly down a gulch. The road smooths and levels, but the clayey surface can get real mucky when wet. A bit farther, the road bends left and reaches the Traverse Mountains divide (**m3.8**).

Here, you can make out Lone Peak's chiseled granite cornice, Box Elder Peak's lofty dome, and Mount Timpanogos' 5-mile-long ridge top. Doubletracks branch in all directions, and all directions are posted with private property/no trespassing signs. Heed the warnings. (Descending the old Hog Hollow Road doubletrack to Alpine is controversial, although it may become part of the BST. Inquire with Draper City or Alpine City for updates.) Simply retrace your tracks to return to the trailhead.

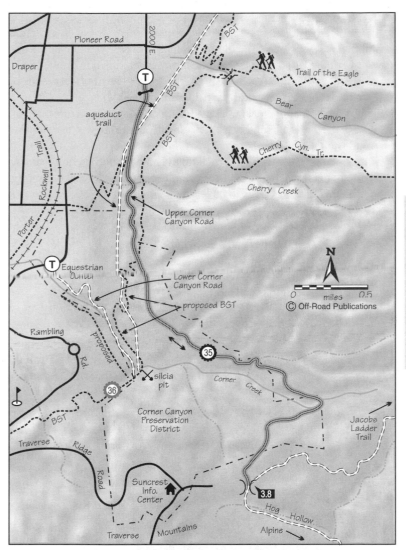

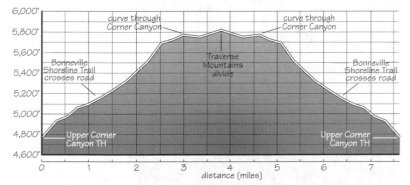

! Know Before You Go

- Public use by vehicles (including mountain bikes) and horses within the Corner Canyon Preservation District is restricted to public roads and trails designated open to such uses. Public use of private lands is prohibited, except by expressed consent of the owner.
- This route is deathly hot at midday during midsummer, so ride early or late in the day. You might be able to sneak out during winter when the road is either dry or frozen.
- *Fido Factor:* The gravel and rock tread can be tough on dogs' paws, and owners must be alert to vehicle traffic. Salt Lake County Ordinance requires dogs to be leashed.

? Maps & More Information

- USGS 1:24,000: Draper and Lehi, Utah
- City of Draper: (801) 576-6500
- City of Alpine: (801) 756-6347
- Public Lands Information Center (at REI): (801) 466-6411

Trailhead Access

From I-15, take Exit 294 (Draper, Riverton). Travel east on UT 71, which becomes 12300 South. Turn right on 1300 East at Hidden Valley Shopping Center then left/east on Pioneer Road (flashing stop light). Drive 1 mile east and turn right on 2000 East. Park near the steel gate after the road turns to dirt.

Mount Timpanogos and Utah Valley come into view when you crest the Traverse Mountains.

Bonneville Shoreline Trail (Draper-Sandy)

JUST THE FACTS

Location:	Draper foothills
Length:	About 8 miles
Type:	One-way
Tread:	Singletrack with a bit of doubletrack
Physically:	Moderate (smooth-riding trails w/ plenty of intermittent terrain changes)
Technically:	2⁺-5 (good hand-built trails w/ some challenging sections.)
Gain:	About 800 feet
Dogs:	Yes, on leash

GO ☐
NO ■ | JAN | FEB | MAR | APR | MAY | JUN | JUL | AUG | SEP | OCT | NOV | DEC |

WHY SHOULD U RIDE THIS TRAIL

A *"work in progress"* is the best way to describe the Draper and Sandy sections of the Bonneville Shoreline Trail (BST). Ongoing housing developments, stalled negotiations with landowners, environmentally sensitive areas and rugged terrain have hampered the completion of a through trail, but ambitious trail building projects have produced many miles of excellent tread to use right now. In time, the trail will run from Little Cottonwood Canyon to Point of the Mountain with links to Alpine in Utah County and other regional trails. Overall, the BST will provide access to an every-expanding network of trails developed by Sandy, Draper, and the Suncrest development.

Details

BST (Sandy section)

Terrain gaps and property disputes have stalled efforts for a through trail in Sandy between Little Cottonwood Canyon and Draper, but you can bike and hike small segments to whet your appetite. The future looks bright because Sandy City administrators are making continuous strides toward completion. Designated trailheads are on Little Cottonwood Canyon Road (about a mile west of the flashing billboard) and at The Boulders private community (about 10245 S. Wasatch Boulevard). Both trailheads provide access to Bells Canyon Trail as well. A third trailhead is at Hidden Valley Park (about 12000 S. Wasatch Boulevard). From there, hand-built trail heads south along the foothills to Draper but is closed at Little Willow Creek because of property and easement disputes. Therefore, linking to the Draper BST is not possible, and you are asked not to cross the blockade. North of the Hidden Valley Park is a "wait-and-see" situation. Private property boundaries and extremely rugged terrain will necessitate creative trail building to link with The Boulders trailhead.

BST (Draper section)

At the time of publication, about 8 miles of the BST had been completed between Upper Corner Canyon Road and Salt Lake County's Point of the Mountain Flight Park for hang gliders. Because of the gravel pit opera-

CENTRAL WASATCH

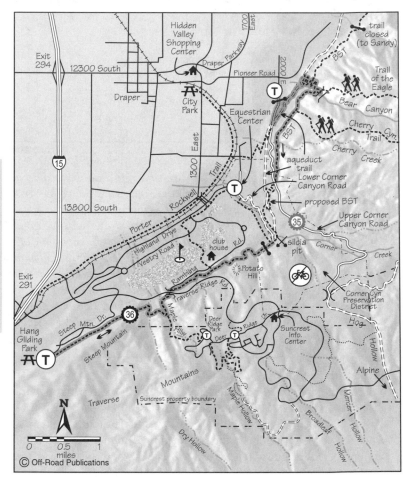

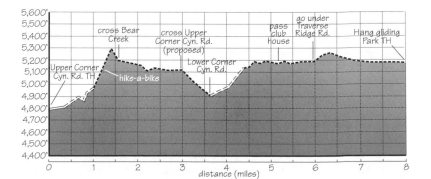

tions and the lack of a safe bicycle corridor around Point of the Mountain currently, the BST is proposed to go over the Traverse Mountains. "Good luck. Suncrest development sits in the way," you're thinking? Think again. Suncrest has an impressive trails master plan and is committed to providing community and regional trails. Kudos to Suncrest!

Here's the low down on the Draper BST. Currently, there are three trailheads: Upper Corner Canyon Road, Andy Ballard Equestrian Center, and Point of the Mountain Flight Park (North Side).

From the Upper Corner Canyon Road trailhead, head up the sandy road for .2 mile (tech 2), and fork left/north on the aqueduct doubletrack, posted with hike, bike, and horse decals (tech 2$^+$). Climb a short modest hill, dip through Bear Canyon, and come to a junction signed for "BST access." Hike-a-bike up this steep, sandy trail and around sharp turns (tech 5) to a second junction and the true "shoreline." (The aqueduct road ends shortly ahead.) Here, the BST heads north to Sandy but is blocked in 1 mile at Little Willow Creek. Check out the trail just the same. Trail builders did an impressive job because Lake Bonneville lapped against barren rock here and left little shoreline on which to put a trail.

Onward. Hike-a-bike up more rugged trail to the junction with Trail of the Eagle (no bikes); then hike down over bedrock (tech 5) to the bridge over Bear Creek. The rest is gravy, as the BST contours on smooth sandy tread back to Upper Corner Canyon Road (tech 2$^+$).

The BST is proposed to cross Upper Corner Canyon Road, descend across the aqueduct trail (foot traffic only), and connect to Lower Corner Canyon Road. There, you ride up Lower Corner Canyon Road to the old silica pit to resume on the BST. Until that section is built, you must return on Upper Corner Canyon Road toward the trailhead, and then fork left about .3 mile before the gate on a trail marked with hike, bike, and horse decals. It crosses the aqueduct trail, descends past a Questar maintenance shack and private homes, and arrives at the intersection of 13200 South and Highland Drive (1750 East). Pedal south on Highland Drive, or take the proposed "Mulch Trail" to the equestrian center. Now head up Lower Corner Canyon Road (tech 3) for 1 mile to its end.

CENTRAL WASATCH

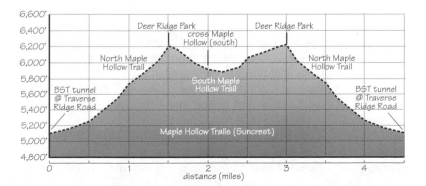

Head west past a gate, and climb out of Corner Canyon to an elevated bench (and a new housing development) that overlooks Draper and the Salt Lake valley. Look for the BST forking left up a steep hill and then veering west (trail alignment is subject to change). The trail levels and rolls through oak brush. Expect some tricky bits: sharp turns, quick ups and down, and chunky tread. After passing Potato Hill and the golf course club house, the BST crosses Rambling Road and goes through a tunnel under Traverse Ridge Road and into Maple Hollow. (Here, you can link to the North Maple Hollow Trail and climb to Suncrest on the Traverse Mountains. See "Option.") Wind through Maple Hollow (proposed), and strike a beeline west for the Flight Park while passing the backyards of private homes. Watch the hang gliders take to flight and then return.

Option: Suncrest Development

In the years to come, the trails at Suncrest might need a small guidebook of their own. This mountain community located on top of the Traverse Mountains is taking a proactive approach to improving the residents' quality of life by proposing nearly 30 miles of trails in their master plan. Of the 3800 acres available for the community, about half will be designated as natural and open space. Trails will be designed for users to travel within Suncrest or to link to trails in Draper and Alpine, including the BST. Foot, bike, and horse travel will be accomodated on shared and use-specific trails. Trail maps will be posted at trailheads and will be available through the Suncrest Information Center and homeowners' association.

Here's a sneak peak of what you'll find. Several miles of trails have been constructed centered about the Maple Hollow area. The South Maple Hollow Trail is a 1.5-mile loop on singletrack with an out-and-back spur on doubletrack that drops off the south side of Traverse Mountain. The North Maple Hollow Trail is a 1.5-mile one-way singletrack between Suncrest and the Draper BST where it passes under Traverse Ridge Road at the intersection of Rambling Road. Both are moderately difficult.

Currently, there are two designated trailhead-parking areas at Suncrest: Deer Ridge Drive and Deer Ridge Park. To find the former, drive up Traverse Ridge Road, and turn right on Deer Ridge Drive (next to the Suncrest Information Center). Drive .6 mile to the junction of Long Branch Drive, and park at the lot on the north side of Deer Crest Drive. (Note: The trail that descends north from this parking lot is *not* Maple Hollow Trail. This trail descends to the midpoint on Traverse Ridge Road and is proposed to connect with the BST at Potato Hill.) The latter trailhead is found by continuing on Deer Ridge Drive another half mile and turning right on Elk Glen Drive. Parking is available at the Deer Ridge Park site, but the park won't be fully constructed until 2004.

To reach South Maple Hollow Trail from the Deer Ridge Drive trailhead, pedal west on the sidewalk along Deer Ridge Drive for .2 mile. The trail veers from the road's edge, descends past old telephone poles and then loops back up on the hollow's west side. The trail affords stunning views of Utah Valley, Utah Lake, and the southern Wasatch Front along the way. As you approach the top of the trail, it crosses under Deer Crest Drive and exits to Deer Ridge Park. North Maple Hollow Trail begins here and descends to the Draper BST.

! Know Before You Go

- Trail access, location, and conditions may change without notice.
- Portions of the BST and adjacent trails cross private property. Obey all signs restricting travel to avoid trespassing.
- Ride on trails and roads posted open to mountain bikes only.
- *Fido Factor:* Pets must be leashed.

? Maps & More Information

- USGS 1:24,000: Draper, Jordan Narrows, and Lehi, Utah
- Public Lands Information Center (at REI): (801) 466-6411
- Bonneville Shoreline Trail Committee: www.bonneville-trail.org; (801) 816-0876
- City of Draper: (801) 576-6500
- City of Sandy: (801) 568-7100
- Suncrest: (801) 553-9300

Trailhead Access

Upper Corner Canyon Road: From I-15, take Exit 294 for Draper, and travel east on 12300 South. Turn right on 1300 East at Hidden Valley Shopping Center, and then go left on Pioneer Road. Drive 1 mile east, turn right on 2000 East, and park where pavement turns to dirt near the steel gate.

Andy Ballard Equestrian Center: Follow the same access as for Upper Corner Canyon Road, but continue south on 1300 East for 1.5 miles past the intersection with Pioneer Road. Go left on Highland Drive for .5 mile to reach the equestrian center. (Note: these trailheads can be easily accessed by taking Wasatch Boulevard and Highland Drive south through Sandy.)

Point of the Mountain Flight Park: From I-15, take exit 291 for Draper and Bluffdale, and go east on Highland Drive for .8 mile. Turn right on Traverse Ridge Road then right on Steep Mountain Drive in .6 mile, and wind through the residential area for 1.5 miles to the end of pavement. Park off to the right near the launch pad and outhouse.

Suncrest: From I-15, take Exit 291 for Draper and Bluffdale. Travel east on Highland Drive for .8 mile, and turn right on Traverse Ridge Road. Drive 3.5 miles to the top, turn right on Deer Ridge Drive near the Suncrest Information Center, and drive .6 mile to the small parking area at the junction with Long Branch Drive.

CENTRAL WASATCH

Fat-Tire Dining Guide (Central Wasatch)

c	(less than $5)
$	($5-$10)
$$	($10-$15)
$$$	(over $15)
B:	Breakfast
BR:	Brunch
L:	Lunch
D:	Dinner

2-Go   Take Out
🚗   Delivery
🍺   Serves Beer
🍷   Serves Wine
🍸   Serves Liquor
☂   Patio Dining

American, Steaks & Seafood

Johanna's Kitchen
9725 S State, Sandy UT 84070
(801) 566-1762
www.johannaskitchen.com
$-$$, B L D (M-Su), 2-Go

Something Good's Always Cooking! American home-style cooking guaranteed to satisfy the heartiest appetite--from "wagon wheels & axle grease" for breakfast; to soups, salads, and specialty sandwiches for lunch; to grilled fish, steaks, and chops for dinner. Pastas and burritos, too. Don't miss "Meatloaf Thursday." Take our fresh-baked cookies, muffins, and scones for the trail. Early-bird and daily specials.

Market Street Broiler
260 S 1300 East, SLC UT 84102
(801) 583-8808
www.gastronomyinc.com
$-$$$, L D (M-Sa), D (Su), 2-Go 🍺🍷🍸☂

"Fresh" is the focus here, where seafood is flown in daily and grilled over mesquite for a unique and savory flavor. Enjoy crisp seafood salads, our famous clam chowder, and an assortment of delicious sandwiches, or choose from chicken, Certified Angus Beef, or hickory-smoked baby back ribs. A neighborhood favorite near the University of Utah.

Market Street Grill (Downtown)
48 W. Market St. (340 South), SLC UT 84101
(801) 322-4668
www.gastronomyinc.com
$-$$$, B L D (M-Sa), BR D (Su) 🍺🍷🍸

Enjoy breakfast (rated "best in town"), lunch, and dinner every day of the week, with an abundant selection of fresh seafood specialties, Certified Angus Beef, chops, chicken, prime rib, pasta, and a variety of fresh, crisp salads. Delectable desserts made from Gastronomy's own bakery. Sunday brunch is always a hit. Zagat rated "Tops" in seafood, food, and popularity.

Market Street Grill (Cottonwood)
2985 E 6580 South, Sandy UT 84121
(801) 942-8860
www.gastronomyinc.com
$-$$$, L D (M-F) D (Sa-Su) BR (Su), 2-Go
🍺🍷🍸

Serving the same delicious fresh seafood, Certified Angus Beef, and specialties as Market Street Grill/downtown. Also featuring a Fresh Fish Market with seafood flown in from around the world, plus a take-home market with deli items, salads, chowder, fresh baked desserts, and select entrees from all Gastronomy restaurants. Summer patio offers spectacular mountain views.

Market Street Oyster Bar*
54 W Market St. (340 South), SLC UT 84101
(801) 531-6044

2985 E 6580 South, Sandy UT 84121
(801) 942-8870
www.gastronomyinc.com
$-$$$, L D (M-F), D (Sa-Su), BR (Su)
🍺🍷🍸

Salt Lake's showcase for dining and conversation, offering a variety of fresh fish and seafood from around the world as well as a selection of chowders and stews, steaks, pastas, sandwiches, and salads. At least a dozen fresh fish specials are offered daily. A convivial setting in which to enjoy the largest selection of fresh oysters in the state. *A private club for members.

Bagels, Bakeries & Delis

Great Harvest Bread Co.
905 E 900 South, SLC, UT 84105
(801) 328-2323

4667 S 2300 East, SLC, UT 84117
(801) 277-3277

5592 S Redwood Rd., Taylorsville, UT 84123
(801) 966-9699
www.greatharvest.com c-$, B L D (M-Sa) ☂

The wholesome high energy food of Great Harvest Bread Co. is the perfect way to gear up for and to get you through any ride in the beautiful Wasatch Range. Everyday, we grind our own wheat for our phenomenal made-from-scratch breads, cookies, cinnamon rolls, and other yummy treats. We also have juices, granola, soup, and sandwiches to go! Eat Great Harvest every day, and it will help you keep your lifestyle healthy.

The Bagelry
905 E 400 South, SLC UT 84102
(801) 355-9111
2233 S. State, SLC UT 84115
(801) 485-3434
5901 S State, Murray UT 84107
(801) 685-9000
c-$, B L D (M-Sa), 2-Go

Proof you can get a *real* bagel in Utah! 16 varieties of fresh-baked bagels, 11 custom-blended cream cheeses, homemade hummus, awesome breakfast and sandwich-style bagels, vegetarian selections, and more. Yogurt parfaits, fresh salads and soups, juices, Chai, soymilk, and Tazo Teas. Don't worry about food for the trail, we'll pack it for you!

Einstein Bros Bagels
1-800-BAGEL-ME
www.einsteinbros.com
c-$, B L D (M-Su), 2-Go 🌲

Fuel for the mind, mouth, and soul--not to mention your legs! Great bagels, plus sandwiches, soups, salads, coffee, and drinks. Rendezvous at any our 20 Wasatch Front locations.

Frank Granato Importing Co.
1391 S 300 West, SLC UT 84115
(801) 486-5644
4000 S 2700 East, Holladay UT 84124
(801) 277-7700
$-$$, B L D (M-Sa), 2-Go

After a long day at the office or long miles on the trail, you are just one stop away from authentic Italian food. Granato's specializes in dine-in or take-out sandwiches, lasagne, pasta, and more. And our extensive selection of imported Italian food products will make your next home-cooked meal the best ever. Between the deli, bakery, groceries, and hot food, all you need to worry about is which nearby trail to ride.

Rich's Bagels
8691 S Highland Dr., Sandy UT 84093
(801) 947-0890
6191 S Highland Dr., SLC UT 84121
(801) 277-3137
c, B L (M-Su), 2-Go

Fuel up at Rich's Bagels--Home of the *original* asiago cheese bagel! We have 12 choices of bagels and tasty cream cheeses, plus made-to-order sandwiches, breakfast bagels, soups, and salads. Get your day buzzin' with specialty coffee drinks. Our homemade muffins and cookies are a sweet treat--take some for the trail, other bikers will be jealous.

Barbeque & Southern

Sugarhouse Barbeque Co.
2207 S 700 East, SLC 84106
(801) 463-4800
www.sugarhousebbq.com
$-$$, L D (M-Su), 2-Go 🌲 🍷 🍸

Award-winning Memphis-style BBQ, offering slow-smoked ribs, pulled pork, beef brisket, chicken, and turkey breast. All freshly smoked twice daily. The ribs and pulled pork are all-time favorites, and the Bourbon Street Jambalaya is a straight from the deep South. From sandwiches to Bill's Big Combo, we will satisfy any appetite. Excellent choice of vegetarian side dishes. The atmosphere is casual and comfortable, so come as you are. A Salt Lake original since 1996.

Brewpubs & Taverns

Bohemian Brewery & Grill
94 E Ft. Union Blvd (7000 South), SLC UT 84047
(801) 566-5474
www.bowhemianbrewery.com
$-$$, L D (M-Su), 2-Go 🌲 🍷 🍸

Brewers of four legendary European lagers, each on tap to refuel those lost carbos. Great meeting place for Salt Lake road rides or after bombing Wasatch singletracks. American keystones and great Central European favorites grace our eclectic menu. Summer patio is open late. Ask for Bohemian Beer at your favorite watering hole.

Fiddlers Elbow*
1063 E 2100 South, SLC, UT 84106
(801) 463-9393
$-$$, L D (M-Su), BR (Su) 2-Go 🌲 🍷 🍸 🌲

Kick back at this Salt Lake original American Roadhouse. Enjoy one of 32 beers on tap and the "Best Comfort Food" in town, including their famous Salmon Fish & Chips. Play billiards, darts, or foosball, and catch your favorite sports event on a dozen TVs (MTB racing and TdF, of course). Don't miss the legendary Sunday Sports Brunch, featuring prime rib, omelets, and bagels with lox--best deal in town at only $9.95. *Must be 21 years old.

Brewpubs & Taverns

Red Rock Brewing Company
254 S 200 West, SLC, UT 84101
(801) 521-7446
 www.redrockbrewing.com
$-$$, L D (M-Su), BR (Su), 2-Go 🏠 ♥ Y ⊤

"Good food, good beer, good friends," what more could you want after a mountain bike ride? Voted "Local's Favorite" for the last 5 years and named National Brewpub of the Year in 2000. Red Rock serves fresh casual fare and award-winning beers, including non-alcoholic brews, too! Centrally located in downtown Salt Lake with plenty of parking. Open late every day. Children are always welcome.

Squatters Pub Brewery
147 W Broadway (300 South), SLC UT 84101
(801) 363-2739
www.squatters.com
$-$$, L D (M-Su), 2-Go 🏠 ♥ Y ⊤

"Good For What Ales You." Salt Lake's original brewpub features an award-winning menu complimented by our chef's interesting and eclectic daily creations and Squatters' fresh brewed beers. Squatters' banquet room and patio provide an urban garden atmosphere for gatherings ranging from apres mountain biking to cocktail parties to wedding receptions. Brewers of Double Gold-Medal winning Full Suspension Pale Ale--take a "growler" to go.

Tracks Restaurant & Brewery
1641 North Main, Tooele, UT 84074
(435) 882-4040
www.tracksbrewing.com
$-$$, L D (M-Su), 2-Go 🏠 ♥ Y

"Make Tracks" to Tooele to dine and drink at Tracks Restaurant and Brewery. The menu showcases the cornerstones of American Pub cuisine: stout-poached bratwurst, linguine carbonara, dry-rubbed pork medallions, chicken picatta, and cornmeal-dusted halibut while the on-site brewery pumps out impressive suds, ranging from Incinerator Pale Ale to Skull Valley Stout. The lively, casual atmosphere is perfect for any occasion. Spend a day car touring or biking the Oquirrh Mountains on the "Tracks Loop": Middle Canyon to Butterfield Canyon.

Burgers & Grilles

Cotton Bottom Inn
2820 E 6200 South, SLC UT 84121
(801) 273-9830
$, L D (M-Su), 2-Go 🏠

The Cotton Bottom Inn is the perfect stop for a quick bite, a cold beer, and a round of pool after a long day of riding Wasatch trails. Famous for its Garlic Cheeseburger, this classic neighborhood tavern is located 10 minutes from all major Salt Lake canyons and just west of Exit 6 (6200 South) off I-215.

Hires Big H
425 S 700 East, SLC UT 84102
(801) 364-4582

835 E. Ft. Union Blvd. (7000 South)
Midvale, UT 84047. (801) 561-2171

2900 W. 4700 South, W. Valley City, UT 84118
(801) 965-1010
www.hiresbigh.com
c-$, L D (M-Sa), 2-Go

Hires Big H has become famous for its sensational Big H Burger, fresh cut french fries, homemade onion rings, fry super sauce, and frosty mugs of root beer. Hires Big H is the "gathering place" where friends and families from all walks of life enjoy tasty food and cheerful service. Carhop service just like the old days. See you there!

Crown Burger
2684 S 3200 West, West Valley City, UT 84119
(801) 972-8566

3190 S Highland Dr., SLC UT 84106
(801) 467-6633

3270 S State, SLC UT 84115
(801) 463-6644

118 N 300 West, SLC UT 84103
(801) 532-5300

377 E 200 South, SLC UT 84111
(801) 532-1155
www.crownburger.com
c-$, L D (M-Sa), 2-Go

Great food that's served fast, not just fast food. Renown for the Crown Burger (cheeseburger piled high with pastrami). Also serving gyros, chicken, fish, and rid-eye steak sandwiches; homemade onion rings, thick-cut fries, and a variety of salads--all prepared to order. Finish with a root beer float. Crown Burgers is a family-owned Salt Lake tradition since 1978.

CENTRAL WASATCH

Cafes

The Singing Cricket Cafe
673 E. Simpson Ave. (2240 S), SLC UT 84106
(801) 487-0056
www.singingcricketcafe.com
$-$$, L D (M-Su), 2-Go 🏠🍷 🍸

We call it Gourmet American Energy Food; our customers call it fabulous . . . and affordable! Chef Lara serves healthy, filling, and creative food that keeps you moving all day long. Join us for a gourmet lunch, an elegant dinner, or an outstanding Sunday brunch served in a cozy contemporary setting furnished by the adjoining Dancing Crane Imports. Valet *bicycle* parking available upon request.

Hard Rock Cafe
505 S 600 East, SLC UT 84102
(801) 532-ROCK (7625)
www.hardrockcafe.com
$-$$, L D (M-Su) 🏠🍷 🍸 🌂

Salt Lake City is still the place for music fans of all ages seeking great food and fantastic memorabilia, and that isn't changing anytime soon. So come on over and check us out at Historic Trolley Square Center, where our bi-level cafe in this delightful neighborhood also features live music in our private club every Saturday night.

Park Cafe
604 E 1300 South, SLC UT 84105
(801) 487-1670
$-$$, B L D (M-Su), 2-Go 🏠🍷 🍸 🌂

Located across the street from Liberty Park, The Park Cafe offers a cozy, intimate atmosphere overlooking the park. During summer, our garden patio is unlike any in the city. It's a great place to visit after a run or ride and is truly one of a kind place to eat in Salt Lake. It's all fresh, homemade, and tasty.

Clubs & Entertainment

Bayou*
645 S State, SLC, UT 84111
(801) 961-8400
$-$$, L D (M-F) D (Sa), 2-Go 🏠🍷 🍸 🌂

Beervana! Utah's greatest beer selection with nearly 200 bottled and on-tap beers from around the world. The food is equally impressive. It's a taste of New Orleans without leaving Salt Lake with Cajun specialties like jambalaya, gumbo, and crawfish etoufee. Gourmet pizzas, sandwiches, and appetizers, too. Live blues and jazz Wed - Sat, plus billiards, darts, and sports on TV. Open late, so stop in after a night of urban freeriding. Bike parking available. ***A private club for members.**

Lazy Moon Club*
32 Exchange Place, SLC UT 84111
(801) 363-7600
$-$$, L D (M-F), D (Sa-Su), 2-Go 🏠🍷 🍸 🌂

Housed in the historic Exchange Place in downtown Salt Lake, this casual but energetic college-style club serves traditional pub fare with mouth-watering burgers and sandwiches, pizzas, wings, and salads, all named with catchy musical lingo. It's all homemade and goes great with the vast beer selection. Watch sports on TV, play pool, and listen to the best local bands nearly every night. Relax under a lunar sky on the brick patio. ***A private club for members.**

Coffeehouses

Salt Lake Roasting Company
320 E 400 South, SLC UT 84111
(801) 363-7572
1-800-748-4887
www.roasting.com
c-$, B L D (M-Sa), B L (Su), 2-Go 🌂

"Coffee Without Compromise." Salt Lake's original coffeehouse known for its unique, eclectic atmosphere. Coffee is fresh-roasted on the premises with over 50 varieties available. Featuring an extensive "lighter fare" lunch/dinner menu that changes daily, along with delectable pastries to accompany the coffee and espresso drink selections. Also located in the downtown SLC Library, which is open on Sunday!

« Got Hoops? UTA TRAX sculpture at 900 E 400 S Salt Lake City.

CENTRAL WASATCH

CENTRAL WASATCH

Juice Bars

Jamba Juice
7194 S Union Park Ave., Midvale UT 84047
(801) 561-9361

3294 S 1300 East, SLC UT 84106
(801) 463-9200

5578 S Redwood Rd., Taylorsville UT 84123
(801) 968-9767
www.jambajuice.com
c-$, B L D (M-Su), 2-Go

Jamba creates delicious, nutritious, all-natural, energizing fruit smoothies and juices. Each re-freshing drink provides 3-6 servings of fruit to get you on your way to Five-A-Day! Also boosted with vitamins, minerals, anti-oxidants, phytonutrients, and optional protein powder. Have a Jamba Bread or Jamba Pretzel for whole-grain nutrition. Together, Jamba offers a perfect light meal before or after a ride and to promote a healthy, happy life. "Your body is a temple, lit-tering is strictly prohibited!"

Greek & Middle Eastern

Cafe Med
420 E 3300 South, SLC UT 84115
(801) 493-0100
c-$, L D (M-Su), BR (Sa-Su), 2-Go 🚙

Serving the best of Mediterranean and Middle Eastern regions, including Greek, Persian, Turk-ish, and Italian cuisines. Start with hummus, spanikopita, dolmas, or curried chick pea soup, then try the popular Turkish yogurt pasta, portabello mushroom ravioli, lamb souvlaki (skewers), or Khoresh-e Bademjan (roasted chicken and eggplant) with basmati rice. Veg-etarians have much to choose from, including meatless lasagne and the vegetarian sampler. The baklava is flaky and sweet, and the saffron-pistachio ice cream is one-of-a-kind. Kids menu available.

Mazza Middle Eastern Cuisine
1515 S 1500 East, SLC UT 84105
(801) 484-9259
c-$ L D (M-Su), 2-Go ⊤ 🚙

Middle Eastern specialties are prepared fresh from scratch. Only the best cuts of lamb, chicken, and beef are used for kabobs and pita sand-wiches. Vegetarians will savor the falafels plus a wide variety of delectable side dishes. The fry sauce for the twice-cooked french fries is a knock out! Voted "Best Bang for the Buck" by *Zagat* and "Best Neighborhood Joint" by *Salt Lake Magazine*. It's always worth the trip.

International & Eclectic

Guru's Enlightened Eating
912 East 900 South, SLC, UT 84105
801-355-4878

940 E. Fort Union Blvd., Midvale, UT 84047
801-352-8161
www.go2gurus.com
c-$, L D (M-Sa), 2-Go ⊤

Enter Guru's and find yourself walking down a winding stone "Path to Enlightenment" where you can order "Stir the Soul" rice bowls, salads of "Enlightened Greens", "Self Fulfilling" pastas, and wraps and burritos that promise to "Ignite the Fire Within." At Guru's you will Enlighten your taste buds, not your wallet. As important as our food is, we are passionate about our mission to support local charities and disadvantaged youth through the Guru's Foundation.

Log Haven
East Mill Creek Canyon, SLC UT 84109
(801) 272-8255
www.log-haven.com.
$$-$$$, D (M-Su) 🍴 🍷 🍸 ⊤

Long considered Utah's finest canyon dining, Log Haven is a beautiful log mansion built in 1920, and located in the heart of the Wasatch National Forest. Bask in fantastic canyon views while dining on Zagat Award-winning cuisine that will excite your palate. The menu changes sea-sonally and features complex pleasures with Pacific Rim, California, Southwest and classic French influences. Located four miles up Mill Creek Canyon and next to the ever-popular Pipe-line Trail.

Italian

Baci Trattoria
134 W Pierpont Ave. (240 South), SLC UT 84101
(801) 328-1500
www.gastronomyinc.com
$-$$$, L D (M-F) D (Sat) 🍴 🍷 🍸

Salt Lake City's hip haven for an extensive menu of traditional Italian favorites, featuring fresh pasta, pizza, and lasagne as well as Certified Angus Beef, veal, lamb, chicken, and seafood specialties. Delicious appetizers, salads, and fresh baked desserts. The colorful, upbeat at-mosphere is a perfect "cool" down after a day of mountain biking, or for any occasion. Adjoining Club Baci is a private club for members.

Cafe Trio
680 S 900 East, SLC UT 84102
(801) 533-TRIO (8746)
$-$$, L D (M-Sa), 2-Go 🏠🍺🍸🍴

Fine dining at affordable prices and friendly, quick service add to the contemporary neighborhood setting, which captures the three-part focus of Cafe Trio. Our "New Italian" cuisine features gourmet pizzas and flatbreads cooked in a wood-burning oven, simple but creative pastas, and hearty entrees that are "delizioso!" Delectable desserts are just reward after a long day in the saddle. Bike parking available, so pedal over anytime.

Confetti's Restaurant
4751 S. Holladay Blvd., SLC UT 84117
(801) 272-9111
$-$$, D (M-Sa), 2-Go 🏠🍺🍸🍴

An unassuming neon sign belies the quality and charm of this restaurant, which creatively blends Italian and Eastern Mediterranean cuisines. Inside, it is simply elegant yet relaxing, with white linen table cloths and straight-backed chairs. Start with delicious stuffed grape leaves and home-baked bread, then move on to pasta primavera, veal picatta, or Moroccan chicken couscous. Savor each morsel, and don't miss the homemade tiramisu for dessert.

Fresco Italian Cafe
1513 S 1500 East, SLC UT 84105
(801) 486-1300
$$-$$$, D (M-Su) 🏠🍺🍸🍴

Our name means "fresh." Award-winning Northern Italian cuisine served in a quaint cottage setting amidst a quiet east-bench neighborhood. Dine on our garden patio during summer or next to a warm fireplace in winter. Polenta antipasto is a must; then select from bountiful pastas, creamy risotto, or delightful entrees from a menu that changes with the seasons. Buon Appetito!

Salt Lake Pizza & Pasta
1063 E 2100 South, SLC UT 84106
(801) 484-1804
$-$$, L D (M-Su), 2-Go 🏠🍺🍸

Located in the historic Sugarhouse neighborhood, SLPP tames your post-ride munchies with traditional Italian and American favorites. Start with Buffalo wings or fresh soup, then sink your teeth into the popular Cajun shrimp or goat's cheese pizza, tomato-basil linguine, burgers and sandwiches, or a crisp Cobb salad. Wash it down with one of 32 beers on tap. Indulgent cheesecakes and decadent desserts will top-off your calorie quota. Great place for families.

Mexican & Southwestern

Loco Lizard
6550 S Big Cottonwood Road (3000 East)
SLC UT 84121
(801) 453-9400

Kimball Plaza at Kimball Junction
Park City UT 84098
(801) 435-7000
$-$$, L D (M-Su), 2-Go 🏠🍺🍸

A contemporary cantina meets Old World Mexico and serves some serious Mexican food. Our award-winning menu combines traditional and regional recipies that are full flavored and varied with a focus on clean, creative, fresh food. Savor our house-made chips, three kinds of salsas, tamales, and tortillas all made fresh daily. House specialties include carnitas, salmon tacos, carne asada, posole, and fresh seafood. Moderate prices and separate children's menu make us a hit with families and large parties.

Barbacoa
4638 S 2300 East, Holladay UT 84117
(801) 273-7231

859 E 900 South, SLC UT 84102
(801) 524-0853

3927 S Wasatch Blvd., SLC UT 84124
(801) 278-8700
www.barbacoa1.com
c-$, L D (M-Su) 2-Go 🍴

Know for their *gigantic* burritos, Barbacoa serves fresh, healthy, gourmet Mexican food at reasonable prices in a casual, quick-service setting. Hand-crafted burritos, tacos, salads, and burrito bowls are filled with mesquite-grilled chicken, carnitos, slow-roasted steak, sauteed vegetables, or famed "barbacoa." Add in cilantro-lime rice, your choice of beans, and top off with fresh salsas to create your own meal. Drop in, they'll get you fed!

Cafe Pierpont
122 W Pierpont Ave. (240 South), SLC UT 84101
(801) 539-8783
www.gastronomyinc.com
$-$$, L D (M-F), D (S-Su), 2-Go 🏠🍺🍸🍴

A Salt Lake favorite for festive Mexican cuisine such as rotisserie chicken, enchiladas, combinations dinners, seafood, and our famous sizzling hot fajitas served with hand-made tortillas. All are served with our complimentary salsa bar. Deserts are scrumptious. Hungry? We dare you to finish off an entire Macho Grande Burrito plate! A great spot for groups and families.

CENTRAL WASATCH

Mexican & Southwestern

Cafe Rio Mexican Grill
3025 E 3300 South, Salt Lake, UT 84109
(801) 463-7250
6985 S Park Centre Dr., Midvale UT 84047
(801) 562-4431
62 E 12300 South, Draper, UT 84020
(801) 572-3125
www.caferio.com
c-$, L D (M-Sa), 2-Go

Huge, flaky tortillas are made before your very eyes then jammed full of USDA Choice chicken, beef, or pork using traditional recipes from the Rio Grande Valley regions. Enchiladas, tacos, salads, home-baked flan, and key-lime pie, too. Customize your meal with endless add-ons, fresh salsas, and baked-on cheeses; "no problemo." Voted "Best Burrito in Utah" by *Salt Lake Magazine* (2002).

Pizza

Big Apple Pizza
2939 E 3300 South, SLC, UT 84109
(801) 485-4534
http://bigapplepizza.citysearch.com/
$-$$, L D (M-Sa), 2-Go

Lady Liberty comes to Salt Lake. This small neighborhood pizzeria serves authentic thin-crust hand-tossed pizzas cooked in stone deck ovens like you would find in New York's Little Italy. The calzones were voted "Utah's Best" by *City Weekly.* Plus hot sandwiches, pasta entrees, salads, and the famous Bender--a pizza bread sandwich filled with crisp veges, hot meats, and melted cheeses. Lunch specials, by-the-slice, and kids menu available. A mile from Mill Creek Canyon and a heartbeat from Central Park.

Pie Pizzeria
1320 E 200 South, SLC, UT 84102
801-582-0195, www.thepie.com
c-$-$$, L D (M-Su)

1300 E 300 South, SLC, UT 84102
801-582-5700, www.thepie.com
c-$-$$, L D (M-Su), 2-Go

Voted "Best Pizza in Utah" 12 years straight. Our dough is hand rolled and hand tossed in Pie-standard, New York (thin) or Chicago (thick) styles. We use the highest quality meats, vegetables, gourmet toppings, and a blend of 100% whole milk Mozzarella, Parmesan, and Romano cheeses. Salads, "zappis," baked subs, and a large beer selection, too. We offer live music, and kids are always welcome! A University of Utah tradition.

Wasatch Pizza
820 E 400 South, SLC UT 84102
(801) 359-2300
792 E 3300 South, SLC UT 84106
(801) 466-7777
2065 E Ft. Union Blvd (7000 S.), SLC UT 84121
(801) 944-0444
1263 E Draper Pkwy (12300 S.), Draper UT 84020
(801) 533-0700
www.utahsbestpizza.com
$-$$$, L D (M-Su), 2-Go

Salt Lake's #1 selling gourmet pizza offers mouth-watering combinations that cater to discriminating tastes. We satisfy the traditionalist, culinary experimenter, carnivore, and vegetarian. Our Italian peasant crust is smothered with your choice of house-made marinara, fresh pesto, olive paste, Cajun, Alfredo, and even Dijonnaise base with over 40 toppings ranging from traditional to exotic: pepperoni and mushrooms to smoked salmon and capers. Hot wings, fresh salads, and desserts, too. Go online for special offers.

Snowbird Ski & Summer Resort

The Keyhole Junction & Cantina
Snowbird UT 84092
(801) 933-2222 x 5100
www.snowbird.com
$$, L D (M-Su)

Serving excellent Southwest fare with a touch of American. The Keyhole Junction has roasted peppers, toasted tortillas and whipped up margaritas for 27 years. Longtime favorites include Fajitas, Chile Verde, Fish Tacos and Wild Mushroom Enchiladas. Expect friendly service, delicious food and great value. The Keyhole Cantina (a private club for members) offers 21 different tequilas for that perfect margarita and local microbrews fill the taps. It's the perfect place to wind down after a day of hiking or mountain biking at the Bird during the summer. No reservations taken. (Cliff Lodge, Snowbird Entry 4)

The Aerie Restaurant
Snowbird UT 84092
(801) 933-2222 x 5500
www.snowbird.com
$$-$$$, D (Tu-Sa)

Serving New American cuisine. Spectacular mountain views seen through 15-foot windows accentuate the fine dining experience at the Aerie, high atop the resort's 10-story flagship hotel. Menu items change from winter to summer, but favorites are carried over by popular demand. The 80+ selection wine list is award-winning. Dinner reservations are recommended; resort casual attire is welcome. Lighter fare is available in the adjoining Aerie Sushi Bar & Lounge (a private club for members). (Cliff Lodge, Snowbird Entry 4)

The Steak Pit
Snowbird UT 84092
(801) 933-2222 x 4060
www.snowbird.com
$$$, D (M-Su) ⌂♥ Y

A favorite with Utahns for over 30 years, the Steak Pit offers aged steaks and fresh seafood cooked to perfection and served in a rustic steakhouse setting. Each table gets a bottomless bowl of salad filled with fresh greens, cherry tomatoes and home-made croutons. Named "One of America's Best Restaurants," you might even like the Steak pit as much as the staff members, many of whom have worked there for over 20 years! No reservations taken. (Snowbird Center, Snowbird Entry 2)

Thai

Bangkok Thai
1400 Foothill Village, SLC UT 84108
(801) 582-THAI (8424)
www.bangkokthai.com
$-$$, L D (M-Sa), D (Su), 2-Go ⌂♥ Y ⌔ ⌱

Voted "Best East Asian" by *Salt Lake Magazine* since 1997. Offering the finest in Thai cuisine, featuring traditional rice, noodle, and wok-fried entrees plus curry dishes made as mild or spicy as you like it. Extensive vegetarian specialties, or join us for "Meatless Monday". Award-winning wine list. Early-bird specials nightly, or go online for other discount offers. Need extra carbs? Then try the fried bananas for dessert.

Vegetarian & Natural Foods

Sage's Cafe
473 East 300 South, SLC UT 84111
801-322-3790; www.sagescafe.com
$-$$, L D (W-Su), 2-Go ⌂♥⌔

Sage's provides an eclectic, cross-cultural menu featuring organic foods and a fresh selection of worldly flavors--all created in house. We offer an impressive selection of beer and wine, triple certified coffees, a great tea menu, fresh pastries, raw foods, and a unique atmosphere. Nightly Chef's Specials feature the freshest seasonal produce. Vegetarian food never tasted so good! Voted "Best Vegetarian" by *City Weekly*.

Oasis Cafe
151 S 500 East, SLC UT 84102
(801) 322-0404
$-$$, B L D (M-Su), 2-Go ⌂♥ Y ⌔

As unique and spiritual as your last ride, the Oasis Cafe offers excellent heart-healthy delights from all over the world. The eco-friendly staff has created a gourmet menu that matches the finest quality around while using organic and natural ingredients. Fresh squeezed juices, international coffees, and an extensive wine and beer list all add to the natural energy connection not far from the trailhead high we have all experienced. Next to the Golden Braid Bookstore.

Wild Oats Natural Marketplace
1131 E Wilmington (2200 South), SLC, UT 84106
(801) 359-7913

645 E 400 South, SLC UT 84102
(801) 366 7401
www.wildoats.com
$, B L D (M-Su), 2-Go ⌔

Discover the world of natural and organic food. We have the largest selection of organic produce in Utah, plus a full line of natural groceries and bulk foods; fresh natural meats, poultry, seafood, and dairy; botanical body care; and pure vitamins, supplements, and herbs. Our full-service deli includes a juice and java bar, sushi and salad bar, fresh baked goods, and a wide variety of vegetarian/vegan dishes for a light lunch or full meal.

Vietnamese & Chinese

Cafe Trang
818 S Main, SLC UT 84101
(801) 539-1638

4835 S Highland Dr., SLC UT84117
(801) 278-8889
$-$$, L D (M-Su), 2-Go ⌂♥ Y

A long-time favorite for Salt Lakers seeking authentic Vietnamese and Chinese cuisine. The expansive menu offers traditional Lo Mein and seafood with vermicelli to the chef's special spicy curry chicken and honey walnut shrimp. Trang's spring rolls with peanut sauce are a must, and the house rice noodles are delicate and smoky. Abundant vegetarian selections--papaya salad and fried bean curd-marinated vegetables are favorites. Voted "Best Vietnamese," so you are sure to find pleasure in every bite.

SOUTHERN WASATCH

37

Lambert Park

Location:	Alpine
Length:	Up to 12 miles
Type:	Loops
Tread:	Singletracks
Physically:	Moderate
Technically:	2⁺-3⁺ (Variably smooth, sandy, rutted, and rocky trails)
Gain:	Variable but less than 1,000 feet
Dogs:	On leash

GO □
NO ■ | JAN | FEB | MAR | APR | MAY | JUN | JUL | AUG | SEP | OCT | NOV | DEC |

Stop the presses! There's new singletrack to be ridden! We're not talking about the one-lane dirt track havens of Park City or Brian Head, but of Alpine. "What the . . . heck," you say? Alpine's newly designated open space, Lambert Park, boasts about 12 miles of multi-use trails within its compact two-square-mile size. Granted that's hardly epic, and you're bound to a high desert plain of sage and scrub oak, but the riding is suprisingly good. Poppies bloom in the spring, and the brushy trees turn to tawny crimson in the fall. You can even sneak out during winter when the trails are frozen. And with Lone Peak and Box Elder Peak towering overhead, the town's name really strikes a cord.

Details

A t the time of publication, only a couple of trails were "official;" the rest were being considered for inclusion by the Alpine Trails Committee. Trail signs consisted of small wooden plaques placed discretely in the brush next to trail junctions. So, if this is your first go round, you might be scratching your head a lot trying to figure things out. Don't worry, be happy. Wanderlust. You can't get helplessly lost.

Directions can be exasperating, but this 7-mile cloverleaf circuit has a good flow and takes in most of the trails. It consists of three parts: a north loop (Rodeo-Middle Trails), a middle loop (Poppy-Ruin Trails), and a south loop (Zag-Ziggy-Corkscrew-Flank Trails). The north and middle loops are moderate, whereas the south loop is moderate⁺ because of more abrupt climbs and rougher tread. It's all good.

From the Rodeo Grounds, pick up Rodeo Trail just down the access road on the south side. You'll dive into a gully with high-banked turns that try to shake you from your saddle like an angry Brahma. Cross a road and veer right on River Trail, which takes a more mellow approach. You'll cross several dirt roads before you come to the Orientation Course kiosk near the L.D.S. church (alternate trailhead). Turn almost 180 degrees, and head up Middle Trail. Cross the water tank dirt road (you can see the cement reservoir uphill), pass Ziggy Trail, and veer right on Poppy Trail, so named for the orange blooms that adorn the area during the spring. Climb through the brush to a Y-junction, and fork left on Ruin Trail. Pass the old stone building, and freewheel back to Middle Trail. "Huck it" off the small jumps—or not—and dodge through the oak and maple. If you've had enough, then take Middle Trail north for a moderate climb back to Rodeo Trail; then take the Uphill Trail to the Rodeo Grounds. Watch out for fast-approaching downhill riders when you re-enter the gulch.

For the south loop, return to the familiar junction of Middle and Ziggy Trails. Climb either Ziggy or Zag Trails, cross the water tank road, and poke around until you find Corkscrew Trail heading south. (If you find yourself way up on the foothills on a tight choppy trail, you are on the Bonneville Shoreline Trail, which is proposed to run all the way to the mouth of American Fork Canyon.) Corkscrew Trail is a downhill delight—fast and furious. Don't let speed blur your anticipated turn onto Flank Trail forking right as you approach the houses. If you exit to Bald Mountain Drive, you went a bit too far. Now chug up Flank Trail to the junction of River and Middle Trails to complete the south loop. Head up to the Rodeo Grounds by climbing Middle Trail, retracing your tracks briefly on Rodeo, and veering off on Uphill Trail.

Got the itch for more miles? Then take another lap (try riding in reverse), or add on Spring Trail for a 2-mile loop and several hundred feet of climbing around the Rodeo Grounds. After several flights at Lambert Park, you'll unlock the right combination of trails that will make you want to return time and again.

! Know Before You Go

• Some trails may cross onto private property. Obey all signs restricting travel. Trails may be closed, rerouted, or renamed without notice.
• This area can be dangerously hot at midday during midsummer.
• Rattlesnakes are know to inhabit these foothills.
• *Fido Factor:* Dogs must be leashed.

? Maps & More Information

• USGS 1:24,000: Lehi and Timpanogos Cave, Utah
• City of Alpine: (801) 756-6347

♪ Trailhead Access

Take Exit 287 from I-15, travel 5.5 miles east on UT 92, go left/north on UT 74 at the four-way stop light, and drive 1.8 miles to Alpine. Go right on 200 North then left on 200 East (becomes Grove Drive), and continue nearly 2 miles to a T-junction where Oak Ridge Drive is to the left. Turn right, travel .3 mile, and turn right on a dirt road for the Rodeo Grounds. Park next to the arena.

SOUTHERN WASATCH

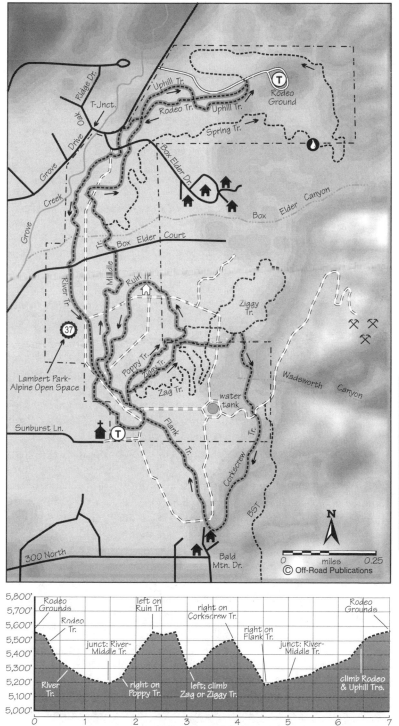

SOUTHERN WASATCH

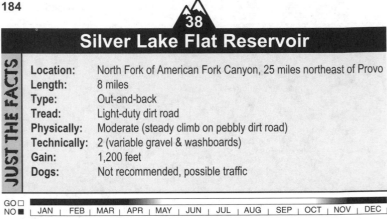

38
Silver Lake Flat Reservoir

JUST THE FACTS

Location:	North Fork of American Fork Canyon, 25 miles northeast of Provo
Length:	8 miles
Type:	Out-and-back
Tread:	Light-duty dirt road
Physically:	Moderate (steady climb on pebbly dirt road)
Technically:	2 (variable gravel & washboards)
Gain:	1,200 feet
Dogs:	Not recommended, possible traffic

GO ☐
NO ■ | JAN | FEB | MAR | APR | MAY | JUN | JUL | AUG | SEP | OCT | NOV | DEC |

WHY SHOULD U RIDE THIS TRAIL

The ride to Silver Lake Flat Reservoir captures the scenic beauty of American Fork Canyon without having to tackle the area's more demanding singletracks. The lightly graveled and washboarded dirt road is a steady climb, so endurance is more important than precise handling skills. With the Mount Timpanogos Wilderness to the south and the Lone Peak Wilderness to the north and west, the sky is filled with alpine motifs. These mountain images reflect off the lake's mirrored surface on a calm day.

Details

From the Tibble Fork Reservoir trailhead pedal up the paved Forest Road No. 008. At the Granite Flat Campground, the road turns sharply right, becomes dirt and gravel, and rises at a moderate grade (tech 2). The climb steepens to a heart-taxing grind past the trailhead for Deer Creek and Dry Creek Trails, but the sight of Tibble Fork Reservoir framed by the massive flank of Mount Timpanogos eases the burden.

A faint doubletrack forks right and is blocked by boulders at a sharp left bend in the main road (**m2.3**). This is the Old Sheep Trail (see Option). Press onward. Soon you are greeted with wondrous sights of the Alpine Ridge, which separates American Fork and Little Cottonwood Canyons, while the weighty presence of Box Elder Peak bears down on your left shoulder. Its ravaged slopes attest to winter's avalanches.

Take a lap around Silver Lake Flat Reservoir (**m3.3**), passing through the Silver Lake Trail trailhead and stepping over the creek on the north side; then simply retrace your tracks back down to Tibble Fork Reservoir. Mount Timpanogos keeps watch over you the entire way.

Option: Old Sheep Trail

Why ride dusty dirt roads when you can explore uncharted doubletracks and singletracks? The old sheepherder's road is a quick, exciting alternative to the otherwise straightforward return from Silver Lake Flat Reservoir. This side route is 3.2 miles long and offers eventful moments, culminating with a cold, deep crossing of American Fork River.

When descending from Silver Lake Flat Reservoir, turn off on the faint doubletrack blocked by boulders (see **m2.3**). Enjoy the unobstructed

SOUTHERN WASATCH

sights of Tibble Fork Reservoir and Mount Timpanogos; then as the trail bends north, watch out for tree limbs and deadfall boobie-trapping the way. Ford the shallow outlet creek of Silver Lake Flat Reservoir and descend steeply on the rugged trail (tech 3$^+$) to American Fork River. If there are no logs to step across, then you must shoulder your bike and jump in. The stream can be icy cold and swift flowing, so grab a stick for balance and cross quickly but cautiously. Loop back to Tibble Fork by descending the dirt road 1.5 miles.

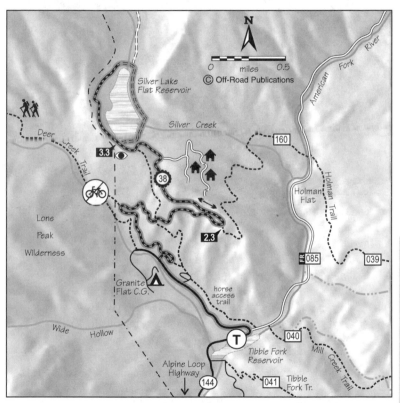

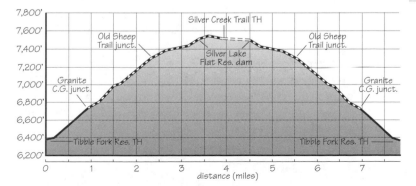

The rugged beauty of the Wasatch Range unfolds at Silver Lake Flat Reservoir.

Know Before You Go

- American Fork Canyon/UT 92 is a recreation fee area: $3 per vehicle for a three-day pass.
- If you're taking the optional Sheep Trail, you should check the flow of American Fork River before you go. The stream can be fast flowing and dangerous to ford during May and June.
- Motorists and OHVs are common on the road to Silver Lake Flat Reservoir and up the North Fork of American Fork Canyon.
- The Tibble Fork trailhead has an outhouse and a water tap.
- Timpanogos Cave National Monument has a snack bar and a pay telephone.
- *Fido Factor:* Dogs are not recommended because of possible traffic.

? Maps & More Information

- USGS 1:24,000: Dromedary Peak and Timpanogos Cave, Utah
- Uinta National Forest (Pleasant Grove Ranger Dist.): (801) 785-3563

Trailhead Access

From I-15, take Exit 287 (Alpine, Highland). Travel east on UT 92 then up American Fork Canyon. Turn left 2.5 miles past Timpanogos Cave National Monument on UT 144 for North Fork. Park in the big lot on the north side of Tibble Fork Reservoir.

SOUTHERN WASATCH

39

Ridge Trail 157 (Ant Knolls-Forest Lake)

<table>
<tr><td rowspan="10">JUST THE FACTS</td></tr>
<tr><td>Location:</td><td>North Fork of American Fork Canyon, 25 miles northeast of Provo</td></tr>
<tr><td>Length:</td><td>13.7 miles</td></tr>
<tr><td>Type:</td><td>Loop w/ out-and-back</td></tr>
<tr><td>Tread:</td><td>6.8 miles singletrack, 4.3 miles dirt road, 2.6 miles doubletrack</td></tr>
<tr><td>Physically:</td><td>Strenuous (solid climb to Pole Line Pass, intermittent climbs on rolling singletrack); less strenuous if you ride only either half</td></tr>
<tr><td>Technically:</td><td>2-4 (variable rocks & ruts on dirt roads; tight singletrack w/ smooth & choppy tread)</td></tr>
<tr><td>Gain:</td><td>2,600 feet</td></tr>
<tr><td>Dogs:</td><td>Yes on Tr. 157; not recommended on dirt roads</td></tr>
</table>

GO ☐
NO ■ | JAN | FEB | MAR | APR | MAY | JUN | JUL | AUG | SEP | OCT | NOV | DEC |

If you want to experience Ridge Trail 157, one of Utah's great alpine singletracks, but don't have a shuttle available for the standard one-way ride, then tap into the trail's northern segment, and loop right back to your car at the same time. In doing so, you'll savor 157's sweetest parts and avoid the nasty descent off the mountain to Mill Canyon Spring. Best yet, the once mandatory bike-on-shoulders hike over the Ant Knolls has been replaced with a scenic contouring trail around it's west side. There, you'll catch bird's-eye views of the upper American Fork basin and of the peaks that profile the tops of Snowbird and Alta ski areas. You'll culminate the ride with a thrilling descent past Forest Lake.

Details

From Dutchman Flat, pedal up the dirt road and cross the bridge over American Fork River. One-half mile farther, fork right on FR 085 for Wasatch Mountain State Park, Midway, and Heber. The 3-mile climb to Pole Line Pass (**m3.9**) is steady and moderately strenuous with tread varying from smooth packed dirt to pea gravel to thick aggregate. Just do it!

If the climb knocked the wind out of you, skip the next out-and-back section, and head south on Trail 157 to loop past Forest Lake; otherwise, head north on Trail 157/GWT, and climb the singletrack through the aspens. (The nearby doubletrack gets you to the same place.) Watch for the usually signed singletrack forking left just past the usually dry livestock pond. It switchbacks aggressively up through a stand of aspens to a small saddle on the ridge. In years past, the GWT went straight up the big hill for the first of two murderous portages. Now, the GWT contours the ridge's west side through pristine aspens and across sloping meadows that open up to stunning views of distant Mount Timpanogos and nearby Alpine Ridge. Snowbird's tram summit can be seen atop Hidden Peak, and the Bird's Mineral Basin area is one of the biggest ski bowls around. Sugarloaf

SOUTHERN WASATCH

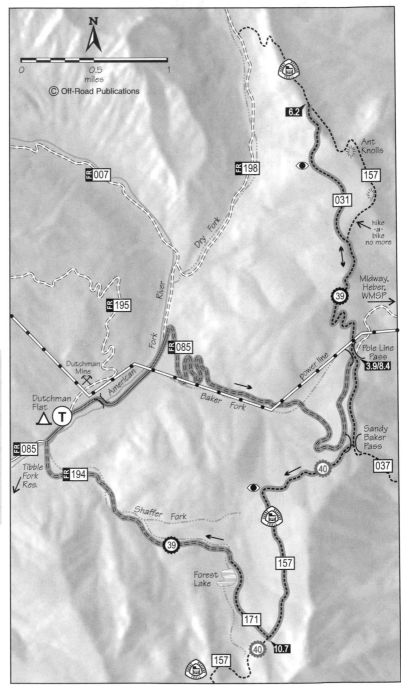

and Devils Castle define neighboring Alta Ski Area. Parts of the new GWT are narrow and choppy (tech 3-4), so watch your front wheel; a fall could be disastrous.

Turn around when you regain the ridge north of Ant Knolls (**m6.2**) to retrace your tracks to Pole Line Pass (**m8.4**). (Yes, you could take the GWT north and descend Dry Fork Trail to upper American Fork Canyon, but don't bother—it's nasty. Besides, the return to Pole Line Pass is too sweet to pass up.) Take Trail 157 south of Pole Line Pass and up a sharp climb that few bikers can ride; then surf through thick sand and rock to Sandy Baker Pass. Angle right to roll through the mixed timber and to bend around the side of

Snowbird's Mineral Fork Basin backdrops the GWT around Ant Knolls.

Mill Canyon Peak. Forest Lake comes into view far below along with a huge swath of timber that has been bowled down from repetitive snow avalanches. In the summer, the trail-side flowers grow so high that you'll take "face-shots" the whole way. About one mile of steady climbing on tight tread (tech 2^+-3^+) takes you to the Forest Lake Trail turnoff (**m10.7**).

It's a steep, straight shot down to the lake on eroded singletrack (tech 4), so ride skillfully to keep from locking up your rear wheel and making matters worse for future riders. Wrap around the lake's north shore, and connect with a doubletrack signed for Shafer Fork Trail and Dutchman Flat. (It dips into a gully.) The rutted and rock-studded jeep road (tech 3^+) drops quickly to American Fork River where you'll face a hub-deep ford. It's ridable, if you don't hesitate, but you'll get soaked just the same. Dutchman Flat is .3 mile uphill.

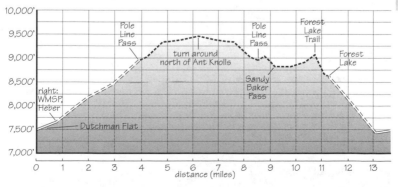

SOUTHERN WASATCH

Know Before You Go

- American Fork Canyon/UT 92 is a recreation fee area: $3 per vehicle for a three-day pass.
- American Fork Canyon and Snake Creek Roads are popular with 4x4s and OHVs, especially on weekends.
- Ridge Trail 157 is popular with equestrians, so ride cautiously and be ready to yield to horses.
- Sheep herding is common in this area.
- The Tibble Fork Reservoir staging area has a water tap and an outhouse. Timpanogos Cave National Monument has a snack bar and a pay telephone.
- *Fido Factor:* Ridge Trail 157 is dog friendly, but the road up to Pole Line Pass can have motorized traffic, and the rocks can be hard on paws. Forest Lake is the only reliable water source.

? Maps & More Information

- USGS 1:24,000: Brighton, Utah
- Uinta National Forest (Pleasant Grove Ranger Dist.): (801) 785-3563

Trailhead Access

From I-15, take Exit 287 (Alpine, Highland), and travel east on UT 92 to American Fork Canyon. Turn left on UT 144 for North Fork 2.5 miles past Timpanogos Cave National Monument. Drive 2.3 miles to Tibble Fork Reservoir; then continue up American Fork Canyon on FR 085. This dirt road is passable by passenger cars but is rough, especially the switchbacks about 2.8 miles up. Park at Dutchman Flat (backcountry campsites), 4.6 miles from Tibble Fork Reservoir.

Big climbs net you sweet singletrack.

SOUTHERN WASATCH

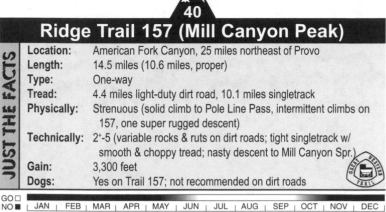

40

Ridge Trail 157 (Mill Canyon Peak)

JUST THE FACTS		
Location:	American Fork Canyon, 25 miles northeast of Provo	
Length:	14.5 miles (10.6 miles, proper)	
Type:	One-way	
Tread:	4.4 miles light-duty dirt road, 10.1 miles singletrack	
Physically:	Strenuous (solid climb to Pole Line Pass, intermittent climbs on 157, one super rugged descent)	
Technically:	2⁺-5 (variable rocks & ruts on dirt roads; tight singletrack w/ smooth & choppy tread; nasty descent to Mill Canyon Spr.)	
Gain:	3,300 feet	
Dogs:	Yes on Trail 157; not recommended on dirt roads	

GO ☐
NO ■ | JAN | FEB | MAR | APR | MAY | JUN | JUL | AUG | SEP | OCT | NOV | DEC |

Like Salt Lake's Wasatch Crest Trail, American Fork Canyon's Ridge Trail 157 is also a world-class singletrack that traces the top of the Wasatch Range. It requires strong legs and acclimated lungs to tackle the numerous climbs plus a full repertoire of riding skills to handle the technical descents. The trail itself is top notch—a blend of buffed and rugged singletracks—but the scenery is truly superlative. The Alpine Ridge, home to the Lone Peak Wilderness, catches your eye early on then fades away as Mount Timpanogos grows to majestic proportions from the ride's mid-point to its end. As solid as these mountains seem, glaciers made easy work of grinding down the volumes of rock into deep bowls and canyons separated by sharp 11,000-foot peaks.

Details

Ridge Trail 157, proper, is 10.6 miles one-way from Pole Line Pass to the summit of the Alpine Scenic Loop Highway. This version starts at Dutchman Flat in American Fork Canyon with a 4-mile warm-up climb to Pole Line Pass because the dirt road is rough on cars.

From Dutchman Flat, pedal north and cross the bridge over American Fork River. Fork right .5 mile farther on FR 085 (signed for Wasatch Mountain State Park, Midway, and Heber), and climb 3 miles to Pole Line Pass (**m3.9**) on alternating smooth, rutted, and choppy doubletrack (tech 2-3⁺). Head south on Ridge Trail 157/GWT (signed for Forest Lake and Alpine Loop), and attack a devilish hill that is nearly impossible to ride; then surf through loose sand and rock down to Sandy Baker Pass. Trail 157 stays right/southwest on a rolling contour through mixed timber (tech 2⁺-3⁺). Sweet!

As you wrap around the flank of Mill Canyon Peak, a tremendous panorama unfolds with American Fork Canyon overshadowed by Box Elder Peak due west and the Alpine Ridge to the north. An eagle's eye can spot Snowbird Resort's tram summit atop Hidden Peak; more conspicuous is the backside of Alta Ski Area's Devils Castle to the east. Below the trail, an swath of bowled down trees conjures up images of Mount Saint

SOUTHERN WASATCH

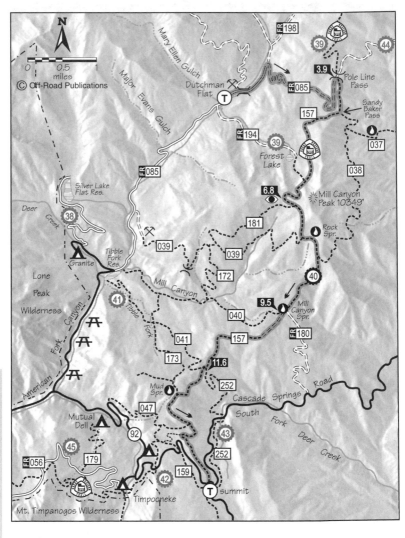

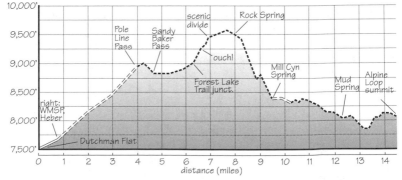

Helen's fiery volcanic winds, but here the fury of winter's avalanches has produced similar results. Climb steadily on tight tread through pockets of aspens while taking wild-flower "face shots" during the height of summer. Just past the junction with Forest Lake Trail, the path

Tibble Fork Reservoir and Box Elder Peak.

crosses a talus slope then tilts upward for periodic hike-a-biking to a small ridge (**m6.8**). Wham! You're slapped in the face with a shocking view of Mount Timpanogos. The Alpine Ridge becomes a fleeting memory

The trail contours past the junction with Holman Trail (see "Option") then comes to Rock Spring. Pass the junction with East Ridge Trail, forking left, and hunker down for 157's notoriously nasty descent to Mill Canyon Spring. Through years of use and abuse by a variety of users, the trail has become a deeply entrenched, rock- and rubble-filled, fall-line drop (tech 4-5). Enter the clearing at Mill Canyon Spring (**m9.5**), and head due south on a doubletrack. (Mill Canyon Trail forks west, see "Option.")

A series of rugged ridge-top pulses and quick paint-shaker descents (tech 3-4) take you to the combined junction of Tibble Fork Trail, No. 041, and South Fork Deer Creek Trail, No. 252 (**m11.6**). Thereafter, 157 rolls more smoothly along the now-subtle ridge. Bound over a half-dozen log bars down to the Mud Spring junction; then savor smooth trail that undulates past scenic outlooks of Mount Timpanogos. A swift descent takes you past Pine Hollow Trail, No. 047, and curves around a grassy meadow. Don't think you're home free just yet because there's a bugger of a climb past the Salamander Flat Trail junction, plus another grinder before you reach the summit trailhead.

Option: Mill Canyon Trail Loop

"We don't need no stinkin' shuttle," you say? Then make an 18-mile loop out of Trail 157 by starting at Tibble Fork Reservoir and ending on Mill Canyon Trail. You'll begin by climbing 8.5 miles and 2,600 feet to Pole Line Pass, just to get warmed up! Hop on Ridge Trail 157, and take it all the way to Mill Canyon Spring. Now, veer right and descend 3.5 miles on Mill Canyon Trail, No. 040. There's never a dull moment, as the trail varies from sweetly buffed to viscously rocky (tech 2-4[+]). When you exit the canyon, you must ford American Fork River to return to the parking area. Don't think you'll keep your feet dry by riding across instead of fording because it's hub deep in spots, but ridable.

SOUTHERN WASATCH

Mountains everywhere: Alpine Ridge behind and Mount Timpanogos in front.

Option: Old Trench Road, No. 181

Old Trench Road offers a reasonable alternative to descending Mill Canyon Trail if your goal is to return to Tibble Fork Reservoir. Is it worth it? It depends on your desire to go where other bikers don't and, more importantly, on your tolerance for rugged trails.

The unsigned Old Trench Road, No. 181, forks right from Trail 157 about .1 mile south of the hike-a-bike at **m6.8**. Look for a lone pine tree with roots sprawled out like an octopus' tentacles on the left side of 157. The path conspicuously follows one of the old erosion control trenches that was cut into the mountain in the 1930s. After a 1.5-mile contour on highly scenic but bumpy singletrack (tech 3⁺), the path descends to a meadow, angles left, and drops to a junction with Holman Trail, No 039. Go right and descend .5 mile to a multisigned junction; go left on Holman Ridge-Cabin Flat Trail, No. 172 (Holman Trail, No. 039, goes right/north). Descend entrenched tread that has been chewed up by horses and motorcycles (tech 3⁺-4⁺) to Mill Canyon Trail in a meadow. Go right and drop down Mill Canyon to American Fork River at Tibble Fork Reservoir. Climbing this route to 157 is torturous (say hike-a-bike).

Option: Holman Trail, No. 039

That's the easy way. Holman Trail is more a pack trail than a mountain bike trail, and you'll be "packing" your mountain bike regularly if you pursue it. Here's the scoop if you have to know. Holman Trail forks right from Trail 157 just before Rock Spring. The initial descent is tight, steep, and loose (tech 3⁺) then becomes steeper and looser after a sharp left bend in a grove of aspens (tech 4⁺-5). Pick you way over rubbly limestone on a faint trail, and angle northward down into a gulch. Now you've done it! Pass a spring, and struggle uphill on choppy tread and through bristly brush that tears at your exposed flesh to the junction with Old Trench Road, No 181. Descend left to the multisigned junction where Holman Ridge-Cabin Flat Trail, No. 172, goes left/south to Mill Canyon Trail, but go right/north on Holman Trail, No. 039—sucker!

You'll descend on pretty good tread at first then climb steadily on an overgrown trail to a highpoint. Go left and drop down rotted tread to a saddle at the base of a knoll (tech 5). Go right, hack your way along the trail, and portage across a landslide. Finally, skitter down the horse-worn trail (tech 5) past a mine, and take a doubletrack down to American Fork Canyon. The reservoir is 1.4 miles downhill. Don't even think about going up Holman!

ⓘ Know Before You Go

* American Fork Canyon/UT 92 is a recreation fee area; $3 per vehicle for a three-day pass.
* American Fork Canyon and Snake Creek Roads are popular with 4x4s and OHVs, especially on weekends.
* Ridge Trail 157 is popular with equestrians, so ride cautiously and be ready to yield to horses.
* Sheep herding is common around Pole Line Pass.
* Rock Spring is a reliable water source, but it's only a trickle.
* The Tibble Fork Reservoir trailhead has a water tap and an outhouse.
* *Fido Factor:* Ridge Trail 157 is dog friendly, but the road up to Pole Line Pass can have motorized traffic. There is water at Rock and Mill Canyon Springs, but over all this is a long, hard run for a dog.

❓ Maps & More Information

* USGS 1:24,000: Aspen Grove, Brighton, Dromedary Peak, and Timpanogos Cave, Utah
* Uinta National Forest (Pleasant Grove Ranger Dist.): (801) 785-3563

Trailhead Access

From I-15, take Exit 287 (Alpine, Highland), and travel east on UT 92 then up American Fork Canyon. Stay straight at the North Fork junction 2.5 miles past Timpanogos Cave National Monument, and drive 6 miles more on the Alpine Scenic Loop/UT 92 to the trailhead/parking area at the road's summit. In the shuttle vehicle, return to the North Fork junction, and drive 2.3 miles to Tibble Fork Reservoir; then take FR 085 up American Fork Canyon 4.5 miles to Dutchman Flat (backcountry campsites). This dirt road is usually passable by passenger cars but is rough, especially the switchbacks about 2.8 miles up.

SOUTHERN WASATCH

41
Tibble Fork Trail & More

Location:	American Fork Canyon, 25 miles northeast of Provo
Length:	15.9 miles
Type:	Loop
Tread:	9.1 miles singletrack, 6.8 miles pavement
Physically:	Strenuous (two solid climbs & one wild descent)
Technically:	2-5 (shoulderless paved roads; smooth to lightly choppy trails; eroded, steep drops on Tibble Fork Tr.)
Gain:	2,800 feet
Dogs:	No, paved roads; yes, trails only if you shuttle

GO □
NO ■ | JAN | FEB | MAR | APR | MAY | JUN | JUL | AUG | SEP | OCT | NOV | DEC |

Here's another installment of the many mountain biking opportunities harbored in American Fork Canyon and anchored by Ridge Trail 157. Gravity is both foe and friend on this double-climb, double-descent circuit that incorporates the Great Western, South Fork Deer Creek, and Tibble Fork Trails. The first two offer consistently good tread and biker-friendly hills. The latter, however, is more Jekyll-and-Hyde, combining sharp, technical drops with remarkably buffed tread. A speedy descent and short climb on paved roads round out the loop.

Details

Head out from the Pine Hollow trailhead by climbing 1.5 miles on the Alpine Loop Highway; then turn right for Timpooneke Campground, and go to the day-use Timpooneke trailhead. Take the Great Western Trail (GWT) past the outhouses toward the wilderness, and cross the footbridge to stay on the GWT. (No bikes in the wilderness.) The mostly smooth trail rises gradually above the creek through shadowy conifers, but there are several quick little ups that will make you shift down and pedal hard briefly (tech 2-3). Go left at a junction to cross the Alpine Loop Highway.

Baby-butt smooth tread smothered with pine needles rises steadily to a small ridge, which offers a view of Mount Timpanogos that will make your eyes bug out. Continue straight, and drop through the timber to a multisigned junction at a footbridge just north of Salamander Flat, or catch a cutoff trail to the right that takes you through Salamander Flat (**m3.4**). Regardless, take the trails east for the summit trailhead. You'll cross a little creek, struggle up a rough hill (tech 4⁺), and climb gradually to where the trail crosses the road. Continue climbing aggressively up the hollow on smooth and choppy tread (tech 3⁺) to the summit trailhead (**m4.5**).

Pick up the trail to Aspen Grove, No. 050, behind the outhouses and take it .1 mile; then fork left on South Fork Deer Creek Trail, No. 252, and cross the Alpine Loop Highway at the Cascade Springs Road junction. South Fork Deer Creek Trail descends directly through mixed timber then down a long grassy, aspen-lined hollow (tech 2⁺-3⁺). Control your speed because the trail is popular with equestrians and sight lines can be limited. Cross Cascade Springs Road, drop down to the footbridge over the creek, and settle into climbing 1.7 miles back up to the ridge. A couple of quick, sharp pitches near the bottom yield to steady, moderate climbing through darkened fir trees. Intersect Ridge Trail 157, and go straight over to descend Tibble Fork Trail, No. 041 (**m7.9**).

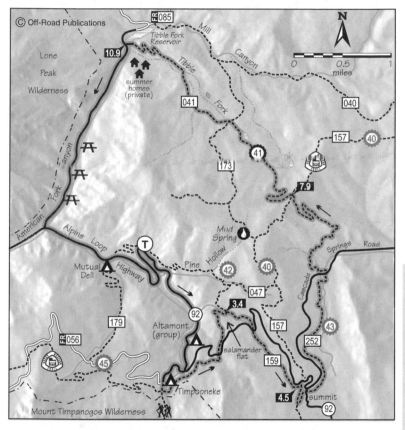

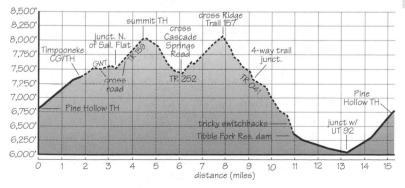

Mount Timpanogos dwarfs James and Peri on Trail 157.

Tibble Fork starts out silky smooth (tech 2⁺), arcs around a pair of switchbacks, and then drops quickly down a roughened hill (tech 4). Roll briefly on smooth tread; then bounce down another eroded hill swarming with roots. Got the hang of it? Curve past a marsh where beavers have been busy, and take in the distant view of the Alpine Ridge; then hunker down for another rough, tricky drop to the four-way junction with Mud Springs Trail. More of the same awaits as you continue down lower Tibble Fork Trail, savoring the smooth, sweet sections and muscling your bike down the choppy parts. The real fun comes after you pass the trail to the summer homes and cross the creek. The trail hangs high on the edge of an oak-timbered canyon and drops you like a pinball through several remarkably tight, eroded turns to the reservoir's dam (tech 4⁺, **m10.9**). Can you ride the turns? Without skidding?

Singletrack is over. What a thrill! To close the loop, freewheel 3 miles down the road to the junction with the Alpine Loop Highway, and chug 2 miles back up to the Pine Hollow Trailhead.

Option: Tibble Fork Beeline (13 miles, loop, mod⁺, 2,300-foot gain)

Naturally, you can skip the South Fork Deer Creek Trail segment and make a beeline for Tibble Fork Trail along Ridge Trail 157. When you reach the junction north of Salamander Flat (**m3.4** above), stay left for Pine Hollow, No. 047, and climb to Trail 157. Then take Trail 157 past Mud Springs and to the Tibble Fork Trail/South Fork Deer Creek Trail junction. Descend Tibble Fork Trail to close the loop as described above. This option cuts off a few miles and a big chunk of climbing. As a corollary, ride

Postcard-perfect scenery is everywhere on the Tibble Fork Loop.

the main route as described to the Alpine Loop Highway summit and take Ridge Trail 157 north to Tibble Fork Trail, or duck onto Mud Springs Trail and shortcut upper Tibble Fork Trail. So many options!

! Know Before You Go

- American Fork Canyon/UT 92 is a recreation fee area: $3.00 per vehicle for a three-day pass.
- These trails are popular with hikers, bikers, motorcycles, and equestrians, so expect and respect other users.
- Stay to the far right side of paved roads, and be alert to motorists.
- If you loath ending with a climb (back to Pine Hollow trailhead), then embark from the North Fork junction. Road-side parking is limited.
- *Fido Factor:* Dogs are not recommended because of the paved road sections. If your dog must come along, then shuttle between Tibble Fork Reservoir and the Timpooneke trailhead.

? Maps & More Information

- USGS 1:24,000: Aspen Grove and Timpanogos Cave, Utah
- Uinta National Forest (Pleasant Grove Ranger Dist.): (801) 785-3563

Trailhead Access

From I-15, take Exit 287 (Alpine, Highland), and travel east on UT 92 then up American Fork Canyon. Stay straight at the North Fork junction 2.5 miles past Timpanogos Cave National Monument, and drive 1.9 miles more on the Alpine Loop/UT 92 to the Pine Hollow trailhead.

SOUTHERN WASATCH

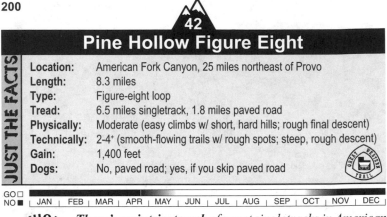

42
Pine Hollow Figure Eight

JUST THE FACTS

Location:	American Fork Canyon, 25 miles northeast of Provo
Length:	8.3 miles
Type:	Figure-eight loop
Tread:	6.5 miles singletrack, 1.8 miles paved road
Physically:	Moderate (easy climbs w/ short, hard hills; rough final descent)
Technically:	2-4⁺ (smooth-flowing trails w/ rough spots; steep, rough descent)
Gain:	1,400 feet
Dogs:	No, paved road; yes, if you skip paved road

GO □
NO ■ | JAN | FEB | MAR | APR | MAY | JUN | JUL | AUG | SEP | OCT | NOV | DEC

There's an intricate web of sweet singletracks in American Fork Canyon between the Pine Hollow trailhead and the Alpine Loop Highway summit trailhead. Some trails are easy, some are tough, and some ride better in a specific direction. You can spend days exploring all the nooks and crannies to piece together a sensible route on your own, or you can follow this figure-eight loop and sample most of the trails at one time. It's a real dandy, and given all the options, it's suitable for a wide range of bikers. In addition to great singletrack riding, you'll feast your eyes on one of northern Utah's most spectacular landmarks: Mount Timpanogos. In summer, the trail-side meadows burst with wildflowers; in autumn, huge groves of aspens drape the mountains in a shawl of golden fleece.

Details

From the Pine Hollow trailhead, pedal up the paved Alpine Loop Highway/UT 92 for 1.5 miles to the Timpooneke Campground junction, and go to the day-use parking area for the Mount Timpanogos Wilderness. Take the wilderness access trail past the outhouse, and cross the footbridge to follow the Great Western Trail (GWT). (No bikes in the wilderness, naturally.) The mostly smooth trail rises gradually above the creek through shadowy conifers, but there are several quick little ups that will make you shift down and pedal hard briefly (tech 2-3). Go left at a junction to cross the Alpine Loop Highway.

Baby-butt-smooth tread smothered with pine needles rises steadily to a small ridge, which offers a view of Mount Timpanogos that will make your eyes bug out. Dart into the timber and drop to a junction at a footbridge (**m3.3**), signed "Salamander Flat (right), Timpooneke TH (reverse), Summit TH (straight), Pine Hollow/GWT (left)." You'll return to this junction after making a loop.

Head left to Pine Hollow on silky tread that pierces opaque fir trees; the trail then exits to a small meadow at the Pine Hollow Trail junction (**m3.8**). Stay straight/right for a short, strenuous climb up the narrow hollow to Ridge Trail 157. Take 157 right/south, curve around the meadow, and climb gradually to the upper Salamander Flat Trail junction. There's

SOUTHERN WASATCH

a tough climb ahead on Trail 157 (tech 4) followed by a second one that's half as hard. (See "Option" for a bailout down Salamander Flat Trail.)

From the west edge of the summit parking area (**m5.8**), take the path signed for Salamander Flat. It starts out by staying close to the road then eases down a hollow, crossing the rocky creek gully several times (tech 3). Cross the road and continue freewheeling, but watch out for one rough drop (tech 4). Come to a four-way junction and stay straight for the GWT; left goes to Salamander Flat (big backcountry camping area), and right rises back to Trail 157 on the Salamander Flat Trail. Cross a trickling creek, and stay straight/right again to return to the familiar junction at the footbridge just north of Salamander Flat (**m6.9**).

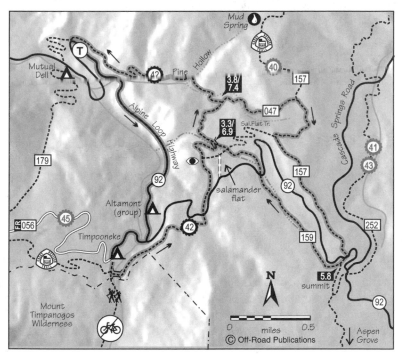

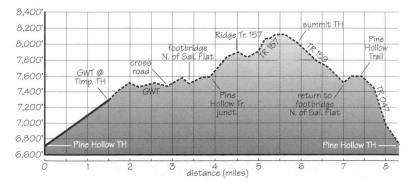

SOUTHERN WASATCH

So many trails; so much fun.

Ride up to Pine Hollow Trail again (**m7.4**), but this time go left and take it 1.3 miles down to the trailhead to complete the ride. This last stretch is the most technical with root and rock drops; tight, eroded tread; and a set of angular, rough switchbacks that are almost impossible to ride (tech 3^+-5). An easier way out is to retrace your tracks to the Timpooneke trailhead and return on the road.

Option: Canine Compatibility

To avoid the paved road section if your dog is coming along, simply start from the Timpooneke trailhead and skip the last descent down Pine Hollow Trail. Total distance out-and-back to Salamander Flat plus the Ridge Trail 157 loop is about 6.6 miles. Control your dog when crossing the road! The Timpooneke parking area can fill up early on weekends.

Option: Salamander Flat Bailout

To avoid the two short, tough climbs on Ridge Trail 157, you can bail out down Salamander Flat Trail as a short cut. It's a quick drop through sharp, steep turns (tech 4) that takes you to, where else, Salamander Flat. Continue to Pine Hollow Trail or bailout back to the Timpooneke trailhead.

Option: Salamander Flat Out-and-back

Don't feel like climbing? Short on time? No problem. Go as far as the Pine Hollow Trail junction (**m3.3**) and return. If you start from the Timpooneke trailhead and skip the road riding, round-trip distance is merely 4 miles and it's rated easy (tech 2-3). That's 4 miles of sweet singletrack with a whopping view of Mount Timpanogos along the way.

Option: South Fork Deer Creek Trail Add-on

Want to log longer miles, climb some hills, and take in the best trails American Fork Canyon has to offer? Simply combine the Pine Hollow figure-eight with the South Fork Deer Creek Trail for a 12-mile combo loop. Total gain is around 2,300 feet. This ride rules! (See "South Fork Deer Creek Trail.")

Option: Mutual Dell Add-on

But wait, there's more. When you return to the Pine Hollow trailhead, don't exit to the road. Instead, bank right to catch a half-mile more of singletrack that drops to UT 92 across from Mutual Dell Camp.

Peri charges up the GWT.

It's a thrilling little descent that is often overlooked. Just be cautious when you exit the trail to the road because there is no shoulder or trailhead. The "cost" of taking this little singletrack stash is pedaling .8 mile up the road to the parking area. It's worth it! But skip the notion of climbing trail No. 179—nasty, nasty.

! Know Before You Go

- American Fork Canyon/UT 92 is a recreation fee area: $3 per vehicle for a three-day pass.
- These trails are popular with hikers, bikers, equestrians, and motorcycles. Expect and respect other trail users.
- Bikes are not allowed in the Mount Timpanogos Wilderness.
- *Fido Factor:* This route is dog friendly, except for the initial 1.8 miles on the paved Alpine Loop Highway. Start at the Timpooneke trailhead and skip the Pine Hollow descent if your dog is coming along.

? Maps & More Information

- USGS 1:24,000: Aspen Grove and Timpanogos Cave, Utah
- Uinta National Forest (Pleasant Grove Ranger Dist.): (801) 785-3563

》 Trailhead Access

From I-15, take Exit 287 (Alpine, Highland) and travel east on UT 92 then up American Fork Canyon. Stay straight at the North Fork junction 2.5 miles past Timpanogos Cave National Monument, and drive 1.9 miles more on the Alpine Loop Highway/UT 92 to the Pine Hollow trailhead.

SOUTHERN WASATCH

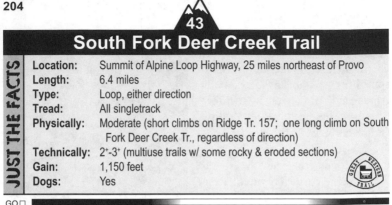

South Fork Deer Creek Trail *is one of the best introductory rides to American Fork Canyon's multitude of singletracks, especially if the prospect of tackling the entire Ridge Trail 157 is a bit daunting. You'll experience the fun riding that Trail 157 has to offer combined* with a remarkable descent and solid climb on South Fork Deer Creek Trail. Although this loop is only 6 miles long, it's 100-percent singletrack. Need scenery? You'll get an eyeful on Trail 157 with close-up views of Mount Timpanogos plus distant sights of American Fork Canyon and Deer Creek Reservoir. Need more miles? The network of trails that radiate from the Alpine Loop Highway offer a multitude of options for die-hard bikers or for anyone with a penchant to explore choice singletracks.

Details

Naturally, you can ride this loop in either direction, and there is little change in difficulty. Out of habit, the loop is described clockwise here. Roll out Trail 157 through pockets of aspens with a couple of quick descents (tech 3-4) and a few short climbs (tech 2-3). Round a broad meadow and pass the Pine Hollow Trail junction; then climb steadily. Over your left shoulder, Mount Timpanogos rises to regal proportions and flaunts its conspicuous glacial topography. The Giant Staircase is a deep, 2-mile-long valley flowing out of Timpanogos Basin, and Wooley Hole is a double-decker cirque to the right. Timp's 5-mile-long ridge top has made it an icon of northern Utah.

Glide on smooth tread to the Mud Springs Trail junction, go right on Tr. 157, and climb strenuously over log water bars (tech 4). The path mellows as it crosses to the ridge's east side before intersecting the Tibble Fork Trail/South Fork Deer Creek Trail junction (**m3.0**).

Go right on South Fork, and freewheel through dense fir trees on a switchbacking course (tech 3) followed by rolling straightaways. Down shift for a short, abrupt hill and descend more switchbacks through the aspens. A quick drop leads to a small footbridge in a meadow followed by a short ramp up to Cascade Springs Road (**m4.7**). Grab your dog! Cross

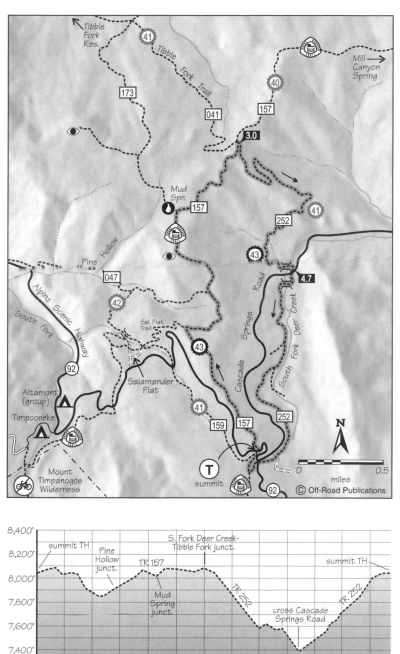

SOUTHERN WASATCH

Singletrack doesn't get much sweeter than on South Fork Deer Creek Trail.

the road to pick up the continued South Fork Deer Creek Trail. The breeze that was in your face on the descent will be replaced by sweat dripping from your brow because now you climb.

The climb is moderate at first as you head up a grassy hollow lined off with aspens; then the grade steepens intermittently to strenuous as you pass a small mud bog. Stay left/straight where a faint pack trail forks right and away from the hollow. A tenth mile farther, veer right and climb through the aspens where a pack trail forks left and stays in the hollow. A wooden post marks the junction. Cross a dirt road, and then cross the Alpine Loop Highway at the Cascade Springs Road junction. In .1 mile, fork right amidst closely packed aspens and chin-high yarrow to return to the summit trailhead (Aspen Grove Trail forks left).

Option: Mud Springs Trail-Tibble Fork Trail Add-On

Up the difficulty rating to strenuous and tip the technical scale to 4+ by veering off on Mud Springs Trail No. 173 for a steep, rough drop to Tibble Fork Trail No. 041 and then by pedaling and pushing back up to Ridge Trail 157. A spur leads to a viewpoint of Mount Timpanogos that few have seen, no doubt. The total digression is 4 miles long.

Ride as described to Mud Springs but go left on No. 173 past the water trough. You'll climb moderately on mostly smooth tight trail to a high scenic meadow. For the special view, go left/west on the faint path. It gets pretty brushy and there's brief hike-a-biking over choppy limestone, but in .5 mile you'll reach the viewing deck. Wow!

Return to the high meadow and take Mud Springs Trail northward.

Make the effort to take the spur from Mud Springs Trail to grab this killer view of Mt. Timp.

"No problem," you'll think as you descend gradually through the fir trees. Then the path angles down sharply, gets loose, and narrows to an eroded trench (tech 3⁺-4⁺). There's no turning back once you reach the four-way junction with Tibble Fork Trail because Mud Springs Trail is all hike-a-biking in reverse. Tibble Fork Trail rises in stair-step fashion with four short murderous hills, say "hike-a-bike." But the trail redeems itself with respites of amazingly sweet tread that pass beaver ponds and silky meadows. A pair of biker-friendly switchbacks precedes the junction with Ridge Trail 157. Continue on South Fork Deer Creek Trail (**m3.0** previously).

Option: Salamander Flat-Pine Hollow Add-On

If you feel like you just got started by the time you finished, then add on this moderate 3.5-mile side loop to Salamander Flat and Pine Hollow.

From the Alpine Loop summit trailhead, head west on Trail No. 159, signed for Salamander Flat. You cross a lightly flowing creek a couple times then intersect the road in .8 mile (tech 3). Cross over and continue descending to a junction just before Salamander Flat (large backcountry camping area). Stay straight for the GWT, and drop to a footbridge just north of Salamander Flat. Go right on smooth gently rising trail through shadowy fir trees to the Pine Hollow Trail junction in a small meadow. Stay right again, and climb strenuously up Pine Hollow to Trail 157. Take 157 back to the summit. This loop rides equally as well in reverse.

! Know Before You Go

- American Fork Canyon/UT 92 is a recreation fee area: $3.00 per vehicle for a three-day pass.
- These trails are extremely popular with hikers, bikers, and equestrians, and Ridge Trail 157 is open to motorcycles. Be especially cautious of horseback riders because many are on guided tours and may not be well skilled at controlling a horse. Ride at prudent speeds so you can stop safely at all times within the distance you can see down the trail.
- *Fido Factor:* This route is dog friendly. Grab your dog when crossing Cascade Springs Road and the Alpine Loop Highway! The only reliable water source is at the bottom of South Fork Trail (**m4.7**).

? Maps & More Information

- USGS 1:24,000: Aspen Grove and Timpanogos Cave, Utah
- Uinta National Forest (Pleasant Grove Ranger Dist.): (801) 785-3563

Trailhead Access

From I-15, take Exit 287 (Alpine, Highland) and travel east on UT 92 then up American Fork Canyon. Stay straight at the North Fork junction 2.5 miles past Timpanogos Cave National Monument, and drive 6 miles more on the Alpine Loop Highway/UT 92 to the trailhead/parking area at the road's summit.

SOUTHERN WASATCH

44

Upper Provo Deer Creek

JUST THE FACTS

Location:	30 miles northeast of Provo, 13 miles southwest of Heber	
Length:	17.3 miles	
Type:	Loop	
Tread:	2.7 miles singletrack, 1.5 miles doubletrack, 12.5 miles dirt road, .6 miles paved road	
Physically:	Strenuous (long, steady climb)	
Technically:	2-4⁺ (gravel, washboards, & rocks on dirt roads; rough singletrack descent; fast doubletrack w/ one wide water crossing)	
Gain:	3,000 feet	
Dogs:	Not recommended, rocky roads & possible traffic	

GO ☐
NO ■ | JAN | FEB | MAR | APR | MAY | JUN | JUL | AUG | SEP | OCT | NOV | DEC |

If you're looking for a solid aerobic workout with long steady miles on a nontechnical climb, then the Upper Provo Deer Creek loop fits the bill. The reward for your effort is a wild descent on singletrack followed by a blazing fast romp on smooth doubletrack accented with one big water crossing. If you're seeking scenery, then you'll find plenty along this loop. The route begins at Cascade Springs where crystalline waters bubble from the hillside and tumble through pellucid pools. Your eyes will feast on peaks of the southern Wasatch Range, Deer Creek Reservoir, and Heber Valley from high points on the ride.

Details

If you are starting from the Cascade Springs trailhead, then return on the paved access road and fork right on the dirt road (tech 2-3) toward Wasatch Mountain State Park and Little Deer Creek Campground. The road gets rough as it rises steeply around a switchback; then it smooths and moderates. Curve right at the turnoff for Little Deer Creek Campground (**m2.7**), and climb steeply up Cummings Parkway for .6 mile to the ridge. You'll spin in low gears up the seven-percent grade for 2 more miles before a short, fast downhill gives your legs a break. The continued climb is steady, if not tedious, but your eyes are kept busy by the views of Little Deer Creek Campground in the narrow valley below, of Mill Canyon Peak and Mount Timpanogos on the western skyline, and of farmlands blanketing Heber Valley like a country quilt to the east.

If your legs have had enough when you reach Middle Mountain, then you can call it quits by taking the doubletrack that forks left at the edge of a big aspen grove (**m6.7**). It drops steeply into the Provo Deer Creek valley, where you then race back past the campground and return to Cascade Springs; otherwise, keep grinding away for 1.5 miles to Snake Creek Road (tech 2⁺) and 1.8 miles more to Pole Line Pass (**m10.0**).

Hop on Ridge Trail 157, attack a short, murderous hill, and surf through sand and loose rocks down to Sandy Baker Pass. Fork left following the sign for Pot Hollow and East Ridge Trail. You'll descend quickly

SOUTHERN WASATCH

and steeply on rough tread around a point and come to a second junction where East Ridge Trail forks right. Go left again and square up for a rugged, free-falling descent down Pot Hollow and past Big Spring (tech 4+). A smoother, faster ATV trail takes you down the lower hollow to the Provo Deer Creek road (**m12.6**). Kick in the after burners like an F-15 Eagle going supersonic, and zoom down the doubletrack, hitting the big wide water crossing at full speed, if you dare. Stay left where the road splits to circle below Little Deer Creek Campground. Finally, retrace your tracks back to Cascade Springs with a couple miles of choppy dirt road.

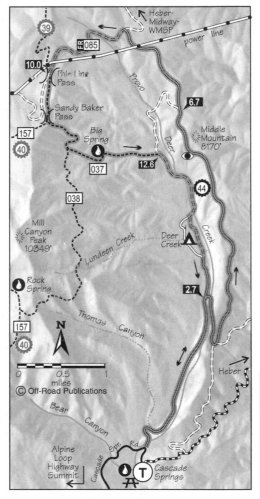

SOUTHERN WASATCH

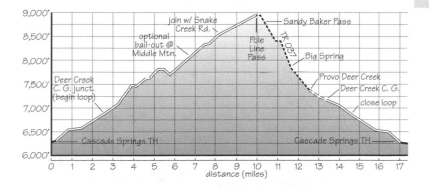

Know Before You Go

- American Fork Canyon/UT 92 is a recreation fee area: $3 per vehicle for a three-day pass. If you access the ride from Heber, then you must pay the recreation fee at Cascade Springs.
- To avoid possible congestion at the Cascade Springs trailhead and several miles of pebbly, washboarded dirt road, drive to and start from Little Deer Creek Campground.
- Little Deer Creek Campground is a fee area maintained by Wasatch Mountain State Park.
- Sheep herding is common in the Provo Deer Creek valley. Be aware of sheep dogs; they might like chasing you as much as they do sheep. If you ride slowly through a herd, you should not have a problem.
- Cascade Springs and Little Deer Creek Campground have water taps and outhouses.
- *Fido Factor:* Dogs are not recommended because of possible vehicle traffic on dirt roads and sheep herding in the area.

Maps & More Information

- USGS 1:24,000: Brighton and Aspen Grove, Utah
- Wasatch Mountain State Park: (435) 654-1791; http://www.stateparks.utah.gov/parks/www1/wasa.htm
- Uinta National Forest (Pleasant Grove Ranger Dist.): (801) 785-3563

Trailhead Access

Via American Fork Canyon: From I-15, take Exit 287 (Alpine, Highland), and travel east on UT 92 then up American Fork Canyon. Stay straight at the North Fork junction (2.5 miles past Timpanogos Cave National Monument), and drive 6 miles up the Alpine Loop Highway/UT 92 to the summit. Just over the summit, turn left on Cascade Springs Road, and descend about 7 miles to the springs' parking area.

Via Provo Canyon: From I-15, take Exit 275 (8th North/Orem, Sundance, Provo Canyon). Travel east on UT 52 then 7 miles up Provo Canyon/US 189, and turn left on UT 92 for Sundance and Alpine Loop. Travel 9 miles on the Alpine Loop Highway/UT 92, and turn right on the Cascade Springs road. Descend 7 miles to the springs' parking area.

Via Heber: Travel 3.3 miles west on UT 113/100 South Street from Heber to Midway. Turn left/south on 200 West. Zigzag through residential areas, and then head south on Stringtown Road. After 1 mile, turn right/west on a dirt road for Cascade Springs, which is about 6 miles away. (The road is suitable for passenger cars but can be rough in spots.)

SOUTHERN WASATCH

45
Timpooneke Road

Location:	American Fork Canyon, 25 miles northeast of Provo
Length:	17 miles
Type:	Out-and-back
Tread:	Light-duty dirt road & doubletrack
Physically:	Strenuous (steady climbs, rocky near the end); moderate if you turn around early
Technically:	1⁺-3 (light chop & smooth dirt early on; rocks & ruts later on)
Gain:	3,000 feet
Dogs:	Not recommended, possible traffic

GO ☐
NO ■ | JAN | FEB | MAR | APR | MAY | JUN | JUL | AUG | SEP | OCT | NOV | DEC |

WHY SHOULD U RIDE THIS TRAIL? *Two off-road routes curve around the north end of Mount Timpanogos: the Great Western Trail and Timpooneke Road. Both routes provide constantly changing views of tall mountains, deep canyons, and broad valleys, but Timpooneke Road is definitely the easier choice. Timp Road, however, is not "easy" because there are long miles to log and big hills to climb if you go the distance. The first half follows a light-duty dirt road; the second leg is choppy doubletrack. Tackle as much as your legs will allow, and then simply turn around. Since the Great Western Trail crosses the road three times, you'll have several opportunities to explore bits of the 3,000-mile, border-to-border trail.*

Details

From the Timpooneke trailhead, take the paved road west; it soon turns to rock-studded dirt with some washboards (tech 2⁺). You'll climb steadily for 2 miles then bend left around a low topographic point. Be sure to glance back over your shoulder because this stretch is exceptionally scenic. Barren peaks and scalloped ridges tower over multi-tiered bowls that are lined off with bounteous forests. Many features have individual names like Pika Cirque, Giant Staircase, and Roberts Horn, but collectively they form the hulking mass known simply as Mount Timpanogos.

The GWT crosses the road in less than a mile from the bend. To the left, the GWT rises moderately to Julie Andrews Meadow. It's not hard to imagine what sights await, so go check it out. To the right, the GWT plunges into Rock Canyon (tech 4) then rises sharply out the other side (tech 3). Let's stay on the road for a contouring curve on mostly smooth-running road through the middle of Rock Canyon.

Round a left bend that overlooks the craggy limestone cliffs of Burned Canyon and offers a good view of Lone Peak in the distance. The GWT crosses the road here after rising out of Rock Canyon and then hangs on Timp's western flank. Stay on the road and climb gradually around the

SOUTHERN WASATCH

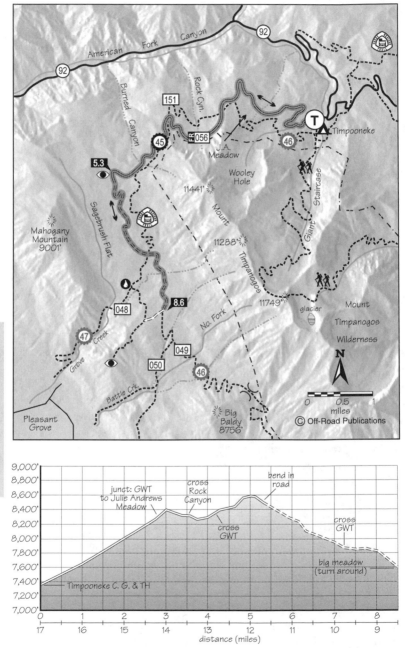

Brad S. and Edgar outrun storm clouds gathering over Mount Timpanogos.

head of Burned Canyon to another left bend in about 1.5 miles (**m5.3**). This is a good turnaround if you're starting to tire because the road will descend continually for the next 3 miles to its end.

You can access the GWT again near an old corral on the left after you round the bend. Thereafter, the road degrades to choppy doubletrack (tech 3) and descends the length of a broad valley called Sagebrush Flat. Mount Timpanogos rises 4,000 above you as one solid rock wall. The road ends at a big meadow just past Grove Creek Trail (**m8.6**), so turn around, climb back up Sagebrush Flat, and roll back to the trailhead.

Option: Great Western Trail

Strong bikers who want to add on some singletrack can tie together the GWT and Timpooneke Road. Here are some tips.

First, skip the section from the Timpooneke trailhead to Julie Andrews Meadow altogether, unless you're a masochist and enjoy hauling your bike up some of the nastiest trail in the Wasatch. No lie! Instead, ride Timp Road as described previously, and catch the GWT through Rock Canyon (tech 3-4[+]). The initial drop is steep, and rugged conditions in the bottom require brief walking; however, the climb out is quite enjoyable.

Cross Timp Road and head up a small but steep ridge in the woods. The trail can get worn from horses and motorcycles (tech 4[+]), so expect to walk sections. A rolling contour takes you past the old corral (near **m5.3** above), where you can bail out to the road. Beyond, the GWT rolls up and down for a mile then descends steeply on rough tread (tech 3-4) to Timp Road near Grove Creek Trail. This section would be very difficult to climb, so plan on returning on the road.

Option: Grove Creek Canyon Overlook

This 2-mile, out-and-back trip takes you to a dizzying overlook of the cliff-hemmed gash of Grove Creek Canyon and of flat-bottomed Utah Valley. From Timpooneke Road's end at the grassy meadow (**m8.6**), turn right/west and cut across the field on a doubletrack. On the meadow's west side, the doubletrack bends south, narrows to singletrack, and then descends gradually over a handful of earthen berms. You'll be rim-rocked on the edge of Grove Creek Canyon with cheery Pleasant Grove and the Orem-Provo metropolis sprawling out below.

! Know Before You Go

- American Fork Canyon/UT 92 is a recreation fee area: $3 per vehicle for a three-day pass.
- You may encounter vehicles on Timpooneke Road. Ride attentively and stay to the right, especially when rounding corners.
- The trailhead has a water tap and an outhouse.
- Bikes are not allowed in the Mount Timpanogos Wilderness.
- *Fido Factor:* Dogs are not recommended because of possible vehicle traffic on Timpooneke Road, and the road's choppy tread may be hard on dogs' paws.

? Maps & More Information

- USGS 1:24,000: Timpanogos Cave, Utah
- Uinta National Forest (Pleasant Grove Ranger Dist.): (801) 785-3563

) Trailhead Access

From I-15, take Exit 287 (Alpine, Highland), and travel east on UT 92 then up American Fork Canyon. Stay straight at the North Fork junction on Alpine Loop Highway/UT 92 about 2.5 miles past Timpanogos Cave National Monument. Turn right for Timpooneke Campground 4 miles farther, and park at the wilderness trailhead past the campground. The lot can fill up on weekends and holidays.

SOUTHERN WASATCH

R.A.T. (Ride Around Timpanogos)

JUST THE FACTS	**Location:**	Provo Canyon, 6 miles northeast of Provo
	Length:	33 miles
	Type:	Loop
	Tread:	15.4 miles singletrack, 1.3 miles doubletrack, 3.4 miles paved trail, 12.9 miles paved roads
	Physically:	Extreme (long miles, big gain, rugged trails)
	Technically:	1⁺-5 (paved trail & roads are easy; GWT is more rough than smooth w/ two burly portages)
	Gain:	6,000 feet
	Dogs:	No, too long, too tough; yes, out-and-back sections

GO☐
NO■ | JAN | FEB | MAR | APR | MAY | JUN | JUL | AUG | SEP | OCT | NOV | DEC |

At a time when "freeriding" is all the buzz and gravity seekers flock to ski resorts during summer months to ride chair lifts just to coast downhill, the R.A.T. (Ride Around Timpanogos) is for old school die-hards who haven't lost sight of the true meaning of "mountain" biking. The ride's long miles, monstrous elevation gain, and two painful portages will redline your physical and mental fortitude. Difficulty aside, R.A.T. exudes alpine beauty by providing an up-close look at four very different faces of the Wasatch's most recognized mountain icon: Mount Timpanogos. So, if you want to go big, really big, then the R.A.T. is for you, and it's what mountain biking is all about.

Details

Cross the footbridge over the Provo River at Canyon Glen Park, and head up the paved Provo-Jordan River Parkway through Nunns Park and under the highway. Across the canyon, Mount Timpanogos catches the morning sun while nearby Bridal Veil Falls stays in a shadowy mist. Exit Vivian Park to US 189, and pedal up the highway, taking the dirt bypass around the tunnel. Fork left up the Alpine Loop Highway/UT 92, and climb steadily past Sundance Resort to the Mount Timpanogos Trailhead at Aspen Grove (**m9.5**). (Bikes do not have to pay the recreation use fee.)

Go past the information kiosk, and chug up the graveled Mount Timpanogos Trail straight toward Primrose Cirque and Roberts Horn, which loom 4,000 feet overhead. (Don't take Stewarts Cascades Trail next to the outhouse.) In .5 mile, fork right on the GWT at a sign stating that bikes are not allowed in the wilderness, and cross a footbridge.

Now the ride really begins. The GWT starts out with a sharp climb on rocky tread (tech 3-4), angling up a warm, sunny slope. The trail moderates briefly in the timber then rises steeply again around several rough switchbacks. Pedal easier as the trail contours gracefully through groves of old-growth aspens underlain with broad leaf plants and wildflowers. Go left at the South Fork Deer Creek Trail junction to arrive at the Alpine Loop Highway summit trailhead (**m12.7**).

SOUTHERN WASATCH

Feeling fresh? If so, then take Trail No. 159 (for Salamander Flat) from the parking area's west edge, and freewheel down the hollow on tight gravelly trail (tech 3). (Pooped? Then retrace your tracks or glide down the highway to call it a day.) Cross the paved road, drop down a rough ramp, and fork left to cut across Salamander Flat (backcountry camping area). Pedal up through the timber to rejoin the GWT at a scenic outlook of Mount Timpanogos. (If you reach the footbridge north of Sala-

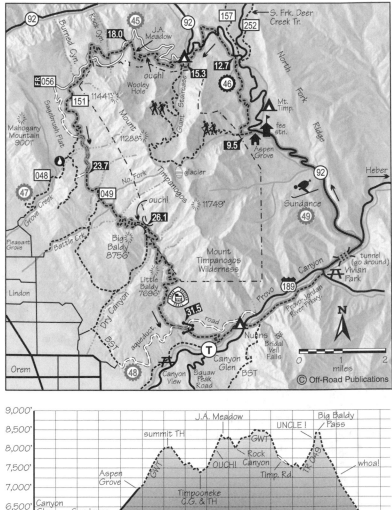

mander Flat, signed for Pine Hollow, go west and climb two turns to the overlook of Timp.) A buffed section of trail takes you across the road and to the Timpooneke trailhead (**m15.3**) where you can restock on water. You're halfway in or half-way out, depending on your outlook.

Bridal Veil Falls.

Go back to the information booth, and head west on the GWT, No. 151. Pedal and push up a set of steep turns, cruise through a swath of blown-down aspens, and cut straight across a small meadow on the edge of campsites. Now comes the first of the ride's two soul-searching portages. The GWT rises directly up a ridge on the edge of a glacial cirque. The trail is so steep and the tread has been so hammered by horses (tech 5) that it's impossible to ride; in fact, even walking is a real chore. The only consolation is the up-close sights of meltwater cascading from winter's vestiges high on the limestone terraces of Wooley Hole. The view north of the central Wasatch Range from Julie Andrews Meadow is straight from the silver screen, but is it worth the agony you just endured?

Fork left on the GWT upon descending from Julie Andrews Meadow, and take a faded doubletrack to the crossing of Timpooneke Road (**m18.0**). A steepening decent (tech 3-4) takes you into the depths of Rock Canyon where you must climb right back out. Except for a rough section at the bottom, the trail is surprisingly ridable as it curves thoughtfully through mixed timber up to Timp Road again. Compare that well-designed section of trail with the next straightaway climb, which has no intention of contouring. Go figure! After rolling through a camp of "leaning" aspens, the trail exits the timber to offer competing views of Lone Peak to the north and of Utah Valley to the south. You'll descend deservedly for over a mile on roughened trail (tech 3-4) across the base of Timp's western rampart before exiting to Timpooneke Road near Grove Creek Trail. If

Alpine Loop Highway past Sundance.

Descending off Big Baldy Pass to Provo Canyon.

you're fried, and realizing that the toughest climb is still ahead, you can bailout down Grove Creek Trail to Pleasant Grove and limp back to Provo Canyon on paved roads; otherwise, take Timpooneke Road (tech 3) to its end and continue on the GWT, signed for Dry Canyon Trail, No. 049 (**m23.7**).

Your destiny awaits as you eye the 1,000-foot-tall pass separating Timp from the knoll called Big Baldy. The approach takes you past the junction for Battle Creek Trail in a vast meadow; through oak, aspen, and fir hillsides; and over three bouldery tributaries (tech 5) of Battle Creek that double as avalanche zones in the winter.

The switchbacks you encounter were built in the late 1990s to ease the climb to the pass, but the reconstruction project only made it halfway up. The new/lower trail will still make your legs revolt. The remaining upper section is a painful fall-line portage over a jumble of rocks—two steps forward, one step back—for one-quarter mile and 300 vertical feet to the pass (**m26.1**). Uncle! It's all downhill from here, but it's hardly anticlimactic.

Don't be suckered into going straight over the pass on the innocuous looking Dry Canyon Trail because it becomes a deep, nasty rut (tech 5); instead, take the GWT on a contour heading left into the aspens on one of the old erosion trenches. It will switchback right to rejoin Dry Canyon Trail. Descend Dry Canyon Trail a couple hundred yards to a lone aspen on the left to resume on the GWT, which again contours on an old trench. If you miss the turn, you'll descend Dry Canyon Trail to Orem (tech 5), and that's something you should avoid. The GWT is no cruise through the park, either, for it clings precariously to steep slopes with roots and

You too might feel crucified after Riding Around Timpanogos.

SOUTHERN WASATCH

rocks in the narrow, loose tread. Two bouldery gulches and bristly oak brush make the initial descent especially arduous (tech 4⁺). The hardships are trivialized by the glorious sights of Mount Timpanogos hovering overhead and of Cascade Mountain's blocky facade rising above Provo Canyon. You'll descend aggressively (tech 3-4⁺) through a dozen turns for over a mile before breaking out to a small meadow and coming to a four-way junction marked by a big rock pile. Go left; then stay left again at a Y-junction to drop to the aqueduct road. (Heavy sigh of relief!)

Go left on the aqueduct road to a junction marked by two steel gates and a cement manhole (**m31.5**); fork right, go round another gate, and then fork left immediately on the GWT (may be unsigned). Choppy singletrack (tech 3⁺) takes you on the south rim of an elevated meadow called Johnson Hole. Plunge down the pebbly GWT to the lower aqueduct road next to where the big water pipe ducks underground like an ostrich, and drop quickly again to the Provo-Jordan River Parkway. Go right 100 feet then left at the outhouse, cross the bridge, and make a bee line for your cooler. You did stock the cooler, didn't you?

Option: Julie Andrews Meadow Bypass

There is no shame in skipping the burly portage up the GWT to Julie Andrews Meadow for the longer but easier climb on Timpooneke Road. You can always take the short spur up to the meadow for the view. Likewise, stay on Timp Road to bypass the Rock Canyon section.

! Know Before You Go

- Bikes are not allowed in the Mount Timpanogos Wilderness.
- This is a big ride; know your ability and that of others in your group.
- You'll be out on the trail all day; pack appropriate clothing, food, water, and tools. Be prepared for rapidly changing alpine weather.
- The Timpooneke trailhead has a water tap. Grove Creek Spring is your only other reliable water source, but purify it just to be safe.
- *Fido Factor:* This ride is too long for dogs, although out-and-back segments are well-suited.

? Maps & More Information

- USGS 1:24,000: Aspen Grove, Bridal Veil Falls, Orem, and Timpanogos Cave, Utah
- Uinta National Forest (Pleasant Grove Ranger Dist.): (801) 785-3563

♪ Trailhead Access

From I-15, take Exit 275 for 8th North Street/UT 52 (Orem), Sundance, and Provo Canyon Recreation Areas. Travel east on 8th North for 4 miles, and follow U.S. 189 up Provo Canyon for 2.6 miles to Canyon Glen Park.

SOUTHERN WASATCH

47
Grove Creek Trail

Location:	2 miles east of Pleasant Grove
Length:	10.4 miles
Type:	Out-and-back
Tread:	Singletrack w/ a touch of doubletrack
Physically:	Strenuous⁺ (steep climb on narrow, rocky trail)
Technically:	3-5 (steep, narrow, rocky trail along edge of a deep gorge)
Gain:	3,000 feet
Dogs:	Yes

GO ☐
NO ■ | JAN | FEB | MAR | APR | MAY | JUN | JUL | AUG | SEP | OCT | NOV | DEC |

WHY SHOULD U RIDE THIS TRAIL?

Grove Creek Trail isn't one of the Wasatch Range's longest climbs, but it is surely one of the toughest, gaining 2,600 feet in about 3.5 miles. Do the math. The trail's steep unrelenting pitch is punishing; its technical traits and precarious placement make it downright unnerving at times. Why bother? Grove Creek is diversely scenic. The path clings to the side of a deep treeless gorge lined off with slabs of laminated limestone. Then it rises to spring-fed meadows that wrap Mount Timpanogos in an emerald skirt. At the route's turnaround, you'll gaze into the canyon's ragged depths and across all of Utah Valley. The descent is a thrill a minute that requires straight shooting and technical prowess.

Details

Take the doubletrack into the canyon, and fork left on the steeply rising singletrack. (The doubletrack ends shortly ahead next to the creek.) Get ready to hoof it because the first climb is heinously steep and loose (tech 5). Pass through a wire fence ominously signed "Grove Creek Trail 048, May Be Hazardous For Horses."

Take a quick break at the upcoming switchback for an impressive overlook of Utah Valley and of the southern Wasatch Front. You'll spend the next mile or so pedaling and pushing apprehensively up the narrow path with ledgy cliffs overhead and precipitous slopes under foot (tech 3⁺-4⁺). You must choose between riding and sightseeing because it's difficult and dangerous to do both simultaneously.

Cross the footbridge over Grove Creek; then pedal and push still more through cool, moist timber. Alas, the path moderates and crosses spacious meadows. The trail splits just beyond a fenced-in spring (**m3.5**). Fork right, break through another meadow, and push your bike up eroded tread through the aspens (tech 4⁺). Head south on a faint path across an immense pasture of verdant, wind-rippled grasses to a doubletrack; turn right and follow it to the field's western edge. The path narrows to singletrack, descends southward over numerous earthen berms, and ends atop cliffs that encase Grove Creek Canyon (**m5.2**). Retracing your tracks down Grove Creek Trail is easier said than done. Watch out for that patch of bedrock (tech 5), and don't look down.

Option: Battle Creek and Dry Canyon Trails

I know what you're thinking. Why not just loop back to Pleasant Grove on Battle Creek Trail or Dry Canyon Trail? They're nasty trails,

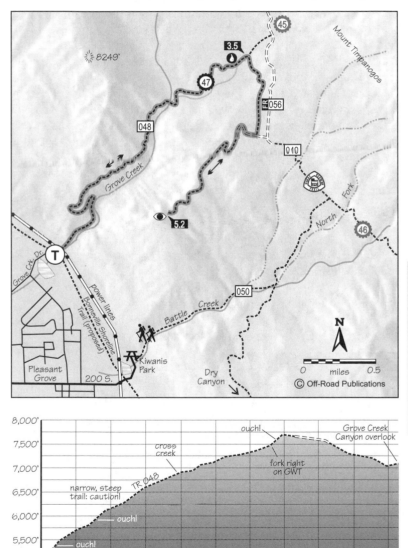

that's why. Upper Battle Creek Trail, No. 050, starts out deceptively invit-ing; then you drop down entrenched trail choked with baby-head rocks and pass through oak brush that shreds your exposed skin. That's the easy part! After dropping to the creek, you'll have to pick your way past the waterfalls and skitter down 20-percent grades on gravelly tread. Ugh!

For Dry Canyon, descend upper Battle Creek Trail to the creek (tech 4-5). Cross over and hack your way up steep, torn-up tread through the oak (tech 5). A piece of sweet trail is hidden in there, but it's followed by more unspeakable portaging. After you top out, you'll head southward on more overgrown trail (tech 3^+-4^+) to a spring. A doubletrack bends left/east to meet Dry Canyon Trail, where you'll drop through the "gates," a narrow passage bound by tall rock walls (tech 3^+-4^+).

But then again, this all could change. The Pleasant Grove Ranger District is committed to renovating upper Battle Creek and the cutover trail to Dry Canyon. Plans are on the drawing board to build a new trail from Dry Canyon around the south flank of Big Baldy and connect with the GWT above the Orem Bonneville Shoreline Trail where it follows the Alta aqueduct road. There, you can ride the near-level dirt road back to Orem on the BST. Looks promising. Check it out and report back.

! Know Before You Go

- Use good judgement when descending Grove Creek Trail. Ride what you can and walk the rest. A fall could be fatal from certain spots along the trail.
- This trail can be deathly hot at midday during midsummer. Potability of spring water along the route is uncertain.
- *Fido Factor:* Trail is acceptable for dogs, except that it's steep, narrow, rough, and exposed to sheer drop-offs at times.

? Maps & More Information

- USGS 1:24,000: Orem and Timpanogos Cave, Utah
- Uinta National Forest (Pleasant Grove Ranger Dist.): (801) 785-3563

♪ Trailhead Access

From I-15, take Exit 281 (American Fork). Travel east on US 89, which becomes State Street in American Fork. After passing under the Union Pacific Railroad bridge in Pleasant Grove, turn left/north on UT 146 (next to the Purple Turtle Cafe) and drive 2 miles. Turn right/east on 500 North, which becomes Grove Creek Drive and leads to the Grove Creek Trail trailhead.

SOUTHERN WASATCH

48
Bonneville Shoreline Trail (Orem)

Location:	Orem foothills
Length:	Up to 4.4 miles
Type:	One-way, out-and-back, or loop
Tread:	1.2 miles singletrack, 3.2 miles dirt road
Physically:	Moderate (undulating trail; one short, tough climb then flat on aqueduct road)
Technically:	1⁺-3⁺ (dirt, pebble, and rock singletracks; smooth dirt road)
Gain:	500 feet
Dogs:	Yes, on leash

GO □
NO ■ | JAN | FEB | MAR | APR | MAY | JUN | JUL | AUG | SEP | OCT | NOV | DEC |

Although Orem's section of the Bonneville Shoreline Trail (BST) is not long, it offers a variety of terrain to ride through and to look at. Currently, just over a mile of hand-built singletrack rolls between the Dry Canyon and Cascade Drive trailheads. Along this stretch, the steep foothills of the Wasatch Range interface sharply with the Utah Valley metropolis. Continuing south, the BST curves high into Provo Canyon along the Alta Aqueduct road and runs beneath the mighty shoulders of Mount Timpanogos. The future looks bright for the BST because in years to come the trail will extend north of Orem through Lindon to Pleasant Grove and eventually to American Fork Canyon.

Details

Pick up the BST under the power lines at the Dry Canyon trailhead. A short, steep, sandy ramp will force most bikers to hoof it briefly, and some choppy spots in the trail farther on will test your bike-handling skills (tech 3⁺). There is a lot of smooth-rolling tread, too (tech 2). Exit the trail to a paved cul-de-sac near an underground water tank in about .7 mile. Cross the pavement to continue on the trail and to reach the Cascade Drive trailhead after another .5 mile.

Heading south from the Cascade Drive trailhead, power up the steeply rising trail, and exit to a dirt road above the Utah Valley Water Purification Plant. Climb past the big water tank, and stay left at all junctions. The road is smooth dirt and gravel (tech 1⁺), but it rises steeply at times. One mile from the trailhead, the road bends left/north around a point, levels high above Provo Canyon atop a band of cliffs, and becomes the Alta Aqueduct road (**m2.2**). Mount Timpanogos is straight in your sights. If you look just below the road and on top of the cliffs, you'll see a secret little singletrack angling down into the brushy canyon, where more singletracks are stashed. Ooh, sweet! (See Options.) Take the perfectly level aqueduct road 2.2 miles to a gate next to a cement manhole (**m4.4**). Here you must decide your next move. Return the way you came, or follow one of the optional routes listed next.

Options: Return routes to Orem from **m4.4** above

Aqueduct road, continued: Continue straight past the gate, stay on the Alta Aqueduct road for another 2.2 miles, and descend to US 189 in Provo Canyon. Return the way you came. Or ride down the highway, catch the paved Provo-Jordan River Parkway (PJRP) from Nunns Park to the Olmstead trailhead, and ride 800 North to 800 East to return to your starting point.

Great Western Trail: Fork right from the Alta Aqueduct road, go around another gate, and *immediately* fork left on singletrack (may not be signed). A choppy descent (tech 3⁺) takes you around Johnsons Hole and down to the PJRP at Canyon Glen Park. Take the PJRP to the Olmstead trailhead, and ride 800 North to 800 East to return to your trailhead.

Mount Timpanogos Park: Only singletrack purists with a good sense of direction, razor-sharp handling skills, and no fear of heights should follow this route. It links to the old mountain bike race course and returns you to the Alta Aqueduct road via that ledgy trail you drooled over earlier. (These trails were originally accessed from Mount Timpanogos Park in Provo Canyon, but pipeline construction in 2004 has since closed or altered access to the trails network.)

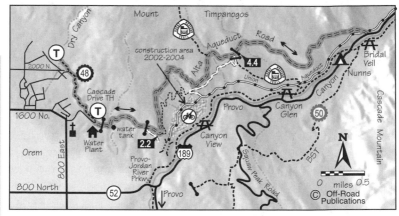

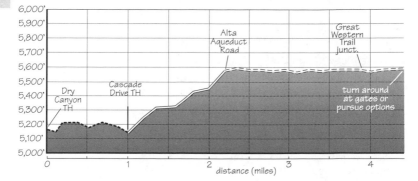

Fork right from the Alta Aqueduct road, go around another gate, and descend swiftly on the pebbly doubletrack into a hollow (tech 3). In .9 mile, the road bends left and descends under the big green Union Aqueduct pipeline. Instead, fork right on a faint trail that dips through a hollow where a silver pipe is exposed. Climb out of the hollow, fork right, and climb briefly along the rim of the hollow.

You're on your own from here because directions are perplexing. Your goal is to reach the north side of the distant cliffs where they pinch out into the brush. Stay above the big green pipeline and out of the construction area. After about a mile of wandering, you'll want to fork right and hike-a-bike briefly up a steep trail that takes you above a wrecked orange truck in a hollow. Here, the trail is merely one step up onto the cliffs. *Caution:* You are exposed to shear drop-offs on this trail, and there are several tricky spots (tech 5). A fall could be disastrous, a la the Portal Trail on Moab's Poison Spider Mesa.

! Know Before You Go

- Obey all signs restricting travel, and stay away from construction areas.
- Rattlesnakes are known to inhabit these warm foothill areas.
- Midday temperatures during the midsummer can reach 100 degrees Fahrenheit.
- *Fido Factor:* Dogs must be leashed and under control at all times.

? Maps & More Information

- USGS 1:24,000: Bridal Veil Falls and Orem, Utah
- Uinta National Forest (Pleasant Grove Ranger Dist.): (801) 785-3563
- City of Orem Recreation: (801) 229-7151
- Mountainlands Association of Governments: (801) 229-3800, www.mountainland.org

Trailhead Access

Dry Canyon trailhead (Lindon): From I-15, take Exit 276 for 1600 North (Orem) and travel east. Go left/north on State Street; then turn right/east on 200 North (Orem)/200 South (Lindon). At about 1500 East in Lindon, turn left on Dry Canyon Drive, which turns from pavement to dirt and leads to the Dry Canyon trailhead.

Cascade Drive trailhead (Orem): From I-15, take Exit 276 for 1600 North (Orem). Where the road bends south and becomes 800 East (in 2.9 miles), turn left on Cascade Drive for the Bonneville Shoreline Trail (north edge of the Orem Cemetery). Turn left at the Utah Valley Water Purification Plant to reach the parking area. From 800 North/UT 52, go north on 800 East and turn right just past the Orem Cemetery for the BST to reach the Cascade Drive trailhead.

SOUTHERN WASATCH

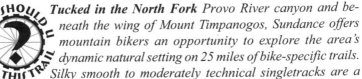

49
Sundance

<table>
<tr><td rowspan="9">JUST THE FACTS</td></tr>
</table>

Location:	10 miles northeast of Orem
Length:	Variable, see below
Type:	One-way downhill or cross country loops
Tread:	Singletracks & dirt roads.
Physically:	Easy-moderate (downhill); moderate$^+$ (uphill)
Technically:	2-4$^+$ (smooth running & variably choppy singletracks; dirt roads)
Gain/Loss:	1,050 feet between Rays Lift summit & the base
Dogs:	No

GO ☐
NO ■ | JAN | FEB | MAR | APR | MAY | JUN | JUL | AUG | SEP | OCT | NOV | DEC |

Tucked in the North Fork Provo River canyon and beneath the wing of Mount Timpanogos, Sundance offers mountain bikers an opportunity to explore the area's dynamic natural setting on 25 miles of bike-specific trails. Silky smooth to moderately technical singletracks are a breeze to coast down for most bikers, and their well-executed design makes them a joy to climb. Weekly races and events, award-winning dining, rustic elegance, an artisan center, and casual atmosphere make Sundance a world-class summer destination the whole family can enjoy.

Details

Riding at Sundance is a matter of connecting the dots because the trail junctions are numbered, not the individual trails themselves. Variations are many, but here are the most popular combinations.

Sunnyside Ride: Novice bikers will enjoy this easy coast from the end of Rays Lift to the base. Dirt roads cross the resort's ski runs and connect with a paved road that takes you to the bottom. Good braking skills are needed to control your speed; otherwise, the ride is as tame as a fawn at a petting zoo.

> **Sunnyside Ride:**
> 3-miles, easy$^+$, tech 1-2 (paved and dirt roads), 850-foot loss

Ride Rays Lift over the summit and down to its end at Arrowhead Lift. Hop on Sunnyside Road, glide down to junction #10 (Long Hollow Road), and cut across the mountain on Mandan Road to #12 under Rays Lift. Pass junction #15, cut under the lift again at junction #18, and go straight through #19 to connect with the paved road. Check out the view of Mount Timpanogos over your shoulder. Glide down the road to the base. (End of lift-#3-#7-#10-#12-#15-#18-#19-#27-base)

Rays Ride: Rays Ride is the backbone of Sundance's lift-served trail system, delivering miles of sweet singletrack that's not too tough, not too easy, but just right. The top half affords sweeping views of the terrain that make Sundance so special. The lower half ducks into thick timber on a forever-turning one-laner.

> **Rays Ride:**
> 3.5 miles, moderate, tech 2$^+$-3$^+$ (singletracks w/ some dirt roads), 1,050-foot loss

SOUTHERN WASATCH

Exit Rays Lift at the summit, and descend the main route left down to junction #9. Fork left on singletrack and drop through a few turns to #11. Cross the dirt Mandan Road and come to #14 at the picnic table in the trees. Go left and then bear right at #15 under Rays Lift. A challenging section of tight turns, rooted tread, and side-swiper trees takes you down to #17 where you go left and cross the dirt road at #18. Now the trail weaves uphill slightly over "the Island," a low knoll covered with aspen,

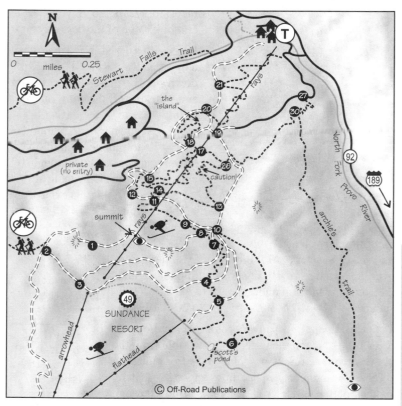

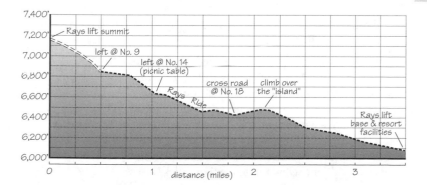

SOUTHERN WASATCH

Brad drops into the timber on lower Archies.

oak, and maple. The sight of Stewarts Cascades and Cascade Cirque are especially striking here. Finally, wind your way down through #20 and #21 to the base. (Lift summit-#9-#11-#14-#15-#17-#18-#20-#21-base.)

Rays Ride has been the centerpiece of Sundance cross-country races for years, so if you like to climb, it's one of the best ways up.

Rays with a Twist: Need more challenge than Rays Ride? Then "twist" down steeper, more technical trails, and "huck it" off the notorious rock drop.

Coast down from the summit of Rays Lift to junction #9, and veer left on singletrack. Drop through #11 and come to the picnic table at #14. Now go right (signed "most difficult"). Bank left on a ski run next to a dirt road (#13), duck back into the trees, and hang your butt off the back for the big rock drop (tech 4⁺). Heed the cautionary signs if you are tentative. Go left at #26 and cross over to #17. Finish off by either going over the Island from #18 or short-cutting to #20 and then cruising the trail under the lift to the base. (Lift summit-#9-#11-#14-#13-#26-#17-#18-#20-#21-base.)

Rays with a Twist:
3.25 miles, moderate, tech 2⁺-4⁺ (singletrack w/ some dirt roads), 1,050-foot loss

Boneyard Loop: Boneyard Loop is an alternate to lower Rays Ride to reach the base. It's accessible from the above-mentioned rides by going right from junction #17 past the maintenance buildings and to #26. There, tight smooth singletrack descends playfully through old growth fir trees and arcs around friendly turns to #30 (Archies Trail). To reach the base, fork left and continue descending around wide, fast turns through mixed timber. Exit to the paved road, and coast downhill. (Go to #17 then #26-#30-#27-base)

Boneyard Loop:
1 mile add-on, moderate, tech 2-3⁺, (singletrack)

Scotts Pond: Get away from the hurried downhillers by sneaking into the woods and actually *pedaling* your bike a bit. This side loop to Rays Ride dives into thickets of oak and maple then curves through a moist hollow cloaked with aspens and broad-leaf ferns. You'll brush by a secluded pond along the way where moose are known to hang out, and the brilliant fall colors will make any New Englander homesick.

Scotts Pond:
2.3-mile side loop, moderate, tech 2⁺-3⁺ (singletrack), 300-foot gain

SOUTHERN WASATCH

Exit the summit of Rays Lift, and go left to descend the main service road to junction #9. Go right past a small shack to #8. A thread of dirt coiled tighter than a temperamental rattlesnake drops you through a canopy of tight-knit oak and maple (tech 3⁺) to #7 at Sunnyside Road. Cross over for more spin-cycle free-wheeling down to junction #4 on Long Hollow Road near the base of Flathead Lift. Cross the road and dart into a grove of old growth aspens that rustle loudly with the slightest breeze. After passing Scotts Pond, stay left at #31 (Archies Loop), and climb moderately through mixed timber to #10 at Mandan Road. Take Mandan Road left to #11, and head

Jerry gets his XC-fix climbing Archies.

to the base on Rays, Rays with a Twist, or Boneyard. (Lift summit-#9-#8-#7-#4-#6-#10-#11-your option to base.)

Archies Trail: When combined with Scotts Pond, Archies makes for the longest trail on the mountain. Archies was an ambitious trail-building project, the end result being a trail that hangs like a high wire act 900 feet above the North Fork Provo River canyon. From one location, you'll enjoy a 270-degree view of

Archies Trail:
4 miles, moderate, tech 2-3⁺ (dirt road and singletracks), 1,050-foot loss

Mount Timpanogos, Cascade Mountain and Provo Peak, and Deer Creek Reservoir. Long traverses across brushy slopes on the upper section and slalom-course turns through tall conifers on the lower section make Archies a descent you should not miss. Conversely, its steady, well-planned grade is a climber's delight.

Downhill on Archies: Exit the summit of Ray Lift, and descend left on the service road to junction #9. Link together #8, #7, and #4, and ride past Scotts Pond to #6. Fork right for Archies Trail, and make a long descending traverse across sun-drenched slopes to a sharp left turn where the trail curves over a ridge and the views are huge; then continue coasting high above the North Fork canyon. The trail is narrow and choppy at times, so you'll have to keep your front wheel on the straight and narrow. Enter the fir trees and come to #30. Go right to bank around a dozen serpentine turns before exiting to the paved road, which you take to the base.

Going uphill on Archies: From the base, go around the horseshoe curve on the paved road, climb .2 mile, and fork left on singletrack for Boneyard and Archies. Climb around gooseneck turns to junction #30 and stay left

SOUTHERN WASATCH

(Boneyard goes right). You'll climb moderately through stately fir trees then across brushy slopes while the North Fork canyon drops farther and farther from beneath your pedals. Power up a short, steep ramp and bank right where the trail curves around a ridge. Views, views, views. A long gradually ascending traverse across a sunny slope with Mount Timpanogos square in your sights leads to #6 on Scotts Pond Loop. Go left to climb clockwise around Scotts then up through #4, #7, and #8 to catch Rays Ride, or go right on Scotts and climb to #10 at Mandan Road. Either way, go over to #11 and descend Rays, Rays with a Twist, or Boneyard to the base. Total distance for the whole loop is between 6.5-7.5 miles.

! Know Before You Go

- Sundance's lift-served trails are open from mid-May to mid-October, weather permitting. Rays Lift operates daily from 10 A.M. to 6:30 P.M. Lift fees are $16 full day, $12 half day (starts at 2:30 P.M.), and $9 twilight (starts at 4:00 P.M.). Lift fees included unlimited rides on Rays Lift. "Trails only" use fee is $8 and includes one free ride on Rays Lift. There is no "free" riding at Sundance. A season pass is available. Call (801) 223-4121 for answers to your mountain biking questions.
- Helmets are required. Bicycle rentals are available.
- Be alert to two-way traffic on all trails. Riders pedaling uphill generally have the right-of-way.
- Bikes are not allowed on hiking trails.
- Sundance operates a mountain bike school and offers individual or group instructions.
- The resort holds weekly citizen's races and ladies-day programs throughout the summer. Contact Sundance for information, schedules, and registration fees.
- Sundance offers lodging, dining, a gift shop, an artisan center, conference facilities, and seasonal theatrical entertainment.
- *Fido Factor:* Dogs are not allowed on the trails at Sundance.

? Maps & More Information

- USGS 1:24,000: Aspen Grove, Utah
- Sundance: (801) 225-4107, www.sundanceresort.com

♪ Trailhead Access

From I-15, take Exit 275 for 8th North Street/UT 52 (Orem), Sundance, and Provo Canyon Recreation Areas. Travel east on 8th North for 4 miles; then drive 7 miles up Provo Canyon on US 189. Turn left for Sundance on UT 92, and drive 2.3 miles to the resort.

SOUTHERN WASATCH

50

Bonneville Shoreline Trail (Provo)

JUST THE FACTS		
Location:	Provo Canyon to Springville	
Length:	4.4 miles (Provo Canyon section); 9.8 miles (Provo-Springville)	
Type:	One-way or out-and-back (double the miles)	
Tread:	6.8 miles singletrack, 7.4 miles doubletrack	
Physically:	Provo Canyon: moderate (one steep climb then flat); Provo-Springville: moderate[+] (short, steep climbs & rolling hills)	
Technically:	2-4 (smooth & choppy singletracks; dirt, gravel, & rock doubletracks)	
Gain:	1,250 feet (Provo-Springville), 750 feet (Provo Canyon section)	
Dogs:	Yes, on leash	

GO ☐
NO ■ | JAN | FEB | MAR | APR | MAY | JUN | JUL | AUG | SEP | OCT | NOV | DEC |

WHY SHOULD U RIDE THIS TRAIL

The Provo-Springville section of the Bonneville Shoreline Trail boasts over 14 miles of designated off-road trails. Except for a short mile-long interruption by paved roads, you can bike from Provo Canyon nearly to Hobble Creek Canyon on singletracks and doubletracks. The section of trail south of Rock Canyon is ideal during early spring and late fall because it receives copious sunshine and dries quickly. The Provo Canyon section is generously shaded, making it more suitable for warmer times of the year. The views of the nearby mountains, deep canyons, and metropolitan valley are stunning and are unique to northern Utah.

Details

Provo Canyon section: The Bonneville Shoreline Trail (BST) forks right from the paved Provo-Jordan River Parkway a couple hundred yards up from Bridal Veil Park. Gear down for a rigorous climb on choppy tread (tech 3[+]). The narrow trail rises sharply through scrub oak for a half mile where it nips the triple support legs of a power line. Catch your breath, and repeat the sequence of climbing in earnest, and then recovering briefly. After rounding two steep, tight, rough switchbacks, the trail levels on an old doubletrack that runs like singletrack. This is the Smith Ditch Road not the ancient Lake Bonneville shoreline, although you would never know it because it's just as flat (tech 2[+]).

Intersect a dirt road in .6 mile, take it to the right through a hollow, and fork left immediately to resume the ditch road/BST. Another .9 mile of level trail takes you to Squaw Peak Road (**m3.0**). Cross over and continue on the ditch road/BST (tech 2). At .7 mile from Squaw Peak Road, the BST forks left in the second of two hollows that the ditch road curves through. If you miss the junction, you'll come to the ditch road's gated end where you can opt to descend a new section of trail to the Indian Road trailhead.

The BST heads steeply up the side of the hollow to a small saddle (tech 3[+]) where it then descends quickly to a four-way junction (**m4.4**). It's hardly worth the effort unless you're planning to drop off the moun-

SOUTHERN WASATCH

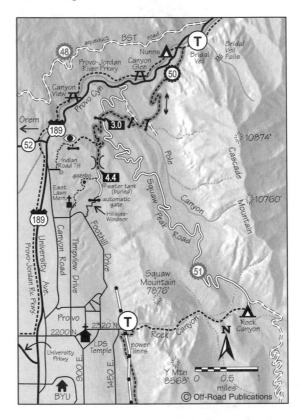

tain and circle back to Provo Canyon on paved roads. If that is your intention, then go straight through the four-way junction, and connect with a
one-lane paved road. When you reach another four-way junction, signed
for Eagle Ridge Ranch, go straight again on the paved road. Go through
the automatic gate (just say "open says-a-me"), and exit next to 1077
Hillside Drive. Descend Hillside Drive and Windsor Drive, go right on
Foothill Drive, pedal along Canyon Road, and link to the Provo-Jordan
River Parkway at the mouth of Provo Canyon (Olmstead trailhead). Bridal

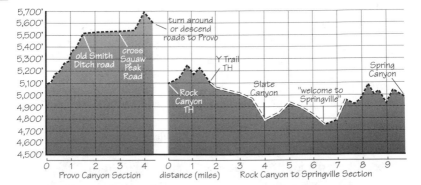

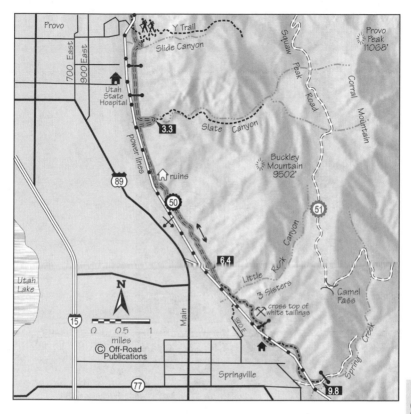

Veil Park is 3.5 miles up Provo Canyon. To reach the Rock Canyon trailhead, take Foothill Drive left/south, weave through residential roads named after Native American tribes (try Sioux to Cherokee to Iroquois), and go left on 2300 North.

Provo-Springville section: This 10-mile section between Rock Canyon (Provo) and Spring Canyon (Springville) follows a braided network of doubletracks along a utility corridor and finishes with a couple miles of tight hand-built singletrack. Trail markers are sporadic, and there are a multitude of junctions. If you miss a turn or get too confused, you can always bail out to a city street and return to Rock Canyon.

Go up the paved road from the gate at the Rock Canyon trailhead, and fork right on another paved lane. Watch for the BST forking right in a couple hundred yards. The singletrack exits the canyon and curves south under the power lines. Tackle two short strenuous climbs (tech 4), and zoom down several steep gravelly hills like a roller coaster screaming toward the earth (tech 4). Climb the paved road to the Y Trail parking area, squeeze through a gap in the fence, and take a doubletrack through Slide Canyon. A sand and gravel utility road (tech 2⁺) takes you high above Provo and Seven Peaks Resort. Go through two gates that define

After making the tough climb out of Provo Canyon, Ross relishes a silky smooth section of Provo's BST.

SOUTHERN WASATCH

Utah State Hospital property, and freewheel down a long hill to Slate Canyon (**m3.3**), so named for the charcoal-gray cliffs that enclose it. On the return, this section will be the longest climb.

Exit Slate Canyon completely by descending the gravel road, but fork left on a dirt road that follows under the power lines and is tagged with pipeline markers. Nearly a mile from Slate Canyon, fork quickly left then right to climb a sandy road south of a rock building that is remnant of an old quarry. Atop the climb, you'll go around a fenced-in underground tank, and you'll overlook a gravel pit. A long gradual descent takes you to a dirt pullout and to a large sign welcoming you to Springville (**m6.4**).

Go through the rock barrier, and continue south on a narrow doubletrack (tech 2). In a half mile, the route narrows to coarse-pebble singletrack and finds an aggressive line through the mouth of Little Rock Canyon (tech 3⁺). The Three Sisters formation is a colossal rock slab towering over the canyon. Directions get tricky here. ("As if they haven't been so far," you say?) Fork left on an unsigned singletrack on the south side of the canyon, climb above the power lines, and cross the top of a mine tailing made of bleach-white limestone. (If you get duped into taking the right/lower fork, you'll exit to a residential area on 970 East in Springville.) A half mile farther, the signed BST goes through a steel gate.

Climb above the power lines again, and roll across the steep foothills on smooth trail (tech 2$^+$) high above Springville and behind a custom home bordered by a black iron fence. The track dips downhill quickly and brushes by a private home so closely that you could pluck a burger off the back-yard grill. A quick hike-a-bike section takes you back uphill on tight peb-bly trail and through the triple support legs of the power lines. Drop down a near vertical descent (tech 4$^+$), link to an old doubletrack, and descend more gradually to Spring Canyon (**m9.8**).

Hope you're feeling fresh because there is a lot of climbing on the return to Rock Canyon. If you bonked, then you might want to ride paved roads from Springville back to Provo and to Rock Canyon.

! Know Before You Go

* The BST is very popular, so expect and respect other trail users.
* Stay on route, and obey all signs restricting travel.
* Midday temperatures during midsummer can reach 100 degrees Fahrenheit, so carry lots of water.
* Rattlesnakes might inhabit these warm foothill areas.
* *Fido Factor:* Dogs must be leashed on the BST. There are no reliable water sources, so carry plenty for your pet.

? Maps & More Information

* USGS 1:24,000: Bridal Veil Falls, Orem, Provo, and Springville, Utah
* Uinta National Forest (Pleasant Grove Ranger Dist.): (801) 785-3563
* Provo City Parks and Recreation: (801) 852-6600
* City of Springville Recreation Department: (801) 489-2730
* Mountainlands Association of Governments: (801) 229-3800, www.mountainland.org

Trailhead Access

Provo Canyon trailhead: From I-15, take Exit 275 for 800 North (Orem) and UT 52. Drive east for 3.6 miles, and enter Provo Canyon on US 189. (The Olmstead trailhead for the Provo-Jordan River Parkway is at the junction.) Drive 3.4 miles up Provo Canyon, and exit for Nunns Park and Bridal Veil Park. Park in the lot at the off ramp.

Rock Canyon trailhead: From I-15, take Exit 272 for University Park-way and Brigham Young University, and travel east. Cross State Street, bend south on University, and turn left/east on 550 West, which becomes 2230 North. Cross University Avenue (stop light) and Provo Canyon Road (stop light). Turn left on North Temple Drive, which becomes 2300 North. Where the road bends south and becomes 1450 East, stay straight/east to reach Rock Canyon.

SOUTHERN WASATCH

51
Squaw Peak Road

JUST THE FACTS	**Location:**	Between Provo Canyon & Hobble Creek Canyon
	Length:	26.8 miles
	Type:	Out-and-back
	Tread:	16.8 miles doubletrack, 10 miles dirt road
	Physically:	Strenuous (long-winded climbs, raging descents)
	Technically:	2-3⁺ (light gravel & washboards on dirt road; ruts & rocks on doubletrack)
	Gain:	4,200 feet
	Dogs:	No to Rock Cyn C.G., traffic. Yes thereafter but possible 4x4 traffic

GO ☐
NO ■ | JAN | FEB | MAR | APR | MAY | JUN | JUL | AUG | SEP | OCT | NOV | DEC |

Squaw Peak Road takes you to some truly outstanding alpine vistas of the Wasatch Range, including three of its wilderness areas: Lone Peak to the far north, Mount Timpanogos in the near north, and Mount Nebo to the south. Distant mountains are only part of the allure, for Provo Peak and Cascade Mountain loom overhead as if they might topple over on you. Far beneath your wheels, the Provo-Orem metro sprawls from the base of the Wasatch Range to Utah Lake. Squaw Peak Road is fast paced and mostly low in technical difficulty, but you'll face several sizeable climbs along the way. Hills that make you sweat and moan on the way in will bring a huge satisfied grin on the return trip.

Details

Although Squaw Peak Road (proper) begins at Provo Canyon, the trailhead for this route is several miles up Squaw Peak Road at Hope Campground where pavement turns to dirt. Begin with 3 miles of steady climbing to a low summit; then descend one-half mile to an overlook of Rock Canyon. Take a break here to peer into this devilish cliff-lined chasm. Its dark gray and treeless limestone walls have been tilted, bent, and broken by what geologist call "tectonics," or movement and deformation of the Earth's crust. You can spy on the residents of Provo far below through the canyon's deep V-shaped notch. Provo Peak and its attendant summits swirl overhead while Cascade Mountain, just north of Provo Peak, is a near-vertical escarpment of rough-cut stone.

A high-speed descent leads to Rock Canyon Campground (**m5.0**) where you begin the route's most formidable climb. Forest Road 027 rises steadily and turns continuously. It's a slow granny-gear grind for mortal mountain bikers or an anaerobic test track for racers in training. The views along the way are very different from traditional Wasatch Front scenes, for you rise through a back basin wedged between the frontal peaks of Squaw and Y Mountains and the predominant Provo Peak crest.

The climb's summit is marked by the Slide Canyon trailhead and a compelling view north of superimposed Wasatch peaks (**m9.0**). Contour

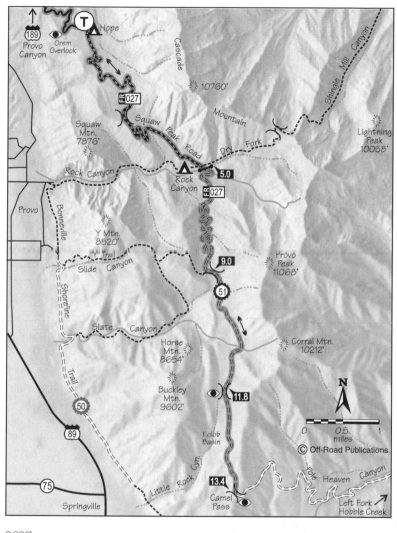

SOUTHERN WASATCH

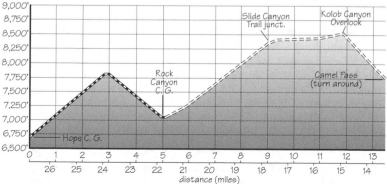

An autumn snowfall drapes Provo Peak.

across the head of Slate Canyon to the saddle separating Horse Mountain from Corral Mountain (**m11.8**). Far below in Utah Valley, Springville cuddles up against the Wasatch Front; Lake Bonneville's ancient terraced shoreline traces the mountains' foothills before fading out of sight around Mount Nebo; and Nebo, the tallest of all Wasatch peaks at 11,928 feet, shapes the southern horizon into a mountainous pyramid.

Two miles of choppy dirt road lead to Camel Pass where the road bends sharply left (**m13.4**). This is your "last-chance Texaco" to turn around and return to Hope Campground. If you continue descending through Pole Heaven Canyon to Hobble Creek, you'll end up over 30 miles from Hope Campground and your vehicle. Plus, you'll want to go straight to the chiropractor after the long jackhammer descent.

Option: Squaw Peak Road Short Course

Naturally, you don't have to go the whole distance. Ride to Rock Canyon Campground and back for a 10-mile, moderate tour on light-duty dirt roads (1,700-foot gain); otherwise, start at Rock Canyon Campground and ride to Camel Pass and back for a 16-mile, moderate[+] ride on doubletracks (2,500-foot gain).

Option: Rock Canyon Trail

Go for broke and start from Provo by climbing Rock Canyon Trail to Rock Canyon Campground. There, you can head south on Squaw Peak Road to Camel Pass. Better yet, go north on Squaw Peak Road, and link up with the Bonneville Shoreline Trail. Decend the BST to the Provo-Jordan River Trail, and loop right back to Rock Canyon via a few paved roads (see

Trailhead Access). Sounds great, huh? Keep in mind that Rock Canyon Trail is a murderous climb that gains nearly 2,000 feet in 3 short miles. That's an average 11-percent grade, and that's steep! Plus, the tread is rock and gravel in many places, which makes the task that much more difficult. Got something to prove? Then go ahead, blow a gasket.

Know Before You Go

- Motor vehicles are common on Squaw Peak Road between Hope and Rock Canyon Campgrounds. Four-wheel-drive vehicles and OHVs frequently travel the remainder of the route.
- Hope and Rock Canyon Campgrounds are Forest Service fee areas. Both have water taps.
- Rock Canyon Trail is extremely popular with hikers, so expect and respect other trail users.
- *Fido Factor:* Dogs are not recommended on this route because of possible vehicle traffic.

Maps & More Information

- USGS 1:24,000: Bridal Veil Falls and Springville, Utah
- Uinta National Forest (Pleasant Grove Ranger Dist): (801) 785-3563

Trailhead Access

From I-15, take Exit 275 for 8th North (Orem), travel east on UT 52, and then veer up Provo Canyon on US 189. About 2 miles up Provo Canyon, turn right on Squaw Peak Road (near milepost 9). Hope Campground is 4.5 miles up the road. A small road-side pullout at the campground's entrance accommodates a couple of vehicles; otherwise, park at your discretion. Do not park in a campsite unless you plan to pay for it.

SOUTHERN WASATCH

52
Bald Knoll-Windy Pass

JUST THE FACTS

Location:	15 miles southwest of Heber; 26 miles northeast of Provo
Length:	22 miles
Type:	Point-to-point
Tread:	13.5 miles singletrack, 4 miles doubletrack, 4.5 miles pavement
Physically:	Strenuous+ (steep climbs, big gain, rugged descents, remote)
Technically:	3-5 (rock-studded dirt road w/ shallow creek crossings; narrow, choppy singletrack w/ steep, rocky ascents & descents)
Gain:	3,500 feet
Dogs:	Not recommended, paved road section required

GO □
NO ■ | JAN | FEB | MAR | APR | MAY | JUN | JUL | AUG | SEP | OCT | NOV | DEC |

Adventures on the Great Western Trail continue. This is a big ride that ventures from one valley to another and crosses mountaintops along the way. You'll ride along the margins of stream-fed canyons, penetrate alpine forests, and gain extraordinary views of the southern Wasatch Range from the day's end, you'll agree that the Great Western Trail is a corridor of diversity.

WHY SHOULD U RIDE THIS TRAIL

Details

S tart out on FR 121 with about 3 miles of rock-studded doubletrack, and cross Right Fork Little Hobble Creek several times. Fork right near an old wooden corral in the broad pastures of Little Valley, and follow a carsonite post marking the Great Western Trail (GWT) (**m3.1**). Fork right again 1 mile farther on another doubletrack tagged with GWT markers. (The left fork is the continuation of FR 121.)

Head up the aspen-clad hollow, chasing the GWT markers, and then fork left on a singletrack that winds up the narrowing canyon. Climb through aspen groves, gently at first then steeply, to a saddle that separates Bald Knoll from Wallsburg Ridge (**m5.9**). Take the path southward and up a set of switchbacks. Thereafter, the narrow path hugs the steep slopes of Bald Knoll at the 8,200-foot mark and penetrates aspen and fir trees underlain by maples, oaks, and ferns.

The trail bends south around Bald Knoll and descends gently to a saddle marked with a solitary tree. Take a deep breath so you can tackle the steep, switchbacking climb over the knoll to the west. It's a hike-a-bike, by and large. The path clips the ridge then bends south and continues rising around a hillside that affords a huge panorama of Provo River's South Fork basin, Wallsburg Ridge, and distant Wasatch peaks. Lightning Peak and a series of glacial holes, simply named First through Fourth, define the west side of the Provo Peak ridge. A sharp, technical descent takes you to Windy Pass where, not surprisingly, the breeze can blow to bothersome levels (**m12.3**).

It's all downhill from here, but don't think you're out of the woods just yet because many sections are rough and require a full repertoire of riding skills (tech 3-4⁺). The GWT plummets north into the head of Water Hollow, wraps around the sheer flank of Lightning Peak, and angles into upper Shingle Mill Canyon. Alpine forests that were plentiful at higher elevations yield to tenacious oak, maple, and alpine sage at these lower, warmer climes. Turn right on a dirt road at the Big Springs trailhead (**m17.0**), go around a steel gate, and take the road down to Trefoil Ranch. Cap off the ride by zooming 4.5 miles down the paved road to Vivian Park.

After hours of climbing, Bart's still smiling and ready for more.

! Know Before You Go

- Windy Pass to Big Springs trailhead is very popular with equestrians and hikers, so expect and respect other trail users.
- You may encounter motorists between Trefoil Ranch and Vivian Park.
- Vivian Park has water taps, restrooms, and picnic areas. Snows Marina, at the turnoff for Wallsburg, has a small convenience store. Wallsburg has a general store.
- *Fido Factor:* The GWT is dog friendly, but you must ride several miles on a paved road at the end of this route. Leave your pick-up vehicle at Big Springs trailhead if your dog is coming along. Even then, it's a long ride with few water sources.

? Maps & More Information

- USGS 1:24,000: Bridal Veil Falls, Charleston, and Wallsburg Ridge, Utah
- Uinta National Forest (Pleasant Grove Ranger Dist): (801) 785-3563

Trailhead Access

Vivian Park trailhead: From I-15, take Exit 275 for 8ᵗʰ North/UT 52 (Orem), Sundance, and Provo Canyon Recreation Areas. Travel 4 miles east on UT 52 then 6 miles up Provo Canyon on US 189 to Vivian Park/ South Fork. From Heber, travel southwest on US 189 and around Deer Creek Reservoir. Turn off for Vivian Park/South Fork about 5 miles below the dam.

Wallsburg trailhead: In the shuttle vehicle, drive from Vivian Park up Provo Canyon, and turn right for Wallsburg on UT 222 about 2.8 miles east of Deer Creek Reservoir's dam and across from Snows Marina. Pass through Wallsburg (pretty much any road will do), and continue 2 miles on Main Canyon Road. Turn right at a junction for Little Valley Road. Curve around a knoll, and stay left at another junction for Little Valley Road. About .5 mile after the pavement turns to dirt, park at the edge of a meadow where several jeep roads fork left. Obey all signs restricting travel.

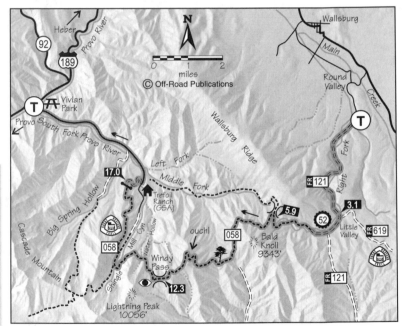

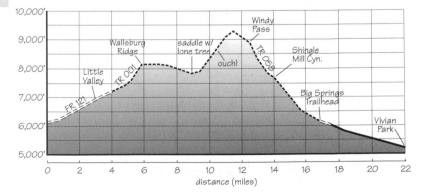

53
Hobble Creek

JUST THE FACTS

Location:	7 miles southeast of Springville
Length:	42 miles
Type:	Loop
Tread:	22.7 miles doubletrack, 6.3 miles dirt road, 13 miles pavement
Physically:	Extreme (long distance w/ steady climbs)
Technically:	2-3$^+$ (gravel & washboards; rock-studded descent)
Gain:	4,500 feet
Dogs:	No, too long

GREAT WESTERN TRAIL

GO ☐
NO ■ | JAN | FEB | MAR | APR | MAY | JUN | JUL | AUG | SEP | OCT | NOV | DEC |

WHY SHOULD U RIDE THIS TRAIL

Whether you're looking for a long-distance, off-road, train-ing ride or a seldom-traveled, fat-tire tour through the Wasatch's hinterlands, you'll enjoy the Hobble Creek loop. You'll crank out 25 miles of moderate hills up to the loop's highpoint then rip around sweeping turns and hop over rocks and ruts on a furious descent. Of course, if you let up on the throttle and allow your eyes to wander, you'll find charming blue-ribbon streams, captivating woodlands, flower-clad meadows, and stunning sights of the southern Wasatch Range.

Details

A thick riparian veil enshrouds Right Fork Hobble Creek, and only its steady gurgling suggests that fat trout await a baited line. Pavement turns to light-duty dirt at the Wardsworth Creek trailhead (**m7.6**), and you begin the long, steady, and shadeless climb to the Right Fork summit (tech 2). Along the way, you'll catch distant views of Provo Peak's faceted ridge. From the summit, a speedy descent on smooth dirt takes you to the junction with the Halls Fork road/FR 132 (**m14.0**).

Several miles of steady, moderate$^+$ climbing alongside Halls Fork Creek bring you to the trailhead for Center Trail, No. 009 (**m17.5**). (See "Center Trail: Halls Fork-Sixth Water.") Your pace will quicken farther along as the doubletrack rolls across hills and vales that flank Strawberry Ridge. Loafer Mountain and Mount Nebo fade on the southern skyline while Provo Peak flashes through aspen groves to the west. Cross Chase Creek, and bend through Slab Canyon 2 miles farther. Pump Ridge is marked by a cattle guard, wire fence, and doubletrack paralleling the fence. Stay on the main road and bend around upper Wardsworth Creek. Continuing the traverse, you come to a prominent right-hand bend, marked by a massive Douglas fir tree and a doubletrack branching south toward Wardsworth Peak (**m26.8**). Stay on the main road, and begin descending the Left Fork Hobble Creek road.

The Left Fork road is steeper and noticeably more rocky than the Halls Fork road (tech 3$^+$), so pick your line carefully. If you dare take your

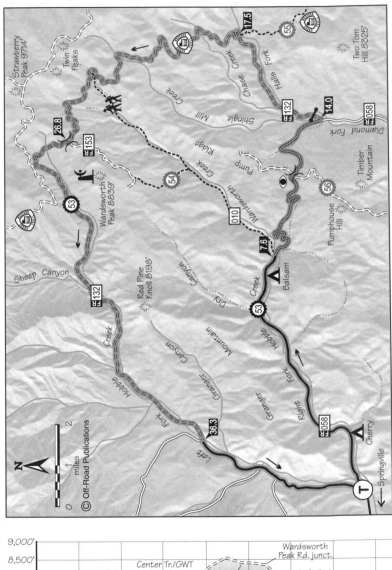

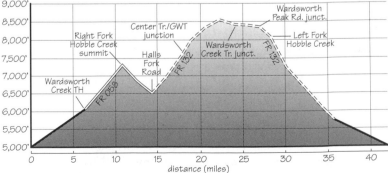

eyes off the bumpy road, you'll catch inspiring angles of Provo Peak and adjacent mountains. A couple of miles down from the summit, the GWT branches north and heads to Little Valley near Wallsburg, but keep descending the jackhammer road. Splash through the Left Fork of Hobble Creek twice; then rejoice when dirt turns to pavement (**m36.3**). Six miles of easy cruising take you back to the junction of Left and Right Forks and the loop's end. Whew! What a long day.

Aspen leaves sprinkle the road with golden glitter.

SOUTHERN WASATCH

! Know Before You Go

- Portions of this loop are remote and seldom visited, except during hunting season at which time this route can be a dangerous choice.
- Vehicles may be encountered on all roads.
- Cherry and Balsam Campgrounds in Right Fork Hobble Creek are Forest Service fee areas.
- *Fido Factor:* This ride is too long and difficult for dogs, and you might encounter vehicle traffic.

? Maps & More Information

- USGS 1:24,000: Granger Mountain, Twin Peaks, Two Tom Hill, and Wallsburg Ridge, Utah
- Uinta National Forest (Spanish Fork Ranger District): (801) 798-3571

Trailhead Access

From I-15, take Exit 263 for Springville. Travel east on UT 77/400 North, cross Main Street, and bend right/south on 1300 East/Canyon Drive, following signs for Hobble Creek Golf Course and Hobble Creek Canyon. The road splits .5 mile past the golf course at the confluence of the Right and Left Forks of Hobble Creek. Park here at your discretion or 1.5 miles farther up the Right Fork road near the Cherry Campground.

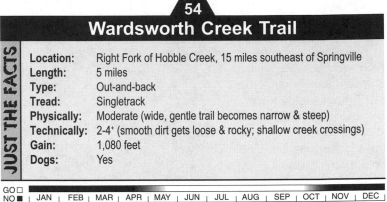

54
Wardsworth Creek Trail

JUST THE FACTS

Location:	Right Fork of Hobble Creek, 15 miles southeast of Springville
Length:	5 miles
Type:	Out-and-back
Tread:	Singletrack
Physically:	Moderate (wide, gentle trail becomes narrow & steep)
Technically:	2-4$^+$ (smooth dirt gets loose & rocky; shallow creek crossings)
Gain:	1,080 feet
Dogs:	Yes

GO □
NO ■ | JAN | FEB | MAR | APR | MAY | JUN | JUL | AUG | SEP | OCT | NOV | DEC |

WHY SHOULD YOU RIDE THIS TRAIL

Wardsworth Creek Trail is a relatively short ride but one that will leave you grinning from ear to ear. Novice to intermediate bikers will enjoy the lower trail's smooth, wide tread. Strong bikers who venture farther up the trail will find that the multiple tiny creek crossings are fun technical challenges. All along the way, the trail hugs the banks of the tumbling creek and passes through a rich mosaic of riparian growth.

Details

The trail splits just up from the trailhead. The main trail forks right and crosses the creek over a log footbridge. (The left fork stays on the north side of the creek, but it's steep and generally unridable.) Shortly ahead, the path crosses back over the creek. For the next mile or so, the trail is an absolute joy (tech 2$^+$) as it snakes through pine, oak, maple, and cottonwood trees that envelop the cascading creek. Then the path rises up a steep hill near a small picturesque waterfall. The errant trails trod by cattle can make things confusing at times. Just stay next to the babbling brook.

The trail turns northward, and heads up a tributary to Wardsworth Creek on what is now the Dry Canyon Cutoff Trail, No 128. The next mile is quite challenging because the narrow, rock- and root-filled path crosses the creek a half-dozen times while rising steeply (tech 3-4). These conditions will test both your handling skills and your strength. Where the creek's flow dissipates, the path enters a grass and sage meadow marked by cattle ponds (**m2.5**). This is the recommended turnaround point because the trail peters out ahead to a braided network of cattle paths that wander every which way. The ride back to the trailhead is quick but, oh, so delightful.

If you continue uphill past the cattle ponds, then you will intersect a doubletrack that goes right to Wardsworth Peak and eventually connects to the Halls Fork road. Left leads to Right Fork Dry Canyon, presumably.

SOUTHERN WASATCH

❗ Know Before You Go

- This route is popular with equestrians, hikers, and anglers, too. Ride courteously and at prudent speeds, especially when descending.
- Cattle range in this canyon, so watch out for "guacamole" in the trail.
- Cherry and Balsam Campgrounds on the Right Fork Hobble Creek road are Forest Service fee areas.
- *Fido Factor:* Trail is dog friendly.

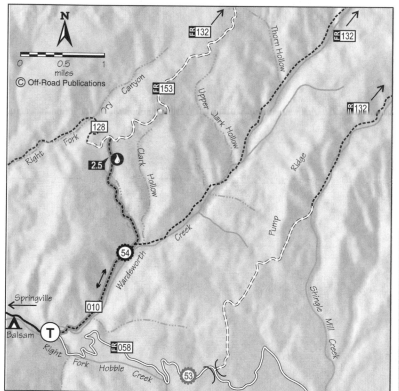

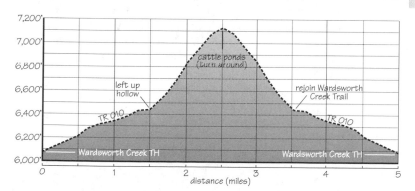

SOUTHERN WASATCH

A double waterfall in Wardsworth Creek.

? Maps & More Information

- USGS 1:24,000: Granger Mountain and Two Tom Hill, Utah
- Uinta National Forest (Spanish Fork Ranger District): (801) 798-3571

Trailhead Access

From I-15, take Exit 263 for Springville. Travel east on UT 77/400 North. Cross Main Street then bend right/south on 1300 East/Canyon Drive, following signs for Hobble Creek Golf Course and Hobble Creek Canyon. Stay right .5 mile past the golf course, and drive 7.5 miles up the Right Fork Hobble Creek road to the Wardsworth Creek trailhead. Parking is limited.

SOUTHERN WASATCH

55
Center Trail (Halls Fork-Sixth Water)

JUST THE FACTS	**Location:**	Diamond Fork, 35 miles southeast of Provo
	Length:	15 miles
	Type:	Loop (clockwise)
	Tread:	4.3 miles singletrack, 8.9 miles doubletrack, 1.8 miles dirt road
	Physically:	Moderate⁺ (moderate climb on dirt road; steep hills on primitive singletrack; route-finding)
	Technically:	2-4⁺ (under maintained trail w/ deadfall, rocks, & steep descents; rutted doubletracks; gravel & washboards on dirt roads)
	Gain:	2,300 feet
	Dogs:	Not recommended, possible vehicle traffic; yes, trails only

GO □
NO ■ | JAN | FEB | MAR | APR | MAY | JUN | JUL | AUG | SEP | OCT | NOV | DEC |

Although the Center Trail may not be the center of attention in the Spanish Fork Ranger District, it offers
adventerous mountain bikers the chance to explore remote areas of the Wasatch hinterlands without completely
severing their ties to the civilized world. The loop begins
with a one-shot climb on good roads alongside glistening streams; then
it traverses rolling, timbered terrain on a promising but sometimes rugged singletrack. A rutted doubletrack descent will keep you hopping. Its
out-of-the-way location keeps the crowds away, so it might be just right
if you're looking for a little solitary exploration.

Details

From Springville Crossing, pedal north on FR 058. (You'll return on FR 029 to the east from Sixth Water Creek.) The smooth dirt road rises gently for a nice warmup (tech 1). Fork right up Halls Fork Road/FR 132 (**m1.8**). The grade steepens progressively, and some rough sections can be strenuous (tech 2-3). Alongside the road, Halls Fork Creek sparkles in the midday sun as it tumbles over rock ledges or pools behind beaver dams. Sage and oak dominate these warm, sunny slopes, but every shaded hollow harbors communities of fir and aspens.

The road bends left sharply at the Center Trail-GWT trailhead (**m5.4**). Hop on the trail and take it south into a small valley, cross fields to a high point, and then descend to a second valley (tech 3⁺). Watch for carsonite posts marking the way. Cross a small creek and head south up a sun-dappled hollow. This section is steep, rough, and can be overgrown, so you may have to walk at times. Another carsonite post directs you south into a broad, sage-filled clearing where the trail can be indistinct, if not undetectable. Veer left/southeast and make your way up the draw. The track is more evident when you reach the meadow's wooded perimeter. Pedal and push your way uphill, generally eastward, through thick under-brush and hip-high wildflowers that crowd the trail. A pair of carsonite posts atop the hill confirm the route (**m7.8**). This is also the trail's highest elevation.

SOUTHERN WASATCH

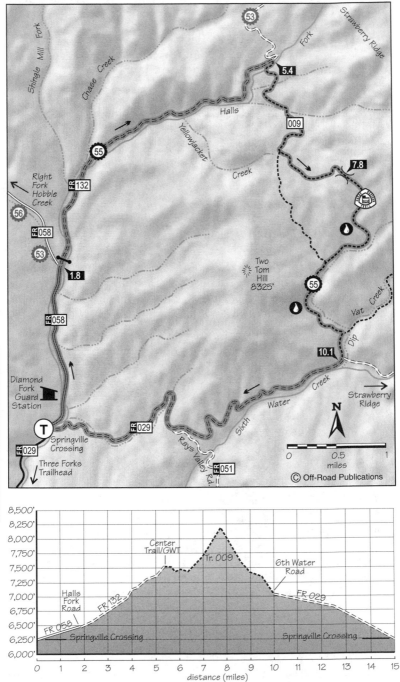

Enveloped by an aspen jungle on the Center Trail.

Begin descending tentatively because the trail can be narrow, overgrown, and booby-trapped with unforeseen obstacles (tech 3$^+$). Zoom downhill through glades of aspens, and pass a fenced-in spring with a cattle trough. Pass another spring and cattle trough in the next clearing, keeping an eye out for trail markers directing you down the valley.

A charming creek cascades through the deepening canyon, but the suddenly rough and rocky trail warrants your full attention (tech 3$^+$-4$^+$). Veer right at a trail junction signed for Dip Vat Creek, and follow the doubletrack to the Sixth Water Creek road (**m10.1**). The road can be deeply rutted from four-wheel-drive vehicles that have squirmed through the mud, so you'll have to shoot straight and balance cleanly to ride the berms and to avoid being sucked into the sinuous furrows (tech 3$^+$). Stay right at the junction with Rays Valley Road, and float down Sixth Water Road another 2 miles back to Springville Crossing.

Option: Sixth Water-Fifth Water

You can add an extra 10 miles by following the Sixth Water Creek road up to Strawberry Ridge and back. In the canyon below the road, Sixth Water Creek is a veritable torrent as it gushes out of the Strawberry Tunnel's

SOUTHERN WASATCH

West Portal. A short distance past the portal, the Center Trail/GWT branches south and heads over to Fifth Water Creek. Although the trail begins as an inviting doubletrack, it turns into an abusive pack trail fraught with protracted slopes, fallen trees, and a tangle of underbrush. Pack along a machete and a small chainsaw because you might need it if you dare explore this stretch!

! Know Before You Go

- Center Trail is remote and seldom traveled, so prepare accordingly.
- Diamond Campground on Diamond Fork Road and Cherry and Balsam Campgrounds on Right Fork Hobble Creek Road are Forest Service fee areas with water taps and outhouses.
- *Fido Factor:* Singletrack is dog friendly, but vehicle traffic may be encountered on dirt roads and doubletracks.

? Maps & More Information

- USGS 1:24,000: Two Tom Hill, Utah
- Uinta National Forest (Spanish Fork Ranger District): (801) 798-3571

Trailhead Access

Via Diamond Fork: From I-15, take Exit 261 for Price and Manti and travel east on US 6. Five miles up Spanish Fork Canyon, turn left/north on FR 029 for Diamond Fork. Drive 10 miles to the Three Forks parking area then 6 miles more to Springville Crossing (trailhead). Park at your discretion.

Via Springville/Hobble Creek: From I-15, take Exit 263 for Springville and travel east on UT 77/400 North. Cross Main Street and bend right/south on 1300 East/Canyon Drive, following signs for Hobble Creek Golf Course and Hobble Creek Canyon. Stay right .5 mile past the golf course, and drive 7.5 miles up the paved Right Fork Hobble Creek Road to the Wardsworth Creek trailhead. Continue on the Right fork road (now light-duty dirt, gravel, and washboards) for 8.5 miles, over the summit, and to Springville Crossing. (Road is generally suitable for passenger cars when dry but might be impassable when wet.)

SOUTHERN WASATCH

⛰ 56
Sawmill Hollow

JUST THE FACTS

Location:	Diamond Fork, 35 miles southeast of Provo
Length:	11.2 miles
Type:	Loop (counterclockwise)
Tread:	1.7 miles singletrack, 3.5 miles doubletrack, 4.8 miles dirt roads, 1.2 miles paved road
Physically:	Moderate (steady climbs & a few, short, steep hills)
Technically:	1-4 (narrow paved road; some washboards on dirt roads; rutted doubletracks; under-maintained singletrack w/ short, steep drops)
Gain:	1,713 feet
Dogs:	Not recommended, possible vehicle traffic

GO ☐
NO ■ | JAN | FEB | MAR | APR | MAY | JUN | JUL | AUG | SEP | OCT | NOV | DEC |

If variety is the spice of life, then you'll find the full gamut of riding conditions on this little circuit in Diamond Fork. You'll start out with an easy climb on the paved Diamond Fork Road, climb moderately on dirt roads to a ridge that overlooks the southern Wasatch Range and its hinterlands, and then dive down a hair-raising singletrack that rivals any amusement park thrill ride. Don't be dismayed if you are not a flying ace. The white-knuckle parts of the trail are short, so if you are willing to dismount and walk a bit, you should fare well on this ride.

Details

Head up the paved Diamond Fork Road for 1.2 miles to Springville Crossing. Continue straight/north toward Right Fork Hobble Creek and Springville on FR 058, which turns to dirt with light gravel and washboards (tech 2⁺). Fork left at the Halls Fork junction to continue on FR 058 (FR 132 forks right), and climb moderately to the summit of Right Fork Hobble Creek (**m6.0**).

Go left/south at the summit on a deeply rutted doubletrack, FR 115, although it may not be signed. Cross an open meadow that offers a grand vista of Provo Peak to the east, and then duck into the conifers. Pump up a couple of steep hills, and cross vast meadows blanketing Timber Mountain. At a T-junction (**m7.4**), turn right on FR 115 (may be marked with a carsonite post), and then fork left 100 yards farther on an unsigned doubletrack. Descend gradually through a meadow toward Mollies Nipple. (Ignore a doubletrack branching left and rising to a grove of aspens and pines on Timber Mountain; it's a dead end.) Keep descending to a forested hollow posted "Sawmill Hollow, Dominguez-Escalante Trail" (**m8.5**). You can tack on a couple extra miles by pedaling out-and-back to Mollies Nipple for some great views of Diamond Fork and Wanrhodes Canyons.

Lower your seat and cinch down your brain bucket. As you start down the singletrack, stay to the right and toward a carsonite post; don't follow the game trail northward and across the meadow. Swing through angular turns; then plummet down steep fall-away slopes through thick

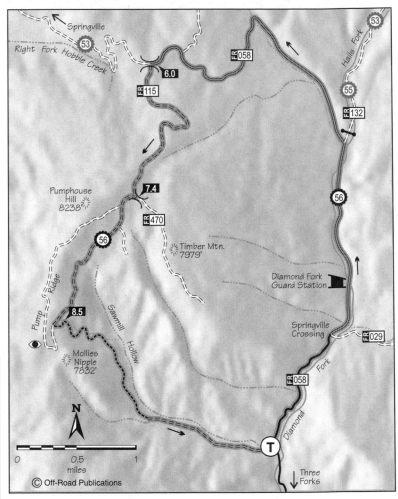

SOUTHERN WASATCH

Springville

Right Fork Hobble Creek

53

FR 058

6.0

FR 115

7.4

FR 470

Pumphouse Hill 8238'

Timber Mtn. 7979'

56

Pump Ridge

8.5

Sawmill Hollow

Mollies Nipple 7832'

Halls Fork

53

55

FR 132

56

Diamond Fork Guard Station

Springville Crossing

FR 029

FR 058

Diamond Fork

N

0   0.5   1
        miles

© Off-Road Publications

T

Three Forks

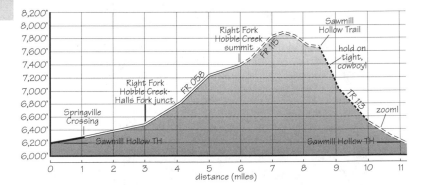

Sawmill Hollow Trail

Right Fork Hobble Creek summit

FR 115

FR 058

Right Fork Hobble Creek–Halls Fork junct.

Springville Crossing

Sawmill Hollow TH

hold on tight, cowboy!

TR 113

zoom!

Sawmill Hollow TH

distance (miles)

Joe races down Sawmill Hollow, and likes it.

brush. Some sections redline the "Oh Sh*t" meter (tech 4⁺). Sure, if you're determined, you might make it down without dismounting or even dabbing a foot, but can you descend cleanly without locking up your brakes and skidding an inch? Now that takes skill!

About one-half mile down, the trail mellows and crosses open fields linked by groves of trees. One last pitch drops to a junction signed "Dominguez-Escalante Trail." Kick in the afterburners and blaze down the jeep road for a mile to the trailhead, but be wary of a half-dozen gullies that cross the road; many are booby-trapped with unforeseen obstacles.

! Know Before You Go

* Doubletracks are impassable when wet.
* Diamond Campground on Diamond Fork Road is a Forest Service fee area with water taps and outhouses.
* *Fido Factor:* Singletrack and doubletracks are dog friendly, but vehicle traffic may be encountered on paved and dirt roads.

? Maps & More Information

* USGS 1:24,000: Two Tom Hill, Utah
* Uinta National Forest (Spanish Fork Ranger District): (801) 798-3571

⌇ Trailhead Access

Via Diamond Fork: From I-15, take Exit 261 (Price, Manti), and travel east on US 6. Five miles up Spanish Fork Canyon, turn left/north on FR 029 for Diamond Fork. Drive 14.5 miles to the Sawmill Hollow trailhead, passing Three Forks parking area in 10 miles.

Via Springville: From I-15, take Exit 263 and travel east on UT 77/400 North. Cross Main Street and then bend right/south on 1300 East/Canyon Drive, following signs for Hobble Creek Golf Course. Stay right .5 mile past the golf course, and drive 7.5 miles up the paved Right Fork Hobble Creek road to the Wardsworth Creek trailhead then 3.5 miles farther on the light-duty dirt to the summit. Start here (**m6.0** in the trail description above), or drive 4.2 miles down to Springville Crossing and 1.8 miles farther to the Sawmill Hollow trailhead. (Right Fork Hobble Creek road is generally suitable for passenger cars when dry but might be impassable when wet.)

57

Diamond Fork Hot Springs Loop

JUST THE FACTS

Location:	Diamond Fork, 28 miles southeast of Provo
Length:	15.1 miles
Type:	Loop
Tread:	9.6 miles singletrack, .7 mile doubletrack, 4.8 miles pavement
Physically:	Moderate$^+$ (steady singletrack climb, rolling paved road, choppy & buffed descent)
Technically:	2-4$^+$ (good singletracks w/ a few dismounts on the descent)
Gain:	2,100 feet
Dogs:	No, paved road; yes on trails only

GO ☐ NO ■	JAN	FEB	MAR	APR	MAY	JUN	JUL	AUG	SEP	OCT	NOV	DEC

Cottonwood Canyon-Fifth Water, a.k.a. *Hot Springs Loop, links together the two core trails of the Diamond Fork area on what is an all-time Wasatch singletrack classic. There are no lofty ridge-top views along this route— unless you opt for the longer Strawberry Ridge loop. You'll trade panoramas for two sweet singletracks that go up one stream-fed canyon and down another. Most importantly, you'll pass right by the Fifth Water hot springs near the ride's end, where you can soak your weary muscles in rock-lined pools fed by natural sulfur springs and then douse yourself under an icy waterfall nearby. But wait, there's more. You can add on more trails and doubletracks to make loops up to 24 miles long. Conversely, you can shorten your day by riding out-and-back on either trail. You name it, Diamond Fork has it.*

Details

Rather than flip through separate chapters for the many variations of the Hot Springs Loop, just see the "Options" listed below for the *Full Monty.* Here's the main loop: up Cottonwood-Second Water Trail, across Rays Valley Road, and down lower Fifth Water Trail.

Cross the footbridge at the parking area, fork right for Cottonwood-Second Water Trail, No. 018, and hop across Cottonwood Creek. You might have to cross the creek several times in the next quarter mile, depending on current trail alignment. The trail rises moderate$^+$ along the creek through stands of oak, maple, fir, and namesake cottonwood trees. Rocky zones and steep micro hills interrupt the path's smooth flow and make for tech 3$^+$ conditions periodically. You'll get a strong whiff of rotten eggs a half mile past the junction for Jocks Canyon Trail (No. 019) because the trail winds past sulfur springs. The trail dips steeply through the creek twice, bends through a rocky gulch (tech 4$^+$), and rises up a short steep hill. Ride along a wire fence on the edge of a thistle meadow, and come to a junction with a dirt road (**m4.6**).

Fork left for Second Water Trail, and pump hard up a steep, pebbly ramp; then hike-a-bike over rock ledges that create a small waterfall in the creek. Watch for a carsonite post directing you across the drainage, and rise up the narrow sage valley to paved Rays Valley Road (**m5.7**). (To make the journey a touch easier, skip this last section of trail, and take the dirt road up to Rays. You'll add on an extra mile in doing so but avoid some tough trail.)

Those heading to Center Trail or Strawberry Ridge will cross the road to continue on Cottonwood-Second Water Trail. Those continuing on the Hot Springs Loop will take Rays Valley Road northward. Four short modest climbs offset by long howling descents take you across Second, Third,

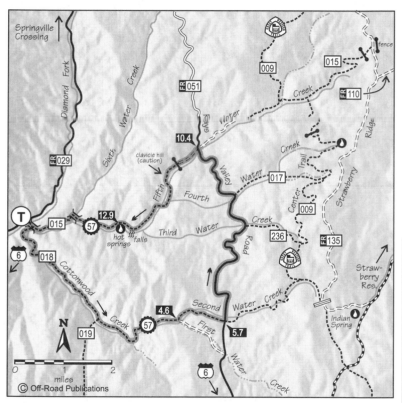

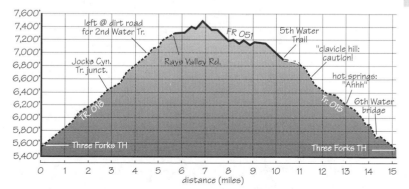

SOUTHERN WASATCH

Waterfalls mean the Fifth Water hot springs are nearby.

and Fourth Water Creeks to the Fifth Water Trail junction (**m10.4**). Keep your eyes peeled because the junction is at the bottom of a particularly fast hill and marked only by a stop sign on the crossroad. (If Rays Valley Road turns to dirt, then you missed it.)

Fifth Water Trail, No. 015, begins as doubletrack then narrows to singletrack after .7 mile. A quick little climb takes you high above the creek and to "Clavicle Hill" where the path drops suddenly over tall rock ledges (tech 5). A fall here could leave you with only one functional shoulder. The water crossing at the bottom of the hill can be swift and deep in the spring. (If flow is high, then try the cheater route to the right. It's tricky because it crosses the steep shale bank, but you'll keep your feet dry.) Cross a tributary then the main creek again to rejoin the cheater route. A lovely stretch of smooth, curving trail winds through fir, juniper, and pinyon; then the bouldery path dives steeply on the edge of the narrow gorge (tech 3-4$^+$). The second waterfall marks the hot springs (**m12.9**). Take a soak; riding the last 2.2 miles with soggy shorts is well worth it.

The trail is much easier (tech 2-3) and remarkably scenic below the hot springs. Tall cliffs of ruddy sandstone conglomerate peppered with fir trees enclose the deep canyon, and after crossing the bridge over Sixth Water, the trail-side creek becomes a torrent of white water. The descent is long and gradual on both silky smooth and choppy tread all the way back to the trailhead, but there are several short, steep rises along the way that will force you to shift quickly to easier gears and pump hard briefly.

Option: Cottonwood-Second Water, out-and-back

This is a no brainer. Just ride up to the dirt road junction (**m4.6** above), and turn around. Total distance is 9.2 miles; gain is 1,300 feet, difficulty is moderate, technical rating is 2-4, and fun-factor is off the charts. You'll miss the Fifth Water hot springs, though.

Option: Fifth Water Trail, out-and-back

Here's the other side of the equation. Ride 2.2 miles from the trailhead to the Fifth Water hot springs then back. The distance is short, the gain is only 700 feet, the difficulty is moderate. In 2001, Diamond Fork was hit by an intense rainfall event that caused flash flooding. Small rock and debris slides slammed the trail, making it a bit rougher and tougher than in the past. Future trail maintenance may restore the tread.

Cross the footbridge at the trailhead, and head straight up Fifth Water Trail along Sixth Water Creek. In 1.1 miles, you'll cross a footbridge over Sixth Water and continue up Fifth Water Creek. Another 1.1 miles takes you to a waterfall at the hot springs. Above the hot springs, the trail gets steep and very rocky at times (tech 3-5). Upper Fifth Water Trail, across Rays Valley Road, is an excellent ride up to the Center Trail junction. Beyond, it gets steep and rough.

Option: Center Trail (20.5 miles, extreme, tech 2⁺-5, 3,700-foot gain)

Making a loop out of the Center Trail is less an "add-on" and more a whole new ride. You'll forfeit nearly 5 miles of smooth, rolling paved road for double the distance of rugged singletrack. Although the Center Trail is part of the multi-use GWT (it's open to motorcycles here), it's never been the center of attention for land managers as a mountain biking trail. Each of the four drainages you cross is preceded by a burly climb with bouts of hike-a-biking and is followed by a thrilling descent that has redeeming moments. Some riders love the Center Trail for its remoteness and ruggedness while others loath it for the same reasons.

Ride up Cottonwood Canyon to Rays Valley Road as described in the Hot Springs Loop previously (**m5.7**). It's 7.5 miles from here to upper Fifth Water Trail via the Center Trail plus another 2.5 miles to Rays Valley Road; allow several hours for this section alone. Cross the road and head up Cottonwood-Second Water Trail, No. 018, for Strawberry Ridge and Center Trail. Dip through the creek and spin up the drainage on clay-dirt tread, which can be gumbo mud when wet, powdery silt when dry, or hardpacked brick when just right (tech 2⁺). Cross the creek a second time, and push up a steep ramp. The trail gets steeper and rockier (tech 4-5) as it bends north and crosses the trickling creek several times on its way up to the Center Trail junction. Get used to it.

Go left, and pedal and push up the rock-riddled trail to a small ridge engulfed by aspens (tech 4-5). There are four more climbs between here and Fifth Water Trail that are just like this one. Ready? A fast descent through mixed timber takes you to the right fork of Third Water Creek (tech 3-4). You can bail out by taking Third Water Trail for 1.5 miles to Rays Valley Road, but the trail is in no better shape than what you've been on. At least you'll be going downhill, though. Otherwise, hike-a-bike out of the gulch, bend through a hollow, and climb on rough, brush-lined tread to a highpoint. Descend swiftly to the left fork of Third Water Creek and repeat the process. Get the hang of it?

Stay straight/north atop the next climb, ignoring a path that crosses east to west, and freewheel on smooth then choppy trail to the right fork of

This would be a choice ride even without the natural hot springs.

Fourth Water Creek. You can take Fourth Water Trail 2 miles to Rays Valley Road, but the trail's condition is unknown. Stay right, cross the gulch, and climb in earnest across brushy sunny slopes that provide distant views of the southern Wasatch Range from the top. Descend to the left fork of Fourth Water Creek, and cross the narrow valley at a fence-bound spring. Climb strenuously once more on alternating smooth and choppy tread, and go through a gated fence at the top. The initial descent to Fifth Water angles northwest into old-growth fir and aspen; then the rutted trail makes a beeline across a sloping meadow and drops quickly to upper Fifth Water Trail, No. 015. You made it! (Heavy sigh.)

Center Trail follows alongside Fifth Water Creek (tech 3-4$^+$) for one-half mile to a creek crossing. There, Center Trail forks right/north for Sixth Water. Don't even think of going that way; it's far worse than any conditions you encountered previously. Continue down on Fifth Water Trail, No. 015, wind through grand cottonwood trees on smooth trail, and stay right on a cheater route to bypass a double water crossing. The trail widens to doubletrack, and you'll swoop around curves to Rays Valley Road. Continue to the trailhead as described previously from **m10.4**.

Option: Strawberry Ridge Loop (24 miles, strenuous$^+$, tech 2$^+$-4$^+$, 3,800-foot gain. Allow 4-6 hours.)

Like Center Trail, this marathon loop, takes you from Second Water to Fifth Water but via Strawberry Ridge and along its gigantic roller-coaster doubletrack. From the ridge, you'll find impressive views of the southern Wasatch Range to the west and of the Uinta Basin to the east. The 8-mile descent on upper and lower Fifth Water Trails is one of the best downhills around and is worth every drop of sweat to reach it. The icing on the cake is knowing that a soak in the Fifth Water hot springs awaits you at the ride's end, but you've probably figured that out by now.

Ride up Cottonwood-Second Water Trail to Rays Valley Road as described in the Hot Springs loop previously, continue up Second Water Trail as described in the Center Trail option previously, but stay right/straight toward Indian Springs at the Center Trail junction. A moderate, .6-mile climb on a good trail takes you up to Strawberry Ridge and to a four-way junction of dirt roads. Go left/ north on the ridge road, FR 135, and climb the first of five moderately strenuous hills. Each climb is offset by a blazing fast descent that is just reward for your effort (tech 2-3⁺).

Watch for FR 110 forking right after 5.3 miles (may not be signed). Continue on the ridge road .75 mile past FR 110—not an inch farther— going up a hill and down to the base of what would be your sixth climb; then fork left on upper Fifth Water Trail, No. 015. The junction may not be signed, so look for a wire fence running along the right side of the ridge road as a marker. Fifth Water Trail begins as doubletrack then narrows at a log barrier (tech 3). After

Miles from nowhere on the Center Trail.

bending sharply left on the top of a small ridge, the trail descends quickly to a (usually) dry fork of Fifth Water Creek for a rock-n-roll ride through mixed timber (tech 3-4⁺). Break out of the woods to a marshy meadow, and continue down the right side of the creek on the edge of low brushy hills. Rock drops and narrow tread can make the trail dicey in spots (tech 4⁺), but there are smooth-rolling sections as well (tech 3). Pass Center Trail forking left to Second Water, and .5 mile farther, cross the creek at the junction where Center Trail forks right for Sixth Water. Wind through grand cottonwood trees on buttery smooth trail, and stay right on a cheater route to bypass a double water crossing. The trail widens to doubletrack, and you'll zoom around swooping curves to Rays Valley Road. Continue to the trailhead as described previously from **m10.4**. Epic!

❗ Know Before You Go

- The Fifth Water hot springs are "clothing optional." County ordinances state that you must be clothed when in the presence of minors or others who request that you be clothed. Ask first, strip later.
- Lower Fifth Water Trail is very popular with anglers, bikers, and hikers (including families with children). Ride cautiously and courteously because sight lines are limited.
- Cottonwood Canyon, Second Water, Center Trails, and upper Fifth Water are open to motorcycles; lower Fifth Water Trail (below Rays Valley Road) is nonmotorized.
- Center Trail is in the middle of prime cattle grazing country. It would

SOUTHERN WASATCH

behoove you to contact the Spanish Fork Ranger District to find out where cattle are ranged seasonally. Cattle can have a significant impact on the trail, and the "guacamole" they leave behind is not the kind you want to serve with tortilla chips.

• *Fido Factor:* Dogs are not recommended on the Hot Springs loop because of the required paved road, but Cottonwood Canyon and Fifth Water Trails are dog friendly. Center Trail loop is dog friendly, but the miles are long. Strawberry Ridge loop is probably too long for dogs, and there are no reliable water sources on the ridge.

❓ Maps & More Information

• USGS 1:24,000: Rays Valley, Strawberry Reservoir NW, and Strawberry Reservoir SW, Utah
• Uinta National Forest (Spanish Fork Ranger District): (801) 798-3571

🎵 Trailhead Access

From I-15, take Exit 261 (Price, Manti), and travel east on US 6. Turn left on FR 029 for Diamond Fork 5 miles up Spanish Fork Canyon. Three Forks trailhead is 10 miles.

Alternatively, you can access the trails from Sheep Creek Road/Rays Valley Road, FR 051. To get there, continue 10.7 miles on US 6 from the Diamond Fork Road junction, and turn left on Sheep Creek Road for Strawberry Reservoir. Cottonwood-Second Water Trail is 9.5 miles.

SOUTHERN WASATCH

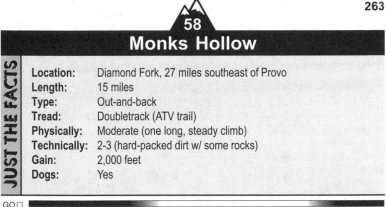

58
Monks Hollow

JUST THE FACTS

Location:	Diamond Fork, 27 miles southeast of Provo
Length:	15 miles
Type:	Out-and-back
Tread:	Doubletrack (ATV trail)
Physically:	Moderate (one long, steady climb)
Technically:	2-3 (hard-packed dirt w/ some rocks)
Gain:	2,000 feet
Dogs:	Yes

GO ☐
NO ■ | JAN | FEB | MAR | APR | MAY | JUN | JUL | AUG | SEP | OCT | NOV | DEC |

WHY SHOULD U RIDE THIS TRAIL ?

As members of the muscle-powered family of recreationists, mountain bikers often frown upon ATVs for their energy-consumptive, exhaust-spitting, and otherwise-deafening attributes. One good thing about ATVs is they can pack down a nice trail at times. Take Diamond Fork's Monks Hollow ATV Trail; it's ideal for mountain bikes. The steady climb is just right for intermediate bikers who are out for a casual tour or for hammerhead bikers in need of training. Along the trail, you'll enjoy distant views of Mount Timpanogos, Provo Peak, and Spanish Fork Peak. At the summit, you'll spy Mount Nebo floating on the southern horizon. The return descent is always thrilling.

Details

From the trailhead, cross over the hollow to the left, and then fork right to follow the trail along the creek's east side. (The rocky ATV trail heading uphill to the east is too steep and rough to climb, but it's a good optional descent.) In about one-half mile, the trail switchbacks up from the creek and delivers a powerful view of Provo Peak to the west. Then the trail contours across the head of a grassy meadow (**m2.5**).

Keep chugging up the narrow doubletrack. You pass a spring enclosed by a log fence nearly 5.5 miles from the trailhead. One mile farther, the trail rises to a subtle divide above Brimhall Canyon (**m6.6**). This is a good turnaround point for novice-intermediate bikers; otherwise, continue for another half mile to a second saddle, which provides an inspiring view of the distant Mount Nebo. Beyond, the trail drops swiftly over a couple of whoop-de-doos, banks around an unexpected turn, and rises steeply to a T-junction with a jeep road. This ridge separates Chicken Hollow from Long Hollow. It's also the route's highest elevation and recommended turnaround (**m7.5**). The return descent is fast and furious. Control your speed and be attentive because turns approach quickly and sight lines are limited.

The Spanish Fork Ranger District plans to build connecting trails from upper Monks Hollow to the Teat Mountain Road, but no dates of completion were available at the time of publication.

Option: Long Hollow

You can descend 4.2 miles through Long Hollow to US 6 instead of retracing your tracks down Monks Hollow. The initial descent is steep, rutted, and marred with loose rocks (tech 4⁺). Thereafter, the ATV trail widens to a doubletrack and descends more gently through stands of aspen, cottonwood, oak, and maple trees. Beyond the power lines, the lumpy and bumpy road continues 2 miles farther to US 6.

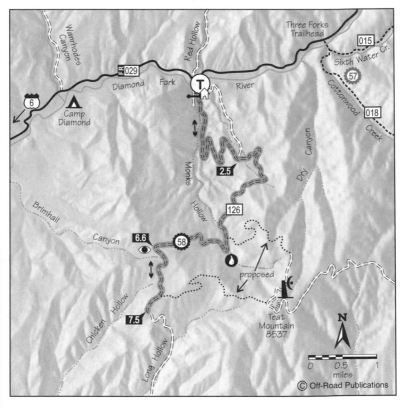

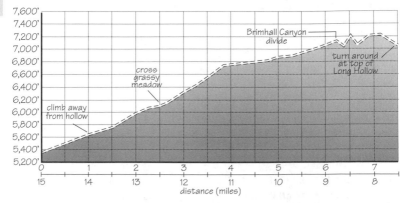

Mount Nebo, the king of the Wasatch, as seen from the top of Monks Hollow.

This option requires a shuttle; otherwise, you'll have to pedal nearly 14 miles on US 6 and Diamond Fork Road back to Monks Hollow. On the way, stop at the Thistle Landslide Overlook and read the interpretive signs about the mudslide that buried the stream-side hamlet in 1983. A "bathtub ring" from the slide-formed lake can still be seen on the hillsides.

! Know Before You Go

- This route is open to ATVs, motorcycles, and nonmotorized uses.
- Diamond Campground on Diamond Fork Road is a Forest Service fee area with water taps and outhouses.
- *Fido Factor:* Trail is dog friendly, but watch out for vehicles.

? Maps & More Information

- USGS 1:24,000: Billies Mountain and Rays Valley, Utah
- Uinta National Forest (Spanish Fork Ranger District): (801) 798-3571

Trailhead Access

From I-15, take Exit 261 for Price and Manti, and travel east on US 6. Five miles up Spanish Fork Canyon, turn left/north on FR 029 for Diamond Fork. The Monks Hollow trailhead is 7.7 miles up paved Diamond Fork Road, just past a particularly scenic redrock canyon. Look for a small bridge over Diamond Fork River posted FR 072.

SOUTHERN WASATCH

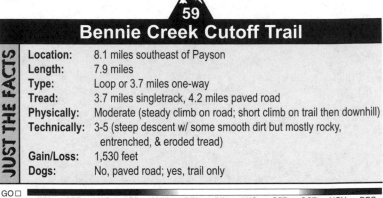

59
Bennie Creek Cutoff Trail

Location:	8.1 miles southeast of Payson
Length:	7.9 miles
Type:	Loop or 3.7 miles one-way
Tread:	3.7 miles singletrack, 4.2 miles paved road
Physically:	Moderate (steady climb on road; short climb on trail then downhill)
Technically:	3-5 (steep descent w/ some smooth dirt but mostly rocky, entrenched, & eroded tread)
Gain/Loss:	1,530 feet
Dogs:	No, paved road; yes, trail only

GO □
NO ■ | JAN | FEB | MAR | APR | MAY | JUN | JUL | AUG | SEP | OCT | NOV | DEC

WHY SHOULD U RIDE THIS TRAIL?

Riding up Bennie Creek Cutoff Trail *is virtually impossible, so that leaves only one other option—riding down—and what a downhill ride it is. After a rolling climb initially, your handling skills and braking power will be put to the test as gravity pulls you down the timbered ravine on smooth and rough tread, over rock and log drops, and through steep-sided gulches. There is never a dull moment. If you shuttle to the top, you'll be down in minutes; if you pedal up the Nebo Loop Road first, you'll get a solid workout and justify your downhill run. Better yet, go big and tack this trail on to one of the other rides around Payson Lakes for a figure-eight loop that culminates with a scintillating descent.*

Details

Naturally, you could shuttle to the Loafer Mountain Trail trailhead, but in the real world of mountain biking there is no such thing as "free" riding. You have to earn your downhill by pedaling to the top first. So, here we go. Directions are pretty straight forward: pedal 4.2 miles up the Nebo Road to the Loafer Mountain Trail (**m4.2**). The average 6.3-percent grade is remarkably steady, so once you pick the right gear, you'll just sit and spin the whole way. If you're with a group, however, there will likely one wise guy (or gal) who will start pushing the pace and set into motion the dreaded undeclared race. Hammer time!

Hop on the Loafer Mountain Trail, No. 098, cross the little creek, and stay left toward Bennie Creek Trail, No. 071, where Blackhawk Trail, No. 084, forks right through a gate. Climb moderately on smooth, packed tread through mixed timber, descend through a hollow, pump hard up a steeper grade crossed with water bars, and drop to a saddle marked by a fence and corral (**m5.2**). That's it for the climbing. Bennie Creek Trail forks right (through the fence) and drops 2,500 vertical feet to Birdseye and US 89. Don't go that way. Continue straight on Trail No. 098, and square up for a tricky little drop over roots and water bars (tech 4⁺). Fork left on Bennie Creek Trail, No. 071, where Loafer Mountain Trail, No. 098, forks right and rises 2,200 feet to the summit. Ouch!

A fast, thrilling descent unfolds as the path drops through maple and fir trees on both buffed and rough sections (tech 3). Yeah, baby! A mile down, the trail follows along the edge of the creek through timber so dark that your sunglasses are a hazard; then it veers away from the canyon until you are high above the creek bottom and into the bright of day. Some of the trees through here are so old that it would take two persons with arms outstretched to completely hug one. A couple of unannounced rock drops may surprise you (tech 4-4⁺), and you'll have to be quick with the shifters to avoid stalling where the trail dips sharply through a side gulch.

The trail breaks out of the timber to a clearing that affords impressive views of Payson Canyon below and of Dry Mountain to the west. Then you're tossed radically down four sharp, eroded turns, one of which is impossible to ride and even difficult to walk (tech 5). More steep, gravelly descending takes you back into the lower gulch of Wimmer Ranch Creek before you are spit out to the trailhead.

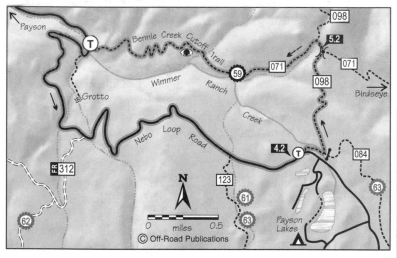

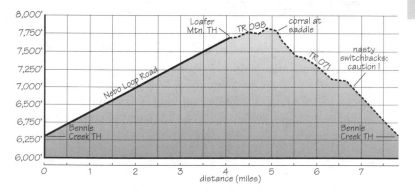

A wild little descent that is well worth the paved-road climb.

Option: The Grotto

This .3 mile-long trail is better for hiking than biking. It's a pleasant jaunt on a hot summer day that leads to a waterfall cascading into a hollowed-out cove of red stone. The shower is utterly refreshing. The trailhead is just up the road from the Bennie Creek Cutoff Trail trailhead.

! Know Before You Go

* This trail is popular with hikers, especially the lower portion, so control your speed and be ready to yield the trail courteously.
* Backcountry camping restrictions apply in Payson Canyon.
* *Fido Factor:* The loop is not recommended for dogs because of the paved road miles. The trail is dog friendly if ridden one-way.

? Maps & More Information

* USGS 1:24,000: Payson Lakes, Utah
* Uinta National Forest (Spanish Fork Ranger District): (801) 798-3571

♪ Trailhead Access

From I-15, take Exit 254 for Payson and UT 115. In Payson, go left on UT 198 for Nebo Scenic Byway; then turn right in .4 mile on 600 East to officially start the Nebo Scenic Byway. Bennie Creek Cutoff Trail is 8.1 miles up Payson Canyon; Loafer Mountain Trail trailhead is 4.2 miles farther.

60

Payson Lakes Loop

Location:	12 miles southeast of Payson
Length:	8.3 miles
Type:	Loop
Tread:	6.6 miles singletrack, .1 mile doubletrack, 1.6 miles paved road
Physically:	Moderate (tough climb on Blackhawk Trail, short hike-a-bike on Box Lake Trail, rest is a piece o' cake)
Technically:	1-4 (good trails throughout, one short hike-a-bike)
Gain:	1,100 feet
Dogs:	No, paved roads; yes, trails only

GO □
NO ■ | JAN | FEB | MAR | APR | MAY | JUN | JUL | AUG | SEP | OCT | NOV | DEC |

WHY SHOULD I RIDE THIS TRAIL?

This little circuit ties together the many connector trails around Payson Lakes into a logical and scenic loop. A few tough spots, like the initial climb on Blackhawk Trail and the short hike-a-bike on Box Lake Trail, prevent the loop from being a family fun ride, unless the tikes have a "go get 'em" attitude. Fortunately, there are out-and-back segments that are perfect for rookies and children. If you make the whole loop, you'll experience some of the area's smoothest trails and visit two pretty lakes. Give it a try; you'll like it.

Details

You can start this loop from one of three trailheads or from Box Lake or Big East Lake. Like any good investor who "buys low and sells high" you'll maximize your trail-riding dividends by starting at the lowest trailhead, climbing first, and ending with a sweet downhill. That means starting at the Jones Ranch trailhead off Nebo Road.

Get your legs warmed up by pedaling .8 mile up the paved Nebo Scenic Byway from the Jones Ranch Trail trailhead to the Loafer Mountain Trail trailhead. Hop on Loafer Mountain Trail, fork right on Blackhawk Trail (No. 084) after crossing a creek, and go through the gate. The trail rises moderate+ through the timber then up a sloping meadow to Bennie Creek Ridge (tech 2-3+). This is the toughest hill on the whole ride, so if you persevere, the rest is gravy. Curve through the timber just below a knoll, and come to a prominent but unsigned Y-junction on the ridge, which is little more than a low, rounded divide (**m2.4**). Blackhawk Trail, marked by a carsonite post, forks left and descends steeply. Stay right/straight and go past a remote backcountry weather station on your right. A fun coasting section exits to the Nebo Road next to a hiking trail sign. Cross the road and take the dirt road to the signed trailhead next to the old Jones Ranch.

The trail is an old doubletrack, but it rides like singletrack and rises gradually up a grassy hollow into the aspens (tech 2). A gentle but swift descent leads to the junction of Rock Spring Trail (No. 101) and Jones Ranch Trail (No.123). Go right on Jones Ranch Trail for .2 mile, and then fork right up the draw on a trail signed for Payson Lakes Campground (tech 2). Enter the fir and aspens and stay left at a faint junction. You'll descend like the wind across a meadow to the Payson Lakes Campground road (**m5.2**). Loafer Mountain is square in your sights.

Go past the entrance station, and take either the road or the paved lakeside trail to the day-use/fisherman parking area for Big East Lake. Stay on the lakeside trail to the north access road, and fork left for Box Lake after coasting downhill for .1 mile. A one-lane road leads to a group picnic

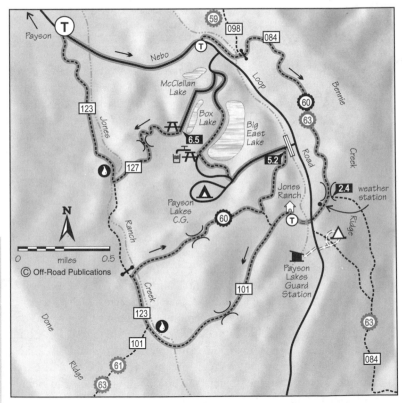

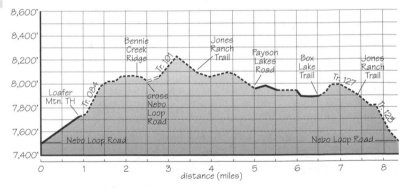

area where you'll hit the dirt again on Box Lake Trail, No. 127 (**m6.5**). Climb quickly through the aspens (tech 3⁺), level out, and hike-a-bike up a short, sharp hill (tech 4⁺). Glide down the hollow to Jones Ranch Trail. Finish off the loop with 1.3 miles of rockabilly singletrack.

Big East Lake.

Option: Payson Lakes Short Course

Skip the climb on Blackhawk Trail and the hike-a-bike on Box Lake Trail for an easy 4-mile loop between Big East Lake and Jones Ranch. Start at the Big East Lake day-use/fisherman parking area (fee required), and ride back to Nebo Road. Ride .4 mile up to the dirt road accessing old Jones Ranch. (The junction is marked with a hiking trail sign alongside Nebo Road. Don't take the Payson Guard Station road .4 mile farther.) Pick up the trail next to Jones Ranch's white clapboard cabins, and follow the main description back to Big East Lake. This ride is family friendly, but use caution when pedaling the Nebo Road because the shoulder is narrow.

! Know Before You Go

- Some of these trails are open to motorcycles. All of them are especially popular with equestrians, so be ready to yield the trail.
- Big East Lake has a developed campground (fee area). Picnic and parking areas at Payson Lakes require a day-use fee.
- Water taps and outhouses are at the Big East Lake day-use/fishermen parking area.
- *Fido Factor:* The loop is not recommended for dogs because of the paved road section. The trails, however, are dog friendly. If your dog must come along, then start at Jones Ranch and poke around on Jones Ranch Trail and Rock Springs Trail.

? Maps & More Information

- USGS 1:24,000: Payson Lakes, UT
- Uinta National Forest (Spanish Fork Ranger District): (801) 798-3571

🔥 Trailhead Access

From I-15, take Exit 254 for Payson and UT 115. In Payson, go left on UT 198 for Nebo Scenic Byway; then turn right in .4 mile on 600 East to officially start the Nebo Scenic Byway. Pass the turnoff for Pete Winward Reservoir in 9.7 miles, and drive 1.8 miles farther to the Jones Ranch Trail trailhead (unsigned). Park in the clearing on the left side of the road. Alternatively, drive another .8 mile to the Loafer Mountain Trail trailhead.

SOUTHERN WASATCH

61 Jones Ranch-Shram Creek Trails

JUST THE FACTS

Location:	10 miles southeast of Payson
Length:	8.8 miles
Type:	Loop
Tread:	5.8 miles singletrack, 1.2 miles doubletrack, 1.8 miles paved road
Physically:	Moderate (steady climb on road, two sharp hills then moderate climbs on Jones Creek Trail, long descent on Shram Creek Trail)
Technically:	3 (trails are universally tech 3 w/ smoother & rougher spots)
Gain:	1,500 feet
Dogs:	No, paved road; yes, trails only

GO □
NO ■ | JAN | FEB | MAR | APR | MAY | JUN | JUL | AUG | SEP | OCT | NOV | DEC |

WHY SHOULD U RIDE THIS TRAIL

Just looking at all the trails around Payson Lakes will make any singletrack purist drool like a dog eyeing a juicy bone. It just so happens that these trails are, indeed, tasty treats. The challenge is unlocking the right combination of trails to get the goods. Jones Ranch Trail has always been the denouement descent to the Blackhawk loop, but it also rides well in reverse, uphill. When it's tied together with the oft-overlooked Shram Creek Trail, you have a dandy little loop. Jones Ranch Trail begins with a couple of short protracted hills but then yields to comfortably steady climbing. Rock Spring Trail is a mix of smaller hills and fast descents. Shram Creek Trail is a real barn-burner on both singletrack and doubletrack.

Details

Start out by pedaling 1.8 miles up the paved Nebo Scenic Byway to Jones Ranch Trail, No. 123. There's not much of a trailhead, so look for a large clearing/staging area on the left/north side of the road and the inconspicuously signed trail on the right/south side. It starts out as an old doubletrack then narrows immediately to singletrack. Now that your legs are sufficiently warmed up, attack a short, sharp, rough hill followed by a longer incline, all within the first quarter mile. Ouch! The trail moderates through the aspens, and then it follows up the shallow, grassy hollow of Jones Ranch Creek (tech 2-3+).

Pass three trails forking left to Box Lake, Payson Lakes, and Payson Lakes Guard Station, respectively, and climb moderately over Done Ridge on what is now Rock Spring Trail, No. 101 (**m3.7**). Descend swiftly on periodically choppy tread, pass Rock Spring on the right, and roll up to Amos Backbone Ridge. Go through the gate, and descend quickly past Lizard Lake, which is off to the right. (Lake is a generous term because by late summer it's little more than a clump of brown dried-up grass.) Pump up a small hill to another gate guarded by two massive Douglas fir trees, and freewheel on rougher tread (tech 3⁺) to the Shram Creek Trail junction in a small clearing (**m5.9**). (Shram Creek Trail, No. 124, may be tagged as No. 122 on older trail signs.)

Now it's time to suck the tender marrow out of that bone you've been gnawing on. Shram Creek Trail darts into old growth aspens and descends lively on rich humus tread splashed with roots and rocks (tech 3⁺). Make a beeline across a meadow, and bounce down a rocky draw. The trail widens to doubletrack and comes to a T-junction in a clearing with the

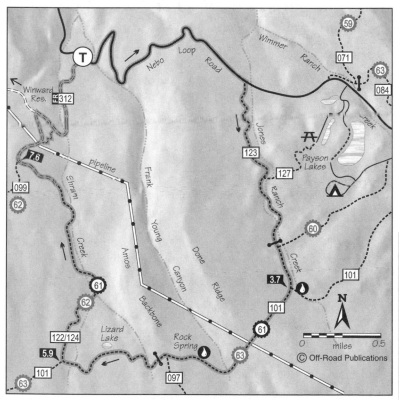

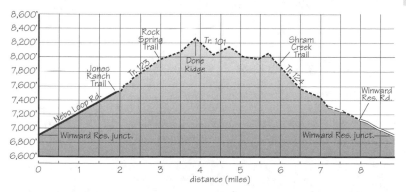

© Off-Road Publications

SOUTHERN WASATCH

SOUTHERN WASATCH

Payson Canyon is for singletrack lovers.

Sheepherder Hill Trail, No. 099 (**m7.6**). Go right and wind through juniper and pinyon. Watch for a singletrack peeling off to the right after crossing the Questar pipeline. It's a quick little twisting drop to the Pete Winward Reservoir road. If you miss it, you'll intersect the road at a T-junction. Regardless, go right and zoom down to the parking area. Watch out for oncoming traffic because many of the curves are blind.

? Maps & More Information

- These trails are very popular with equestrians, so be ready to yield the trail. Motorcycles are also permitted.
- Nearby Payson Lakes has a developed campground (fee area).
- *Fido Factor:* The loop is not recommended for dogs since it requires nearly 2 miles of paved road. The trails, however, are dog friendly.

? Maps & More Information

- USGS 1:24,000: Payson Lakes, UT
- Uinta National Forest (Spanish Fork Ranger District): (801) 798-3571

Trailhead Access

From I-15, take Exit 254 for Payson and UT 115. In Payson, go left on UT 198 for Nebo Scenic Byway; then turn right in .4 mile on 600 East to officially start the Nebo Scenic Byway. Park at the turnoff for Pete Winward Reservoir in 9.7 miles.

62

Sheepherder Hill Trail

JUST THE FACTS

Location:	10 miles southeast of Payson
Length:	12.7 miles
Type:	Loop
Tread:	6.4 miles singletrack, 4.1 miles doubletrack, 2.2 miles dirt road
Physically:	Moderate⁺ (solid climb up Shram Creek Trail; crude contouring & eroded tread on Sheepherder Hill Trail)
Technically:	2-5 (trails are more rough than buffed)
Gain:	2,000 feet
Dogs:	Not recommended on dirt roads. Yes, on trails.

GO ☐
NO ■ | JAN | FEB | MAR | APR | MAY | JUN | JUL | AUG | SEP | OCT | NOV | DEC |

"Been there, done that?" Then try Blackhawk Trail's alter ego: Sheepherder Hill Trail. You'll veer far away from the Payson Lakes trail complex and tap into a path that only horseback riders and roaming cattle seem to know about. After the initial climb on Shram Creek Trail, you'll fly down Santaquin Canyon Road, and then link up with Sheepherder Hill Trail, a.k.a. "Three Drainages Trail," so named because the path contours crudely across three densely forested gulches. "Crudely" because there are countless micro-hills along the way, and the sometimes choppy, off-camber tread can make you work hard. The more this trail is ridden, the more solid the tread will become, so get a gang together and go ride. Sheepherder Hill Trail will thank you for it.

Details

Head up the dirt Pete Winward Reservoir Road for .9 mile, and fork left on a doubletrack that soon crosses the Questar gas pipeline. (The nearby Sheepherder Hill Trail will get you to the pipeline cut, too, but that trail is easily missed.) Go another .5 mile to a clearing amidst juniper and pinyon, and fade left on the doubletrack, which becomes Shram Creek Trail, No. 124 (may be erroneously tagged No. 122, **m1.5**). (Sheepherder Hill Trail, your return route, is straight ahead and is marked by a carsonite post.) The track narrows to a single lane, rises quickly up a bouldery gulch (tech 4⁺), and runs the length of a broad meadow that affords views of nearby mountains and distant metropolitan valley. Power up a couple more hills amidst aspens (tech 3), and fork right on Rock Spring Trail. Climb in earnest for another mile through old knotty aspens to Santaquin Canyon Road (**m4.3**).

Tuck it down the dirt road (tech 2⁺) to Santaquin Meadows (**m6.5**), but be cautious rounding the corners because the gravel can be slippery, and you never know when you might encounter oncoming vehicles. A half-mile climb on doubletrack takes you to a fence and to a sign for Sheepherder Trail, No. 099. Pedal and push 100 yards more, and stay

SOUTHERN WASATCH

right/straight on the trail marked with white trail diamonds. Take the old doubletrack .25 mile; then fork right on singletrack marked with white trail diamonds just past a cattle trough next to a spring (**m7.4**).

Exit the aspens to a small clearing, and make your way down the draw but not too far. You'll drop through a rough, steep turn then climb away from Big Spring Creek to contour "crudely" across the canyon's steep-sided slope. Curve through a hollow of dark, dank timber, while powering over abrupt terrain changes and hopping roots, stumps, and rocks in the tread. The variety of users this trail attracts (nonmotorized and mo-

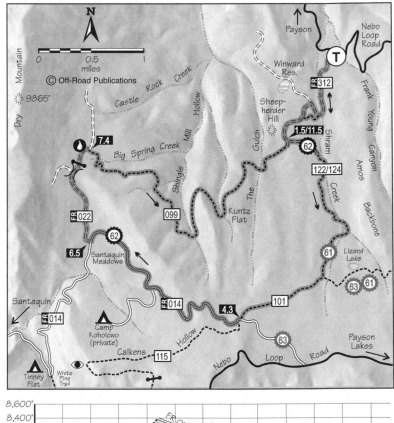

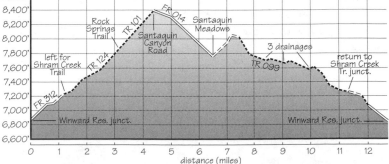

Lindsey leads Amy on
Rock Spring Trail.

torized) plus roaming cattle have badly damaged portions of the trail, and the tread has sloughed off camber in spots. No bother. Just more tricky bits for you to negotiate (tech 3-5). Other sections, however, are remarkably smooth. Bend through Shingle Mill Hollow (lightly flowing creek), and dismount where the trail kisses an outcrop of volcanic breccia, or igneous conglomerate. Bank around another tight gulch (third one so far), and feel the pull of gravity while descending on firm tread in the timber. Watch for a faint Y-junction. You'll want to fork right to return to the juniper-pinyon meadow to close the loop (**m11.5**). Simply retrace your tracks to Pete Winward Road and back to the parking area, or fork right just past the Questar pipeline cut to catch one last little bit of singletrack.

Option: Calkens Hollow Trail

You can add on 3.8 miles (out-and-back) by taking the seldom-traveled but promising Calkens Hollow Trail (tech 3) to the Santaquin Canyon Overlook when you exit Rock Spring Trail to Santaquin Canyon Road. Don't be dismayed by the rude little ramp at the start or by the abrupt creek crossing a few hundred yards in. The rest of the trail rides nicely on an undulating course through mixed timber (tech 2^+-3^+). The trail drops about 200 feet over its 1.7-mile length.

SOUTHERN WASATCH

So many choices.

If you're the Curious George type, you'll wonder where the rest of Calkens Hollow Trail goes. Past the overlook, it first rises steeply up a ridge to a fence then drops wickedly to the White Pine Hollow Trail in upper Santaquin Canyon. Be forewarned, lower Calkens Hollow Trail gets hammered by cattle (tech 4-5), and when you reach the canyon, you *must* portage about one-quarter mile down the rushing, bouldery White Pine Creek through a "gate," or narrows, of closed-in rock cliffs. This could be dangerous during spring run off. Beyond, White Pine Hollow Trail is quite pleasant. Lower Calkens Hollow Trail would have great potential if it received regular maintenance, especially after cattle get to it. Bummer!

! Know Before You Go

- These trails are popular with equestrians and motorcycles, so ride cautiously, especially on the downhill stretches.
- *Fido Factor:* Dogs are not recommended because of possible traffic on Santaquin Canyon Road; however, the trails are dog friendly.

? Maps & More Information

- USGS 1:24,000: Payson Lakes, Utah
- Uinta National Forest (Spanish Fork Ranger District): (801) 798-3571

Trailhead Access

From I-15, take Exit 254 for Payson and UT 115. In Payson, go left on UT 198 for Nebo Scenic Byway; then turn right in .4 mile on 600 East to officially start the Nebo Scenic Byway. Park at the turnoff for Pete Winward Reservoir in 9.7 miles.

63
Blackhawk Trail

JUST THE FACTS	**Location:**	11 miles southeast of Payson
	Length:	17.1 miles
	Type:	Loop
	Tread:	13.9 miles singletrack, .9 mile dirt road, 2.3 miles pavement
	Physically:	Strenuous (short climbs add up quickly; route finding near Blackhawk C.G.)
	Technically:	1-3⁺ (buffed & choppy trails, roughest west of Blackhawk C.G.)
	Gain:	2,400 feet
	Dogs:	No, paved roads required; yes, trails only

GO □
NO ■ | JAN | FEB | MAR | APR | MAY | JUN | JUL | AUG | SEP | OCT | NOV | DEC |

Although the Blackhawk Trail has not been widely publicized over the years, it is regarded as a mountain bike classic, especially by those who have pledged their allegiance to the B.O.S.S. (Brotherhood of Secluded Singletracks). Now, you too can become a charter member, but initiation into the "club" is no easy task because Blackhawk Trail will whoop the butt of anyone who underestimates it. Blackhawk is a tough ride, but your efforts will reap huge rewards with mile after mile of Grade-A-Choice singletracks. The loop circles the Payson Lakes area on the edge of the Mount Nebo Wilderness and penetrates pristine timber, which during the height of autumn color will impress any homesick New Englander. With its solid climbs, thrilling descents, and lively rolling tracks, it's a wonder Blackhawk has stayed out of the limelight, until now.

Details

Hop on the Loafer Mountain Trail, No. 098, cross a small creek, and fork right through a gate for Blackhawk Trail, No. 084. You're off. The tight trail rises through aspen and maple then up the length of a broad field at a moderate⁺ grade (tech 2-3⁺). After the trail reenters the woods, it mellows, loosely contours the west slope of Bennie Creek Ridge, and comes to a prominent Y-junction (**m1.6**). "Ridge" is a generous term because here it's more a low rounded hill than a knife-edged divide. The main trail forks left, marked with a carsonite post, but *don't* take it. If you do, you'll descend on chewed-up tread and face a nasty little climb in short order. Instead, fork right/straight (unsigned), pass a remote weather station on your right, and exit to the Nebo Road. Take the road a few hundred feet, and veer left from it on a trail near a hiking decal next to a log barrier. Cut across a large backcountry camping area to pick up the continued Blackhawk Trail (may be unsigned). Are you with me?

Now, descend on roughened tread to a junction where trail signs confirm your route and point you right/south for Blackhawk Trail, No. 084, and Blackhawk Campground (**m2.3**). Descend swiftly across a sloping grassy field, and stay left/straight at a junction signed for Blackhawk C.G. and Blackhawk Loop Trail, No. 102 (Blackhawk Trail, No. 084, forks right and uphill). After the little creek crossing in Paces Hollow, the trail rises over a small timbered ridge and weaves through charming groves of aspen and maple that explode with color in autumn. (New England has nothing on this place come September.) Cross the Questar gas pipeline, go through a gate, and cross a dirt road that accesses the campground's disposal

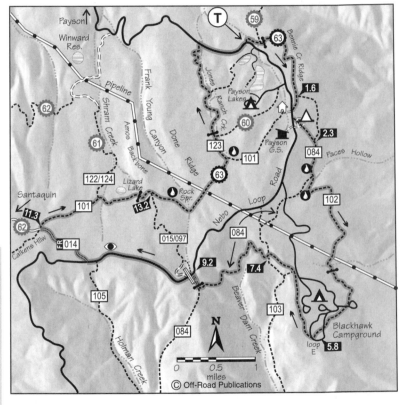

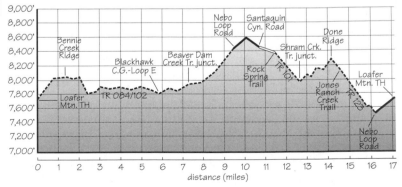

Ron leads the "brotherhood" around Blackhawk Trail.

ponds. When you intersect a paved road (group picnic area), go right 50 feet to pick up the signed trail. Cross more paved campground roads, and cut across a big meadow in the middle of the campground. The trail resumes next to site E-10D (Loop E) and is signed "Blackhawk Loop Trail, No 102" (**m5.8**). Are you still with me?

Climb into the timber and cross a doubletrack. (It accesses the campground at a site that has a good view of Mt. Nebo if you want to break for lunch.) The trail rounds the head of Beaver Dam Creek through thickets of oak and maple and descends in lively fashion. But then you must undo the freewheeling by climbing in earnest up to a four-way junction on a small ridge (**m7.4**). This is the end of Blackhawk Loop Trail, No. 102. Beaver Dam Trail, No. 103, forks left, but who knows what treasure or turmoil awaits to be discovered that way? Go straight over the ridge and into the timber on Blackhawk Trail, No. 084. (You'll notice that Blackhawk Trail, No. 084, also forks right, signed for the campground. It's a murderously steep climb and is not a good choice if you wish to bail out.)

Climb and glide over several short, steep hills; then climb continually for over a mile along the western rim of the Beaver Dam Creek basin (tech 2-3+). This the longest climb on the loop, but the views of the Wasatch Plateau off to the east are your compensation. During prolonged dry spells, the tread turns as powdery as cake flour; when wet, it's slicker and stickier than snot. Other times, it's hard-packed and just right. Reach a log barrier, and climb the doubletrack to the right/north to Nebo Road (**m9.2**). Blackhawk Trail continues westbound to Holman Canyon Trail, No. 105 (brutally steep), and then into the great unknown, so if you chase Blackhawk any farther, you're on your own!

SOUTHERN WASATCH

Singletrack bliss a la Payson Canyon.

Continue or bail out? If you're still feeling fresh, then take Nebo Road left for 1.4 miles to Santaquin Canyon Road, FR 014. Take five at the Utah Valley Overlook along the way for a cheery view of "happy valley." If you're cooked, then see the "Options" that follow.

Cruise down FR 014 (dirt road) for .9 mile, and hop on Rock Spring Trail, No. 101 (**m11.3**). A mile-long, rippin' fast descent on smooth and bumpy singletrack (tech 2-3) takes you to the junction with Shram Creek Trail. Stay on Rock Spring Trail, climb a short pro-tracted hill, pass Lizard Lake off to the left, and tackle a trio short uphill spurts. A longer, steeper, rougher climb (tech 3-4) takes you to a gated fence on Amos Backbone Ridge. Cross a high meadow, and come to the junction with Tie Fork Spur Trail (a.k.a. Frank Young Canyon Trail, No. 015/097). It's signed "Nebo Loop Road, right/south" (**m13.2**). Descend swiftly past Rock Spring, but you're not "done" climbing until you crest Done Ridge.

Revenge is sweet because you'll pedal nary a stroke for 2 miles down Jones Ranch Trail, No. 123, to Nebo Road, except for one little blip in the terrain. At first the descent is a bit choppy (tech 3); then it smooths to soft dirt (tech 2). Gravity is a powerful force, so harness your speed. Be alert to other trail users, and yield courteously to them. Stay left at three junctions; just follow the trail down the hollow. Upon exiting to the Nebo Loop Road, limp .9 mile uphill to the trailhead. All hail to the B.O.S.S.!

Option: Bailouts

If you're having an off day, experiencing mechanical problems, or the skies look threatening, then consider these two bailouts to cut the day short. 1) Blackhawk Campground: Simply take the paved roads through the campground to Nebo Loop Road. It's a long steady climb, but it's the fastest way out. Nebo Loop Road is a fast glide back to the trailhead. If you get a burst of energy along the way, tap into Rock Spring Trail at Jones Ranch by taking the access road .2 mile north of the Payson Lakes Guard Station. An easy climb takes you over to Jones Ranch Trail, No 123. 2) Tie Fork Spur Trail, a.k.a. Frank Young Canyon Trail: If you made it all the way around to the Nebo Loop Road (**m9.2** previously), then you can short-cut the loop and knock off a whole bunch of climbing by taking the Tie Fork Spur Trail/Frank Young Canyon Trail, No. 015/No. 097. The path forks from Nebo Loop Road road at the cattle guard. It starts out faint and rough but improves to a fun little one-laner after it crosses the nearby doubletrack. (If you take the doubletrack, you might miss the trail and reach a dead end in a hollow after a half mile.) Tie Fork Spur Trail/Frank Young Canyon Trail intersects Rock Spring Trail, No. 101, just east of Amos Backbone. You'll have to tackle the climb over Done Ridge, but you'll reap the reward of descending Jones Ranch Trail, No. 123.

Option: Sheepherder Hill Trail

It's tough to pass up the descent on Jones Ranch Trail because it's so sweet, but if you want to "go big," then add on Sheepherder Hill Trail for a jumbo 22.6-mile loop all the way around the top of Payson Canyon. (Tack on 3.8 more miles by riding out-and-back on Calkens Hollow Trail, too. Turn around at the overlook of Santaquin Canyon.)

Know Before You Go

* Trail signs and numbers for Loafer Mountain Trail, Blackhawk Trail, and Blackhawk Loop Trail can be confusing.
* These trails are popular with equestrians, so ride attentively and yield the trail. Be especially cautious when descending Jones Ranch Trail. Some trails are open to motorcycles.
* *Fido Factor:* The loop is not recommended for dogs since it involves two paved-road sections; however, all trails are dog friendly. If riding with your dog, take the optional Tie Fork Spur/Frank Young Canyon Trail to Rock Springs Trail. When you reach the paved Nebo Road after descending on Jones Ranch Trail, have a buddy retrieve your vehicle from the trailhead instead of running your dog up the road.

SOUTHERN WASATCH

? Maps & More Information

* USGS 1:24,000: Birdseye and Payson Lakes, Utah
* Uinta National Forest (Spanish Fork Ranger District): (801) 798-3571

Trailhead Access

From I-15, take Exit 254 for Payson and UT 115. In Payson, go left on UT 198 for Nebo Scenic Byway; then turn right in .4 mile on 600 East to officially start the Nebo Scenic Byway. The Loafer Mountain Trail trailhead is 12.3 miles up the highway. (Jones Ranch Trail is just shy of milepost 10, and the Loafer Mountain Trail trailhead is near milepost 11.)

Fat-Tire Dining Guide (Southern Wasatch)

c (less than $5)	
$ ($5-$10)	2-Go Take Out
$$ ($10-$15)	🚗 Delivery
$$$ (over $15)	🍺 Serves Beer
B: Breakfast	🍷 Serves Wine
BR: Brunch	🍸 Serves Liquor
L: Lunch	⊥ Patio Dining
D: Dinner	

Burgers & Grilles

Fuddruckers
210 W 1300 South
Orem UT 84058
(801) 235-9885
www.fuddruckers.com
$, L D (M-Su), 2-Go 🍺

"Worlds Greatest Hamburgers," from 1/3 to 1 pound of USDA Choice beef. You choose the temperature and pick the toppings: portabello mushrooms, bacon, avocado, tomato, cheeses, and more! Or try the steak or the grilled chicken sandwich--all guaranteed to satisfy the carnivore in any mountain biker. Vegetarians rejoice; order our garden burger, bread bowl of fresh soup, stuffed baked potato, or crisp salads. Wash it all down with old-fashioned milk shakes, bottomless fountain drinks, or a cold beer. Give into you cravings!

Bakeries & Delis

Great Harvest Bread Company
898 N State
Orem UT 84057
(801) 224-0303
www.greatharvest.com
1774 N University Pkwy.
Provo UT 84604
(801) 373-9816
www.greatharvestprovo.com
c-$, B L D (M-Sa), 2-Go ⊥

Wanna know what makes our bread the best in town? The secret is our own freshly ground whole wheat flour, all-natural ingredients, and no preservatives. Come in for a free slice and taste the difference! If you like our bread, you'll love our sandwiches. They are out of this world! Homemade soups, too. And skip the pre-fab energy bars--our cookies, muffins, and granola are real food for real energy. Take some for the trail.

Coffeehouses & Juice Bars

Juice N Java
280 West 100 North
Provo UT 84601
(801) 375-5409
c, B L D (M-Su), 2-Go

We really do mean fresh. Our produce is delivered daily. We juice carrots, apples, oranges, grapefruit, and for added nutrition ginger, parsley, beets, celery, cucumber, pineapple, lemon, lime, banana, and seasonal berries. We also specialize in a large variety of traditional Italian drinks, cappuccino, latte, mocha, coffee, tea, hot chocolate, blended drinks, and chai--all to promote good health, to sustain energy, and to delight the palate.

Jamba Juice
117 N State
Orem UT 84057
(801) 426-6400
www.jambajuice.com
c-$, B L D (M-Su), 2-Go

Jamba creates delicious, nutritious, all-natural, energizing fruit smoothies and juices. Each refreshing drink provides 3-6 servings of fruit to get you on your way to Five-A-Day! Also boosted with vitamins, minerals, anti-oxidants, phytonutrients, and optional protein powder. Have a Jamba Bread or Jamba Pretzel for whole-grain nutrition. Together, Jamba offers a perfect light meal before or after a ride and to promote a healthy, happy life. "Your body is a temple, littering is strictly prohibited!"

Eclectic & Cafes

Guru's Enlightened Eating
45 East Center St.
Provo, UT 84606
801-377-6980
www.go2gurus.com
$, L D (M-Sa), 2-Go ⊥

Enter Guru's and find yourself walking down a winding stone "Path to Enlightenment" where you can order "Stir the Soul" rice bowls, salads of "Enlightened Greens", "Self Fulfilling" pastas, and wraps and burritos that promise to "Ignite the Fire Within." At Guru's you will Enlighten your taste buds, not your wallet. As important as our food is, we are passionate about our mission to support local charities and disadvantaged youth through the Guru's Foundation.

SOUTHERN WASATCH

Eclectic & Cafes

Fresh Food Junkies Cafe
500 S State
Orem UT 84058
(801) 221-7788
$, L D (M-Sa), 2-Go ☂

Fresh Food Junkies Cafe has become the hot house for addicts of the finer food in life. If you need to curb your cravings for a pulled-from-the-bone, slow-roasted-this-morning turkey sandwich, or if it's simply an urge for our mouth-watering fresh-made salsa, our menu will suppress the any Junkies' appetite. From sandwiches and salads to wraps, soups, and fruit smoothies, *no one* in search of filling their belly with the finest food in Utah Valley will leave disappointed. Be fit, be healthy, be a Fresh Food Junkie.

Italian

Buona Vita Italian Restaurant
98 W Center
Provo UT 84601
(801) 377-4522
$-$$, L D (M-F), D (Sa), 2-Go

Mountain biking and Italian food--here's to the "Good Life." Established in 2001 in Provo, Buona Vita is rapidly gaining popularity. Recently voted "Top 10" in Utah County and "Best Italian" at their Los Angeles location. Chef Allan Galeano and a friendly staff present an authentic menu including salads, pastas, thin-crust Italian pizzas, raviolis, and a selection of chicken and seafood entrees. Portions are generous, so come hungry. Don't miss the all-you-can-eat lunch specials.

Mexican & Southwestern

Cafe Rio
2250 N University Ave., Provo UT 84606
801) 375-5133

1847 N 1120 West, Provo UT 84604
(801) 818-2791
www.caferio.com
$, L D (M-Sa), 2-Go

Huge, flaky tortillas are made before your very eyes then jammed full of USDA Choice chicken, beef, or pork using traditional recipes from the Rio Grande Valley regions. Enchiladas, tacos, salads, home-baked flan, and key-lime pie, too. Customize your meal with endless add-ons, fresh salsas, and baked-on cheeses, "no problemo." Voted "Best Burrito in Utah" by Salt Lake Magazine (2002).

Los Hermanos Mexican Restaurant
16 W Center
Provo UT 84601
(801) 375-5732

395 N State
Lindon UT 84042
(801) 785-1715
$-$$, L D (M-Sa), 2-Go (🏠 Provo only)

Voted "Best Mexican Restaurant in Utah County," Los Hermanos is well-loved for their signature specialty drinks, sizzling fajitas, and delectable seafood entrees. At Los Hermanos, you get a 22-year-plus tradition of quality, value, and great friendly service. Serving traditional Mexican favorites. Relax and dine in, take it to go, or let us cater your next party.

Pizza & Subs

Zubs Pizza & Subs
520 N Main
Springville, UT 84663
(801) 489-9484
$-$$, L D (M-Sa), 2-Go 🚐

Zubs Pizza and Subs is famous for their fresh toasted subs. Each sub is a mountain of delectable ingredients. You can really sink you knobbies into these babies. If pizza is more your style, then make a singletrack in for one of the freshest pizzas you've ever had--it's clean burning fuel. Dude, this food is grub! Located on route to your favorite trail in Hobble Creek and Diamond Fork Canyons.

Vegetarian & Natural Foods

Sage's Cafe
473 East 300 South
SLC UT 84111
801-322-3790
www.sagescafe.com
$-$$, L D (W-Su), 2-Go 🏠 🍷 ☂

Sage's provides an eclectic, cross-cultural menu featuring organic foods and a fresh selection of worldly flavors--all created in house. We offer an impressive selection of beer and wine, triple certified coffees, a great tea menu, fresh pastries, raw foods, and a unique atmosphere. Nightly Chef's Specials feature the freshest seasonal produce. Voted "Best Vegetarian" by *City Weekly* (2002).

SOUTHERN WASATCH

WEST OF THE WASATCH

64
Stansbury Island Mountain Bike Trail

JUST THE FACTS

Location:	45 miles west of Salt Lake City
Length:	10.4 miles
Type:	Loop (clockwise)
Tread:	5.8 miles singletrack, 3.2 miles doubletrack, 1.4 miles dirt road
Physically:	Moderate (tough intial climb then flat w/ micro-hills)
Technically:	1⁺-5 (sharp, unridable switchbacks on initial climb; smooth & choppy trail w/ exposure thereafter; steep, gravelly descent; smooth dirt roads w/ light sand & washboards)
Gain:	1,050 feet
Dogs:	Yes

GO☐
NO■ | JAN | FEB | MAR | APR | MAY | JUN | JUL | AUG | SEP | OCT | NOV | DEC |

WHY SHOULD U RIDE THIS TRAIL?

Stansbury Island is an enticing *alternative to driving ump-teen hours to southern Utah's canyon country when lo-cal mountain trails are snowbound. Developed for nonmotorized use, the Stansbury Island Mountain Bike Trail takes advantage of Mother Nature's craftsmanship by following the elevated shoreline bench of ancient Lake Bonneville. The initial 650-foot climb to the bench trail is a bitter pill to swallow because it's steep and rocky, and the switchbacks are virtually unridable; however, once you reach the shoreline, you'll pedal along a near-level traverse. This skeletal landmass is as bleak and bizarre as the moon, but you know you're on Mother Earth when your eyes fall upon the Great Salt Lake's rippled waters, upon steely mountain peaks both near and far that are trimmed with verdant green, and upon a distant metropolis boasting one million inhabitants.*

Details

Head south on the singletrack across the sun-baked foothills, and fork left when you intersect a doubletrack. Along the approach, you can trace the nine switchbacks that lead up to your anaerobic destination. (Ugh!) The initial climb on the rocky doubletrack can be de-moralizing (tech 3-4), but don't give up. After the trail bends right, it levels and offers a brief respite. Then you'll curse the steep, angular switchbacks and rejoice over the flatter stretches in between. You cross the ancient lake's wave-cut shoreline after turn number six at 4,940 feet and then climb a bit more to the pass (**m1.2**). Drop through four more tight turns, and stay left at a junction with a doubletrack to catch the shoreline once again. You'll stay glued to this elevation for 4 miles.

At times, the shoreline's narrow rocky lip barely accommodates your two-inch wide tires (tech 4); other times, the smooth terrace is broad enough to build a house on (tech 2). Acrophobes and bikers with rudimentary handling skills may find some sections especially unnerving. Where the trail crosses Tabbys Canyon, a doubletrack forks right and offers a rea-

WEST OF THE WASATCH

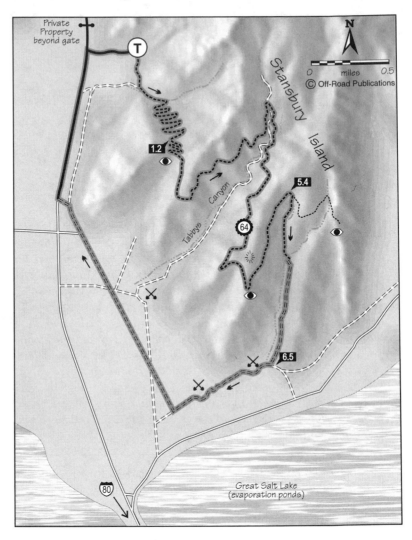

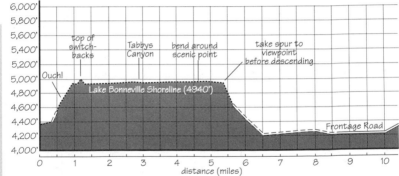

The trail catches the shoreline bench of Lake Bonneville; Deseret Peak in the Stansbury Mountains towers over the West Desert.

sonable bailout off the mountain. Curve around two points that provide overlooks of the salt evaporation ponds on the mountain's southern tip and of the magnificent Oquirrh and Stansbury Mountains. Nearly a mile farther, the trail bends through a canyon where a trail forks right and descends sharply (**m5.4**). That's your route down, but if you chase the bench trail another .4 mile, you'll reach a knobby viewpoint that is the best yet. Here, the Wasatch Range can be seen stretching over 60 miles from Ogden's Ben Lomond to Salt Lake's Lone Peak, and the big blue of the Great Salt Lake is an evaporative vestige of its ice age predecessor.

The initial descent is steep and gravelly (tech 4), so be cautious. Connect with a pebbly doubletrack, and race down to the flats. Fork right on a dirt road (**m6.5**); then veer right again on a doubletrack marked with a carsonite post, provided it hasn't been the target of a "sportsman's" bullet. Stay right, generally, at subsequent junctions to take the doubletracks around the island's western base and back to the trailhead. Don't worry if you miss a turn. You'll just connect with the island's main road anyway.

Option: Out-and-back and Tabbys Canyon climb

Nothing says you *have* to descend off the shoreline to return to the trailhead. Singletrack purists should simply turn around and retrace their tracks to "double-your-pleasure, double-your-fun." But if doubling your pleasure means doubling your vertical, then drop off the mountain as described, and climb back up to the shoreline via Tabbys Canyon: When you reach the old gravel pit, fork right on a doubletrack that leads up the discernable hollow. The 1.5-mile-long climb is altogether ridable and only moderately technical (tech 3), which is more than you can say about the unspeakable climb from the trailhead.

WEST OF THE WASATCH

Sage and Aspen take Brad for a ride on Stansbury Island.

! Know Before You Go

- Stansbury Island is best enjoyed March-May and September-November. It's dangerously hot during midsummer, and insects can be savage.
- Although the route is short, take lots of water; there is no shade.
- The Stansbury Island road north of the trailhead is private property and is closed to the public. Riding around the island is not allowed.
- There are no services at the trailhead or on Stansbury Island. Visitor services can be found in Grantsville and Tooele.
- *Fido Factor:* The trail is canine compatible, but there are no water sources, so carry extra for your pet. Keep your dog close to your side when riding the doubletracks back to the trailhead because this is a popular area for freelance target shooting.

? Maps & More Information

- USGS 1:24,000: Corral Canyon and Plug Peak, Utah
- Bureau of Land Management (Salt Lake Field Office): (801) 977-4300, www.blm.gov

♪ Trailhead Access

From Salt Lake City, travel 36 miles west on I-80 to Exit 84 (Grantsville, UT 138). Go right at the exit then left/west on the paved Frontage Road for Stansbury Island. After crossing the railroad tracks twice, the road turns to all-weather dirt. There is a Y-junction about 3.5 miles from the exit. Stay straight to reach the main trailhead, which is 3 miles farther. (Right leads to the trail's southern access point.)

WEST OF THE WASATCH

65
Stansbury Front Trail

JUST THE FACTS		
Location:	Stansbury Mountains, 50 miles west of Salt Lake City	
Length:	10.5 miles	
Type:	One-way	
Tread:	ATV trail & doubletracks	
Physically:	Moderate⁺ (several moderate to steep climbs on rough tread)	
Technically:	2⁺-4⁺ (steep, rocky climbs & descents w/ some smooth stretches)	
Gain:	2,500 feet	
Dogs:	Yes	

GO □
NO ■ | JAN | FEB | MAR | APR | MAY | JUN | JUL | AUG | SEP | OCT | NOV | DEC |

WHY SHOULD U RIDE THIS TRAIL

The Wasatch-Cache National Forest is not restricted solely to the Wasatch Range. Beyond the Oquirrh Mountains and west of Tooele, you'll find the Wasatch-Cache NF in the Stansbury Mountains, home to the Deseret Peak Wilderness. Formerly the Mack Canyon Trail, the Stansbury Front Trail runs the length of the Stansbury Mountains through sunny foothill chaparrals of juniper and pinyon. Although the trail is a designated motorcycle and ATV route, mountain bikers will find that the tight dual-track is well suited for pedal-pushers. With only a muscle-powered motor, however, bikers may find some sections especially challenging.

Details

Go across the road from the Boy Scout Campground, and take the lower doubletrack to the signed trailhead. The ATV trail begins with a modest hill (tech 3⁺), contours a bit across juniper and pinyon slopes, and then descends into a forested gulch (tech 2⁺). This is the fare for the day. Cross the Mining Fork road, and continue north following signs for the Mack Canyon Trail-Big Hollow Trail. A difficult hill ahead is littered with loose volcanic cobbles (tech 4⁺) and can be a short hike-a-bike depending on how much the motorcyclists and ATVers have "juiced" their throttles and torn up the tread. Cross a wire fence, and descend a mile to a small picnic area in North Willow Canyon (**m3.0**).

Take the doubletrack downhill/east, following a sign for O. P. Miller trailhead. Swing through an S-turn, cross the creek, and then look for the continued trail heading north and uphill through a wooden gate (may not be signed). Climb the steep trail to a low ridge, and then drop into Davenport Canyon. You may find a sign here confirming your route. Another sharp ascent takes you to a saddle on a small ridge marked with a fence. Descend to Baker Canyon, which has no road accessing it. After rising gently past a spring, the trail bends southeast, rounds a prominent point, and then traverses northward. You'll find good views of the Stansbury Mountains and of the south shore of the Great Salt Lake from this part of

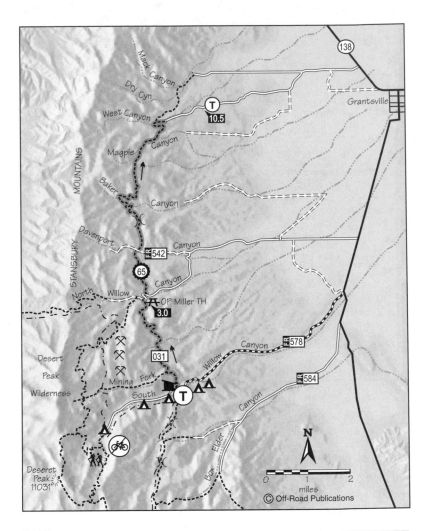

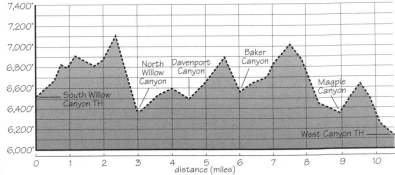

the trail. Descend through a pair of angular turns to Magpie Canyon. You must conquer one more agonizing hill before descending to West Canyon. Finally, race down the West Canyon doubletrack for about a mile to the parking area (**m10.5**).

Option: Stansbury Front Trail (South)

But wait, there's more. The Stansbury Front Trail also heads south from the Boy Scout Campground in South Willow Canyon toward Box Elder and East Hickman Canyons. In years past, though, this stretch proved exceedingly difficult with little contouring and many protracted hills to climb. Go blow your gasket, and then report back.

! Know Before You Go

- This multiuse trail is open to motorized and nonmotorized travel.
- Mountain bikes are not allowed in the Deseret Peak Wilderness.
- There are several Forest Service campgrounds in South Willow Canyon, but none has a water tap. The nearby guard station has a water tap that usually works. Grantsville offers minimal visitor services but does not have a bike shop. Bike shops in Tooele come and go like the annual rise and fall of the Great Salt Lake.
- *Fido Factor:* Trail is canine compatible, but be aware of motorized users. Some creeks and springs may dry up by mid to late summer, so carry lots of water for your pooch.

? Maps & More Information

- USGS 1:24,000: Deseret Peak East and North Willow Canyon, Utah
- Public Lands Information Center (at REI): (801) 466-6411
- Wasatch-Cache National Forest (Salt Lake Ranger District): (801) 733-2660; www.fs.fed.us/r4/wcnf/unit/slrd/index.shtml

Trailhead Access

From Salt Lake City, travel about 40 miles west on I-80 and take Exit 88 for Grantsville. To reach the northern trailhead in West Canyon, take Main Street (Grantsville) west then north, following posts with bike and horse decals. Turn left/west, signed for the West Canyon trailhead, and drive several miles to the parking area. (This dirt road is generally suitable for passenger cars.)

To reach the southern trailhead, return to Grantsville, drive south on 400 West for 5.1 miles, and go right on the South Willow Canyon road. The trailhead is 5.2 miles farther at the Boy Scout Campground.

WEST OF THE WASATCH

66
Cedar Mountains

Location:	61 miles west of Salt Lake City
Length:	55.7 miles
Type:	Loop
Tread:	Light-duty dirt roads throughout
Physically:	Extreme (long miles, rolling hills, two significant climbs)
Technically:	1⁺-3⁺ (smooth dirt & gravel roads w/ intermittent choppy sections)
Gain:	4,000 feet
Dogs:	No, too long

GO ☐
NO ■ | JAN | FEB | MAR | APR | MAY | JUN | JUL | AUG | SEP | OCT | NOV | DEC |

WHY SHOULD U RIDE THIS TRAIL ?

Just a few kilometers short of a metric century, the Cedar Mountains loop is ideal for endurance junkies who want to log long miles and spend all day in the saddle. The generally smooth dirt roads lend to a fast pace, but the rolling hills and the two passes you must climb rack up the elevation gain quickly. Utah's west desert is bleak and utterly desolate at first glance, but what may seem to be a wasteland to nuclear power proponents bears intrinsic beauty. In spring, the desert's tenacious plants burst with verdant, or new green, and the nearby Stansbury Mountains, home to the Deseret Peak Wilderness, instill alpine beauty. All sorts of critters hop, scurry, and slither between the brush, while pronghorn antelope and wild horses make their home among the namesake junipers. Distant salt flats flicker through the rising heat waves, and more mountains back up against the western skyline. Whether you view them as utterly monotonous or delicately balanced, the Cedar Mountains define an inseparable part of Utah's varied landscape.

Details

Head south from the Hastings Pass road junction on a gradual descent that lets you cruise at high speeds. Go left at a junction in 2 miles, dive into a gulch, and plow down the sandy wash. (The right fork leads to a big rusted tank at Redlam Spring.) The road bends south upon exiting the canyon. On your left, the Stansbury Mountains rise more than 6,000 feet above Skull Valley to heights over 11,000 feet. Less striking, but conspicuous just the same, is a "bathtub ring" on the low knoll to your right, which marks the wave-cut shoreline of ancient Lake Bonneville. Watch for more benches like this throughout the ride. They tell the tale of an ice-age lake that covered nearly all of northern Utah and made islands out of the Cedar and nearby mountains.

Cross a cattle guard, go straight through a four-way junction, and pedal swiftly for several more miles on the smooth packed-dirt and light-gravel road. A small climb makes you shift to easier gears briefly; then you come to a junction at Eightmile Spring. Go right to continue on a southern bearing.

After nearly 7 miles of rolling terrain and variable tread (tech 2+), the road rises abruptly over a 200-foot-tall pass aside Black Knoll (tech 3+). A small tongue of chunky lava on the knoll's east side is a telltale sign that it was a volcanic vent in recent geologic time. Fork right at a T-junction in 3.9 miles. The road then bends left (there's a wilderness study area post on the right) and arrives at a three-way junction (**m22.3**). You're at the base of knoll with charred trees from a recent wildfire.

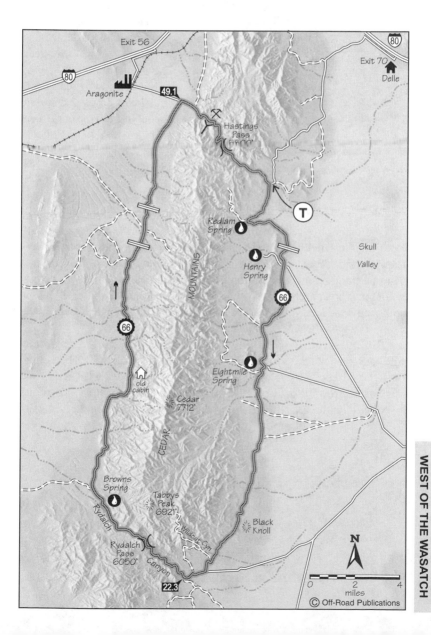

Deseret Peak draws home a weary biker after rounding the Cedar Mountains.

If you're feeling fresh, go right to climb Rydalch Canyon; otherwise, turn around, and return to the trailhead. Keep in mind that you'll climb 800 feet in the next 2.3 miles. More importantly, you'll have to climb nearly 1,000 feet more over Hastings Pass after another 30 miles. The climb to Rydalch Pass is a moderate[+] spin overall; the last one hundred yards to the top is a low-gear pump. The road's sand and gravel base stays packed down pretty firm, so put your head down and grind. Freewheel down from the pass (tech 2-3), and begin the loop's "back nine." You can stock up on water at Browns Spring, where the road exits the canyon. The water flows from a steel pipe, so it should be clean.

At first, the west side road is baby-butt smooth (tech 1[+]). Good thing because you'll want to knock off these miles as quickly as possible, for the terrain is more hapless than ever. The Bonneville Salt Flats appear as a bleach-white mirage off to the west. Can you imagine the desperation of pioneer travelers who toiled across the flaming hot, parched crust on their westward trek to California? If you cock your head left, you'll catch a sight of Ibapah Peak in the Deep Creek Range. It's the tallest peak in western Utah at 12,087 feet.

Six miles from Rydalch Canyon, the road angles uphill steeply for .5 mile, and the tread turns to chunky gravel with rocks (tech 3[+]). Thereafter, you'll cruise easily again on generally smooth dirt and sand. There's not much visual reward out here other than a turn-of-the-century one-room log cabin 1.7 miles after the climb and some junipers that were charred from

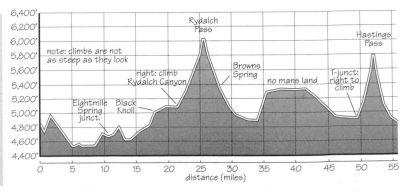

Left: Long lonely miles. Right: "Home, home on the range . . ."

a recent wildfire. Still, keep your eyes on the desert for pronghorn antelope and wild horses. Pronghorns are the sprint champions of the animal
world, for they can attain a speed of nearly 70 miles per hour for short
durations. You'll reconnect with civilization after hours of nomadic wandering when the smoke-belching stacks of the Aragonite plant come into
view. Over the next 6 miles, you'll go straight at a four-way junction, cross
two cattle guards, and come to a T-junction (**m49.1**).

Go right to climb over Hastings Pass; left leads to the Aragonite plant.
As you enter the canyon, you pass a metal post with an inscription that
commemorates this route as the Hastings Cut-off (see the chapter, "Crossroads of the West"). Farther up the canyon, you pass a deep cut in the
hillside where a seam of aragonite was once mined. Take home a piece of
the milky white calcium carbonate as a souvenir. Like Rydalch Canyon, the
climb to Hastings Pass is moderate overall, but it rises steeply for the last
couple hundred yards. Zoom down the other side with the Stansbury
Mountains in your sights once again, and you're done.

Option: Grassy Mountains

This is less an option and more a separate ride in itself. Like the
Cedars, the Grassy Mountains, located north of I-80, is circled by dirt
roads. The loop is about 40 miles and gains 2,000 feet, so it's a bit less
daunting than the Cedar loop. Still, it's a long haul, and you need to be
good with a map to navigate the dirt roads. You can't afford to stray off
course because the loop clips the USAF Utah Test and Training Range.

Take Exit 62 from I-15, and drive north on an all-weather dirt road for
5.5 miles. Fork left on a light-duty dirt road, and angle northwest across
Puddle Valley toward the Grassy Mountains for 4.5 miles. Park near an old
well and a tank at a four-way junction on the east side of Cobble Hill.

To ride the loop, head south for about 6 miles to a T-junction. Go right,
climb over a pass on the south end of the Grassy Mountains, and take the
second right fork. Hug the base of the mountains, cross Finger Ridge, and
descend swiftly while heading north along the mountains' west side. Con-

WEST OF THE WASATCH

nect with the main west-side road near a gravel pit, and take the main road north for 2 miles; then fork right, and climb German Valley. Upon descending, and where the road exits from the mountains to Puddle Valley, fork right on a doubletrack that runs the length of the mountains on their east side to return to the starting point.

You can shortcut the southern end of the Grassy Mountains by about 10 miles if you climb the canyon west from the trailhead. But you'll have to sell your soul to Satan (or at least to Larry) to find the secret cutoff at the top!

! Know Before You Go

- This is a long ride. Know your ability and that of others in your group. Be self-sufficient, and carry ample food and water.
- Brown Springs is reported to flow perennially, but the purity is uncertain.
- Most roads are impassable when wet, so be sure you have a clear forecast before you ride. If you get stuck in the rain, you may have to wait a day or two for the clayey road base to dry before you can get out. Slogging through the mud is less than desirable.
- Midday temperatures during midsummer can exceed 100 degrees Fahrenheit, so target this ride for spring and fall.
- *Fido Factor:* Dogs are not recommended because of the long distance and the lack of water.

? Maps & More Information

- USGS 1:100,000: Bonneville Salt Flats, Rush Valley, Tooele, and Wildcat Mountain, Utah
- Bureau of Land Management (Salt Lake Field Office): (801) 977-4300, www.ut.blm.gov/salt_lake/index.html

Trailhead Access

From Salt Lake City, drive 50 miles west on I-80 toward Reno, and take Exit 70 for Delle. (Note: The following access mileages are cumulative from Delle.) Drive west from the gas station on the south Frontage Road (light-duty dirt), and fork left at an unsigned junction in 2 miles. Go left/south at a fork in 4.1 miles. (The right fork angles northwest to a distant radio tower.) Stay on the main dirt road to another junction at 10.1 miles; go left again. (Here, the main road is simply making a 90 degree bend left/south.) At 11.2 miles, the main road makes a quick dog leg bend right then left. Hastings Pass road forks right from the left bend. Park at your discretion near this junction. Access roads are generally suitable for passenger cars but can be rutted and rough in spots. All roads are impassable when wet.

Copper Pit Overlook

<table>
<tr><td rowspan="12" style="writing-mode: vertical-rl;">JUST THE FACTS</td></tr>
<tr><td>Location:</td><td>Oquirrh Mountains; 7 miles southeast of Tooele.</td></tr>
<tr><td>Length:</td><td>9.8 miles</td></tr>
<tr><td>Type:</td><td>Loop w/ out-and-back</td></tr>
<tr><td>Tread:</td><td>1.2 miles semi-primitive singletrack, 1.8 miles dirt & cobblestone doubletrack, 6.8 miles light-duty dirt roads</td></tr>
<tr><td>Physically:</td><td>Moderate⁺ (grunt work to Butterfield Pass then less severe)</td></tr>
<tr><td>Technically:</td><td>2-4⁺ (gravel & rock on dirt roads; doubletracks vary from silky smooth to stacked-up cobbles; singletrack is semi-primitive)</td></tr>
<tr><td>Gain:</td><td>2,200 feet</td></tr>
<tr><td>Dogs:</td><td>Not recommended, possible traffic; yes, trail only</td></tr>
</table>

GO ☐
NO ■ | JAN | FEB | MAR | APR | MAY | JUN | JUL | AUG | SEP | OCT | NOV | DEC |

WHY SHOULD U RIDE THIS TRAIL? *Alter ego to Salt Lake County's* Butterfield Canyon road, Tooele County's Middle Canyon road also provides access to the overlook of Kennecott's Bingham Canyon Mine. Like Butterfield Canyon, Middle Canyon is a steep choppy climb, but on this return, you can sneak away from the road and tap into a sweet little singletrack stashed in White Pine Canyon. This tasty treat is not without its consequences, for it concludes with a tire-bashing descent on a doubletrack that rides like a dry, rocky streambed. Full suspension is a godsend. So, mix it up a bit, and go see what the neighbors in Tooele are riding.

Details

D ownshift to granny gear and rev up the rpms for the no-holds-barred climb from the trailhead to Butterfield Pass (**m1.3/m6.6**). At times, the gravel, washboard, and rock road (tech 2-3) rises at grades that push 15 percent. Yes, that's steep, and you'll wish you had lower gears. If you lift your nose from the handlebar, however, your eyes will gravitate to the grass-veneered limestone ledges of White Pine Canyon and to its treeless, glacial-carved peaks. You'll head that way after you return from the copper pit overlook.

Fork left at Butterfield Pass, and continue climbing 2.7 miles to the Sunrise Overlook aside West Mountain, this time at a more tolerable grade (**m3.9**). An entire mountain once stood where the gaping mine now rests. Currently, the copper pit is nearly 4,000 feet deep and 2.5 miles wide, and it's getting bigger and deeper daily. From 1863-1900, there was no pit because the mining was in underground tunnels, and the miners were searching for gold, silver, and lead. At the turn of the twentieth century, the precious metals played out, and Daniel Jackling and Robert Gemmell proposed mining the copper, which was in abundance although at low grades. Their plan for mass production was considered a folly, but they proved that the profit margins could be great, and the Utah Copper Company began large-scale surface operations. Even with ore grades as low as two percent, or 40 pounds of copper per ton of waste rock, the mine has since produced more copper than any other mine in history.

Descend back to Butterfield Pass, and fork right on a doubletrack that heads southwest into the trees. In .8 mile, the track narrows to a singletrack, and the trail-side oak and maple form a wooded tunnel. Sweet. Heed the sign warning of a washout ahead and dismount! All good things must come to an end when the path crosses White Pine Canyon Creek and connects with a doubletrack that is fraught with river cobbles. The culminating descent is sketchy and requires good handling skills (tech 4). Farther down, the track is more biker friendly as you return to the trailhead.

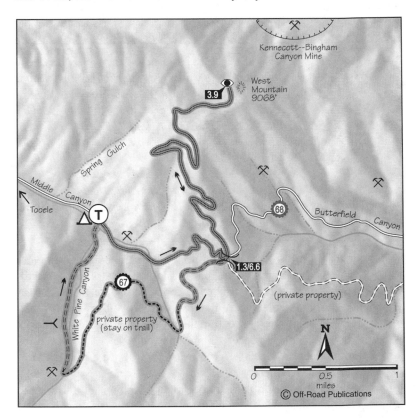

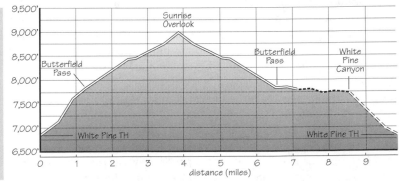

! Know Before You Go

- The route through White Pine Canyon crosses private property. Stay on the trail and respect the land so access privileges will continue.
- *Fido Factor:* Dogs are not recommended because of possible vehicle traffic, and the tread is rocky on the Middle Canyon road.

? Maps & More Information

- USGS 1:24,000: Bingham Canyon and Lowe Peak, Utah.
- Bureau of Land Management (Salt Lake Field Office): (801) 977-4300, www.ut.blm.gov/salt_lake/index.html
- Kennecott-Bingham Canyon Mine: www.kennecott.com
- *Bicycle Tooele County* (fold-out brochure) available from Tooele County Department of Parks and Recreation: (435) 843-4000.

Trailhead Access

From the intersection of Main and Vine in Tooele, take Vine up Middle Canyon for the Oquirrh Overlook. After 7 miles, the narrow paved road turns to dirt and gravel at the White Pine Canyon camping area (no water available). Park and embark here.

White Pine Canyon Trail is sweet before it gets nasty.

WEST OF THE WASATCH

68
Butterfield Canyon

Location:	Oquirrh Mountains, 27 miles southwest of Salt Lake City
Length:	13.6 miles
Type:	Out-and-back
Tread:	Light-duty dirt roads
Physically:	Strenuous (steady, steep climb; paint-shaker descent)
Technically:	2-3⁺ (variable washboards, gravel, & rocks)
Gain:	3,000 feet
Dogs:	Not recommended, rocky roads & possible traffic

GO □
NO ■ | JAN | FEB | MAR | APR | MAY | JUN | JUL | AUG | SEP | OCT | NOV | DEC |

WHY SHOULD I RIDE THIS TRAIL? *Butterfield Canyon does not tolerate wimps or whiners, for it rivals other gut-busting climbs like Snowbird's Peruvian Gulch Road, Farmington Canyon Road to Francis Peak, and the Ben Lomond Trail. On the way up, you'll wish for ultra-low gears; upon descending, you'll long for plush dual suspension. If you're indefatigable and reach Sunrise Overlook, you'll be rewarded with an endless panorama of northern Utah's Wasatch Front. Plus, you'll gain a staggering overlook into the world's largest man-made excavation, Kennecott's Bingham Canyon Mine, which has been dubbed "The Richest Hole on Earth."*

Details

From the outset, Butterfield Canyon Road rises moderately through groves of hardwoods, and it's quite pleasant biking. Haunting ruins of the once-bustling mining days dot the hillsides. Old cabins, mining structures, and tailings tell the stories of individuals and small startups who prospered then vanished as ore-rich mineral veins were discovered and played out.

The road forks after one-half mile; stay right on the well-traveled dirt road. Now the climb begins, and you face a half-mile-long, merciless grind up Spring Gulch at a near 20-percent grade. Gravel, rocks, and washboards compound the difficulty. After a left-hand turn, you'll welcome gentler grades and a chance to recover. But, the respite is short lived and is followed by sustained 10-percent inclines all the way to the canyon's top (**m4.2**).

At the pass, turn right on a dirt road that rises up the Oquirrh's northern crest. Although this ascent is no less demanding than Butterfield Canyon, it's more easily endured because the surrounding mountains are surprisingly scenic. White Pine Flat sits in a magnificent cliff-lined cirque across the pass. From selected turns on the road, you can peer down into Butterfield Canyon and across the Salt Lake Valley to the Wasatch Front. The road ends at the Sunrise Overlook aside West Mountain (**m6.8**).

As if on the rim of the Grand Canyon, you'll stand here silent and awestruck by the immensity of Kennecott's Bingham Canyon Mine. Here, unlike the natural chasm cut by the Colorado River, man and machine have leveled an entire mountain and dug down to its core. How big is the copper mine? It's over one-half mile deep and 2.5 miles wide at the top. That means the world's tallest building, the Sears Tower in Chicago, would reach only half way up. A quarter million tons of material are removed from the pit daily, seven days a week, 365 days a year. Over five billion tons have been removed since it opened in 1906. The giant electric shovels in the mine can scoop up 98 tons in a single bite—about the weight of 50 cars. And those haulage trucks that look no bigger than MatchBox© cars stand over two stories tall; their tires alone are nearly 10 feet high and cost about $20,000. Perhaps the Romans would have been impressed by this modern-day Colosseum.

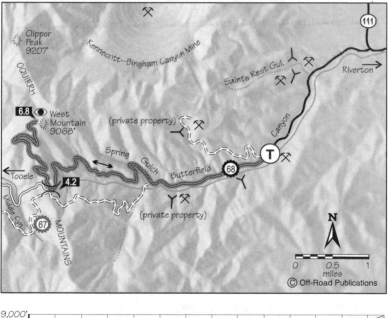

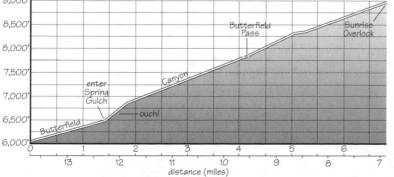

Kennecott's Bingham Canyon Copper Mine is the "Richest Hole on Earth."

! Know Before You Go

- All lands adjacent to Butterfield Canyon are private property. Stay on existing roads, and obey signs restricting travel.
- Be alert to vehicle traffic, especially when rounding blind curves.
- *Fido Factor:* Dogs are not recommended because of possible vehicle traffic, rocky road surfaces, and lack of water.

? Maps & More Information

- USGS 1:24,000: Bingham Canyon, Lowe Peak, and Tickville Spring, Utah
- Bureau of Land Management (Salt Lake Field Office): (801) 977-4300, www.blm.gov
- Kennecott-Bingham Canyon Mine: www.kennecott.com

Trailhead Access

From I-15, take Exit 294 (Draper, Riverton), and travel west on 12300 South/UT 71. After 11 miles, the road bends sharply right and becomes UT 111; turn left toward Butterfield Canyon. There are numerous pullouts over the next 3 miles. Thereafter, the paved road turns to dirt and gravel. This is where the route's mileage begins.

WEST OF THE WASATCH

Settlement Canyon

69

JUST THE FACTS

Location:	2 miles southeast of Tooele
Length:	8.6 miles
Type:	Loop w/ out-and-back
Tread:	4.1 miles singletrack, 1.5 miles doubletrack, 3 miles paved road
Physically:	Moderate (Left Hand Fork Trail is steep, Dark Trail is a breeze)
Technically:	1-3$^+$ (paved roads, pebbly doubletracks, under maintained tread on Left Hand Fork Trail, mostly smooth dirt on Dark Trail)
Gain:	1,850 feet
Dogs:	No, paved roads; yes, trails only

GO □
NO ■ | JAN | FEB | MAR | APR | MAY | JUN | JUL | AUG | SEP | OCT | NOV | DEC |

WHY SHOULD U RIDE THIS TRAIL?

Two vastly different trails in Tooele's Settlement Canyon are linked together for a ride that is well worth the half-hour drive from the Wasatch Front. If you live in Tooele, then it's just a stone's throw away. Left Hand Fork combines paved road, doubletrack, and singletrack for a steady 2.5-mile, 1,500-foot climb that is sure to get your heart pumping. Dark Trail is just the opposite: half as long, mellow, and well-suited for families. Even the die-hard bikers who make the climb up Left Hand Fork will appreciate cooling down their weary legs on Dark Trail. If you pack up the tent along with your bikes, then you can camp overnight in Settlement Canyon and explore other nearby routes the next day.

Details

Glide down the paved road from the toll booth about .1 mile, and look for a doubletrack peeling off to your right under the power lines. That's Dark Trail and your return route. Continue up the paved road about a half mile, and turn left for the moderately steep, .6-mile climb to Camp Wapiti (private). When you reach the camp's gate, search for a little path on the left that links to a doubletrack running alongside the fence. Once around the camp, the pebbly road (tech 2$^+$) rises moderate$^+$ past backcountry campsites to the city's fenced-in spring (**m1.8**). You'll find a faint trail on the right side of the fence, which goes up a dry creek that looks like a ditch. (The trail forking to the right and heading up the timbered slope is a horse path.) Gear down and pump hard, for the path heads straight up the drainage without a single switchback to ease the grade (tech 3$^+$). Some sections are mercilessly steep, others are quite tolerable, if not enjoyable. You'll fill your lungs with the rich scents of the forest, and ride through a canopy of oak, maple, aspen, and fir. Reach a fence at the pass (**m3.1,** private property beyond), take five, and then let gravity pull you back down the trail past the camp and to the canyon road. Revenge is sweet!

Don't head back to the trailhead just yet because more singletrack awaits. If you thought Left Hand Fork Trail was Mr. Hyde, then Dark Trail is Dr. Jekyll—rather, Dr. Jekyll's sweet ol' granny. Head up the paved

WEST OF THE WASATCH

canyon road for a mile to where it crosses over the creek, plus another hundred feet (**m6.9**). Veer right and into the dirt pullout; then cross the old cement sluice to tap into Dark Trail (may be unsigned). If you reach a camping area alongside the paved canyon road, you missed it.

Dark Trail starts out a bit choppy (tech 3), and you'll have to duck your head under a rock overhang. Farther on, the wide path hugs the bank of Settlement Canyon Creek for a mellow cruise through thickets of oak and maple that turn the otherwise-drab canyon into a fire storm of crimson

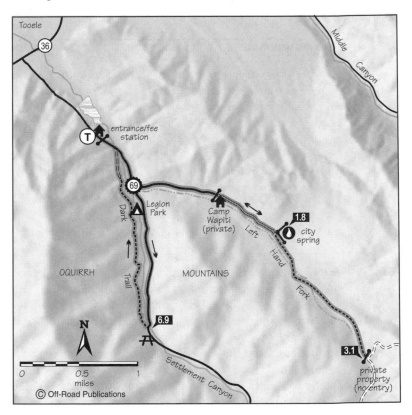

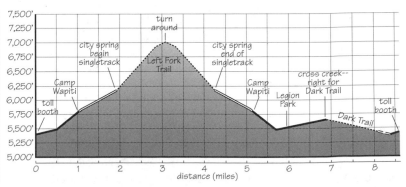

during autumn (tech 2). Pass Legion Park across the creek in about a mile (no access path), and exit the trail to a doubletrack a half mile farther. Connect with the paved canyon road, and you're home free.

Option: Dark Trail (3.3 miles, out-and-back, easy, tech 2, 300 feet)

If you don't feel like grinding your legs to hamburger on the Left Hand Fork climb, or if the kids are tagging along, then settle on riding only Dark Trail. The easiest approach is to ride the paved canyon road about 1 mile past Legion Park and coast back on the trail. Riding out-and-back on Dark Trail is only a touch harder (easy[+]), but you'll double your singletrack pleasure. For the latter, take the doubletrack located about .1 mile down the paved canyon road from the toll booth. It's just before the road crosses a little bridge/culvert. Stay to the right of the main power line road, and follow the posts with horse decals.

! Know Before You Go

* Left Hand Fork Trail and Dark Trail are very popular with equestrians, so ride attentively and yield the trail.
* Camp Wapiti is private.
* Day-use fee for Settlement Canyon is $2 per vehicle; camping fee is $5. There is no fee for bikes entering the canyon. Settlement Canyon is open from mid-April through October, weather permitting, from 9 A.M. to 9 P.M. on weekdays and 8 A.M. to 9 P.M. on weekends.
* Settlement Canyon is surrounded by private property, so stay on designated routes.
* *Fido Factor:* As a whole, this ride is not recommended for dogs because of the paved roads. Left Hand Fork above Camp Wapiti is canine compatible. Dark Trail is dog friendly, if ridden out-and-back.

? Maps & More Information

* USGS 1:24,000: Stockton and Tooele, Utah
* Bureau of Land Management (Salt Lake Field Office): (801) 977-4300, www.blm.gov
* Tooele County Parks and Recreation: (435) 843-4000
* Settlement Canyon: (435) 882-9041

↟ Trailhead Access

Drive 1 mile south of Tooele (from Vine Street), and fork left on Settlement Canyon Road for Camp Wapiti. Park at the toll booth after 1 mile.

Dark Trail.

WEST OF THE WASATCH

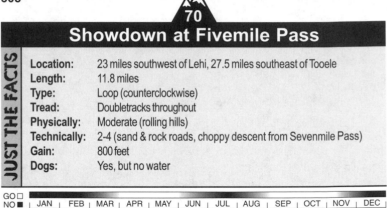

70
Showdown at Fivemile Pass

Location:	23 miles southwest of Lehi, 27.5 miles southeast of Tooele
Length:	11.8 miles
Type:	Loop (counterclockwise)
Tread:	Doubletracks throughout
Physically:	Moderate (rolling hills)
Technically:	2-4 (sand & rock roads, choppy descent from Sevenmile Pass)
Gain:	800 feet
Dogs:	Yes, but no water

GO □
NO ■ | JAN | FEB | MAR | APR | MAY | JUN | JUL | AUG | SEP | OCT | NOV | DEC |

If you were amping out in spin classes or suffering on cold, damp road rides all winter while your buddies were carving up the fresh powder, then put the hurt on them at the Showdown at Fivemile Pass Mountain Bike Race. This springtime tradition, held on the first weekend of May, has become a proving ground to sort out who was putting miles on their bike and who was putting pounds on their gut during the off-season. Even if you're not hellbent on making the podium, the race course's rolling desert doubletracks are perfect for logging quality early-season miles.

Details

The first half of the race course is nearly impossible to describe because there are so many spur roads heading every which way. This version bypasses part of the race course but gets you to the same place—the road leading up to Sevenmile Pass. Still, you'll need a good sense of direction. Just keep the Thorpe Hills at your side, and don't go wandering across the desert. If you've raced here before, then you have first-hand experience on the little hike-a-bike section that the race promoter tossed in—just for grins (he's grinning while you're suffering). This route skips the portage by linking together roundabout roads.

Head south from the Fivemile Pass staging area on a rutted doubletrack with a deepening arroyo on your left side. In 0.7 mile, go straight through a four-way junction. You'll close the loop on the left fork and shun the widowmaker climb up the knoll on the right fork. Come to a big Y-junction where the road levels (**m1.0**), and go right/straight, while sighting across the hapless Rush Valley Desert to the distant Sheeprock Mountains. (The race course forks left here and hugs the Thorpe Hills.) Go straight through another multiple junction, stay right at a Y-junction, and aim for the gravel pit about a half mile off. Are you with me? You're on track if you pass a sign stating that you're entering public lands and that it's illegal to discharge that pistol you're packing. Stay left of the gravel pit on a south bearing, and come to a prominent Y-junction a mile farther. Stay right, and round the base of a low knoll. (The left fork leads to the race course's infamous hike-a-bike. Go hoof it if you want.) Cruise easily for 0.7 mile,

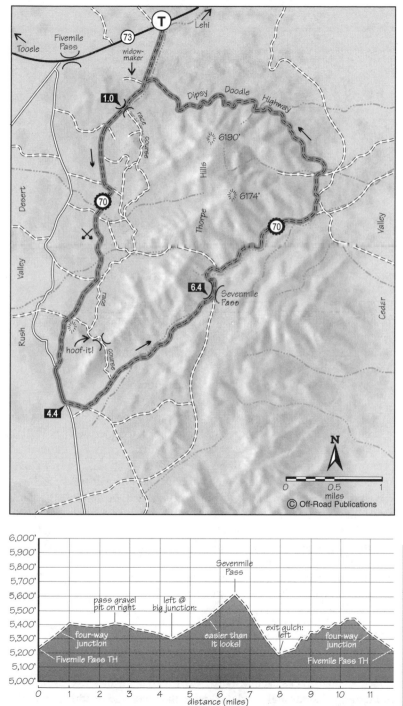

Racers take to the course with gusto, long before the suffering begins.

merge with a good dirt road, and then come to a major Y-junction (**m4.4**). Go left/west and climb gradually for 2 miles to the broad sage saddle at Sevenmile Pass (**m6.4**). (Along the way, you pass a four-way junction. To the left is a kamikaze downhill, if you opted for the hike-a-bike section on the official race course.) From the pass, Lone Peak's chiseled granite cornice rises like a Gothic castle in the Wasatch Range.

The road drops into the head of a broad canyon that narrows to a tight rock and sand gulch (tech 3-4). Surf's up; catch a wave through the pockets of sand and gravel. Exit the canyon to the edge of Cedar Valley, and fade left/north on a smooth, sandy doubletrack toward the distant Oquirrh Mountains. Veer left through a four-way junction, and stay along the base of the Thorpe Hills on the variably choppy dual-track (tech 2^+-3^+). A mile and a half from where you exited the canyon descent, the track bends northwest along what has been dubbed the Dipsy Doodle Highway. Here, a series of short ups and downs and quick turns hugs the foothills through the juniper and pinyon. Stay left at a junction where you can see the parking area in the distance and descend speedily to the familiar four-way junction. Sprint to the finish, or take another lap. Better yet, take three more laps; that's what men's pro racers have to do, and the winners are clocking in at two hours thirty minutes. Whoa!

Option: Fivemile Pass (North)

This is where the whole Showdown began. The original Fivemile Pass race course was held on the north side of the highway and also followed a maze of dual-tracks used heavily by off-road enthusiasts. Racers raved about the secluded singletrack tucked in the pines and the thrilling high-

If you have time to admire the scenic Oquirrh Mountains during the Showdown · race, then you're dogging it. Hammer!

speed luge run down a dry wash with high-banked turns. The route was abandoned because it crossed the old Manning Canyon Mine, where heavy metal toxins have been detected in its tailings. The mine area is closed for environmental reclamation, and you are advised to stay out of the area. Other portions of the old race course are still available, but unless you can remember the route you'll get lost for sure.

! Know Before You Go

- This area is designated open to OHVs, so keep your head up for traffic.
- If you explore the north side of Fivemile Pass, keep out of the Manning Canyon Mine area. Toxins have been detected in its tailings, and you don't want to be kicking up the dust.
- *Fido Factor:* This route is canine compatible, but there is no water on route, and the rocky tread may be hard on dogs' paws.

? Maps & More Information

- USGS 1:24,000: Fivemile Pass and Goshen Pass, Utah
- Bureau of Land Management (Salt Lake Field Office): (801) 977-4300, www.blm.gov
- Intermountain Cup Race Series: www.intermountaincup.com

🏃 Trailhead Access

From I-15, take Exit 282 for Lehi, and travel 23 miles on UT 73 from the center of town to Fivemile Pass. From Tooele, drive 12 miles south on UT 36 then 15.5 miles southeast on UT 73 to Fivemile Pass.

WEST OF THE WASATCH

71
Lake Mountains

Location:	25 miles west of Provo
Length:	29 miles
Type:	Loop (clockwise)
Tread:	13.5 miles doubletrack, 4 miles dirt road, 11.5 miles pavement
Physically:	Strenuous (long distance, tough climb, steep descent)
Technically:	1-3⁺ (gravel & washboards on dirt roads, loose rocks & ruts on doubletracks, narrow shoulder on paved road)
Gain:	3,300 feet
Dogs:	No, paved roads & too long

GO □
NO ■ | JAN | FEB | MAR | APR | MAY | JUN | JUL | AUG | SEP | OCT | NOV | DEC |

WHY SHOULD U RIDE THIS TRAIL?

Like Butterfield Canyon *in the Oquirrh Mountains, your goal on the Lake Mountains loop is a mountain pulpit opposing the Wasatch Front. But on this ride, you'll over-look Utah Lake instead of a gaping copper mine. If you're training for the upcoming race season, then this is one of the first big hill climbs to melt out in the spring. So, get off the stationary trainer and get into the mountains.*

Details

The loop begins with many flat miles along Utah Lake's western shore. Granted, the pedaling can be rather mundane, but the scenery is entrancing. Across the lake, the Wasatch Range changes its complexion continually as your eyes fall upon Mount Timpanogos' 5-mile-long summit, Provo Peak's spiked arête, and Mount Nebo's triple-peaked crown. You pass under power lines after 10.5 miles. About 1 mile farther, turn right on a dirt road marked solely by a stop sign (**m11.5**).

It's a gradual 3-mile dirt road climb (tech 2) to Soldiers Pass (**m14.5**). From the notch, you have a clear view of the Stansbury Mountains and of the desolate and deserted Cedar Valley. Fork right when descending, and continue downhill on what seems to be the less-traveled road. One mile from the pass, the road passes a cement structure presumably used for a gravel pit operation. The road then dips through a gulch and bends right/north. Climb gently for about 2 miles across sunny sagebrush prairies; then fork right on a faint, rock-studded doubletrack. (You've gone too far if you come to a yellow- and orange-colored pumice pit. Backtrack about one-quarter mile.) Within one-half mile, the gravel road enters Mercer Canyon. The 4-mile climb ahead is steep, rocky, and utterly monotonous (tech 3⁺). Other than some lonely junipers scattered on the canyon's dreary gray limestone slopes, there is little scenic gratification. Entertain yourself by whistling a tune from an old sitcom, like *The Brady Bunch*, by pondering the meaning of life, or by analyzing Bill Cosby's universally profound question, "Why is there air?"

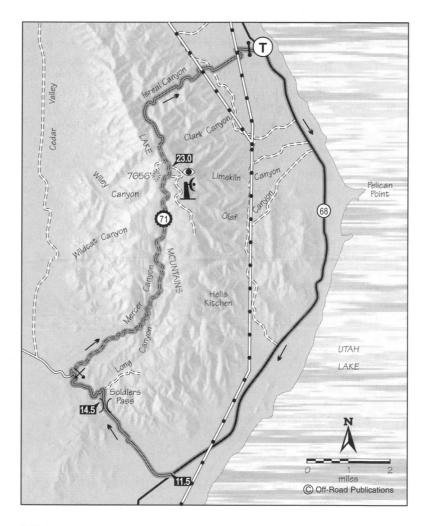

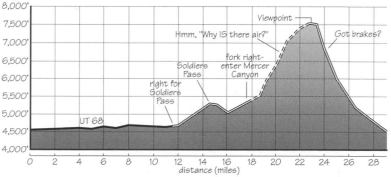

Glades of aspens at the summit enlighten the route with hints of alpine promise. Ignore the first rutted doubletrack forking to the right. Stay straight for one-half mile, and *then* fork right on a doubletrack that climbs to a treeless knoll north of a red pyramid benchmark (**m23.0**). Finally, you have attained your goal, a bird's-eye view of north-central Utah. Nearly the entire Wasatch Range, from Ogden's Ben Lomond to Nephi's Mount Nebo, can be seen hovering over Salt Lake and Utah Valleys. Legs willing, pedal up to the white cones marking the Lake Mountains' true summit for an equally expansive view across western Utah.

The upper portion of Israel Canyon is a "ride-the-brakes-'til-they-smoke" descent with grades dropping at over 15 percent. Fortunately, the road is not technically difficult (tech 2⁺). The grade lessens after the road breaks out of the canyon, but the ride is still fast and furious all the way back to the trailhead.

Know Before You Go

- This route can be very warm during the summer, especially the unshaded climb up Mercer Canyon. Regardless of the season, insect repellant is recommended for the ride along Utah Lake.
- The summit can be much cooler than the valley, so pack along appropriate clothing.
- Muscles weary after the ride? Then check into nearby Saratoga Springs for a soak in its natural hot springs.
- *Fido Factor:* Dogs are not recommended because of the paved roads, long miles, and lack of reliable water sources.

? Maps & More Information

- USGS 1:24,000: Lincoln Point, Pelican Point, Saratoga Springs, and Soldiers Pass, Utah
- Bureau of Land Management (Salt Lake Field Office): (801) 977-4300, www.blm.gov

Trailhead Access

From I-15, take Exit 282 for Lehi. Travel 4 miles west on UT 73, and turn left/south on 10800 West/UT 68 for Elberta. After 3.6 miles, UT 68 makes a prominent bend to the left/southeast; 1.7 miles past the bend, turn right on an unsigned dirt road marked by a wire gate (property status unknown). This is Israel Canyon. Park at your discretion.

Oh yeah, "Why *is* there air?" Mr. Cosby says, ". . . to pump up volleyballs." Go figure!

WEST OF THE WASATCH

APPENDIX

Master List of Rides (Alphabetical)

º: optional route to a main trail/chapter.

Sources of Additional Information

Federal Government

Uinta National Forest

Supervisor's Office
88 West 100 North
Provo, UT 84603
(801) 342-5100
www.fs.fed.us/r4/uinta/

Pleasant Grove Ranger District
390 North 100 East
Pleasant Grove UT 84062
(801) 785-3563

Spanish Fork Ranger District
44 West 400 North
Spanish Fork, UT 84600
(801) 798-3571

Wasatch-Cache Nat'l Forest

Supervisor's Office
8236 Federal Building
125 S State St
S LC UT 84138 (801) 236-3400
www.fs.fed.us/r4/wcnf/

Ogden Ranger District
507 25th St.
Ogden, UT 84403
(801) 625-5112
www.fs.fed.us/r4/wcnf/unit/
ogden/index.shtml

Salt Lake Ranger District
6944 S. 3000 E.
Salt Lake City, UT 84121
(801) 733-2660
www.fs.fed.us/r4/wcnf/unit/
slrd/index.shtml

Public Lands Info. Center
c/o R.E.I.--Recreational Equipment Incorporated
3285 East and 3300 South
Salt Lake City, UT 84109
(801) 466-6411

Bureau of Land Management

Salt Lake Field Office
2370 South 2300 West
Salt Lake City, Utah 84119
(801) 977-4300
www.blm.gov

State Government

Utah Dept. of Natural Resources
1594 W North Temple
SLC UT 8484114
(801) 538-7200
www.nr.utah.gov
Division of Parks & Recreation
(801) 538-7220
www.stateparks.utah.gov
Division of Wildlife Resources
(801) 538-4700
www.wildlife.utah.gov

Antelope Island State Park
4528 West 1700 South
Syracuse, Utah 84075-6868
(801) 773-2941
www.stateparks.utah. gov

Utah Geological Survey
Natural Resources Map and Bookstore
1594 W North Temple
Salt Lake City UT 84114
1-888-UTAHMAP
(801) 537-3320
www.mapstore.utah.gov

County Government

Davis County
Department of Community and
Economic Development
28 East State Street
P.O. Box 618
Farmington, UT 84025
(801) 444-2300
(801) 451-3278
www.co.davis.ut.us

Mountainlands Association of
Governments
586 East 800 North
Orem UT 84097
(801) 229-3800
www.mountainland.org

Junction City Services
Ogden Travel and Information
Source)
www.ogden-ut.com/

Salt Lake County Parks and
Recreation
2001 So. State St.
Suite S4400
Salt Lake City, UT 84190
(801) 468-2299
www.co.slc.ut.us/
www.parks-recreation.org/

Tooele County Parks and
Recreation
47 S. Main
Tooele, UT 84074
(435) 843-4000

Union Station Visitor Information Center
2501 Wall Avenue
Ogden, UT
(801) 625-5306

Utah County Parks
c/o Utah County Public Works
Department
2855 South State Street
Provo, Utah 84606
(801) 370-8624
http://www.co.utah.ut.us/
Dept/PubWrks/Parks/
Index1.asp

Weber County Parks and Recreation
1181 N. Fairgrounds Dr.
Ogden, UT 84404
(801) 399-8491

Local Government

Alpine City
20 N Main
Alpine, Utah, 84004
(801) 756-6347

Town of Alta
P.O. Box 8016
Alta, UT 84092
(801) 363-5105
www.townofalta.com

Draper City
12441 S 900 East
Draper UT 84020
(801) 576-6500

Ogden Trails Network
c/o Ogden City
2549 Washington Boulevard
Ogden, Utah 84401
www.ogdencity.com/
index.cfm/ogdentrails.main

Orem City
Parks and Recreation
580 W. 165 South
Orem UT 84508
(801) 229-7151

Pleasant Grove City
Parks and Rec. Department
41 E 200 South
Pleasant Grove
(801) 785-6172

Pleasant Grove City
Community Development
(801) 785-6057

Provo City
Parks and Recreation
351 W. Center St.
Provo, UT
(801)852-6600
www.provo.org/parks/

Salt Lake City Mayor's Office
Administrative Affairs
451 South State
Salt Lake City, Utah 84111
(801) 535-7704

Salt Lake City Watershed Management:
1530 S. West Temple
Salt Lake City, UT 84115
(801) 483-6705
www.slcgov.com

Sandy City
440 E 8680 South
Sandy UT 84070
(801) 568-2900

Springville City Recreation Department
50 S Main
Springville, UT
(801) 489-2730

Ski Areas

Alta Ski Area
8920 S Collins Road
Alta UT 84092
(801) 359-1078
www.alta.com

Powder Mountain
PO Box 450
Eden UT 04010
(801) 745-3772
www.powdermountain.com

Snowbasin
3925 E. Snowbasin Rd.
Huntsville, UT 84317
(801) 620-1000
www.snowbasin.com

Snowbird Ski and Summer
Resort
P.O. Box 929000
Snowbird, UT 84092-9000
(801) 742-2222
www.snowbird.com

Solitude Mountain Resort
12000 Big Cottonwood Can-
yon
Solitude, UT 84121
(801) 534-1400
www.skisolitude.com

Sundance
RR3 Box A-1
North Fork Provo Canyon
Sundance, Utah 84604
(801) 225-4107
www.sundanceresort.com

Trail Organizations

Bonneville Shoreline Trail
Committee
P.O. Box 58325
SLC, UT 84158
(801) 816-0876
www.bonneville-trail.org

International Mountain Bike Association (IMBA)
PO Box 7578
Boulder, CO. 80306
(303) 545-9011
1-888-442-4622
www.imba.com

Leave No Trace
www.lnt.org

Tread Lightly
298 24th Street Suite 325
Ogden UT 84401
1-800-966-9900
www.treadlightly.org

Weber Pathways
P. O. Box 972 Ogden, Utah, 84401
801-393-2304
www.weberpathways.org/

Miscellaneous

Suncrest Development
2021 E Village Green Circle
Draper UT 84020
(801) 553-9300

Intermountain Cup Race Series
www.intermountaincup.com

Mill Creek F.I.D.O.S.
(Friends Interested in Dogs and Open Spaces)
www.millcreekfidos.org

About the Author

"Everyday's a holiday," says author Gregg Bromka when he's mountain biking in Utah's Wasatch Front. "Why go anywhere else when the trails are this good?"

What started as a hobby for Gregg in 1988, with the first version of this Wasatch guidebook, has evolved into an obsession to scout out mountain biking trails throughout Utah. His pursuit to share his experiences has lead to more than a half-dozen guidebooks over the years, with additional projects in the making. Through his efforts, may you discover the joy of off-road bicycling in Utah.